The New Politics of State Health Policy

STUDIES IN GOVERNMENT AND PUBLIC POLICY

The New Politics of State Health Policy

Edited by
Robert B. Hackey
and
David A. Rochefort

 University Press of Kansas

Published by the University Press of Kansas (Lawrence, Kansas 66049), which was
organized by the Kansas Board of Regents and is operated and funded by Emporia
State University, Fort Hays State University, Kansas State University, Pittsburg State
University, the University of Kansas, and Wichita State University.

Library of Congress Cataloging-in-Publication Data

The new politics of state health care policy / edited by Robert B. Hackey and
    David A. Rochefort.
        p. cm. — (Studies in government and public policy)
        ISBN 0-7006-1084-7 (cloth : alk. paper) — ISBN 0-7006-1085-5 (pbk. : alk. paper)
        1. Medical policy—United States—States.   2. Medical care—United States—
    States.   I. Hackey, Robert B.   II. Rochefort, David A.   III. Series.
    RA395.A3 N47 2001
    362.1'0973—dc21   2001017546

British Library Cataloguing in Publication Data is available.

Printed in the United States of America
10 9 8 7 6 5 4 3 2 1

Contents

Preface

Robert B. Hackey and David A. Rochefort

Public policy shifts can arise as much from ambivalence as from a clear sense of purpose.

During the early 1990s, the American polity turned toward, and then decisively away from, a comprehensive solution to the problems of a health care system widely perceived to be in crisis. At the time, proposed remedies, including most notably the plan of the Clinton administration, seemed to many to be too complicated, too dependent on "big government," and too capable of producing perverse outcomes. Despite rising levels of uninsurance, fiercely escalating costs, and a host of other systemic concerns, powerful organized interests and their allies managed to stymie the health reform process, offering no more coherent alternative in its place than an unfettered private market.

Meanwhile, the broader landscape of American politics and public policymaking was also being redefined in these years, as the balance of power between federal and state governments—always a simmering dispute—tilted once again toward the states. Perhaps the most pivotal instance of devolution occurred in welfare, but the process was much more far-reaching than this. States acquired increased authority on a variety of policy fronts from education to criminal justice, combined with the encouragement to fashion their own innovative and distinctive programs.

At the nexus of these two watersheds, U.S. health politics and policymaking entered a new era beginning in the mid-1990s. The purpose of this book is to describe many of the major developments that have already taken place as states grapple with the health care challenge and to identify the forces that will be shaping this state response for years to come. What results is an analysis covering topics as diverse as managed care, health insurance expansion, mental health care, and public health administration. Of equal interest is the performance of legislatures, executives, courts, and bureaucracies as key political institutions within the state health policy process.

This project has the most humble of origins, as we are willing to admit now that the finish line has been crossed. The truth is that we launched this book on a drizzly spring Saturday in Worcester, Massachusetts, over lunch at an Irish pub. It was to this unpretentious spot we had retreated following what can only be described as a disappointing turnout for a panel session on state health policy that was organized for a regional political science meeting. In our hearts we knew that this panel had only scratched the surface of crucial new issues and that a much greater audience could, and should, be attracted with the proper kind of discussion of this topic.

It has been our good fortune to attract an exceptional group of contributors for this effort (those familiar with the children's story "Stone Soup" will know just how this feat was accomplished). In fact, some of the most distinguished scholars in the academic field of health policy analysis are present in this group, adding to the significance, not to mention the potential readership, of this work. Preparing an edited volume such as this entails numerous tasks that can be taxing, even torturous, for editors and contributors alike. For their forbearance and cooperation throughout this endeavor, we express sincere appreciation to all our collaborators. We hope this final product will redeem all of our past claims on your knowledge, time, and goodwill.

We also acknowledge secretarial support and other forms of assistance that were given to this project by our respective institutions. At Providence College, Mary Politelli and Donna Rocchio provided secretarial support coupled with a good sense of humor; the health policy and management program and the management department provided a wonderfully collegial environment for writing; and Thomas Canavan, the college's vice president for academic affairs, offered both encouragement and a new computer to speed the process of writing this book. At Northeastern University, Janet Joseph and Barbara Chin in the political science department provided valuable secretarial assistance, and Rachel Rashti, a graduate student, did an extraordinary job indexing the work. At the University Press of Kansas, Fred Woodward nurtured and supported this project from its inception; his enthusiasm for our work and his insistence on firm but realistic deadlines were crucial in shepherding this book through the publication process.

Finally, as parents in families with young children, we are grateful both to our spouses and to our children for tolerating the long nights, missed weekends, and other absences that were often necessary to bring this project to completion.

Introduction

James A. Morone

State governments have always gotten mixed reviews. Alexis de Tocqueville thought that America's republican habits sprang directly from state politics. Governing those "little countries" offered just the right civic education because it involved no "wealth or glory" and plenty of pragmatic decisions—where to open a canal or to cut a road. Yet, in the end, Tocqueville did not show the states much respect. The federal government, he concluded, was "infinitely better conducted." Even back in the 1830s, the feds were more wise, more fair, more skillful, more moderate, more consistent—his list rolls on and on (Tocqueville 1969, 154–163).

A century and a half later, we are still echoing Tocqueville's ambivalence. On one side, we have grand "laboratories of democracy." States are incubators of populist policies, pragmatic problem solvers often harassed by the regulations and mandates pouring down on them from Washington. On the more skeptical side, observers continue to see political weaklings driven by Tocqueville's "despotism of the majority." The states, in the more skeptical view, will all plunge to the social-welfare bottom the moment their federal nanny turns its back (Tocqueville 1969, 154).

Which perspective gets it right? The essays in this collection sum up to a clear answer: both. In health politics, each view is about half true.

Health policy adds an unusual dimension to state politics: speed. The governments themselves evolve glacially. Health policy offers a quicksilver difference—there is always something new. Most policy innovations get no traction as bright ideas follow one another in dizzy succession. As the last decade opened, many states were wrestling with the patchwork universal coverage of all-payer systems. The 1990s seemed to promise "a new, more aggressive role for state

---

This introduction draws on research I am conducting with Beth Kilbreth. I wish to thank Beth as well as the Robert Wood Johnson Foundation for providing funding.

1

government in health policy" (Goldberger 1990, 857). Then along came the Clinton administration and its national health care reform; the action bounced right back to Washington. The Clintons failed, of course, and a great Republican backlash followed; in the next election the GOP won control of eleven new state legislatures, ten new governorships, and both houses of Congress. Forget the maladroit government, we were now in a bold new market era. Managed care swiftly remade American health care. Another backlash followed. Within two years, one thousand different bits of regulatory legislation were flowing through the states. In Washington, Democrats and Republicans clashed over different patients' rights bills and conspired on a children's health insurance program (CHIP)—the largest expansion of government insurance coverage in three decades. When the states failed to sign up enough children, reformers began casting about for a better approach. Stay tuned for more.

Note the pattern. The latest health policy solution comes along, stirs a buzz, animates a political coalition, wins or loses, disappoints, provokes a backlash (in this business, even the losers manage to get up a backlash), then gives way to the next hot policy fix. What are we missing in all the flux? Governance. In the chase for health policy solutions, we rarely pause to consider the difficult art of governing.

The chapters that follow all grapple with precisely that issue. Each essay explores the interplay between state government and health policy. If a single moral runs across the essays, it is this: health care policies will be only as effective as the governments that make them. In this introduction, I trace that theme across four major dimensions of contemporary state health policy.

THE MESSY DEVOLUTION

Perhaps the most famous metaphor in American politics reminds us that American federalism is *not* like a layer cake—it is a marble cake. Programs and authority swirl together, up and down, constantly intermingling different layers of government (Grodzins 1966). Today, that metaphor fits better than ever.

Ten years ago, states were experimenting with all kinds of creative programs. Oregon proposed its daring mix of technocracy, democracy, and rationing. New York was concocting the children's health program that inspired CHIP. A dozen states from Vermont to Washington were tinkering toward universal coverage. Today, in contrast, almost every major state health policy is wrapped around a federal program and is nourished by federal funds. The states operate largely within the broad boundaries set by federal choices. But most contemporary programs come from Washington with a difference—they grant state officials unprecedented elbow room.

Social policies sprawl across multiple levels of government. The federal government legislates, funds, regulates, and delegates. The states put their distinctive stamps on the programs (Tennessee's Medicaid grows into TennCare, Wisconsin's into BadgerCare) as well as design the administrative framework and match the funds. Then, they often pass authority to the local level. For example, twelve states (including California, New York, and Ohio) are now operating "county administered" welfare systems—choices that were once jealously held by Washington have moved all the way down the federal chain (Nathan and Gais 1999).

This new federalism comes with a serious shortcoming. It runs blind. The different governments do not much monitor the programs they pass on. Rather, as this book shows, they rely on advocacy groups to raise the alarm when guidelines are violated or goals subverted. For example, the 1996 welfare reform pushed states to introduce abstinence education in their schools. It might have been a largely symbolic gesture. However, a Conservative Christian group sprang up to monitor each state and grade the abstinence effort—Louisiana pulled an A, while Rhode Island (along with most of the other large northeastern states) flunked. Or take Medicaid. Officials in New York City dramatically flaunted program guidelines by refusing to sign up eligible recipients when they first applied. It took lawsuits from local advocacy groups to even put the violations on anyone's political agenda. Local Medicaid administrators eventually provoked court orders, stern letters from the regional office, and even federal spies, but through it all some New York City Medicaid offices clung adamantly to their outlaw (or noncompliant) policies.

The result loads the distinctive bias of interest group pluralism into ostensibly universal programs. State and local governments introduce variations in national policies. Many are creative efforts; some violate national guidelines and subvert programmatic goals. But even dramatic violations may go undetected unless private groups have the resources to blow the whistle.

CAPACITY: BASHING THE STATE GOVERNMENTS

Once upon a time, good old boys ran the states with winks and backslaps. No more. Beginning in the 1960s, state governments became professional operations. "Goodbye to good-time Charlie," wrote Larry Sabato (1978). After growing steadily more sophisticated for some twenty years, state officials began hitting new limits— ardent grassroots efforts to scale back government. Tax rebellions began in the 1970s and in many places are still blazing. Take Oregon, for example. The health policy reports all trumpet creative policies and savvy politicians. The big news on the ground, however, is a string of increasingly fierce tax limitations. The estimable Governor John Kitzhaber has spent much of his final year in office fighting antitax initiatives and referenda. The antitax, antigovernment energy helped propel conservative Republicans to a majority in both houses of the legislature.

Grassroots outrage also clamped term limits on local politicians in eighteen states. The limits drain legislatures of expertise and stability. Advocates may cheer the return of Andrew Jackson's ideal—citizens "rotating" through political office—

but that venerable democratic wish still comes with the same old price: less effective governance. Term limits make it far more difficult for the legislatures to grapple with the intricacies of health care policy (Morone 1998).

The antigovernmental impulse finds important allies among religious conservatives. Defeated at the national level (by President Clinton's endless escapes) and disappointed in their political organizations, Conservative Christian activists have returned to the grass roots. They run for local seats on school boards, town government, and state legislatures. From these positions they resist active government and its social policies.

In some cases, political influence drains from the legislatures into the bureaucracy. Health issues, with their arcane language, rules, and regulations, always tend to push power into bureaucratic hands. Imposing limits on the legislatures quickens the trend (Morone 1994).

Of course, bureaucracies face their own rounds of bashing: budget limits, hiring freezes, personnel reductions, and—with each new administration—reorganization. In Connecticut, Governor John Rowland campaigned with a blueprint for lean, efficient bureaucracy that he called "the scroll." True to his word, Rowland dazzled organizational experts with 46 different reorganizations of his social welfare bureaucracy in his first term alone. Governor George Pataki shook up the New York bureaucracy but, like a true moderate, limited himself to a single reorganization.

The chapters that follow map out the different features of the state institutional frames: governors, legislatures, bureaucracies, interest groups, and grassroots advocates. Of course, every state is unique, as this book makes plain. Each state sums the pieces into a different political whole, a different health policy regime. Nevertheless, a general trend appears through all the differences. State governments face growing responsibilities with declining resources; good-time Charlie will not return. But the officials that replaced him face complex policy issues, partial devolution from Washington, and growing citizen demands—often with a diminished governing capacity.

IDEOLOGY

State politics are always framed by the local ideology.* Watch for two very different political philosophies running through state health policies.

First, there is that familiar political science standard, liberalism (if the term is unfamiliar to you, just think of it as American individualism). Liberal politics focus attention on the boundary between private and public spheres. Every individual or group pursues its own interests in the public arena; the action turns on negotia-

---

*The argument about moral politics developed in this section is drawn from my forthcoming book, *Hellfire Nation* (Morone 2001).

tions among stakeholders. Private lives are protected from government meddling. Liberalism's great social policy question is where to draw that line between public and private. Americans have been especially vigilant (sometimes even belligerent) about restricting the public or governmental sphere. The consequences run across our politics, from the familiar political storms provoked by national health insurance to the agonizing about "crowding out" private insurance with public programs. Every political proposal gets scrutinized for the same fatal flaw: does it exceed government's legitimate authority?

A second, less familiar ideological tradition turns politics to morality. Moral politics cross that boundary between public sphere and private life. Political programs, along with their partisans and their beneficiaries, are weighed as morally worthy or unworthy. Those who fail to measure up become illegitimate, even dangerous. Negotiations among stakeholders disappear. Instead, the moral others need to be controlled (the tobacco industry), transformed (lazy poor people on the dole), or disciplined (unruly teenagers).

Moral politics become especially salient when government benefits are involved. Representative Nancy Johnson is quoted in this book defending the expansion of children's health insurance: "There are millions of families with uninsured children who are working hard, paying taxes and playing by the rules." In short, worthies: "They deserve our help." Contrast that image with the picture drawn by Tennessee Medicaid director Brian Lapp, when his program fell into fiscal crisis (largely because managed care failed to live up to the exaggerated expectations of cost saving): "We have a spoiled population that wants everything for nothing. . . . Why is it that the poor can afford cigarettes at $3 a pack and their alcohol? . . . There's a portion of them who drive up to the doctor's offices in a BMW. . . . What is their purchasing priority?" (Kilborn 1999).

Note the markers of contemporary moral failure: alcohol, tobacco, and the moral hazard of blithely consuming medicine. Meanwhile, the old welfare cheat's Cadillac has turned into the uninsurable's BMW. Fierce images of deserving and undeserving—of vice and virtue—lurk beneath the pragmatic give-and-take of stakeholder politics. All sorts of issues can quite suddenly get entangled in morality.

In many states, school health clinics triggered vehement opposition. Conservatives feared that the student health services would prescribe birth control and counsel abortions. In Pawtucket, Rhode Island, a federally funded school breakfast triggered a similar moral backlash. Breakfast ought to be the parent's responsibility; talk at the school board quickly went from the poor parents to the money they wasted on beer. Even managed care debates occasionally spill into the language of good and evil. "People who are sick will be allowed to die," declared *Time* magazine (quoting a physician), thanks to the "chilling . . . bottom line mentality that is taking over" (Church 1997).

The most sustained moral outrage always seems to swirl around poverty politics. New York City's tough approach to Medicaid offers a classic example. So did the entire debate that surrounded welfare reform. "Although few people discuss it openly," wrote William Tucker in the *American Spectator,* "what welfare reform is really about is illegitimacy. The real goal of the reform is to promote marriage and family formation" (1996, 21).

In short, moral images matter. They freight dull policy discourse ("crowding out" or the "take up rate") with vivid pictures of good and bad, of unfortunate victims who need our help and villains cheating us out of our hard-earned cash. Political scientists often overlook this dimension to our politics. But it surfaces— repeatedly in the essays that follow. Once again, Tocqueville got it right: "I think I can see the entire destiny of America contained in the first Puritan who stepped ashore" (1969, 279).

ILLUSIONS: THE TECHNICAL FIX

A nation skeptical of its own government often leaps at solutions that might run automatically, mechanically, without conscious political choices hammered out by the despised bureaucrats or politicians. The urge has a long legacy in American politics. However, few policy areas have churned out quite as many technical fixes as health care. All kinds of formulas, schemes, and metaphors promise technically correct public choices. Examples run to scientific planning, free market competition, DRG reimbursement methodologies, and—remarkably—citizen participation.

As described in this book, Oregon reformers attached costs and benefits to various health procedures (the technical formulas), took them to the people gathered in community meetings (for democratic legitimacy), and then to the legislature for final judgments about what health services would be funded. Squads of public officials flew in from around the world to learn about the Oregon method of scientific/democratic rationing. They all left empty-handed. There were no lessons to export. Beneath all the technical smoke and mirrors lay the old secret of good government: savvy politicians building political coalitions and making political judgments.

The often repeated lessons of health care competition echo the Oregon experience. Markets are political constructions that require constant tending. Imaginary contests between governments and markets pose a false choice. The real question is how to get the two properly working together. Even fiercely competitive health care markets do not leave the government behind. On the contrary, the more we rely on market forces, the more pressure we put on our public officials. Well-functioning markets require active, nimble oversight. That's true for three reasons: health care has a public side (we're not going to let people die on the streets); someone has to design, enforce, and adjust the rules of fair play (no ducking the bad risks); and finally, we have to control the inevitable fast-talking hucksters. Try organizing markets with improper public supervision and public backlash will follow fast (Morone 1992).

As states shoulder their new responsibilities, they will not find better programs in more precise algorithms or more robust methodologies. Improving our policies means recruiting talented men and women into strong, stable, public service organizations. Unfortunately, the dominant urge goes just the other way: slash budgets, freeze hiring, bash the bureaucrats.

These are flush times in most states. Budgets often balance. Tobacco settlement money pours in. Economies hum in high gear. But the prosperity does not reach everyone. Signs of trouble are also all around us: 2 million Americans in jail, 7 million on the brink of becoming homeless, 44 million without health insurance. Their distress ought to remind us of another, fading, national ideal: what Franklin Roosevelt called the quest for "a morally better world" where every American shares "the elementary decencies of life" (Roosevelt 1936).

Where is a reformer to begin? The political lessons from the states all point us toward the same conclusion: Our public policies are only as good as the governments that design them.

REFERENCES

Church, G. 1997. "Backlash Against HMOs: Doctors, Patients, Unions, Legislators Are Fed Up and Say They Won't Take It Anymore." *Time,* April 14.

Goldberger, S. 1990. "The Politics of Universal Access: The Massachusetts Health Security Act of 1988." *Journal of Health Politics, Policy and Law* 15 (4): 857–886.

Grodzins, M. 1966. *The American System: A New View of Governments in the United States,* ed. Daniel Elazar. Chicago: Rand McNally.

Kilborn, P. 1999. "Tennessee Talks of Rolling Back Health Plan for Uninsurables." *New York Times,* May 1.

Morone, J. A. 1992. "Hidden Complications." *American Prospect* 10 (Summer): 30–39.

———. 1994. "The Bureaucracy Empowered." In *The Politics of Health Care Reform,* ed. J. Morone and G. Belkin. Durham, NC: Duke University Press.

———. 1998. *The Democratic Wish.* New Haven, CT: Yale University Press.

———. 2001. *Hellfire Nation: Moral Politics in America.* New Haven, CT.: Yale University Press.

Nathan, R. P., and T. L. Gais. 1999. *Implementing the Personal Responsibility Act of 1996: A First Look.* Albany: Nelson A. Rockefeller Institute of Government, State University of New York.

Roosevelt, F. D. 1937. Second Inaugural Address, "I See One-Third of a Nation Ill-Housed, Ill-Clad, Ill-Nourished." In *The Public Papers and Addresses of Franklin D. Roosevelt.* 6 vols. New York: Macmillan.

Sabato, L. 1978. *Goodbye to Good-Time Charlie.* Lexington, MA: Lexington Books.

Tocqueville, A. de. 1969. *Democracy in America.* Trans. George Lawrence. Garden City, NY: Doubleday.

Tucker, W. 1996. "The Moral of the Story." *American Spectator* (October): 21–25.

1

State Health Policy in Transition

Robert B. Hackey

Reflecting on the current state of the American health care system often produces a sense of déjà vu. Thirty years ago, New York governor Nelson Rockefeller appointed a steering committee composed of leading business and academic leaders to assess the state of the nation's health care system. The following excerpt from the committee's findings, published in 1971, suggests that while much has changed in the health care system, several powerful themes have endured over the past three decades:

> Despite enormous advances and progress in the past 20 years, we have found irrefutable evidence of major weaknesses in the health care system as it exists today. Among them are: inadequate care for many people, especially the poor and the aged, and particularly in the ghettos and rural areas; rapidly rising costs and spiraling inflation; maldistribution of manpower and needless duplication of facilities; restrictive licensing and certification requirements; inefficient and irrational organization; too few incentives to control costs and too many incentives to inflate them; [and] widespread discontent accompanied by rising expectations. (State of New York 1971, 1)

Policymakers confront many of the same challenges as Nelson Rockefeller, but the landscape of state health policymaking looks dramatically different today. In the last ten years, the rapid growth of managed care was accompanied by the widespread dismantling of state planning and regulatory systems created during the 1970s and 1980s. The repeal of state hospital rate-setting laws and certificate-of-need controls did not mark the end of state regulation of the health care indus-

I am grateful to Tom Oliver and Dave Rochefort for their thorough and insightful comments on an earlier draft of this chapter and to Bob Vogel and Dave Stewart for drawing comparisons between past and present efforts at health care reform.

try but rather signaled the emergence of a new set of policymaking assumptions and approaches to controlling costs, promoting quality care, and ensuring access to care. To a large degree, what has happened to state regulation of health providers in the 1990s symbolizes the changes in the health care market. The evolution of market forces in health care, however, has produced demands for new forms of regulation.

States emerged as the principal catalysts of health care reform during the 1990s. States' interest in new approaches to improving access to health insurance and controlling health care costs predated the national debate over comprehensive health care reform proposals from 1992 to 1994. The policy stalemate that led to the demise of national reform in Congress in 1994 effectively ceded responsibility for policy innovation to the states. Indeed, even where Congress did enact significant legislation to reform the health insurance market and expand health insurance coverage for children, federal policymakers followed in the footsteps of earlier actions by the states. Legislation establishing minimum hospital stays for mothers and newborns and federal insurance market reforms merely ratified the existing status quo; more than 40 states had passed versions of each bill by the time it emerged from Congress.

LOOKING BACKWARD

In 1987, Lawrence Brown described health policy in the 1980s as a "decade of transition," a period characterized by a "system in which measures of competition and regulation that had been unthinkable ten years earlier were not only present but accepted and applauded" (1987, 12). After decades of accommodating provider interests in the design and implementation of Medicare and Medicaid, the 1980s reflected a growing willingness by the federal government to use its market power to reshape the health care marketplace. Congress endorsed a new prospective payment system (PPS) for Medicare payments to hospitals for inpatient care in 1983, ending nearly two decades of retrospective, cost-based reimbursement. Three years later, the Reagan administration won congressional approval for its proposal to terminate federal support for health planning programs (Mueller 1988).

As the decade drew to a close, Congress authorized the development of a new prospective payment methodology for physician services after a highly contentious legislative debate over the design of the new system (Oliver 1993). These federal cost-containment initiatives produced a ripple effect throughout the health care system as hospitals, home care agencies, and physicians scrambled to adapt to the federal government's new efficiency incentives. Their efforts resulted in reduced lengths of stay in the hospital, increased use of outpatient procedures, and recruitment of a veritable army of professional coders to maximize reimbursement under the new regulatory framework.

Improving Access to Health Insurance

By the early 1990s, access to health care had joined cost containment at the top of the nation's health policy agenda. Governors and legislatures established blue-ribbon study commissions, built coalitions in support of reform, and passed legislation to expand health insurance coverage. Following the election of Harris Wofford to the U.S. Senate in 1991—on a campaign platform that emphasized universal health insurance—health care reform quickly occupied a prominent position in the 1992 presidential campaign. As presidential candidates vied for voters' support with dueling health care reform proposals, states followed several paths to increase health insurance coverage. While some states (such as New York and Vermont) sought to reshape their health care systems through global budgets or single-payer health care, others (like Florida and California) created health insurance purchasing alliances or other variants of managed competition (e.g., Washington State).

Several states followed Hawaii's lead by passing plans that mandated employers to provide health insurance benefits or subsidized health insurance for low-income families and employees of small businesses. Such plans, however, ran afoul of the Employee Retirement Income Security Act of 1974 (ERISA), which preempted states from requiring employers to provide health insurance coverage for their workers. By limiting the ability of states to shift the cost of expanded coverage to the private sector, ERISA created a substantial fiscal barrier to compre-hensive health care reform. Several states sought to encourage employers to offer coverage through the use of tax incentives or subsidies, while others passed reforms designed to increase the availability of individual and small group insurance policies. Still others formed purchasing cooperatives to increase the market power of small groups or created high-risk pools for "uninsurable" patients.

As Deborah Stone (1992) has argued, states will find it difficult, if not impossible, to take the lead in increasing access to health insurance without substantial assistance from the federal government. Even with a strong domestic economy, states lack the fiscal capacity to fully finance expanded coverage for millions of working poor and middle-class families who lack health insurance. In particular, several issues present major obstacles for reformers who look to state governments as a vehicle to achieve universal coverage. State legislators fear the economic consequences of reform, both in terms of the commitment of new budgetary resources and in a loss of competitive advantage. States also face a variety of new budgetary commitments, ranging from education reform to rebuilding crumbling infrastructures and tax cuts. Health care reform is a priority issue for state governments, but many other influential interests are also competing for scarce resources in state capitols.

After the failure of the Clinton plan, Congress undertook a series of incremental steps to increase access to health care. Legislators first guaranteed insurance portability with the passage of the Health Insurance Portability and Accountability Act (P.L. 104-191) in 1996. The law signaled a new role for the federal government in regulating the insurance market by requiring all insurers to renew their policies except when subscribers failed to pay their premiums and prohibiting discrimination against individuals on the basis of health status (Ladenheim 1997). The practical impact of the new law was less dramatic, however, since its passage followed in the footsteps of similar legislation in more than 40 states. Furthermore, P.L. 104-191 had a limited impact on access to health insurance, for its protections only applied to individuals who had insurance for at least 18 months. Significantly, legislators placed no limits on the price of individual policies and did not require insurers to extend coverage to previously uninsured persons.

A lack of federal leadership to improve access to health care is particularly troubling, for the percentage of full-time workers covered by employer-sponsored health insurance continues to decline. By 1999, more than 44.3 million Americans lacked health insurance at some point during the previous twelve months (Campbell 1999). In just one example of what has become a national trend, a 1998 study estimated that the number of uninsured Californians increased from 4.7 million to 6.6 million from 1988 to 1996 (American Health Line 1998b). Although Congress approved a significant expansion of federally subsidized health insurance benefits for children living in poverty in the Balanced Budget Act of 1997, federal policymakers have been unable to agree on a strategy to increase either the availability or affordability of private health insurance for workers, the unemployed, and their dependents. As a result, responsibility for mending the gaping holes in the health insurance safety net currently rests squarely on the shoulders of state governments.

The second and more significant expansion of health insurance coverage in the mid-1990s occurred in August 1997, when President Clinton signed the State Children's Health Insurance Program (SCHIP) into law. The legislation promised states $24 billion over five years to extend health insurance to children in families with incomes below 200% of the federal poverty line, but as the chapters by Frank Thompson and William Brandon, Rosemary Chaudry, and Alice Sardell point out, the implementation of the law has varied widely among states. While some states (e.g., Arkansas, Tennessee, and Wyoming) have established low-income eligibility thresholds, others have opened enrollment to children in families earning as much as 350% of the federal poverty level (e.g., New Jersey).

The new program afforded states great flexibility in implementing plans, either through expanding Medicaid eligibility, creating a new freestanding health insurance program for children, or designing a combination Medicaid/CHIP program. Participation in CHIP is voluntary, but by the end of 1999 all 50 states and the District of Columbia had received approval for their plans to expand health insurance to uninsured children. By late 1999, more than 1.9 million children were enrolled in state CHIP programs (HCFA 1999b). CHIP was the most significant federally funded expansion of health insurance coverage since 1965, but its design reflected the "devolution revolution" that took Washington by storm in the 1990s.

As Thompson points out in Chapter 2, states vary widely in their degree of success in enrolling eligible children. Fully implemented, the Medicaid mandates and CHIP would go a long way toward reducing the number of children in the United States who lack health insurance. First, however, states must deal successfully with what Thompson describes as the "take-up" challenge, as more than half of the 11 million uninsured children in the United States meet the income qualifications to be enrolled in Medicaid or CHIP but are not currently enrolled. Although the federal government has created a web site *(www.insurekidsnow.gov)* to promote awareness of the programs, many poor families lack Internet access, and outreach efforts vary widely from state to state.

Apart from legislation banning "drive-through deliveries" (see Declercq and Simmes 1997), Congress and the president also left the regulation of the managed care industry in the hands of state governments. Efforts to enact a "patient's bill of rights" in the 105th and 106th Congresses floundered in a sea of partisan wrangling over expanding medical savings accounts (MSAs) and restrictions on patient lawsuits. Debates over managed care reforms exposed a widening fault line among congressional Republicans, as rank-and-file members openly challenged the leadership of the House to support bipartisan reform (Carey 1999; Congressional Quarterly 1998). The inability of federal policymakers to craft national standards to regulate managed care providers and expand health insurance coverage to uninsured workers and families effectively turned over responsibility for developing innovative approaches to protect patients and ensure fair competition among providers and payers to the states.

States have filled the policy vacuum at the federal level by expanding access to care for the uninsured in several ways. Medicaid demonstration waivers, new regulations governing the behavior of managed care organizations, empowering consumers with information about the cost and quality of health care services, and overseeing a wave of mergers and conversions among hospitals and health plans defined a new role for states in competitive health care markets. In many states, dramatic changes in the health insurance marketplace forced state policymakers to grapple with difficult questions regarding access to care and competition in the health care industry. The decision of insurers to withdraw from Kentucky, Washington State, and other states that embraced individual insurance market reforms such as guaranteed issue, community rating, and rating bands to increase access to health insurance policies created a crisis atmosphere in many state capitols (Hackey 2000b). In early 2000, the fiscal crises facing several of the nation's most prominent HMOs (e.g., Harvard Pilgrim Health Care, Tufts Health Plan, and

Oxford Health) led legislators and advocates to contemplate a much greater role for state governments in regulating, and in some cases subsidizing, the private health insurance industry.

Public Health Promotion and Disease Prevention

Although states made substantial progress in expanding access to health care for the poor and underserved, significant disparities in health status and health care outcomes persist among different racial and socioeconomic groups and among regions in the United States. A chorus of causes and problems competes for attention and resources from policymakers and the public. During the 1990s, problems such as AIDS, food safety, hepatitis B and C, injury prevention initiatives, lead poisoning, low birthweight babies, needle exchange programs, teen pregnancy, universal vaccination, to name just a few, demanded attention from cash-strapped state and local governments. As William Waters notes in Chapter 10, public health programs have frequently been asked to spread a limited pool of resources among a growing number of claimants.

The extraordinary financial windfall generated by state lawsuits against the tobacco industry unleashed a wave of optimism within the public health community—at last, advocates believed, billions of dollars would be available to adequately fund health education and promotion programs; society had dedicated resources for the foreseeable future. Exuberance, however, was quickly tempered by political reality: rather than serving as a trust fund to bankroll public health programs, in many states the tobacco settlement became an exercise in distributive politics. Legislators and interest groups found many ways to spend the unexpected windfall, but a relatively small proportion of the settlement has been dedicated to antismoking programs to date (Goodman 2000). In an ironic twist, several southeastern states have enacted legislation dedicating settlement funds to assist tobacco growers and their communities; other states have used their settlement payments to balance budgets, enhance K–12 education, lower college tuition, control floods, or create "rainy day" funds (Murray 2000). In short, while a substantial portion of the multibillion-dollar settlement has been dedicated to a variety of health care programs, public health programs continue to have a political problem.

The central role of the states in shaping health care reform in the 1990s raises several important questions. First, how have states adapted to the rapid changes within the health care industry over the past decade? Second, do states possess the requisite administrative and fiscal capacities to carry out their new roles? Third, how have traditional advocacy coalitions at the state level changed in recent years? Finally, how have these changes reshaped the landscape of state health care policymaking? Taken together, these four core questions constitute the primary agenda for this book, and each will be explored in different settings and policy arenas in the following chapters.

UNDERSTANDING POLICY CHANGE

State health care policies in the 1990s reflect the changing dynamics of the health care system itself. As states have embraced market-oriented solutions in health care, existing regulatory programs and institutions became less relevant for solving contemporary problems. State health care regulation has continued to expand along with the growth of market-oriented reforms, for as James Morone (1992, 41) observed more than five years ago, "All markets are political constructions. To make them work, we have to agree on rules and enforce them reliably." The transformation of state health care policy over the past decade reflects several fundamental changes in the principal policy assumptions and objectives undergirding state regulation of health providers and third-party payers. In particular, several developments have transformed state health care policymaking over the past decade. These changes have led to an overall transformation of the assumptions underlying state health policy choices, the adoption of new policy tools, efforts to harness the power of competitive markets, and the development of new standards to govern the behavior of providers and purchasers of care.

First, current policy choices are the product of new assumptions about the most effective approach for controlling runaway costs and promoting access to quality care. Second, new policy assumptions have led to the adoption of new policy instruments. By the mid-1990s, many states had jettisoned efforts to allocate resources through planning and regulatory controls in favor of reforms that promote accountability among providers and payers. Third, rather than setting prices, policymakers have sought to maintain competition in the market by regulating the mergers and conversions of health providers and health plans. Finally, policymakers have largely abandoned the pursuit of universal health insurance coverage at the state level through comprehensive reform in favor of incremental reforms targeted at well-defined groups of uninsured residents.

New Policy Assumptions

Frank Thompson (1981, 8) has argued that "a health policy is a hypothesis. It specifies that if $a, b, c, \ldots$ are done at time one, then $x, y, z \ldots$ will result at time two." For example, the basic hypotheses underlying state cost-containment efforts have changed dramatically over the past decade. In the 1970s and early 1980s, states sought to rationalize the health care system through citizen participation in local and regional planning programs and certificate-of-need review of new capital investments and services. Policymakers in several states embraced prospective hospital rate-setting programs to control inpatient hospital costs and created enormously complicated all-payer regulatory systems designed to promote efficiency within the hospital industry (Hackey 1998; McDonough 1997).

The declining popularity of hospital rate-setting and other "command and control" regulatory models in recent years is the result of three interrelated trends:

the growing reliance on managed care among both public and private health insurers, the emergence of a new "policy image" (Baumgartner and Jones 1991) for rate-setting and certificate of need, and legal challenges to state regulatory programs.

Few developments have had greater impact on prevailing attitudes toward health care cost containment than the rapid growth of managed care over the past decade. Nationwide, HMO enrollment rose from 30.3 million in 1988 to 81.3 million in 1999 (Interstudy 1999). However, while the annual rate of growth in HMO enrollment exceeded 10% from 1994 to 1998, total HMO enrollment growth fell to a 6.5% annual growth rate as the decade drew to a close. The slowdown in the rate of HMO enrollment reflected both the widening backlash against managed care among policymakers and the public and a natural plateau, as most states completed their transition to Medicaid managed care by 1999. The rapid growth of managed care during the 1990s, however, ultimately made most hospital rate-setting programs obsolete.

The new policy image of rate-setting is very different from what it was 20 years ago, when regulation was hailed as an essential component of government efforts to control rising health care costs. The effectiveness of inpatient hospital rate-setting programs in controlling costs declined as more patients received care in outpatient settings and fewer patients were covered by indemnity-based health insurance. State hospital rate-setting systems came under fire from both providers and payers in the late 1980s (Hackey 1998). The complexity of both rate-setting and certificate-of-need programs contributed to growing dissatisfaction among providers and payers alike, who lobbied state legislators for relief from onerous reporting burdens and lengthy rate appeals processes. Although payers and policymakers welcomed regulatory controls as a necessary lever to influence the behavior of the hospital industry in the 1970s and early 1980s, the rapid growth of managed care led payers to view rate-setting as an obstacle that precluded them from negotiating volume discounts with provider networks.

In addition, legal challenges to rate-setting programs in New York and New Jersey during the early 1990s cast doubts upon the future of rate regulation. Although the U.S. Supreme Court ultimately upheld the authority of states to regulate inpatient hospital rates, a series of lower court decisions raised doubts about the future of rate-setting and led state policymakers to explore alternative approaches to cost control. Taken together, these developments undermined political support for state rate-setting programs among key stakeholders.

By the early 1990s, a fresh consensus was emerging among policymakers, payers, and providers over the most effective approach to health care cost containment. As traditional forms of price and entry regulation fell out of favor, the rhetoric of the marketplace began to dominate policy debates. Thirteen states repealed their certificate of need (CON) statutes in the late 1980s following the termination of federal support for health planning; by 1997, more than two dozen other states that retained CON requirements had modified their restrictions on capital investments and new services (Hackey and Fuller 1998). The focus on competition among health plans and providers as a means of controlling costs during the 1993–1994 debate over health care reform in Congress effectively redefined the health policy agenda by introducing a new policy hypothesis. Markets, not regulation, now offered the best chance of controlling costs, improving quality, and expanding access to care.

Instead of waiting for final congressional action, states pressed ahead with their own health care reform strategies. Florida created regional health insurance purchasing cooperatives as a means of controlling costs and improving access to care for small businesses and the uninsured, while California created a state purchasing cooperative in 1992 and debated the adoption of a single-payer health care system in a public referendum. Even as the momentum for comprehensive reform waned, states followed the new policy hypothesis by embracing procompetitive solutions aimed at maximizing their purchasing power. With encouragement from the Clinton administration, states enrolled a growing proportion of their Medicaid caseloads into managed care plans in the mid-1990s.

The growing role of competition in the health care system has changed the nature of state health care regulation but not the demand for it. States adopted new regulations in an effort to protect patients and providers from the worst excesses of managed care and market competition (Hellinger 1996). Decisions regarding the allocation of capital and the rate of payment for health providers, however, have increasingly been delegated to the private sector. Rather than being asked to manage the organization, financing, and delivery of health care in accordance with a systemwide plan, state policymakers now face a new set of challenges in harnessing market forces for public purposes. The competitiveness of health care markets, however, varies widely from state to state and within states (Kronick et al. 1993). Indeed, even after a decade of steady increases in managed care penetration, many states still lack the basic prerequisites of a competitive market for health insurance (Fossett et al. 1999).

Promoting Accountability

The changes in the health care industry in the 1990s closely follow Paul Starr's (1982) predictions about the consequences of expanding corporate control over hospitals and medical practice. The rapid growth of for-profit hospital chains, coupled with increased managed care penetration, led to growing tensions between hospital administrators and their medical staffs. To control the use—and hence, the cost—of expensive diagnostic tests and inpatient hospital services, managed care organizations (MCOs) developed new guidelines, or "practice standards," which participating providers were expected to follow in treating common diseases or conditions.

Each of these developments contributed to a gradual erosion of the professional autonomy of practicing physicians and sparked new conflicts over appropriate patient care between physicians and third-party insurers (Marlow 1998). Ironically, while for decades the American Medical Association (AMA) attacked proposals for government-sponsored health insurance as a threat to the quality of medical care, utilization review standards and practice guidelines adopted by Blue Cross and other private health insurers now constitute the greatest threat to the professional autonomy of physicians. By the late 1990s, national surveys reported that more than a quarter of the nation's primary care doctors felt that they were expected to practice beyond their areas of expertise (Gentry 1999).

In a competitive health care system, state governments may establish rules to protect patients and providers from unfair competitive practices. State legislators have pursued several strategies to foster accountability among health plans. First, states have regulated the relationships between participating physicians and health plans and by legislating new standards of medical practice for selected procedures. Second, states have increased consumer access to information about health providers by publishing profiles of physicians and health plans and by developing "report cards" to evaluate the quality of care for selected procedures such as cardiac surgery provided by different institutions or physicians (Langreth 1998). Finally, states have strengthened the ability of consumers to sue health providers as a means of discouraging health plans from denying necessary care.

As David Rochefort's discussion of the backlash against managed care in Chapter 5 illustrates, public confidence in the promise of competition to control costs and improve the quality of patient care has plummeted in recent years (Jacobs and Shapiro 1999). By April 2000, an NBC News/*Wall Street Journal* poll revealed that the voters viewed HMOs' and insurance companies' practice of "limiting medical treatment because of cost" as the "first priority for health care reform" (*Wall Street Journal* 2000). As public trust in HMOs has declined, many plans have undertaken ambitious new advertising campaigns aimed at reassuring subscribers (Jeffery 1998a).

The push for new restrictions on MCOs benefited from a highly favorable policy image (Ginsburg and Lesser 1999; Rodwin 1999). In stark contrast to debates over purchasing alliances, global budgets, and various managed competition proposals earlier in the decade, proposed patients' rights legislation such as minimum maternity stays was understandable, popular, and seemingly easily implemented. As Declercq and Simmes (1997) have noted, despite ambiguous evidence in support of restrictions on early discharge, the symbolic potency of legislation designed to benefit new mothers and babies overshadowed arguments from insurers that a "one size fits all" policy governing maternal discharge was unnecessary.

The rapid diffusion of state legislation banning "drive-through deliveries" foreshadowed a new era of state regulation, as policymakers responded to pleas from a multiplicity of groups for protection from the vagaries of managed care. State legislators imposed new mandates on MCOs in an incremental fashion in the late 1990s. The success of drive-through delivery legislation encouraged other medical specialists to seek legislative protections. By 1999, 37 states had passed direct access laws that either allowed women to designate their OB/GYN as a primary care provider or provided for an annual visit to an OB/GYN without a referral from a gatekeeper (Stauffer 1999). More than 20 states enacted legislation that would allow patients with serious medical conditions to continue to visit their current physician for a predefined period as long as he or she agrees to accept payment from the patient's health plan. As the 1990s drew to a close, however, more states turned to procedural reforms such as the right to appeal adverse decisions rather than substantive regulations that established standards of care (Frankford 1999).

As a means of empowering consumers, states are disseminating information about the quality of medical care. Two assumptions undergird this strategy. First, armed with information about providers, citizens will become more sophisticated consumers as they select health plans and providers. Second, the widespread availability of information will encourage providers to act responsibly and will offer a powerful incentive for providers suffering from deficiencies in quality control or cost-effectiveness to improve their performance. With performance data readily available to consumers and the mass media, providers who fail to improve their standing will face the loss of patients to more highly ranked providers or health plans. Although few assessments of the impact of consumer guides to health care services have been completed to date, initial results from Missouri's experience with consumer reports on obstetrical services (Longo et al. 1997) and the decrease in mortality rates for cardiac surgery in New York (New York State Department of Health 1995) suggest that comparative performance studies offer powerful incentives to providers to improve the quality of patient care.

Policymakers have embraced both legislation and rulemaking to increase consumer access to information. Several states have published consumer guides to managed care plans and provider networks. In 1996, Massachusetts introduced the nation's first statewide physician profiling system. Although much of the information was already available in the public domain, accessing data about particular physicians was difficult since data were gathered by different agencies (Donohue 1997). Consumer demand for the new service was overwhelming; the Board of Registration in Medicine's Internet web site logged more than 800,000 requests for profiles in its first four months of operation, and the board was mailing more than 1,000 profiles per day (Pfeiffer 1997; Lederberg 1997).

The start-up cost for establishing the new profiling service in Massachusetts was $250,000; annual operating costs were estimated at more than $100,000 (Donohue 1997). By 2000, medical licensing boards in 14 states offered physician profiles online through the Association of State Medical Board Executive Directors' "DocFinder" Internet web site (http://www.docboard.org). Patients can also access online information about their physicians' board certifications from the American Board of Medical Specialties (http://www.certifieddoctor.org). Critics of Massachusetts' physician profiling system argued that public disclosure of malpractice claims and settlement information would encourage physicians to avoid high-risk cases and decrease physician interest in settling malpractice claims outside of court in fear of blemishing their public profiles (Donohue 1997).

In addition to profiling physicians, several state health departments have published "report cards" on cardiothoracic surgery to assist patients and third-party payers seeking specialty care. The New York State Department of Health gathers data from all health care facilities in its SPARCS data set and publishes annual reports on costs and patient outcomes to assist hospitals in identifying potential quality problems (New York State Department of Health 1995). In addition, the state contracted with the RAND Corporation to study the appropriate utilization of cardiac surgery in New York in 1990 (Leape et al. 1993). Comparative data on cardiac surgery in New York are now also available on the Internet; patients can download information about adjusted mortality rates, expected death rates, and surgical volume for both hospitals and surgeons (see the "information for consumers link" at *http://www.health.state.ny.us*).

Beginning in 1992, Pennsylvania's Health Care Cost Containment Council also published a "Consumer's Guide to Coronary Artery Bypass Surgery" that compared both hospitals' and surgeons' expected and actual mortality rates and listed the average charges for procedures in each of the state's hospitals (see the comparative listings online at *http://www.phc4.org*). Like other provider profiles, however, efforts in New York and Pennsylvania were criticized by some institutions that received poor ratings for providing incomplete or misleading information that did not include appropriate adjustments for differences in case mix and severity of illness.

By facilitating patient choice through dissemination of comparative data about the performance of physicians and health plans, states seek to empower consumers and modify the behavior of providers. Implicit in this approach is the threat of exit: unless poorly performing providers change their behavior, patients will take their business elsewhere. As Marc Rodwin (1997) observes, however, policies that encourage patients to leave substandard providers may discriminate against the poor, who tend to have fewer health insurance choices, and fail to account for the fact that the departure of patients with chronic or high-cost illnesses is likely to improve the fiscal health of MCOs. In addition to policies that facilitate patient choice among plans and providers, Rodwin argues that policymakers must enact new protections for patients who elect to remain with their current health plan. New mechanisms need to be created to resolve patient grievances, fund independent ombudsmen to advocate for patient needs, and increase consumer participation in governing health plans.

Since 1996, several states have enacted laws designed to increase the voice of patients and providers in seeking relief from MCOs. Patients and providers who have been unable to resolve their differences over covered benefits or access to care through MCOs' own internal appeals procedures may contest adverse decisions from utilization review companies and health plans by lodging a formal complaint with an independent agency such as the state Department of Health (Johnson and DeBlois 1997). Physicians also have turned to state medical boards as a vehicle for challenging the rulings of HMO medical directors who decide that services are not "medically necessary"; in 1997, an Arizona state appeals court upheld the authority of the state medical board to review the necessity of proposed patient treatments (Jeffery 1998b). Texas legislators created a dispute resolution process for physicians whose contracts are terminated by MCOs and established an independent external review process to handle patient appeals regarding the denial of coverage for care on the grounds of medical necessity (Demkovich 1998c).

Although the National Association of Insurance Commissioners estimated that Americans would file more than 35,000 complaints regarding health insurance coverage in 1998, to date states that have instituted independent reviews of coverage denials have not witnessed a significant increase in the volume of patient appeals; indeed, most patients who are denied coverage never appeal adverse decision from MCOs (Johnson and DeBlois 1997; Demkovich 1998a). In 1997, Texas became the first state in the United States to allow patients to take their grievances with MCOs to court (California and Louisiana have subsequently followed suit). The Texas statute, which was upheld upon appeal, permits patients to sue their health plan for damages if they are injured as a result of a plan's decision to deny coverage for medical treatment (McGinley 1998). To date, however, a relatively small percentage of patients have challenged adverse determinations by MCOs.

Each of the reforms described above seeks to hold health care providers and health care plans accountable for their actions. By mandating coverage for certain medical procedures or guaranteeing direct access to providers, legislators have responded to growing consumer frustrations over the propensity of managed care plans to disallow coverage for services patients had come to expect. Although new mandates established new rights for patients, they also limited the ability of MCOs to control costs. New legislative requirements to disseminate information to subscribers about managed care or to establish independent external review programs for patient appeals were also designed to foster accountability among MCOs by discouraging plans from inappropriately denying coverage for services in an effort to control costs. At the same time that state regulators imposed new restrictions on MCOs in the name of ensuring quality patient care, however, legislators increasingly turned to competition among health plans to control the cost of health coverage for Medicaid beneficiaries and state employees.

Harnessing the Market

By the early 1990s, Medicaid had become a "budget buster" in most states. A combination of factors led to rapid growth in program costs. Loopholes in federal reimbursement criteria enabled states to use a variety of creative financing arrangements to qualify existing state services for federal matching funds. Collaborative arrangements between hospitals and state governments led to the enactment of provider taxes, provider donations, and inter- and intragovernmental transfers to maximize revenues for both hospitals and state governments using disproportionate share hospital payments (Coughlin et al. 1994).

Beginning in the mid-1980s, Congress significantly expanded the scope of mandated services for poor women and children through the use of unfunded mandates. By 1990, new federal mandates required states to expand Medicaid eligibility to all pregnant women and infants whose income fell below 133% of the federal poverty line and granted continuous eligibility to women throughout their postpartum period. Furthermore, Congress required states to expand coverage for poor children: children whose family income fell below 133% of poverty were eligible for Medicaid benefits until they reached the age of 6; by 2002, all children under the age of 18 whose family income is up to 100% of poverty will be eligible for benefits (Holahan et al. 1995). Although the federal government assumed more than 50% of total program outlays in all states, the new requirements effectively forced states to share in the cost of expanded coverage.

Prior to 1990, only one state—Arizona—had received a waiver to enroll all of its Medicaid-eligible population into managed care. Soon after taking office in 1993, the Clinton administration revamped the federal waiver process and encouraged states to shift AFDC-eligible Medicaid beneficiaries into managed care under sections 1915 and 1115 waivers permitted by the Social Security Act. The number of Medicaid beneficiaries enrolled in managed care increased nearly tenfold from 1983 to 1993, largely as a result of the use of section 1915 waivers. Between 1993 and 1997, more than 30 states applied for waivers to move Medicaid enrollees into managed care programs or to modify eligibility for Medicaid or both (HCFA 1998). As a result, the number of Medicaid beneficiaries enrolled in managed care plans has soared from fewer than 800,000 in 1983 to more than 16.5 million in 1998 (Rosenbaum and Darnell 1995; HCFA 1998). Nationwide, the percentage of Medicaid beneficiaries enrolled in managed care rose from 9.5% in 1991 to 53.6% in 1998 (HCFA 1998); by 1998, 30 states (along with Puerto Rico) had enrolled more than 50% of their Medicaid population in managed care organizations, while 12 other states had enrolled from 25 to 49% (HCFA 1999a).

The previous track record of Medicaid managed care programs in the 1970s highlights the challenges facing policymakers charged with overseeing the implementation of such programs (Welch and Miller 1988). In 1971, California launched a voluntary managed care system to serve Medicaid beneficiaries by contracting with established HMOs and prepaid health plans (PHPs) that were specifically formed to serve Medicaid beneficiaries. The programs were a disaster for the poor. Providers used fraudulent marketing strategies; large numbers of enrollees who did not select a plan were assigned to one by default; enrollees desiring to leave the plan were retained for inordinate time periods; and in the case of PHPs, medical care was of poor quality and often nonexistent (Jesilow, Pontell, and Geis 1993). To discourage the formation of undercapitalized programs designed specifically for the poor, Congress required in 1976 that prepaid plans that accepted Medicaid patients enroll at least 50% of their members as private patients. After the 1976 amendments, the use of managed care programs declined rapidly. In response to state demands for more flexibility in administering Medicaid, Congress relaxed the restrictions imposed on Medicaid managed care programs in 1981; the prohibition against "Medicaid only" HMOs was eliminated by the Balanced Budget Act of 1997.

Medicaid expansions emerged as one of the principal vehicles for improving access to care for the uninsured during the 1990s. To date, however, although millions of poor children and families are now eligible for Medicaid coverage, actual enrollment of uninsured families has not kept pace with recent extensions of eligibility. Although CHIP and many Medicaid managed care waivers have expanded access to care for the poor, such programs fail to address the health insurance needs of millions of working- and middle-class families. In California, for example, the UCLA Center for Health Policy Research estimated that nearly 500,000 children and 5 million adults would not qualify for assistance from either the Medi-Cal program or the state's new Healthy Families initiative (American Health Line 1998a). These examples illustrate an important limitation of current efforts to expand access to health care services for underserved families: in the absence of comprehensive and ongoing outreach efforts, state and federal policies that increase eligibility for benefits are unlikely to significantly reduce the number of uninsured children and families.

Setting Standards for Competition

In an increasingly competitive health care system, states are under pressure to establish guidelines to protect providers and consumers from "unfair competition" among cost-conscious purchasers in several areas. First, the conversion of nonprofit Blue Cross plans presents both a challenge and an opportunity for states. Competitive pressures forced many Blues to drop community rating, introduce HMOs or managed indemnity plans, or otherwise emulate the marketing and organizational strategies of their for-profit competitors. Conversions provide policymakers with an opportunity to negotiate long-term benefits for the community through the creation of charitable foundations and grant programs.

Second, the rapid growth of large for-profit hospital chains such as Columbia/HCA and Tenet and the "merger mania" among nonprofit institutions in the early 1990s forced legislators to grapple with issues of corporate accountability and governance for nonprofit health care institutions. In several states, proposed mergers or acquisitions of nonprofit institutions with out-of-state proprietary chains set off a firestorm of controversy, while the emergence of competing care networks within states raised concerns about the competitiveness of the health care system. Third, the emergence of for-profit hospitals and the death of state rate-setting programs in many states also raise difficult policy questions about the provision of charity care in a market-driven health care system. Finally, state policymakers are under increased pressure from providers to preserve their right to participate in health plans that increasingly resort to some form of selective contracting to control costs.

Proposals to convert several of the nation's largest Blue Cross plans from nonprofit to for-profit status brought the issue of state oversight of health care mergers and conversions to the top of many state legislative agendas. As Judith Bell (1996, 61) observed during the heyday of Blue Cross conversion activity in 1996, the "culture of health care used to value the care of the vulnerable; now it is increasingly devoted to the care of the shareholders. One issue in this turn toward the market is simply what happens to all the public resources that have gone into building America's health charities." In the debate over health plan conversions, this question is typically addressed through a cy pres proceeding; the cy pres doctrine holds that judicial approval is required before the assets of a nonprofit corporation or charitable trust can be used for purposes other than those defined in the organization's charter or articles of incorporation (Peregrine 1997). As nonprofit hospitals sought to affiliate themselves with larger for-profit networks, and health plans that had enjoyed the benefits of their nonprofit, tax-exempt status opted to create for-profit holding companies to raise capital for expansion, new participants joined debates over health care policymaking. In particular, state attorneys general entered the fray in many states to challenge proposed mergers and seek notification and public disclosure of information related to the proposed transaction (Singer 1997).

Turning to the courts rather than the legislative process, attorneys general in many states alleged that for-profit mergers and conversions represented a departure from the charitable purpose for which the "charitable trusts" had been founded and supported by the public. Although the nature of the review process varied from state to state, the attorneys general sought to preserve the charitable assets that had been dedicated for public purposes by donors. By the end of the 1990s, state officials were actively engaged in the process of knowledge and policy diffusion, as New England's attorneys general were actively collaborating on a wide range of issues, from takeovers to rising prescription drug costs and nursing home bankruptcies (Anand 1999).

Conversions raised new challenges for state regulators who faced the daunting task of valuing nonprofit assets (DeLucia 1996; Singer 1997). In March 1997, the National Association of Attorneys General issued recommendations to guide the development of legislation governing the conversion of health plans and hospitals to for-profit status. The association called for requirements that would provide for advance notice of proposed conversions to state regulators and the public, independent valuations of charitable assets, and prohibitions against excessive compensation or profits for officers or directors associated with the transaction (*State Health Watch* 1997). Hospital conversions have also been challenged on the grounds that the merger or sale of institutions to for-profit organizations constituted a breach of directors' fiduciary duties of care and loyalty (Singer 1997).

In addition to regulating conversions of nonprofit health plans and hospitals, state governments must also cope with a continuing crisis in financing charity care. The expansion of for-profit hospital chains into new markets has raised concerns among providers and policymakers over the provision of charity care to the poor and uninsured. As the percentage of patients enrolled in managed care continues to multiply, hospitals find it increasingly difficult to finance uncompensated care for the medically indigent, for opportunities to shift costs to traditional indemnity payers have diminished.

The deregulation of state rate-setting systems also raises new concerns for urban teaching hospitals and institutions that serve a large proportion of uninsured and publicly insured patients. In the past, rate-setting systems in New York and other states assessed a surcharge on hospital charges to fund uncompensated care pools that were distributed among institutions on the basis of need. In the wake of deregulation, providers will be required to negotiate with third-party payers to fund graduate medical education and uncompensated care. In Massachusetts and New York, third-party insurers and other purchasers of health care have complained bitterly about the imposition of new surcharges on hospital bills to finance uncompensated care; Blue Cross officials in Massachusetts threatened to slash payments to hospitals in response to a surcharge of 5.06% assessed on all hospital bills. After five years of wrangling, New Jersey legislators approved a new financing mechanism for the state's $400 million charity care system that doubled the state's cigarette tax and ended a 19% surtax on hospital charges (*State Health Notes* 1998b).

Physicians have increasingly turned to legislative solutions to counterbalance the use of selective contracting and other exclusionary tactics by health care plans. In an increasingly competitive marketplace, many health plans sought to extract substantial volume discounts from hospitals, pharmacies, physicians, and mental health professionals; others dropped providers whose costs exceed those of a peer group from their networks. In short, the success of providers in supplying cost-effective care increasingly determines their access to paying patients. In response, provider groups in many states pressed state lawmakers to enact "any willing provider" laws that would prohibit third-party insurers from excluding physicians. In addition, the use of primary care physicians as "gatekeepers" to limit access to medical specialists sparked a wave of grassroots activity at the state level as obstetricians and gynecologists lobbied for legislation that would either guarantee women the right to an annual visit or allow OB/GYNs to serve as primary care providers for their patients. To date, 37 states have enacted direct access laws that mandate that health plans must afford women an opportunity to visit their OB/GYN without a referral from a gatekeeper (Stauffer 1999; American College of Nurse-Midwives 1998).

In the late 1990s, a growing number of states created new protections designed to ensure that physicians will function as advocates for patients rather than as cost control agents for health insurers. In 1998, Pennsylvania enacted a patients' bill of rights (SB 91) that responded to the growing concern among policymakers and the public over managed care discussed by Rochefort in Chapter 5 of this volume. It called for providers and health plans to use "sound medical principles, not financial incentives," as the basis for patient care (*State Health Notes* 1998a). In response to heavy lobbying by consumer groups and state medical societies, 48 states passed restrictions against "gag clauses" that prohibit physicians from disclosing information about medical treatments that are not covered by the patient's insurance plan (Stauffer 1999). Gag clauses assume a variety of forms, from prohibiting physicians to discuss treatment options that are not covered by the patient's health plan to recommending care outside of the plan's network (Miller 1997). Although MCOs complained that public concern about gag rules and other restrictions on the autonomy of physicians was overblown, public anxiety over the possibility that patients would be denied care fueled a nationwide backlash that emboldened policymakers to pass new legislation designed to hold health insurers accountable for the well-being of their subscribers.

Managed care also contributed to the growth of collective bargaining among physicians as doctors organized to protect themselves from MCO restrictions on working conditions, reimbursement, and medical practice (Bologna 1998). As hospitals have cut staff in response to tighter budgets, physicians have become increasingly militant in challenging HMOs and other managed care organizations. In January 1998, the AMA endorsed a campaign by doctors in Chicago to organize a union at a suburban hospital. In December 1999, the unionization drive took another dramatic step forward as residents and interns at Boston Medical Center voted to unionize by a vote a 177 to 1 (Knox 1999), marking the first time that residents and interns at a private hospital had cast ballots for federally protected union representation. Unionization was not even an option for most doctors in training until November 1999, when the National Labor Relations Board ruled that since doctors in training provide basic care, they are workers, not students (who have no right to collective bargaining).

The ability of managed care to control health care costs—once its principal appeal to policymakers and private purchasers—has recently been called into question. For most of the 1990s, HMO premium increases had been modest, and in some cases, businesses were able to actually win premium decreases. By 2000, however, rising costs for prescription drugs and several years of below average premium increases had taken their toll on managed care companies' financial health, and a growing number of HMOs reported double-digit premium increases, increased copayments for subscribers, and higher cost sharing (Cohn and Moore 2000).

THE POLITICAL CONTEXT OF STATE HEALTH POLICYMAKING

The events of the past decade have raised new hopes—and questions—for those who turn to the states as leaders in health care reform. According to James Morone, "Properly functioning medical markets place extraordinary demands on government or special private agents, or both. The task requires far more skill than the grosser judgments required by the global budgeting of national health insurance" (1992, 41). Critics of the devolution of health care policymaking to the states argue that in an economic downturn, states will be hard-pressed to maintain the fiscal effort required by recent expansions of health insurance coverage for children and the working poor.

Additionally, federal policy continues to limit the options available to state officials interested in restructuring health care financing. While many states have expanded Medicaid eligibility, created high-risk insurance pools, subsidized or regulated charity care, and increased access to care for pregnant women and children, the actual achievement of universal health insurance coverage via state initiatives faces many obstacles. In particular, the federal Employee Retirement Income Security Act of 1974 limits the ability of states to regulate health plans offered by self-insured businesses.

The ability of states to develop and implement effective policies to control costs and limit the excesses of for-profit medicine is shaped by the nature of their health policy regimes (Hackey 1998). Different regimes reflect "fundamental differences in (1) the nature of the decision-making and implementation process and (2) the ability of state agencies to change the behavior of health providers. While the range of participants in health care policymaking does not vary considerably from one state to the next, the relationships among state officials and private interests will change from one regime to another" (Hackey 1998, 14).

Under *imposed* regimes, state officials preside over a regulatory apparatus that can be used to further the state's interests or limit the activities of providers and payers. Conversely, *market* regimes represent a fundamentally different view of the proper role of state government in regulating the health care industry; under these circumstances, policy choices are designed to nurture competition among providers and payers, with minimal intervention by the state. In a *negotiated* regime, health policy choices reflect a lack of consensus over both the means and ends of state intervention in the health care industry.

Policymaking in an imposed policy regime resembles an authoritative decision-making process; state officials regularly seek to circumscribe the activities of providers and payers through legislative mandates or administrative rulemaking (Hackey 1998). Regulatory policy is shaped within institutions created and controlled by the state rather than through private or quasi-public agencies or commissions. Bolstered by strong political support from the legislature and the governor, state officials within imposed regimes enjoy considerable autonomy; a high degree of policy cohesion (Robertson 1993), a broad statutory mandate, and the expertise of a highly professionalized state bureaucracy favor state-led solutions to policy problems.

The introduction of Medicaid managed care in Tennessee in the mid-1990s illustrates the conditions that lead to the creation of an imposed regulatory regime in a competitive health policy environment. Although Tennessee did not possess either a strong health bureaucracy or a well-developed managed care industry prior to the 1990s, TennCare was developed as a means to rescue the state from a fiscal crisis; Governor Ned McWherter capitalized on the crisis atmosphere to reinvent the organization and financing of health care in the state in under two years. Prior to 1993, only 6% of the state's population was enrolled in any form of managed care plan (Brown 1996); by 1997, 100% of the state's Medicaid caseload was enrolled in managed care. During its first year, TennCare survived a "walkout" by nearly a third of all participating Blue Cross physicians and scathing studies by the Tennessee Hospital Association and the legislature's own oversight committee (Meyer and Blumenthal 1996). As Tennessee's experience demonstrates, imposed regimes are characterized by state-sponsored policies designed to promote competition as a means of controlling Medicaid costs and by aggressive implementation of new restrictions on providers and payers to protect patients' rights in the face of staunch industry opposition. The ongoing fiscal crisis associated with Medicaid in Tennessee, however, illustrates the difficulty of building the requisite capacity to sustain the long-term consolidation of state power over the health care industry.

In states where public officials are unable to impose regulation on the industry, they may nevertheless be able to negotiate a partnership with societal interests to achieve their goals. Negotiated regimes are defined by ongoing active participation of industry groups and other interested parties in the design and implementation of policy. Collaboration, rather than conflict, is the norm in a negotiated policy regime; although societal interests and public officials frequently spar over the most appropriate means to achieve policy objectives, negotiated regimes favor brokered compromises that reflect the interests and concerns of key stakeholders. Public/private partnerships are a hallmark of negotiated regimes, as state officials enlist the support of businesses and other payers to control costs or improve access to care.

As Hanson (1994, 56) notes, health care policymaking in Florida is best described as a negotiated regime, for disagreements among key interest groups provided Governor Lawton Chiles with an opportunity to use the prospect of radical, comprehensive reforms to prod elderly advocates, nonprofit hospitals, and for-profit providers to accept a compromise. The state has also taken an active role in stimulating price competition among MCOs by creating a network of community health purchasing alliances (CHPAs) that enables small businesses to purchase competitively priced health insurance. Oliver (1998) argues that Medicaid managed care reforms in Maryland also illustrate the dynamics of policymaking under a negotiated regime; here health providers joined public and private purchasers of health services in calling for the end of the state's "High-Cost User Initiative" to control Medicaid costs in favor of mandatory enrollment in managed care. Private purchasers were active partners in reinventing the state's Medicaid system through the development of its HealthChoice program, which mandated enrollment in managed care for most Medicaid beneficiaries, thus reflecting the collaborative character of policymaking under a negotiated regime.

In contrast to both imposed and negotiated regimes, market regimes embody an enduring faith in the ability of private groups such as payers, providers, and businesses to solve public problems with little intervention by the state. Under these circumstances, policymaking is effectively ceded to providers and private third-party payers. Apart from tasks that are either mandated by federal guidelines or necessary to protect the health and safety of the public in the form of basic operating standards, the state's role is similar to other private purchasers of care. The limited role of state officials is further reflected in a weak statutory mandate; under a market regime, state agencies have limited authority and resources with which to monitor industry performance, oversee new construction, or evaluate providers.

New Hampshire's experience with health care cost containment over the past two decades illustrates the dynamics of policymaking under a market regime (Hackey 1998). The Granite State has consistently shunned regulatory initiatives in favor of policies designed to promote competition. Support for market competition is strong among Democrats and Republicans alike. The state constitution explicitly endorses competition as a policy goal, arguing that "free and fair competition in the trades and industries is an inherent and essential right of the people." An extraordinary cash transfusion from Medicaid disproportionate share hospital (DSH) payments in the early 1990s helped to nurse the state's hospitals back to health without a significant expansion of state oversight or regulatory controls over the industry.

Although New Hampshire applied for a waiver to enroll its AFDC/TANF–eligible Medicaid beneficiaries in managed care, the state did not invest in the capacity building necessary to implement a successful Medicaid managed care program. By the end of 1998, fewer than 8% of the state's Medicaid population were enrolled in managed care (HCFA 1999a). Few significant differences exist among Democrats and Republicans on policy issues, as candidates from both parties support low taxes and conservative fiscal policies. Barring a major fiscal crisis, proposals to augment the scope or intensity of state controls over the health care industry or to significantly expand health coverage using public funds will find little support here.

ADMINISTRATIVE AND FISCAL CHALLENGES FACING STATE GOVERNMENTS

The devolution of policymaking to the states focuses new attention on the capacity of state health bureaucracies to design and implement cost-effective delivery systems that protect the needs of vulnerable populations and promote the health of the public.

Managed Care and Medicaid

The steady growth of Medicaid managed care enrollment over the past decade presents several important challenges for policymakers. As "prudent purchasers" in a competitive marketplace, state officials must ensure that patients in risk-based managed care plans are not underserved. States must also devise and implement standards to hold health plans accountable for the quality of care provided to beneficiaries and either reward or punish plans that fail to achieve core performance goals (Fossett et al. 1999). In addition, states have an interest in preserving the viability of safety net providers that have served the poor and disabled while nurturing the development of alternative delivery systems to provide more cost-effective care to program enrollees.

The characteristics of an effective indemnity insurer (e.g., traditional fee-for-service Medicaid programs) are quite different from the actuarial and managerial skills required to negotiate managed care contracts and monitor plan performance. The shift to capitated financing brings the administrative competence of state agencies designated to implement Medicaid managed care programs to the forefront. As Hurley (1998, 33) notes, "Buyer performance has been critical to the origins and evolution of managed care—both in pursuit of greater value for money and in stimulating the formalization of organized delivery systems capable of meeting buyer requirements and demonstrating adequacy of performance." Low capitation rates may provide financial incentives for MCOs either to underserve Medicaid enrollees or to refuse to participate in the new system altogether. The shortfall between the administrative capacity of existing state Medicaid programs and the demands of the new medical marketplace led many states to hire outside consulting firms to draft Medicaid managed care waiver applications and, in several cases, to actually manage ongoing program operations (Fossett et al. 1999). The use of specialized consultants underscores the importance of building the bureaucratic capacity of state Medicaid agencies, however, since the need for specialized expertise in developing managed care contracts and assessing patient outcomes is ongoing, not episodic.

Existing fee-for-service–based Medicaid information systems are ill-equipped to facilitate quality improvement in a managed care environment. Under traditional fee-for-service Medicaid systems, utilization review programs focused on the identification of outliers as a means of controlling overpayments. In contrast, effective Medicaid managed care systems require ongoing assessment of patient outcomes, enrollees' satisfaction, and the financial health of participating health plans. To accomplish these tasks, states must invest in capacity-building, as the data sets, specialized personnel, and computer systems needed for ongoing outcomes assessments do not currently exist in most state Medicaid bureaucracies. Previous state experiences with hospital rate-setting and health planning programs suggest that the bureaucratic capacity and professionalism of state health bureaucracies will be a crucial explanatory variable in predicting the success or failure of market-based Medicaid reforms.

State Medicaid agencies must also hold providers accountable for caring for the needs of different subgroups of enrollees (Rosenbaum 1998). Most states have limited experience in designing managed care contracts that hold plans accountable for the quality of patient care, mandate standardized data collection, and assess the adequacy of provider networks, patient appeals processes, and coverage of "medically necessary" services (Fossett et al. 1999).

Enrolling poor, disabled, and elderly beneficiaries in managed care presents state policymakers with several difficult implementation challenges. As Hurley and Draper (1998) observed, the full statutory benefits guaranteed to Medicaid beneficiaries often exceed those offered by MCOs' standard benefits packages. To make certain that all enrollees, and patients with special needs in particular, receive services that they are entitled to, states must conduct ongoing performance evaluations of HMOs, assess the quality of service coordination for patients with chronic conditions, and ensure that the capitation rates paid to MCOs are adequate to provide an appropriate level of care.

Capacity Building and Public Health Promotion

The question of state administrative capacity also surfaces in William Waters's discussion of public health policy in Chapter 10. Despite the well-documented success of prevention programs, most states have devoted few resources to smoking cessation initiatives, injury prevention programs, trauma system development, and other health promotion efforts. As Waters notes, public health programs appear to be invisible to both policymakers and the public. On one level, public health programs have a political problem in that the constituencies for many publicly funded screening programs and preventive services (e.g., needle exchange programs to prevent the spread of HIV/AIDS) are disproportionately members of poor and minority communities who have few institutional resources. In addition, "investments" in prevention programs are less visible and tangible than new roads, police officers, or tax cuts. Success, moreover, is frequently a nonevent; the success of a statewide meningitis vaccination program, for example, is demonstrated by the absence of a future epidemic. Although successful, this result is largely invisible from a political perspective—no ribbon cutting ceremonies or dedications will applaud this achievement.

Many in the public health community hailed the 1997 tobacco settlement as the dawn of a new era in financing public health infrastructure. As Buckle and Thomas-Buckle point out in Chapter 9, the settlement marked a turning point in tobacco control policy because it produced a commitment from the industry to restrict advertising and provided states with an infusion of new resources to support health promotion initiatives and the treatment of publicly insured persons with tobacco-related illnesses. The promise of the settlement remains illusory in most states, however, as a substantial proportion of the revenues have been dedicated to balancing state budgets rather than promoting the health of the public. Without a commitment of resources to hire staff, developing and implementing new health promotion campaigns is difficult. Indeed, states that have achieved the most success in curbing youth smoking have funded aggressive tobacco control programs through higher tobacco taxes. The existence of dedicated funding sources enabled state health departments in California, Florida, Massachusetts, and Michigan to implement comprehensive mass media campaigns and peer education programs aimed at reducing teen smoking (see *www.getoutraged.com* for an example of such initiatives).

Infrastructure issues continue to plague state and local health departments even as the economy remains strong. During the recession of the early 1990s, furloughs, hiring freezes, and tight budgets plagued many state health departments; in a difficult fiscal climate, support for gathering and analyzing health care data waned in many states. In the absence of new resources to assess health risks and behaviors, fielding effective health promotion campaigns will be difficult at best. Although federal planning programs such as *Healthy People 2010* set lofty goals for improving health, without adequate resources public officials will find it virtually impossible to achieve many of these objectives.

THE NEW POLITICAL DYNAMICS OF STATE HEALTH POLICYMAKING

The changing health care marketplace brings new challenges for state governments. During the 1970s and 1980s, third-party payers regularly collaborated with state officials in pursuit of regulatory solutions to control spiraling health care costs. In Massachusetts, New York, and other states, Blue Cross plans banded together with business groups to form legislative coalitions in support of state hospital rate-setting and moratoria on the construction of new health care facilities (Hackey 1998). As the 1990s drew to a close, however, business and third-party payers shunned state regulation in favor of privately administered solutions to control health care costs. The political interests of the state officials and third-party payers that supported rate-setting and health planning in previous decades diverged under the stresses of the competitive marketplace. In their place, new political coalitions, often with strange bedfellows such as social workers and hospital executives, emerged to press for protective legislation and bargaining advantages.

Businesses have pursued several avenues to control the cost of health benefits without state intervention. Firms continue to pass on a significant percentage of total health care costs to employees in the form of higher cost-sharing or premiums (Duchon et al. 2000). In addition, while many small businesses have dropped coverage for their employees or reduced their share of employee premiums, a growing percentage of large firms have limited their contribution to employee health plans to the cost of the lowest priced plan in an area that meets certain "performance standards." By capping contributions for employee health benefits, firms have found a way to reduce their overall exposure to rising health care costs;

employees, in turn, have fled traditional indemnity plans in favor of lower-cost managed care plans.

In the new health care policymaking environment, providers, not payers, have sought protection from state governments. In an ironic twist, government regulation of medical practice, which was once reviled by provider groups as a threat to the professional autonomy of practicing physicians and a precursor to "socialized medicine," is now both accepted and welcomed. In the face of aggressive third-party purchasers of care, providers continue to seek legislative protections designed to limit the ability of MCOs to restrict access to specialists, define relationships between doctors and patients, and exclude certain providers from participating in health care networks. In the new millennium, state health policy is a brave new world where traditional alliances and patterns of policymaking have crumbled under the pressures of the competitive marketplace. The political interests of the parties that had supported rate-setting and health planning diverged in response to rising managed care enrollments, selective contracting, and large-scale hospital mergers. New political coalitions emerged to press for protections and bargaining advantages: purchasers endorsed competitive strategies to control costs, patients struggled to preserve access to specialists and choice among providers, and physicians sought to maintain their decision-making autonomy and financial independence.

In the chapters that follow, several of the policy dilemmas facing state officials over the next decade will be examined. In the next chapter, Frank Thompson analyzes the shifting relationship between the states and the federal government in the 1990s by exploring both recent developments in Medicaid and the capacities and interests of state and federal actors in the health policy process. Michael Dukakis discusses the role of governors in setting the health policy agenda at the state level and evaluates the effectiveness of different gubernatorial leadership strategies in achieving meaningful health care reform. John McDonough and Robert McGrath explore the central role played by state legislatures and their members in formulating health policy. Taken together, these chapters set the institutional context of state health policymaking and offer a framework for understanding the evolution of contemporary state policy initiatives.

The authors of the next five chapters look at current controversies in state health policy. David Rochefort examines the recent evolution of a popular backlash against managed care and the strategies used by state policymakers to regulate the managed care industry. The discussion by William Brandon, Rosemary Chaudry, and Alice Sardell of the new Children's Health Insurance Program explores the dynamics of state policy design and implementation that accompanied the passage of the largest federally funded expansion of health insurance for the poor in the past three decades. Chris Koyanagi and Joseph Bevilacqua review the development of managed mental health care over the past decade and discuss the evolution of state parity laws to preserve access to mental health services in an environment dominated by managed care providers. The case study by Jonathan Oberlander, Lawrence Jacobs, and Theodore Marmor of the Oregon Health Plan

(OHP) debunks several important myths about the implementation of rationing as a cost-containment tool at the state level by analyzing the political dynamics that have sustained the OHP as well as the technical difficulties state officials encountered in implementing the plan. Suzann Thomas-Buckle and Leonard Buckle's discussion of the evolution of state legislation against the tobacco industry to recover the cost of treating patients with smoking-related illnesses fuses the study of public health promotion and Medicaid policy. Finally, William Waters offers an insider's perspective on the challenges facing state officials in implementing public health promotion programs in the current political and fiscal climate. In the concluding chapter, Thomas Oliver discusses what recent patterns in state health policy can teach us about agenda-building and the diffusion of policy innovation across the states.

REFERENCES

American College of Nurse-Midwives. 1998. "State and Federal Action on Primary Care and Direct Access to Obstetrical and Gynecological Providers." Online at *http://www.midwife.org/prof/diracces.htm* (October 24).

American Health Line. 1998a. "California: Health Programs Fail to Enroll Children." Online at *http://cloakroom.com* (January 29).

———. 1998b. "California: Study Finds Ranks of the Uninsured Growing." Online at *http://cloakroom.com* (January 29).

Anand, G. 1999. "Attorneys General Meet on Health Care." *Wall Street Journal,* October 27.

Baumgartner, F., and B. Jones. 1991. "Agenda Dynamics and Policy Subsystems." *Journal of Politics* 53:1044–1074.

Bell, J. 1996. "Saving Their Assets: How to Stop Plunder at Blue Cross and Other Nonprofits." *American Prospect* 26 (May–June): 60–66.

Bologna, M. 1998. "AMA Backs Physicians' Campaign Seeking to Bargain Collectively." *BNA's Health Law Reporter* 7 (5): 171–172.

Brown, D. 1996. "Deluged by Medicaid, States Open Wider Umbrellas." *Washington Post,* June 9.

Brown, L. D. 1987. "Introduction to a Decade of Transition." In *Health Policy in Transition,* pp. 1–16. Durham, NC: Duke University Press.

———. 1993. "Commissions, Clubs, and Consensus: Reform in Florida." *Health Affairs* 12 (2): 7–26.

Campbell, J. A. 1999. *Health Insurance Coverage: 1998.* Washington, DC: U.S. Census Bureau. Available online at *http://www.census.gov/prod/99pubs/p60-208.pdf.*

Carey, M. A. 1999. "New GOP Managed Care Bill Puts Hastert in Predicament." *Congressional Quarterly Weekly Report* (September 11): 2109–2110.

Cohn, L., and P. Moore. 2000. "Managed Care Takes to the Sickbed." *Business Week* (May 15): 44.

Congressional Quarterly. 1998. "Lawmakers Agree on Need for Changes in Managed Care—But Only in Principle." *Congressional Quarterly Almanac:* 14.3–14.15.

Coughlin, T., L. Ku, J. Holahan, D. Heslam, and C. Winterbottom. 1994. "State Responses to the Medicaid Spending Crisis: 1988 to 1992." *Journal of Health Politics, Policy and Law* 19 (4): 837–864.

Declercq, E., and D. Simmes. 1997. "The Politics of 'Drive-Through Deliveries': Putting Early Postpartum Discharge on the Legislative Agenda." *Milbank Quarterly* 75 (2): 175–202.

DeLucia, M. 1996. "Protecting the Public Interest: The Sale of Nonprofit Health Care Organizations." *New Hampshire Bar Journal* (December): 36–39.

Demkovich, L. 1997. "Nonprofit Hospital Conversions Remain Topic A on State Agendas." *State Health Notes* 18 (no. 258): 1, 6.

———.1998a. "Bomer: Overseeing Patient Protections." *State Health Notes* 19 (no. 283): 2.

———. 1998b. "Hospital Rate-Setting in Maryland: Regulation in a Managed Care World." *State Health Notes* 19 (no. 285): 1–2.

——— 1998c. "So Far, So Good: State Managed Care Reforms Ruffle Few Feathers." *State Health Notes* 19 (no. 283): 1, 5

Donohue, J. P. 1997. "Developing Issues Under the Massachusetts 'Physician Profile' Act." *American Journal of Law and Medicine* 23 (1): 115–158.

Duchon, L., C. Schoen, E. Simantov, K. Davis, and C. An. 2000. *Listening to Workers: Findings from the Commonwealth Fund 1999 National Survey of Workers' Health Insurance.* Online at *http://www.cmwf.org.*

Fossett, J. W., M. Goggin, J. S. Hall, J. Johnston, C. Plein, R. Roper, and C. Weissert. 1999. *Managing Accountability in Medicaid Managed Care: The Politics of Public Management.* Albany, NY: Nelson A. Rockefeller Institute of Government.

Frankford, D. 1999. "Regulating Managed Care: Pulling the Tails to Wag the Dogs." *Journal of Health Politics, Policy and Law* 24 (5): 1191–1200.

Friedman, E. 1998. "What Price Survival? The Future of Blue Cross and Blue Shield." *JAMA* 279 (23): 1863–1869.

Gentry, C. 1999. "Doctors Voice Concern Over Expectations of Care." *Wall Street Journal,* December 23.

Ginsburg, P., and C. Lesser. 1999. "The View from Communities." *Journal of Health Politics, Policy, and Law* 24 (5): 1005–1013.

Goodman, E. 2000. "Shock Tactics for Smokers." *Boston Globe,* January 23.

Hackey, R. B. 1998. *Rethinking Health Care Policy: The New Politics of State Regulation.* Washington, DC: Georgetown University Press.

———. 2000a. "Making Sense of Medicaid Reform." *Journal of Health Politics, Policy and Law* 25 (4): 855–863.

———. 2000b. "The Politics of Reform." *Journal of Health Politics, Policy and Law* 25 (1): 211–223.

Hackey, R. B., and P. F. Fuller. 1998. "Institutional Design and Regulatory Performance: Rethinking State Certificate of Need Programs." *New England Journal of Public Policy* 13 (2): 53–72.

Hanson, R. 1994. "Health Care Reform, Managed Competition, and Subnational Politics." *Publius: The Journal of Federalism* 24 (Summer): 49–69.

Health Care Financing Administration (HCFA). 1998. "National Summary of Medicaid Managed Care Programs and Enrollment." Online at *http://www.hcfa.gov/medicaid/trends98.htm.*

———. 1999a. "Medicaid Managed Care State Enrollment: December 31, 1998." Online at *http://www.hcfa.gov/medicaid/omcpr98.htm.*

———. 1999b. *The State Children's Health Insurance Program Annual Enrollment Report (October 1, 1998–September 30, 1999).* Washington, DC.

Hellinger, F. 1996. "The Expanding Scope of State Legislation." *JAMA* 276 (13): 1065–1070.

Holahan, J., T. Coughlin, L. Ku, D. Lipson, and S. Rajan. 1995. "Insuring the Poor Through Medicaid 1115 Waivers." *Health Affairs* 14 (1): 200–217.

Hurley, R. 1998. "Have We Overdosed on a Panacea? Reflections on the Evolution of Medicaid Managed Care." In *Remaking Medicaid: Managed Care for the Public Good,* ed. S. M. Davidson and S. A. Somers, pp. 20–40. San Franscisco: Jossey-Bass Publishers.

Hurley, R., and D. Draper. 1998. "Special Plans for Special Persons: The Elusive Pursuit of Customized Managed Care." In *Remaking Medicaid: Managed Care for the Public Good,* ed. S. M. Davidson and S. A. Somers, pp. 245–276. San Franscisco: Jossey-Bass Publishers.

Interstudy Publications. 1999. *HMO Industry Report 9.2.* Minneapolis, MN.

Jacobs, L., and R. Shapiro. 1999. "The American Public's Pragmatic Liberalism Meets Its Philosophical Conservatism." *Journal of Health Politics, Policy and Law* 24 (5): 1021–1031.

Jeffery, N. 1998a. "HMOs Image Worries Spur Campaigns." *Wall Street Journal,* September 21.

———. 1998b. "New Threat for HMOs: Doctor Discipline Boards." *Wall Street Journal,* July 13.

Jesilow, P., H. Pontell, and G. Geis. 1993. *Prescription for Profit: How Doctors Defraud Medicaid.* Berkeley: University of California Press.

Johnson, L., and A. DeBlois. 1997. "Managed Care: Complaints and Regulations." *Medicine and Health/Rhode Island* 80 (6): 203–205.

Jones, B. 1998. "Doctors Take Stand Against Cost Cutting." *Providence Journal-Bulletin,* July 17.

Knox, R. 1999 "BMC Residents, Interns Vote to Unionize." *Boston Globe,* December 22.

Kronick, R., D. Goodman, J. Wennberg, and E. Wagner. 1993. "The Marketplace in Health Care Reform: The Demographic Limitations of Managed Competition." *New England Journal of Medicine* 328:148–152.

Ladenheim, K. 1997. "Health Insurance in Transition: The Health Insurance Portability and Accountability Act of 1996." *Publius: The Journal of Federalism* 27 (2): 33–51.

Langley, M., and J. Sharpe. 1996. "IRS, State Officials, and Courts Get Involved, Tangling Deals." *Wall Street Journal Interactive Edition,* October 18; online.

Langreth, R. 1998. "Do Your Homework: How to Learn about Your Doctor—Before You Pick One." *Wall Street Journal,* October 19.

Leape, L., L. Hillborne, R. Park, S. Bernstein, C. Kamberg, M. Sherwood, and R. Brook. 1993. "The Appropriateness of Use of Coronary Artery Bypass Surgery in New York State." *JAMA* 269 (6): 753–760.

Lederberg, M. B. 1997. "Rhode Island's New Physician Profiles." *Medicine and Health/Rhode Island* 80 (11): 380–381.

———. 1998. "Physician Unions: The Wave of the Future?" *Medicine and Health/Rhode Island* 81 (3): 104–105.

Longo, D., G. Land, W. Schramm, J. Fraas, B. Houskins, and V. Howell. 1997. "Consumer Reports in Health Care: Do They Make a Difference?" *JAMA* 278 (19): 1579–1584.

Marlow, A. 1998. "The Professional Decline of Physicians in the Era of Managed Care." *New England Journal of Public Policy* 13 (2): 87–102.

McDonough, J. E. 1997. "Tracking the Demise of State Hospital Rate Setting." *Health Affairs* 16 (1): 142–149.

McGinley, L. 1998. "Texas Law Allowing Patients to Sue Health Plans for Damages Is Upheld." *Wall Street Journal,* September 21.

Meyer, G., and D. Blumenthal. 1996. "TennCare and Academic Medical Centers." *JAMA* 276 (9): 672–776.

Miller, T. 1997. "Managed Care Regulation in the Laboratory of the States." *JAMA* 278 (13): 1102–1109.

Morone, J. A. 1992. "Hidden Complications: Why Health Care Competition Needs Regulation." *American Prospect* no. 10 (Summer): 40–48.

Mueller, K. J. 1988. "Federal Programs to Expire: The Case of Health Planning." *Public Administration Review* 48:719–725.

Murray, S. 2000. "Most States to Spend Tobacco Settlement on Improving Health Care, Survey Says." *Wall Street Journal,* March 8.

New York State Department of Health. 1995. *Coronary Artery Bypass Surgery in New York State, 1991–93.* Albany, NY.

Oliver, T. R. 1993. "Analysis, Advice, and Congressional Leadership: The Physician Payment Review Commission and the Politics of Medicare." *Journal of Health Politics, Policy and Law* 18 (1): 113–174.

———. 1998. "The Collision of Economics and Politics in Medicaid Managed Care: Reflections on the Course of Reform in Maryland." *Milbank Quarterly* 76 (1): 59–98.

Peregrine, M. 1997. "Charitable Trust Laws and the Evolving Nature of the Nonprofit Hospital Corporation." *Journal of Health and Hospital Law* 30 (1): 11–20.

Pfeiffer, B. 1997. "Six States Join Forces to Offer Doctor Profiles That Include Malpractice Claims on the Internet." *State Health Watch* 4 (2): 1, 8.

Robertson, D. 1993. "The Return to History and the New Institutionalism in American Political Science." *Social Science History* 17 (1): 1–36.

Rodwin, M. 1997. "The Neglected Remedy: Strengthening Consumer Voice in Managed Care." *American Prospect* 34 (September–October): 45–50.

———. 1999. "Backlash as a Prelude to Managing Managed Care." *Journal of Health Politics, Policy and Law* 24 (5): 1115–1126.

Rosenbaum, S. 1998. "Negotiating the New Health System: A Nationwide Analysis of Medicaid Managed Care Contracts." In *Remaking Medicaid: Managed Care for the Public Good,* ed. S. M. Davidson and S. A. Somers, pp. 197–218. San Francisco: Jossey-Bass Publishers.

Rosenbaum, S., and J. Darnell. 1995. *Medicaid Section 1115 Demonstration Waivers: Implications for Federal Legislative Reform.* Washington, DC: Kaiser Commission on the Future of Medicaid.

Singer, L. 1997. "The Conversion Conundrum: The State and Federal Responses to Hospitals' Changes in Charitable Status." *American Journal of Law and Medicine* 23 (2/3): 221–250.

Starr, P. 1982. *The Social Transformation of American Medicine.* New York: Basic Books.

State Health Notes. 1998a. "Bill of Rights." No. 280 (July 6): 3.

————. 1998b. "Charity Care I, II." No. 268 (January 19): 3.

State Health Watch. 1997. "Attorneys General Weigh in on Conversions." 4 (April): 7.

State of New York. 1971. *Report from the Governor's Steering Committee on Social Problems on Health and Hospital Services and Costs.* Albany, NY: Author.

Stauffer, M. 1999. Managed Care: A Decade of Reform. *State Health Notes* 20 (December 6): 7.

Stone, D. 1992. "Why the States Can't Solve the Health Care Crisis." *American Prospect* 3 (Spring): 51–60.

Thompson, F. 1981. *Health Policy and the Bureaucracy.* Cambridge, MA: MIT Press.

Wall Street Journal. 2000. NBC News/*Wall Street Journal* Quarterly Poll, April/May 2000. Washington, DC: Hart-Teeter. Online at *http://interactive.wsj.com/documents/poll20000128.htm.*

Welch, W., and M. Miller. 1988. "Mandatory HMO Enrollment in Medicaid: The Issue of Freedom of Choice." *Milbank Quarterly* 66:618–639.

PART I

The Institutional Context

2

Federalism and Health Care Policy: Toward Redefinition?

Frank J. Thompson

No assessment of the "new" politics of state health policy can safely proceed without considering developments with respect to one of the most critical features of the American political system—federalism. The interaction and balance of power between the national government and the states strongly affect who gets what, when, and how from government in the health care arena. The fabric of federalism constantly changes. Those who chronicle such developments frequently devote their attention to major formal policy shifts as manifested in new legislation or federal court opinions. But it is equally important to consider the transformation of intergovernmental dynamics and power that emerges from the implementation process. In the contemporary administrative state, implementing agents at the federal, state, and local levels possess vast discretion to shape the processes, outputs, and outcomes of health care programs. Shifts in the commitments and resources of these agents at different levels of the federal system can markedly alter the nature of health politics.

Paying particular attention to two major initiatives, Medicaid and the Children's Health Insurance Program (CHIP), this chapter assesses efforts to redefine the federal-state relationship in the health care arena during the 1990s. In retrospect, the decade of the 1990s emerges as a period of incremental devolution. Proponents of a more radical shifting of authority and responsibilities came up short. But policymakers took meaningful steps to enhance state prerogatives in the health sphere via legislation and the tools of the administrative presidency. This development took place while federal officials increasingly espoused and publicized a new doctrine of intergovernmental management. Fueled by the Clinton administration's National Performance Review and the passage of the Government Per-

I wish to thank Claire Lutz, Beryl Radin, and an anonymous reviewer for helpful comments on a prior version of this chapter.

formance and Results Act of 1993, this doctrine emphasized performance-based accountability. Extolling the virtues of "performance partnerships" with the states, the federal government proposed to shift intergovernmental relations from a form of political accountability based primarily on compliance with federal rules concerning process to one focused on a bottom line—on achieving measurable objectives and goals (National Performance Review 1993; 35–37, 45). The degree to which this new doctrine actually took root and led to a redefinition of the relationship between the federal government and the states in the health care arena remains open to question. But at a minimum it changed the language and tenor of their interaction.

To advance understanding of health care policy and federalism, this chapter first provides a more detailed overview of federal grant programs, the importance of Medicaid in this context, and the character of devolution during the 1990s. Discussion then turns to a general consideration of the capacity and commitment of the states. Do states have the wherewithal in terms of resources and skills needed to meet the challenge of increased responsibility? How committed are they to assuring that all of their residents have access to health care of quality? Following a general response to these questions, the chapter focuses more specifically on questions of state capacity and commitment as they interact with one of the most important new policy initiatives of the 1990s, the effort to provide more children with health insurance via Medicaid and CHIP. A final section draws on the initial experience with CHIP to assess the prospects for greater performance-based accountability in intergovernmental management. It evaluates this initiative as part of a broader effort to create a more transparent federalism, one where higher quality information would enhance prospects for both accountability and policy learning.

THE MEDICAID COLOSSUS AND INCREMENTAL DEVOLUTION

The *Catalogue of Federal Domestic Assistance* (U.S. Office of Management and Budget 1998) lists some 245 health care programs in the Department of Health and Human Services; over a third of them seek to attain their goals by providing grants to states or localities. Some of these grants claim a small share of the federal purse and target specific groups or diseases. For instance, the Centers for Disease Control provides monies to states so that they can support early detection programs for breast and cervical cancer. At the other end of the scale, Medicaid, a major entitlement program administered by the Health Care Financing Administration (HCFA), provides an open-ended grant to the states to subsidize a broad range of services for low-income people.

As Table 2.1 indicates, the federal government spent about $123 billion on health grants to states and localities in 2000. Given the matching requirements built into grants, this amount stimulated appreciable state spending as well. Since

Table 2.1 Federal Outlays for Grants to State and
Local Governments, Health and Other

(in millions of dollars)		
Year	All Grants	Health	Health Percentage of All Grants
1965	10,910	624	6
1970	24,065	3,849	16
1975	49,791	8,810	18
1980	91,385	15,758	17
1985	105,852	24,451	23
1990	135,325	43,890	32
1995	224,991	93,587	42
2000*	284,072	123,340	43

*Estimate
Source: U.S. Office of Management and Budget, *Historical Tables, Budget of the United States Government, Fiscal Year 2001* (Washington, DC: Government Printing Office 2000), pp. 204–212.

1965 (the year when Medicaid became law), the percentage of all federal grants going to health policy has risen from 6% to 43%. Within this policy sphere, Medicaid easily qualifies as the king of the hill. As of 2000, for instance, outlays for Medicaid amounted to 94% of all federal monies flowing to states and localities for health programs and 41% of all federal grants. Medicaid, a joint federal-state program, provides health insurance for 35 to 40 million low-income individuals. Medicaid as a program varies so much from one state to the next that it makes considerable sense to see it as 50 different programs (more if one includes the District of Columbia and U.S. territories). But even this assertion fails to capture its full diversity. In a sense, Medicaid in each state amounts to two different programs, one that provides access to medical care for mothers and children and another that provides access to long-term care for the elderly and disabled.

The devolution debate that swirled around the health care arena in the 1990s largely revolved around Medicaid. The 104th Congress, which came to Washington in 1995, was the first in decades in which the Republicans controlled both houses. With support from Republican governors, who held office in the majority of states, this Congress passed legislation to transform Medicaid from an open-ended federal entitlement where the national government matched whatever states chose to spend to a block grant that capped the federal government's funding obligation. This Medigrant legislation gave states vast authority to shape their programs but at the price of a less generous federal subsidy. The initiative died when President Clinton vetoed it.

But if the president resisted this massive shift of authority to the states, he did encourage other initiatives that tilted power in their direction. The tools of the administrative presidency (Nathan 1983), especially a more liberal interpretation of existing federal law, constituted one vehicle for accomplishing this shift. Section 1115 of the Social Security Act had long provided HCFA with the authority to approve comprehensive waivers for demonstration projects. Although presidential administrations prior to Clinton had approved more modest waivers under alternative statutory authority, they had been extremely reluctant to sign off on these major waivers, doing so only for Arizona in the early 1980s. The arrival of the Clinton administration marked the abandonment of this stringent approach. Federal officials quickly began to entertain and endorse section 1115 waivers that promised a dramatic restructuring of state Medicaid programs. Officials in Tennessee, for instance, won approval for a plan called TennCare that promised to open Medicaid eligibility gates to an anticipated half million new enrollees and to place primary responsibility for service delivery in the hands of managed care organizations that contracted with the state on a capitated, rather than a fee-for-service, basis. As of mid-1999, 19 states had received HCFA endorsement of their comprehensive waiver requests, and 17 had proceeded to implement them (U.S. Health Care Financing Administration 1999).

Federal willingness to grant section 1115 comprehensive waivers opened up new channels for the forces of state politics to express themselves. The waiver process provided a forum for negotiation and bargaining between HCFA and the states. To be sure, state administrators expressed frustration with this process. A top Medicaid official in one state complained that he had to run the gauntlet of responding to "ten questions phrased in 650 different ways" and that HCFA, "like any good bureaucrat [,] knows just the poisoned question to ask which ties you in knots because you can't explain it in two and half minutes" (Thompson 1998b, 279). But the fact remains that many states ultimately got much of what they wanted from this waiver process.

Although in the early 1990s Medicaid devolution primarily proceeded through the tools of the administrative presidency, statutory changes in 1997 also afforded the states significant new authority in several spheres. The Balanced Budget Act of that year repealed legal provisions enacted in 1980 and 1981 (the Boren Amendments) that had made state payment rates for Medicaid services especially vulnerable to court challenge by providers. The new law also bolstered state authority to require Medicaid recipients to enroll in managed care organizations (Fossett 1998, 123–124). Among other things, states gained the right to lock Medicaid enrollees into managed care plans for as much as a year unless the recipient could mount a well-documented appeal. Prior law had allowed Medicaid enrollees to exit from any plan simply by giving 30 days' notice. The new policy also permitted states to limit Medicaid enrollees to a choice between two plans or even to just one in rural areas. In addition, the Balanced Budget Act wiped out a provision that required managed care plans contracting with Medicaid to draw at least 25% of their enrollees from sources other than Medicaid, the so-called 75/25 rule. In opening up these possibilities for state policymakers, the act added certain requirements that states collect data related to quality assurance. Overall, however, the new law meant that the federal government would be a less potent player in the politics of Medicaid managed care within the states.

The Balanced Budget Act of 1997 also opened the gates for states to participate in a new federal policy initiative. Concerned about the growing number of uninsured children, the federal government through CHIP made states an offer that they could not refuse. Authorized as Title XXI of the Social Security Act, CHIP promised states a more generous federal match than they received under Medicaid if they agreed to cover more children. The statute imposed certain requirements on the states concerning benefit packages (which could be less comprehensive than those offered by Medicaid) and maintenance of effort (participating states could not backslide on their Medicaid eligibility criteria for children). But on balance the CHIP legislation gave states vast discretion to design their programs. By early 2000, all 50 states had launched CHIP initiatives.

Although states enhanced their power position relative to the federal government during the 1990s, developments stopped short of the "devolution revolution" favored by some Republicans in the 104th Congress. Important federal mandates remained. Of particular note, federal laws approved in 1989 and 1990 continued to require that state Medicaid programs extend coverage to pregnant women and children under age 6 from families with incomes up to 133% of the federal poverty line. They also mandated that states gradually extend Medicaid coverage to all uninsured children younger than 19 from poor families by 2002.

In the case of Medicaid, the 1990s also witnessed the closing of the federal door to special state financing practices that had allowed many states, through provider taxes and donations, to increase the percentage of Medicaid expenditures paid for by the federal government (the federal match rate) to a level appreciably higher than that authorized by law (Thompson 1998a, 36–41). Even more fundamentally, federal policymakers demonstrated no inclination to free states from the constraints of the Employee Retirement Income Security Act (ERISA). As interpreted by the federal courts, this law significantly limits state opportunities to impose certain regulations on private employers that would expand access to health insurance.

But if the federal government did not take a giant step toward devolution, it took important strides in that direction. This development, along with the distinct possibility that the 1990s may be a way station to even greater devolution in the health care arena, makes the enduring issues of state capacity and commitment important to consider.

THE EBB AND FLOW OF STATE CAPACITY

The case for buttressing the power of states in the intergovernmental framework draws strength from sanguine assessments of the degree to which their capacity has improved over the last four decades both in absolute terms and relative to the federal government. Most of this assessment focuses on the governing capacity of the states—the extent to which they can formulate democratically responsive, coherent, plausible policy and implement it efficiently, effectively, and accountably. Observers note several developments (Conlan 1998, 310). For one thing, changes in the 1960s assured more equitable political representation as the barriers to voting by minorities subsided and legislative districts came to be drawn on the basis of one person, one vote. For another, many legislative bodies met more frequently, had more diverse memberships, and expanded their professional staff support. So, too, reforms in many states bolstered the authority of governors, allowed them to serve for more terms, and assigned them more support staff. With personnel patronage less prominent, the administrative agencies of state government also attracted greater numbers of well-credentialed employees.

To a lesser degree, this sanguine assessment of the states also emanates from appraisals of their fiscal capacity, wealth, and formal rights to tax their assets for public purposes. Some analysts credited states with moving to develop "well-balanced revenue systems that are adequate to fund their principal responsibilities and less vulnerable to cyclical swings in the economy" (Conlan 1998, 310). Still others anticipate that variation among states in their fiscal capacity will decline, thereby reducing the need for federal intervention to redistribute funds from richer to poorer states. So too, the strong economy of the 1990s and the settlement of major suits against tobacco companies have enhanced the flow of revenues into state coffers and generally bolstered the fiscal position of state governments.

General then-and-now comparisons of state capacity using 1960 as the baseline do in fact support the view that state governing and, possibly, fiscal capacity have increased. But this gross comparison can in critical respects be misleading for purposes of assessing the implications of devolution. At least three complicating factors present themselves (Thompson 1998b). First, political scientists have yet to reach a firm consensus on the characteristics of governing capacity and how to measure it. In the 1990s, challenges to the conventional wisdom about how to do "good government" have multiplied and intensified. Traditionally, for instance, analysts have tended to portray better paid legislatures with abundant support staffs as a plus for the formulation of coherent policy and the preservation of democratic accountability. More recently, however, some discussions of health policy reform at the state level have turned the case for legislative professionalism on its head. In this revisionist view, such professionalism may fuel gridlock especially in an era of greater partisan differences and divided governments (that is, where the same party does not control the governorship and both houses of the legislature). In this regard, some see considerable advantage to term limits for legislators and to a kind of "amateurism" that can allow policymakers to avoid analysis paralysis in making decisions about health policy (Leichter 1996). Existing empirical studies of state legislatures prompt skepticism about these claims for term limits (Carey, Neimi, and Powell 1998), but definitive analyses of the implications of term limits for health policy formation await completion.

The conventional thinking about the key markers of "good" public administration have faced even greater challenge. The 1990s have fueled a conviction among advocates of "reinvention" that the progressive administrative reforms of the past have come full circle to impede efficient and effective implementation (Thompson and Riccucci 1998). Reformers criticize states and localities for sustaining rule-encrusted, antiquated personnel, procurement, and budget systems that hamstring managers.

Second, assessments of state capacity need to acknowledge more fully its fluidity and the potential for backsliding. A very strong case exists that the 1960s and 1970s amounted to a great leap forward in state capacity. After assessing this capacity over the last two decades, however, a more mixed picture emerges. As Hackey (1998, 50) notes in his discussion of regime changes in state governments, "State administrative capacities are not static, but expand and contract over time with changes in funding, personnel policies, and policy priorities." Without adopting a glass–half empty perspective or gainsaying positive developments, certain trends present in the 1980s and 1990s raise troubling questions about the ability of states to sustain their governing and fiscal capacity.

From an administrative perspective, for instance, the ideology of downsizing that was so pervasive in the 1990s may well have fueled the perennial propensity of state policymakers to underestimate the resources needed to achieve implementation success. Fueled in part by developments in the private sector, politician after politician has taken pride in calling for a reduction in the number of "bureaucrats" employed by government. A more objective analysis of the evidence suggests that the larger problem may well be the hollowing out of government whereby a growing disparity exists between the demands placed on administrative agencies by policymakers and the employees present to meet these demands. From the vantage point of broader democratic governance, other troubling signs have emerged. For instance, one analysis suggests that at the very point when state governments are acquiring new powers, media coverage of them is in "steep decline." It suggests that press "bureaus are shrinking, reporters are younger and less experienced, stories get less space and poorer play" (Layton and Walton 1998). Under such circumstances, the already difficult task of building an informed citizenry who can participate efficaciously in state politics becomes all the more formidable.

Or consider issues of state fiscal capacity. Analysts have long understood that state capacity to deal with cyclical downturns in the economy tends to be less than that of the federal government due to legal requirements that states balance their budgets and their inability to print money. Over the last 25 years, however, the repeated triumphs of the antitax movement have further eroded the fiscal capacity of many states. As of the late 1990s, over half of the states had added tax or expenditure limitations to their constitutions or statutes. These provisions assume myriad forms, but all of them add to the hurdles that state policymakers must jump to increase tax rates or appropriate monies beyond a certain increment. The provisions tend to add decision sites to the fiscal policy process (e.g., require voter approval of a choice made by the legislature) or mandate that supermajorities (e.g., a two-thirds vote of both houses of the legislature) approve certain tax or expenditure decisions (National Conference of State Legislature 1999). These measures make it all the more difficult for states to increase their support for Medicaid or other health programs through greater tax effort.

Third, assessments of state capacity need to consider the challenge of rising expectations. The critical issue is not so much whether state capacity has increased or decreased, but its status relative to the policy promises being made. The great expansion of state initiatives to enroll more Medicaid recipients in managed care serves as a case in point. In many respects, the administrative challenges of managed care systems exceed those that states faced under the old fee-for-service system. The degree to which states will be able to develop and sustain the capacity to be prudent purchasers in their dealings with managed care firms remains a very open question (Fossett 1998). As will become evident later in this chapter, the gap between policy promises and the capacity of states to deliver on them also looms large in the case of recent initiatives to insure more children.

State Commitment

The devolution of greater authority and responsibility to the states also raises important questions about their commitments in the health care arena. Commitment in this context refers to the degree to which processes of policy formulation and implementation in a state manifest greater effort to assure that all of its residents have access to health care of good quality. These commitments derive from complex interactions among a critical cast of players—the governor, legislators, state administrators, local officials, judges, interest groups, federal officials, and the media, among others. They reflect political processes shaped by a state's institutional configuration, culture, economy, and more. Commitment presents many thorny problems of conceptualization and calibration, and no single measure can express it definitively. Table 2.2 points to a range of indicators that cast light on state commitment in the case of Medicaid. It suggests that one can discern much about the level of such commitment by examining data on formal policy provisions concerning eligibility and service packages, certain expenditure information, and statistics pertaining to enrollment.

The particular politics of the 50 states yields widely differing levels of commitment to Medicaid and CHIP. State commitment also tends to vary over time. But the dominant concern in the devolution debate has centered less on state variation than on the view that the shift of greater responsibility to the states (especially if it also entails federal funding cuts) will, other things being equal, erode the public sector's overall commitment to providing health insurance to low-income people. To an unfortunate degree this debate has revolved around the thesis that devolution will fuel a "race to the bottom." Among other things, this metaphor suggests a certain pace of state response (e.g., a rapid decline rather than

Table 2.2 Selected Indicators of State Commitment to Medicaid and CHIP

Category	Indicator	Relevance
Formal Policy (e.g., as embedded in statutes)	Eligibility criteria	The greater the income and assets of those who can qualify for benefits, the greater the commitment.
	Service packages	A broader scope of subsidized services indicates greater commitment.
Expenditures on the program from state sources	Expenditure per capita	A greater amount signals generalized commitment.
	Expenditure per poor person	A larger number suggests a higher level of commitment relative to the magnitude of the problem.
	Expenditure as a proportion of total state personal Income	Points to the effort states make to fund the programs relative to their wealth.
	Expenditure per enrollee	Not easily interpretable but could cast light on program quality (e.g., adequate pay rates for providers) or efficiency, or service mix.
Enrollees	Number of program benefi- ciaries as percent of popula- tion below certain income levels (e.g., 150% of Poverty)*	Suggests how committed a state is to assuring that all low income citizens have health insurance.
	Take-up rate	Calibrates the degree to which those legally qualified for program benefits get signed up to receive them.

*Ideally, it would be best to express this ratio as beneficiaries divided by those below income level X minus the number who have health insurance from a source other than Medicaid or CHIP. The data needed to make this refined estimate tend to be unavailable on a state-by-state basis.

slow erosion) and certain causal dynamics (e.g., that states will respond to the policies of geographically contiguous states) that may not be valid.

But the limits to this specific model do not gainsay the distinct possibility that certain forms of devolution will in fact weaken the health care safety net (as measured, for instance, by aggregate decline in the indicators suggested by Table 2.2). The central tenet of this pessimistic perspective stresses the salience of economic development policy to state policymakers and the pressures of competitive or "market-preserving" federalism (Weingast 1995). This perspective has two prongs. First, it suggests that affluent individuals and businesses not only have the usual political resources to help them prevail in state politics (e.g., vigorous lobbyists, generous campaign contributions), but they also have the ability to exit. To the degree that a state's commitment to Medicaid and CHIP leads to higher taxes, policymakers run the risk that business and the affluent will flee to lower tax states eager to attract them, thereby diminishing the fiscal capacity of the more generous state. Second, and to a lesser degree, the perspective has roots in the view that generous states can become a health care magnet for low-income people, that these people will choose to remain in or move to a state that offers liberal health insurance benefits. This magnet effect could also strain state resources.

The degree to which the dynamics of interstate economic competition in fact yield these effects has not been definitively determined. But in an era when labor and capital are increasingly mobile, state policymakers have valid reasons to fear that greater tax effort to support Medicaid, CHIP, or other redistributive programs could fuel the flight of business and the well-off (Donahue 1997). Many state policymakers also believe that generous benefits will make their states a health care magnet, even though little if any evidence exists to support the view that low-income people move for this reason (Thompson 1998b, 272; Schram and Soss 1998). On balance, the quest to position their states well in the competition for economic development exerts strong pressure on state officials to limit their support for redistributive policies in the health care arena.

But this long shadow of competitive federalism should not obscure the fact that state health policy commitment can still be appreciable and vary substantially. For example, states such as Minnesota, New York, and Washington have adopted and substantially funded their own programs to extend health insurance to more children. Moreover, almost all states that participate in Medicaid offer more benefits than the federal government mandates as a basic condition of state participation in the program (even as most stop far short of providing the maximum benefits that federal law would permit). In some instances, state commitment helps compensate for diminished fiscal support from the federal government (Nathan et al. 1987).

In considering the forces indigenous to state politics that can counteract the downward pressures induced by interstate economic competition, two models in particular have received attention. One focuses on the influence of federal and state bureaucracies in the policy process. In their assessment of "when federalism works," Peterson, Rabe, and Wong (1986) voice skepticism about the prospects for redistributive programs when the federal government delegates substantial discretion to states or localities for their implementation. They suggest, however, that these adverse effects may well be muted to the degree that administrative professionals dominate the implementation process and elected politicians play a minor role. Under this "depoliticized" model, the commitment to the redistributive program largely emerges from negotiations between federal and state administrators. Possessing similar graduate degrees and outlooks, they often share a commitment to the program. The concept of "picket fence federalism" (Walker 1981) is consistent with this view. This concept posits that administrative alliances between federal and state administrators matter greatly in shaping program delivery, even to a point that accountability to elected officials becomes attenuated. This bureaucracy-dominated politics may well apply to many small intergovernmental grant programs that tend to fly below the radar screen of elected officials, including (perhaps) CHIP. But Medicaid is the elephant in the living room that state political officials and key interest groups cannot ignore. Given the program's vast budget implications, state and federal administrators constitute a small subset of the players jousting with one another to shape Medicaid.

A second model emphasizes the role of provider influence in state politics. In New York State, for instance, hospitals, nursing home operators, and unions representing health care workers have fiercely resisted efforts by the Pataki administration to cut Medicaid spending. (In 1999, one union representing health care workers paid for a television advertisement broadcast around the state that featured a woman with multiple sclerosis pleading with the governor not to cut off her support.) But the degree to which health care providers possess political muscle varies greatly from state to state. Moreover, it is also important to recognize the policy biases of provider-dominated state politics. Above all it tends to emphasize higher payment rates for certain kinds of institutional providers for acute and long-term care. While better paid providers may well be a plus for Medicaid beneficiaries, this policy bias may also enervate efforts to expand eligibility. The state of New York, for instance, ranks near the top in Medicaid expenditures per enrollee but far lower in Medicaid enrollees as a percentage of all poor people within its boundaries (Boyd 1998, 78–79).

In addition to the causal forces embedded in these two models, an array of other factors also affects state health policy commitments. For instance, studies indicate that more affluent states with higher proportions of citizens who identify themselves as liberals tend to evince greater commitment (Boyd 1998).

In considering the health policy commitment of states, it is important to keep in mind that, from the perspective of accomplishing national goals to reduce the number of uninsured, the politics of some states matters much more than that of others. The ten most populous states in the nation (California, Texas, New York, Florida, Pennsylvania, Illinois, Ohio, Michigan, New Jersey, and Georgia) govern over half of the total population of the United States. A transformation in Texas politics leading to a greater health policy commitment in that state would do much more on a national basis to reduce the number of uninsured children than similar transformations in the ten least populous states (especially because Texas currently ranks near the bottom among states in its commitment to covering children).

Capacity, Commitment, and Uninsured Kids

The federal initiative to extend health insurance coverage to more children, a major policy thrust of the 1990s, casts additional light on the interplay between state capacity and commitment. The Medicaid mandates of 1989 and 1990, which gradually require states to cover all poor children younger than 19, survived attempts to repeal them when President Clinton vetoed the Republican Medigrant proposal. The passage of CHIP with bipartisan support in 1997 reinforced this policy commitment.

Of pivotal importance for the possible emergence of a "new" politics of state health policy, this effort to insure more children occurred in a period of safety net delinkage. The new welfare reform law, the Personal Responsibility and Work Opportunity Reconciliation Act of 1996, replaced Aid to Families with Dependent Children (AFDC), an entitlement program born in the New Deal, with a program called Temporary Assistance to Needy Families (TANF). The measure stressed time limits for receiving cash assistance, work requirements, and the reduction of welfare caseloads. As federal policymakers moved to cut the numbers on welfare, however, they went out of their way to delink eligibility for cash benefits from eligibility for Medicaid. This meant that children from low-income families no longer on cash assistance (or who had never received welfare) would constitute an increasing proportion of those targeted for assistance under Medicaid and CHIP.

The take-up challenge. Fully implemented, the Medicaid mandates and CHIP would go a long way toward reducing the number of children in the United States who lack health insurance. But forging a link between formal policy and actual performance requires states to deal successfully with the take-up challenge. Take-up refers to the proportion of children legally qualified for Medicaid and CHIP who actually get enrolled in these programs. As of 1997, the Bureau of the Census estimated the number of uninsured children under the age of 19 to be 11.6 million (U.S. Department of Health and Human Services 1999a). By one calculation, from one-half to two-thirds of them met the income qualifications to be enrolled in Medicaid or CHIP. The decoupling of health care assistance from welfare payments threatens to exacerbate the take-up problem. Sophisticated (albeit far from definitive) estimates suggest that as of the late 1990s the take-up rate for children who also qualify for cash assistance was nearly 80%. But for children from families not on welfare, the Medicaid take-up rate was less than 60%, and the CHIP rate was not quite 50% (Selden, Banthin, and Cohen 1998, 1999).

A state committed to elevating take-up rates would typically need to succeed at four tasks, among others. First, it would need to publicize the programs effectively since many potential beneficiaries lack accurate information about Medicaid and CHIP benefits. The legislation authorizing CHIP acknowledged this problem and called for state plans to deal with outreach, but Medicaid remained another matter. As Sally Richardson (1999), a senior HCFA official noted, Medicaid has long been based on a "field of dreams approach: if we offer it they will come." Historically, states and localities have done little to advertise or otherwise promote Medicaid to low-income people. When welfare benefits and Medicaid benefits were tightly linked, this tended to matter less since those applying for income support automatically got placed in the program. But in an era of delinkage and declining welfare rolls, mastery of the take-up challenge may well require a major culture change in Medicaid agencies.

Second, a committed state would have to demonstrate the value of program benefits to potential beneficiaries. Many low-income people seek to avoid the stigma of signing up their children for "welfare medicine" (Perry et al. 2000). They also correctly sense that a lack of health insurance will not bar the health care door when illness strikes since hospital emergency rooms are generally required by law to treat their children if they get sick. Moreover, confronted with a spate of day-to-day problems, many low-income people tend to pay little attention to health insurance until a member of their family gets sick. Hence, state officials need to send signals to parents that enrolling their children in Medicaid and CHIP is not a demeaning admission of their second-class status in society and that such enrollment brings valuable new health benefits.

Third, a state committed to higher take-up rates would need to find ways to reduce the transaction costs of becoming enrolled to potential beneficiaries. Many states force applicants to surmount countless enrollment obstacles, such as geographically remote eligibility offices, long waiting times to see an intake worker, and lengthy application forms that require potential beneficiaries to spend hours documenting their residence, income, and assets. Reducing these and related barriers would provide more fertile soil for take-up to grow.

Fourth, a state committed to higher take-up rates for children would need to make redetermination processes more client-friendly. Where welfare bureaucracies do more frequent and exacting monitoring to assess whether Medicaid and CHIP enrollees continue to meet income and related requirements for eligibility or automatically drop beneficiaries from the rolls for failure to take certain actions, many legally qualified children lose their health insurance. Under the Balanced Budget Act of 1997, states have the option of providing "continuous eligibility" to help prevent this churning of the rolls. The law allows them to provide 12 months of eligibility to children under Medicaid and CHIP without any redetermination process.

Although these four steps seem likely to boost take-up rates, the degree to which states would successfully undertake them remains an open question. In part, states face limits to their capacity. For instance, considerable uncertainty shrouds the question of how to use public information campaigns as policy instruments (Weiss and Tschirhart 1994). Even the most committed state officials cannot be sure which outreach strategies will most efficiently and effectively enhance knowledge of CHIP and Medicaid among low-income families. The commitment of states to boosting the take-up rate is also far from assured. Aside from the forces of interstate economic competition that normally constrain state commitment to redistributive policies, existing federal policies also function as a flashing yellow light as state officials consider how aggressive to be in signing up children for health insurance. In this regard, the CHIP legislation cautioned states that their insurance initiatives should not fuel "crowd out," a phenomenon that occurs when government insurance programs encourage employees or their employers to drop work-related coverage. Workers, for instance, might drop out of their employer's plan on grounds that the benefits offered by CHIP were more generous. In the plans states submitted to HCFA for approval, they had to incorporate a strategy for preventing crowd out. Some states, for instance, proposed to impose a requirement that children had to be without insurance for six months prior to enrolling in CHIP (U.S. General Accounting Office 1999).

The "quality control system" that remains in place for Medicaid also cautioned states against becoming too zealous in a quest for higher take-up. States that go all out to avoid errors of stringency in their review of applications (denying applicants who in fact meet eligibility criteria) run a higher risk of errors of liberality (putting people on the rolls who do not meet legally stipulated income and asset tests). Medicaid law and regulations call for automatic fiscal penalties on states that "make erroneous excess payments for medical assistance to an ineligible individual or family" that exceeds the "allowable error rate" (*U.S. Code*, Title 42, sec. 1396b). This system has played a significant role in shaping the culture of welfare bureaucracies responsible for processing applications. As one seasoned administrator noted, a Medicaid director can be "seriously criticized for not signing up people for Medicaid who are eligible. He or she can be fired for running up the eligibility error rate" (Waldman 1999).

HCFA tries to lead. As state officials contemplated insuring more children, they faced an implementation process where federal officials were determined to play a significant role. Federal interest in how states coped with the take-up challenge involved the president himself, an unusual occurrence in intergovernmental relations. In February 1997, President Clinton urged states to be aggressive in locating and signing up children who were already eligible for Medicaid. By the end of 1997, however, observers reported that the president was "dismayed" that states had not made more progress in this regard. Nancy-Ann Min DeParle, the HCFA administrator, told the media that "the President has talked to me personally about this and has made clear that he wants to see results" (Pear 1997). In early 1998, the president took an additional step to dramatize his concern when on February 18 he appeared with First Lady Hillary Rodham Clinton at the Children's National Medical Center to announce new efforts to enroll the millions of uninsured children entitled to health insurance. Joining the president at the event was a parent whose child had recently been enrolled in Medicaid because of a local outreach effort. Throughout his second term, the president periodically commented on or displayed other signs of interest in efforts to solve the take-up challenge.

In addition to these highly visible signals of presidential concern, the federal government attempted to enhance take-up through several other tactics. One initiative involved the mobilization of disparate federal agencies. In early 1998, President Clinton directed eight federal departments to report back within 90 days on their plans to foster take-up. By June 1998, this Interagency Task Force on Children's Health Insurance Outreach had responded with a 64-page report (U.S. Department of Health and Human Services 1998). Acknowledging that prior "children's health insurance outreach efforts have not been very successful," the report went on to offer over 150 action steps for ameliorating the problem. Proposed measures covered a broad range of activities. The Internal Revenue Service, for instance, pledged to post information promoting enrollment at its 400 walk-in centers, while HCFA, among other things, vowed to develop a model application form designed to reduce the transaction costs for applicants.

Another cluster of federal tactics revolved around eliciting support from a broad spectrum of private groups. The White House and HCFA paid particular attention to building collaborative relationships with public interest groups that represented critical players at the state and local level, at times contracting with them. These groups included the National Governors' Association, the National Education Association, the American Public Human Service Association, and the American Hospital Association. Federal officials also solicited support from corporations. For instance, ABC and NBC promised to run public service adds touting CHIP with a toll-free number (877-KIDS-NOW) that people could call for information. K-Mart vowed to put this number on shopping bags and diaper boxes in its stores. Foundations also agreed to help. The Robert Wood Johnson Foundation, for example, committed millions of dollars to fund community coalitions to conduct innovative outreach initiatives aimed at enrolling children in Medicaid and CHIP (Pear 1999b).

Other tactics involved HCFA in transmitting a steady stream of missives to state Medicaid and CHIP officials. Many of these communications emanated from a growing concern within HCFA about spillover from the passage of welfare reform legislation. In stressing the reduction of TANF caseloads, the new law licensed welfare bureaucracies to practice an array of diversion activities designed to keep people off the rolls in the first place (Thompson and Nathan 1999). These activities included lump-sum payments to would-be applicants, job search requirements, and counseling to direct applicants to alternative sources of assistance. Although federal policy specified that this emphasis on cutting the number of TANF enrollees should not apply to Medicaid (with the partial exception of resident aliens), HCFA officials worried that state efforts to reduce welfare caseloads through diversion and other means would depress the take-up rates for health insurance.

Consequently, HCFA persistently sought to clarify the rights of individuals who had been denied access to or had exited from TANF. In January 1998, for instance, HCFA sent an official letter to state health officials reminding them to coordinate TANF and Medicaid programs so as to avoid inappropriate denials of Medicaid applications. In September 1998, HCFA followed up with a more extensive letter recommending 16 steps that states should take to increase CHIP and Medicaid enrollments. These recommendations included adoption of a brief two-page common application form for both programs, elimination of any assets tests, the extension of office hours for eligibility workers, and the development of a follow-up process for families who failed to complete the application process for health insurance. HCFA reinforced this message in the spring of 1999 when it joined with the Administration for Children and Families within the Department of Health and Human Services to issue a 28-page *Guide to Expanding Health*

Coverage in the Post-Welfare Reform World (U.S. Department of Health and Human Services 1999a). As a former Medicaid official observed, this document, which sought to "provide a how-to guide describing how to extend eligibility to the maximum limits of the law," reflected a "major change in stance" from the historic behavior of HCFA on this subject (Moore 1999).

Finally, HCFA officials occasionally relied on admonition and the threat of sanctions in their efforts to break down barriers to take-up. In this regard, the case of New York City attracted the most attention. In New York State, local governments play pivotal roles in implementing and financing safety net programs such as Medicaid. New York City, of course, stands head and shoulders above all other jurisdictions in the state in importance. (Indeed, the city has a larger population than all but 11 states.) Under the banner of discouraging dependence and prioritizing work, the Giuliani administration moved to convert welfare offices (once called "income maintenance centers") into "job centers" where applicants sought assistance from a "financial advisor." These offices pursued an aggressive diversion strategy by strongly encouraging applicants to seek employment or to get help from their families or city food pantries rather than file applications. Moreover, intake workers as a matter of routine took an application only after an individual visited the office a second time. In the wake of these practices, caseloads in New York City began to drop appreciably not only for cash assistance but for food stamps and Medicaid as well (Swarns 1998). Advocates for the poor soon complained about the practices of the city's welfare offices, and the Legal Aid Society eventually joined with other groups to sue the city.

Faced with these developments, HCFA intervened. Officials at the agency's regional office served notice that the requirement that applicants return a second time to acquire an application for Medicaid violated federal requirements. HCFA officials also sent strong signals to state officials that they were not doing enough to monitor practices in New York City. In January 1999, a federal district judge sided with the Legal Aid Society, and consequently city officials promised to produce a plan to bring its practices into compliance with federal and state law. Shortly thereafter, state Medicaid officials dispatched three undercover investigators who visited eight welfare offices in New York City and found that in four of them the intake workers indicated that they would have to return on another day to get the Medicaid application forms (Swarns 1999). In May 1999, the federal district court approved a corrective action plan submitted by the Giuliani administration.

But HCFA officials in the New York regional office entertained few illusions that the problem had been solved. Concerned about reports of steep declines in Medicaid rolls in New York State (not only in New York City but also on Long Island and upstate), Sue Kelly, the regional administrator for HCFA, sent a letter to state officials in May 1999, expressing concerns about delays in processing Medicaid applications. She indicated that HCFA would initiate a review of the state's Medicaid program requiring state officials to provide documentation of "all monitoring activities" directed at the local administration of the program and of any meetings that had occurred between state Medicaid officials and their local counterparts. The review might also entail visits by federal officials to local welfare offices (Hernandez 1999).

The case of New York City and general concerns that take-up continued to be problematic throughout the country prompted a more general emphasis on tougher tactics by the summer of 1999. In early August, President Clinton announced that he would instruct HCFA to "conduct comprehensive on-site reviews of Medicaid enrollment and eligibility processes" in all states. Federal officials were to interview state officials and check case files to "assess compliance with current laws and develop recommendations for improvement" (Pear 1999a).

Early returns from the states. As the 1990s closed, the degree to which states would muster the capacity and commitment to help the United States significantly increase the number of children with health insurance remained unclear. Undoubtedly, the Medicaid mandates of 1989 and 1990 and CHIP had motivated all states to put more generous eligibility policies on the books. These formal policy commitments varied greatly among the states. In Connecticut, for instance, uninsured children younger than 19 from families with incomes up to 300% of poverty were eligible for either Medicaid or CHIP. In contrast, South Carolina generally provided eligibility to 150% of poverty (U.S. General Accounting Office 1999, 41).

But will these policy promises founder on the shoals of implementation, especially on the take-up problem? Some positive signs exist. Most states have launched outreach initiatives targeted at potential CHIP beneficiaries—general media campaigns, school-based initiatives, efforts designed by local community groups and other vehicles. These initiatives have also attracted more applicants to Medicaid, a program that continues to do little to advertise its benefits. In Massachusetts and Michigan, for instance, those handling CHIP applications have found two children to be eligible for Medicaid for every one that met the requirements for CHIP. In an effort to remove the stigma of signing up for "welfare medicine," many states have devised more attractive names for their programs (e.g., MiChild in Michigan). A significant number of states have reduced the transaction costs of obtaining eligibility by simplifying or combining forms, by allowing families to submit applications via mail or telephone, by increasing the number, geographic distribution, and operating hours of enrollment sites, and by implementing follow-up systems to ensure that families complete the application process. Some states have also moved to make it easier to remain on the rolls by reducing the frequency of redeterminations (U.S. General Accounting Office 1999).

But the available evidence, while far from definitive, also points to the limits of state commitment. Very few states, if any, have taken full advantage of the discretion offered to them to maximize the eligibility of children for Medicaid and CHIP. Their behavior with respect to continuous eligibility also signals the limits of their commitment. Arguably, no single measure could do more to bolster take-up rates than granting children who qualify for Medicaid or CHIP one year of eligibility without redetermination. This step would reduce the churning of the rolls and the resulting loss of eligibility by many qualified families. It would probably heighten the willingness of parents to put up with the hassle involved in applying for health insurance for their children. In the case of CHIP, just over half of the states appear to have opted for continuous eligibility for one year (National Governors' Association 1999, 133–134; U.S. General Accounting Office 1999, 78). However, states willing to adopt this option for Medicaid, a program that insures vastly more low-income children than CHIP, numbered about 10 (Lewin and Associates 1999).

By mid-1999, CHIP programs had managed to enroll about 1.3 million children. Responding to this number, President Clinton announced that he was "a little disappointed" and that he had expected at least 3 million enrollees by this point (Pear 1999a, 1). By the end of 1999, the number of CHIP participants had risen to nearly 2 million. The degree to which this represents an impressive start-up for a new program can be debated, but given that CHIP had been on the books for only two years by this point, a negative assessment of state performance would be premature. In the case of Medicaid, HCFA data indicate that from 1996 to 1997, the enrollment of nondisabled children dropped by about 3% with declines occurring in well over half of the states (Thompson and Nathan 1999). Valid data on Medicaid enrollments are not readily available for the years following the birth of CHIP when more vigorous outreach began to occur. As the case of New York testifies, however, early returns suggest unexpected declines in the Medicaid rolls in many states, slippage that cannot be readily explained by the robust economy. As the millennium ensues, the jury remains out on whether the "new" politics of state health policy will enable most states to cope successfully with the take-up challenge.

Implications. The initiative to insure more low-income children points to a number of propositions relative to the new politics of state health policy. Three in particular stand out. First, although the 1990s emerged as a decade of devolution, much of what transpired with respect to children reflects an old assumption—that states would not do much more to deal with the problem of uninsured children in the absence of federal mandates and more generous subsidies. The movement toward safety net delinkage is, however, an important new development. At least until an economic downturn ensues, a growing proportion of those who are qualified for CHIP and Medicaid will not be eligible for cash assistance from government.

Second, the children's health initiative reinforces not only the proposition that implementation be kept at center stage to fathom the politics of state health policy but also the tendency for "all implementation to be local." As developments in New York City demonstrate in an especially vivid way, state Medicaid agencies face their own cluster of thorny challenges in bolstering take-up, no matter how committed their own staffs are to this objective. Systems governing Medicaid and CHIP enrollment are not tight command-and-control structures where state officials can count on frontline workers to execute orders promptly and faithfully. To the contrary, these systems tend to be loosely coupled, fragmented administrative arrangements where county welfare offices or the state's own local bureaucracies possess vast discretion to shape whether individuals get signed up and stay eligible. If anything, the 1990s may have further fueled centrifugal forces through a kind of second-order devolution from states to counties (Nathan and Gais 1999). Even in cases where state government operates welfare offices (rather than local governments as in New York), grassroots forces shape and yield variation in their style, methods, and values (Weissert 1994).

Third, within the implementation arena, the children's health initiative suggests more about the limits to federal clout in state health politics than its potential. To be sure, the White House and HCFA experienced some success in shaping the implementation agenda—in getting states to pay more attention to take-up issues than they would have otherwise. Moreover, the steady flow of information about the do's and don'ts of federal law and best practices may well have bolstered the capacity of at least some states to deal more effectively with Medicaid and CHIP enrollment. But HCFA had a much more difficult time persuading states that it could impose sanctions for poor performance, that it had a "gorilla in the closet" if states skirted the letter and spirit of the law in their enrollment practices. In part this challenge flows from the rhetoric and tone of intergovernmental relations in the 1990s. In a period marked by an emphasis on "partnership," where some go so far as to call states the "customers" of the national government, it becomes more difficult for federal administrators to adopt an aggressive posture (Scheberle 1997, 8, 13).

But HCFA faces an even more fundamental problem in convincing states of its capacity to delay, block, or withdraw federal funds if they do not live up to the spirit and letter of federal law. Of particular importance, HCFA in many respects flies blind, lacking the staff and other resources to get high-quality information about enrollment practices in the states. In the case of New York City, an attentive media and advocacy groups served as HCFA's eyes and ears. But these forces are nowhere near as abundant in many other states and local jurisdictions. Even in the highly unusual case where HCFA receives a direct order from the president to investigate state practices, the limits to HCFA's staff and the sheer complexity of health insurance enrollment systems (state officials themselves often do not know much about practices in local offices) make monitoring difficult.

Nor can federal officials easily impose sanctions on errant states in highly discretionary situations where these officials lack ready access to pertinent information. State administrators know that under these circumstances HCFA can make their lives more difficult, requiring them to attend more meetings and mandating that they keep more records and submit more documentation. But they correctly sense that HCFA is reluctant to risk the political reverberations (e.g., angry governors or members of Congress) that the application of sanctions can produce. Hence, HCFA must often depend on allies involved in state politics. The New

York City case shows how local advocacy groups may haul officials into court, generate adverse publicity, and succeed in getting a court order. Federal law and regulations often matter less for what HCFA can do about their enforcement than for how groups in state politics can seize upon them. To be sure, the national government can in some cases credibly use the threat of sanctions to motivate states. The quality control system that aims to discourage eligibility errors leading to excess payment does shape state behavior. It has two features that promote this result: first, it depends on routinely collected information, and second, the fiscal penalties flowing from the system tend to be automatic and formally specified in law and regulation (as opposed to highly discretionary on HCFA's part). Neither condition, however, applied to HCFA in its dealings with the states concerning the take-up challenge.

ACCOUNTABILITY, LEARNING, AND FEDERALISM

The 1990s not only witnessed the incremental devolution of more authority to the states in the health care arena, but it also featured the rise of a new doctrine of intergovernmental relations. This doctrine averred that the national government in its dealings with the states ought to pay less attention to process and procedural requirements (often derided as red tape) and more attention to performance (an amalgam of outputs and outcomes). It proposed that states have ample discretion over the how of program implementation but be held accountable for results (Galston and Tibbetts 1994). The doctrine of performance-based accountability made modest headway in penetrating the Medicaid program in the 1990s, but it did find expression in the legislation authorizing CHIP. Section 2107 of the new law stresses that states must have "strategic objectives and performance goals" approved by the federal government and must submit data in a format to be determined by the secretary of health and human services that would enable the national government "to evaluate and compare the effectiveness of state plans under this title." Although the law did not go into great detail, it underscored one critical bottom line—the need to increase "creditable health coverage among targeted low-income children and other low-income children." The law required states to provide annual reports to HCFA and conduct a more comprehensive evaluation of their programs by March 31, 2000.

Espousing performance-based accountability is, of course, one thing and achieving it another. HCFA officials initially hoped to establish a uniform reporting system that would assure that states provided comparable data on various aspects of their programs; the agency also aspired to shape the evaluation methodologies that states employed. But providing this direction proved to be difficult for HCFA. From an early point, many states had a hard time producing basic program information, and HCFA officials soon felt compelled to extend the deadline for the submission of annual reports. It also became evident that the evaluation due in 2000 would ultimately depend on data and methodologies chosen by the states themselves.

Although HCFA worked through such private groups as the National Governors' Association, the American Public Human Services Association, and the National Academy of State Health Policy to enhance the sophistication and comparability of information that the states would submit, recognition soon sank in that the reports produced by the states would be extremely uneven in quality and would not yield information that would allow policymakers to compare the performance of one state to that of others (Riley 1999). By August 1999, concern about the difficulties of obtaining high-quality information concerning CHIP prompted seven senators involved in the creation of the program to write Donna Shalala, secretary of health and human services, lamenting "the lack of reliable data" needed "to evaluate whether we have made overall progress in reducing the number of uninsured children" (Pear 1999a).

Capacity, commitment, and information. To some degree, the initial experience with performance accountability under CHIP can be understood as a predictable start-up problem since it often takes time to get systems of all kinds in place. However, CHIP's initial difficulties also point to ongoing and enduring issues of capacity and commitment with respect to the collection of program information and its uses in a political system marked by federalism. Political scientists have long understood that information asymmetry tends to correlate with power asymmetry. This understanding (especially as expressed in principal agent theory) yields a pessimistic prediction concerning the willingness of states to provide the national government with information useful in fostering political accountability and policy learning (Moe 1984; Scheberle 1997; Weiss and Gruber 1987). It leads to the hypothesis that, other things being equal, state administrators will prefer to provide information about program inputs (their efforts) rather than outputs and outcomes and will have no special interest in providing data that facilitate comparisons of their performance with that of other states. Even those who evince substantial sympathy for a strong state role acknowledge that federalism is often a "barrier reef" that thwarts efforts to learn from program experience (Nathan 1988, 128).

The resistance of state agencies to collecting and submitting information need not be viewed as the action of self-interested agents with an inclination to shirk their responsibility to federal principals. To the contrary, this reluctance can be seen as principled. State administrators know that, no matter how good a job they do, many factors affecting program performance will be beyond their control. They also understand that elected policymakers at the state and federal levels (some of whom may be longtime opponents of the program) stand ready to misinterpret and reach inappropriate judgments about the program from the data produced. Rather than yielding learning and a strengthening of the program, the release of certain data could lead to its premature termination. As if these factors were not sufficient, state officials resent the substantial costs of reporting systems, especially when the information that is collected seems to have little immediate value for the management of their programs. In some instances, states simply do not have the capacity to produce the requested reports. Fragmented, decentralized administrative arrangements tend to compound the problem. For instance, New York State must rely on counties (some of which are very small mom-and-pop governments) to produce a range of information about social service programs.

The early experience with CHIP, therefore, fits the dominant hypothesis about the limited program information that states would produce at least over the short term. Only energetic leadership by HCFA stood much chance of yielding a different outcome, but an array of factors undermined prospects for such leadership.

HCFA faced commitment and capacity problems of its own. Passage of the Health Insurance Portability Act of 1996 and the Balanced Budget Act of 1997 substantially increased the agency's workload. New provisions with respect to Medicare—a program administered by the federal government through contractors—reinforced the agency's long-standing propensity to attend first to this program and to let the states handle Medicaid and CHIP. Moreover, HCFA faced pressing demands to deal with Y2K problems that could adversely affect Medicare and Medicaid. As HCFA's responsibilities grew, Congress failed to provide additional personnel to the agency. Suffering from an acute staffing shortage, HCFA could not afford to assign large numbers of its employees to the task of working with the states and shaping CHIP during its start-up phase. By 1999, Congress had moved to add personnel to HCFA, but by that point much water was under the bridge with respect to state reporting and evaluation methodology.

HCFA's experience with Medicaid also provided little ground for optimism that states would be able to provide data about CHIP quickly. Starting in 1972, HCFA had struggled for well over a decade to persuade states to establish the Medicaid Management Information System (MMIS), a system that adopted uniform definitions and provided reasonably valid, reliable, and comparable data on the number of different types of Medicaid enrollees and the vendors serving them. Even then, HCFA staff had to toil constantly to uncover and correct errors in the data that states submitted to the agency. In the case of MMIS, the law gave HCFA a set of financial penalties, subsidies, and awards that could be dangled before the states to provide incentives for them to cooperate (Thompson 1998a, 42–46). The CHIP legislation provided federal officials with no such arsenal.

The limits to the federal government's capacity also became evident when its own statistical agencies proved less able to provide basic data than might have initially been expected. The national government has several highly professionalized statistical agencies, such as the Bureau of the Census and the National Center for Health Statistics, that routinely gather pertinent data related to the health care system; it clearly possesses comparative advantage relative to the states in this regard. If nothing else, it might seem that the federal government could provide data on such critical baseline variables as the number of uninsured children within a state's boundaries. And, in fact, the CHIP legislation assumed that this capacity existed when it established the U.S. Bureau of the Census as the official scorekeeper for purposes of allocating grants to the states. Each March, the bureau collects data on the number of persons without health insurance throughout the prior calendar year via the Current Population Survey (CPS). Congress distributes CHIP funds in part on the basis of these estimates; states with more uninsured children receive more money. In contemplating state efforts to gauge their progress toward insuring more children, some assumed that the CPS data would provide a ready baseline that would facilitate fruitful comparisons across states, but this has proven to be wishful thinking.

At least two major factors have encouraged states to question the validity of the March CPS as a gauge for marking their progress. First, experts differ on the degree to which the CPS presents valid data, with many suggesting that it systematically overestimates the number of uninsured children and underreports the number covered by Medicaid.* Disagreement persists on the magnitude of this discrepancy, some seeing it as relatively minor. Others, however, argue that the actual number of uninsured children may in fact be from one-half to two-thirds of that reported by the March CPS (Lewis, Ellwood, and Czajka 1998: Ullman, Bruen, and Holikan 1998; U.S. Department of Health and Human Services 1999b). Second, and of particular relevance in an era of devolution, the national surveys of the federal government do not as a rule produce highly valid and reliable estimates at the state level. In the case of less populous states, federal officials attempt to compensate for small sample sizes by combining the three most recent years of data. But this practice still yields estimates from year to year (the three-year average) that show sufficient variation to raise questions about the accuracy of the number. Hence, even on so basic a matter as counting the number of uninsured (let alone the more complex calculation of the take-up rate), doubts about the federal government's capacity to collect reliable data let states off the hook.

Toward a more transparent federalism. Viewed broadly, the quest to foster performance-based accountability and to learn from the experience of intergovernmental grant programs can be seen as part of an effort to advance a more transparent federalism. Such transparency increases to the degree that policymakers at all

---

*Part of the error in CPS estimates of the uninsured probably stems from differing time frames that surveyors and respondents have in mind. The Census Bureau probes whether the respondent lacked insurance for the entire preceding calendar year. Many respondents reply as if they have been asked about their insurance status at the time the question is posed. These point-in-time estimates of the uninsured yield higher numbers concerning the magnitude of the problem than those that accurately probe health insurance experience over a longer period, such as one year.

levels, citizens, and other players have ready access to a rich supply of program-related information on a state-by-state basis that permits reasoned comparisons among states. If economists preach the virtue of transparency for markets, policy analysts should be alert to its virtues in the context of federalism. A more transparent federalism could provide useful insights for both national and state policymakers and galvanize a more informed politics of health policy. As the experience with Medicaid and CHIP suggests, progress toward transparency will not come easily. By the same token, however, one should not assume that the barriers to transparent federalism are insurmountable.

Surmounting these barriers will require leadership by the national government. Even if state officials have the capacity and commitment to assemble program data, they have no natural inclination to coordinate with other states to ensure uniform definitions and methodologies. For this to occur, the national government must provide direction in this sphere even as it may be devolving still greater authority to the states in other domains.

A more transparent federalism will in part rest on federal efforts to enhance state reporting systems. In their role as implementing agents, states have a unique opportunity to build information systems that routinely provide data related to workload and performance. The experience with MMIS and other data systems in the health care arena points to two major lessons in this regard. First, states will gradually move to supply uniform data only if legislation gives the federal bureaucracy an array of fiscal rewards and penalties to use in dealing with the states. These may include generous matching grants for the establishment of appropriate information systems or fiscal penalties for failure to have the specified systems in place or for not producing acceptable reports in a timely way. Second, even with these carrot-and-stick enticements, it will tend to take a long time and considerable negotiation between federal and state administrators to institutionalize the capacity to produce valid, reliable, and timely data.

The effort to achieve transparent federalism will also require the national government to enhance its own capacity to bypass the states in data collection, to gather critical statistics on its own. In this respect, officials need to pay as much attention to the social indicator movement of the 1960s as the performance management advocates of the 1990s. In March 1966, President Lyndon Johnson recommended the development and assembly of social indicators and the preparation of a report to Congress. Subsequently, a bevy of highly respected social scientists worked with the leadership of the Department of Health, Education, and Welfare to produce *Toward a Social Report,* which was presented to President Johnson in January 1969 just as he was leaving office (U.S. Department of Health, Education, and Welfare 1970). Although the Nixon administration did not sustain the social indicator movement in an explicit sense, efforts to monitor the health care system have gradually moved forward through several presidential administrations.

The first decade of the new millennium could galvanize significant progress toward transparent federalism if three events occurred with respect to social indicators. First, with an eye toward indicators that would assist in the performance assessment of a range of categorical programs, federal officials would, in collaboration with their state counterparts, examine blind spots in the current data system and seek to develop new indicators. Such a development could enhance efficiency in the quest for performance-based accountability. For instance, observers note that given the size of CHIP, it is difficult to justify the cost of collecting the state-level data needed to evaluate the program (Halfon et al. 1999). But if the problem gets cast as one of developing a bank of indicators that could help federal and state policymakers assess the performance of Medicaid, CHIP, and other health programs targeted at low-income children, the benefits of the effort look much more reasonable relative to the expenditure involved. Second, progress toward improved social indicators would depend on further refinement in measurement to ensure high-quality, credible data (as in the case of estimates of the uninsured). Third, sample sizes would need to be sufficient in each state to provide valid estimates of developments within its boundaries.

Ultimately, of course, enhancing the federal government's capacity to galvanize a more transparent federalism requires political support. Such support may at first glance seem highly unlikely. In an era dominated by the dogma of downsizing, the perennial propensity of elected officials to give short shrift to issues of administrative capacity looms ever larger. Through budget cuts and other means, the statistical agencies of the federal government have not escaped the consequences of this mentality. Moreover, sensing that statistics can mobilize political participation, stir debate, and ignite calls for the federal government to do something about a problem, conservatives who seek to limit the government's role generally or the national government's role in particular may well find the quest for better data on health care conditions unappealing. The absence of a significant social movement also augurs poorly for the development of better social indicators. The initial era of "statistical enthusiasm" in this country in the 1820s and 1830s emanated from a social movement that saw the need for "moral statistics" useful in monitoring health, education, and crime in the broader society (Starr 1987, 24; Davis 1972, 158, 172). So, too, the pursuit of social indicators in the 1960s occurred at a time when the civil rights movement and the "war on poverty" ranked very high on the nation's agenda. The early years of the twenty-first century are unlikely to be animated by a similar impulse for reform.

But other factors suggest that progress toward a more transparent federalism may well be feasible. As both CHIP and the welfare reform act of 1996 attest, the Republican-controlled Congresses of the late 1990s have demonstrated a big appetite for collecting information about program developments in the states. In fact, state officials frequently complain about the burden these requirements impose on them. This pattern is consistent with the finding that in a period unlikely to yield great new reform initiatives, the oversight of existing programs becomes increasingly salient in Congress (Aberbach 1990). The rapid development of ever more sophisticated information technology also tends to tilt lawmakers in this direction as does the chronic propensity in Western cultures to see the quest for more information as good in itself and almost independent of the costs of collecting it (Feldman and March 1981).

Nor should the impact of a highly technical politics driven by professionals in and out of government be discounted. Although public endorsement of a social indicator initiative reminiscent of the 1960s would do little other than to create a political backlash, a steady push to improve the bank of social indicators available on a state-by-state basis—a push that flies below the radar screen of high politics and emphasizes technical issues—may well foster progress. In this vein, revisions to the CHIP legislation enacted in November 1999 appropriated $10 million per year so that sample sizes could be increased in the Current Population Survey and other adjustments made in order to yield "statistically reliable annual State data on the number of low-income children who do not have health insurance" (Title VII, sec. 2, *Medicare . . . Refinement Act*).

Success in advancing a more transparent federalism will not, of course, guarantee the adoption of "better policy" by the federal and state governments. It will not necessarily foster enhanced understanding of the causal dynamics affecting health programs, but it could at least provide a better platform for pursuing such insight. In the case of Medicaid and CHIP, for instance, it would permit more refined estimates of the take-up rates in the various states. Researchers could then explore the degree to which factors such as outreach efforts, eligibility intake procedures, and redetermination practices account for variation in these rates. Nor will the richer flow of information embedded in transparent federalism necessarily carry the day in state politics. Knowledge is not always power. A vast array of forces may lead policymakers to ignore this expanded bank of indicators. But if a transparent federalism cannot assure a more enlightened state politics, it can at least improve prospects for performance-based accountability and learning.

CONCLUSION

The forces of federalism, especially those rooted in Medicaid, leave a heavy imprint on health care policy in the United States. As the 1990s dawned, states already possessed vast discretion to shape a wide range of intergovernmental grant programs. Via the tools of an administrative presidency and legislative action, the decade featured the further devolution of authority and responsibility to the states in the health care arena. This devolution stopped short of the vision embedded in the Republican Medigrant proposal of 1995. Nor did it signal a retreat in federal willingness to send dollars to the states for health care programs. But on balance, developments further signaled that state political forces shaping policy formation and implementation would be increasingly important in determining who gets what in the health care arena.

As more authority and responsibility gravitate to the states, the question naturally arises as to whether they are up to the challenge in terms of their capacity and commitment. Problems of conceptualizing and measuring these two concepts preclude a definitive judgment. Debate persists on whether the state glass is half empty or half full. In terms of capacity, states have clearly progressed relative to their position in the 1960s, but this does not mean that they have continued on an upward trajectory in the period since 1980. Moreover, state capacity must be judged in terms of what policymakers ask state agencies to do. As the case of take-up in the Medicaid and CHIP programs vividly illustrates, the policy expectations directed toward states can greatly exceed their current capacity at least over the short term. As for their commitment to assuring that all of their citizens have access to health care of good quality, states vary greatly. Without endorsing the specifics of the race-to-the-bottom thesis, there seems little question that the politics of interstate economic competition mingle with the general political weakness of low-income people to serve as a major constraint on state commitment. In the case of the children's insurance initiative, for instance, almost all states have done more than the minimum required to sustain their flow of federal funds. But they have not taken to the limit the discretion offered to them by the federal government in order to insure more children.

Issues of capacity and commitment also surface in considering another key development of the 1990s: the pervasive endorsement of the doctrine of performance-based accountability. Movement toward a more transparent federalism in the health care arena could facilitate such accountability and enhance prospects for policy learning. But as the experience with the child health insurance initiative suggests, the creation of a rich supply of valid and timely performance-related information on a state-by state basis will be difficult. Whatever their general strengths, states as a group lack the commitment and capacity to fuel a movement toward more transparent federalism. Whether political forces will allow the federal government to enhance its statistical capacity and lead the way toward this form of federalism remains an open question.

Will the first decade of the new millennium feature a further tilt toward devolution in the health care arena? Much depends on the outcome of the elections in the years 2000 and 2004. Greater Republican dominance in the nation's capitol would significantly increase prospects for a major devolution of additional rights and responsibilities (including fiscal burdens) to the states. Greater Democratic dominance would tend to slow devolution or in some cases bring it to a halt. But whatever the dominant political coalition, it seems highly unlikely that the decade born in 2000 will feature either a major shift in power back to the national government or a clean sorting out of federal and state functions in the health care arena. The federal government and the states will continue to jockey for leverage in the politics of state health policy.

REFERENCES

Aberbach, J. D. 1990. *Keeping a Watchful Eye.* Washington, DC: Brookings Institution.
Boyd, D. B. 1998. "Medicaid Devolution: A Fiscal Perspective." In *Medicaid and Devolution: A View from the States,* ed. F. J. Thompson and J. J. DiIulio Jr., pp. 56–105. Washington, DC: Brookings Institution.
Carey, J. M., R. G. Neimi, and L. W. Powell. 1998. "The Effects of Term Limits on State Legislatures." *Legislative Studies Quarterly* 23 (May): 271–300.
Conlan, T. 1998. *From New Federalism to Devolution.* Washington, DC: Brookings Institution.
Davis, R. C. 1972. "The Beginnings of American Social Research." In *Nineteenth-Century American Science: A Reappraisal,* ed. G. H. Daniels, pp. 152–178. Evanston, IL: Northwestern University Press.
Donahue, J. D. 1997. *Disunited States.* New York: Basic Books.
Feldman, M. S., and J. G. March. 1981. "Information in Organizations as Signal and Symbol." *Administrative Science Quarterly* 26 (June): 171–186.
Fossett, J. W. 1998. "Managed Care and Devolution." In *Medicaid and Devolution: A View from the States,* ed. F. J. Thompson and J. J. DiIulio Jr., pp. 106–153. Washington, DC: Brookings Institution.
Galston, W. A., and G. L. Tibbetts. 1994. "Reinventing Federalism: The Clinton/Gore Program for a New Partnership among the Federal, State, Local, and Tribal Governments." *Publius* 24 (Summer): 23–48.
Hackey, R. B. 1998. *Rethinking Health Care Policy: The New Politics of State Regulation.* Washington, DC: Georgetown University Press.
Halfon, N., et al. 1999. "Challenges in Securing Access to Care for Children." *Health Affairs* 18 (2): 48–63.
Hernandez, R. 1999. "Inquiry Grows as Rolls Fall for Medicaid." *New York Times,* June 8.
Layton, C., and M. Walton. 1998. "Missing the Story at the Statehouse." *American Journalism Review* (July/August): 42–63.
Leichter, H. M. 1996. "State Governments and Their Capacity for Health Care Reform." In *Health Policy, Federalism, and the American States,* ed. R. F. Rich and W. D. White. Washington, DC: Urban Institute Press.
Lewin and Associates. 1999. *Implementing Continuous Eligibility: Costs and Considerations.* Oakland, CA: Med-Cal Policy Institute.
Lewis, K., M. Ellwood, and J. L. Czajka. 1998. *Counting the Uninsured: A Review of the Literature.* Washington, DC: Urban Institute.
Medicare, Medicaid, and SCHIP Balanced Budget Refinement Act of 1999 (H.R. 3426).
Moe, T. M. 1984. "The New Economics of Organization." *American Journal of Political Science* 28 (4): 739–777.
Moore, J. D. 1999. Personal correspondence, April 8.
Nathan, R. P. 1983. *The Administrative Presidency.* New York: Macmillan.
———. 1988. *Social Science in Government: Uses and Misuses.* New York: Basic Books.
Nathan, R. P., et al. 1987. *Reagan and the States.* Princeton, NJ: Princeton University Press.
Nathan, R. P., and T. Gais. 1999. *Implementing the Personal Responsibility Act of 1996: A First Look.* Albany, NY: Nelson A. Rockefeller Institute of Government.
National Conference of State Legislatures. 1999. *http://www.ncsl.org/programs/fiscal/1fp104.htm* (June).

National Governors' Association. 1999. *1998 State Children's Health Insurance Program Annual Report*. Washington, DC: National Governors' Association and National Conference of State Legislatures.

National Performance Review. 1993. *From Red Tape to Results: Creating a Government that Works Better and Costs Less*. Washington, DC: Government Printing Office.

Pear, R. 1997. "Clinton Ordering Effort to Sign Up Medicaid Children." *New York Times,* December 29.

———. 1999a. "Clinton to Chide States for Failing to Cover Children." *New York Times,* August 8.

———. 1999b. "President Set to Establish a Toll-Free Number to Enroll Children in Health Insurance Plan." *New York Times,* February 23.

Perry, M., S. Kannel, R. B. Valdez, and C. Chang. 2000. *Medicaid and Children: Overcoming Barriers to Enrollment*. Washington, DC: Kaiser Commission on Medicaid and the Uninsured.

Peterson, P. E., B. G. Rabe, and K. K. Wong. 1986. *When Federalism Works*. Washington, DC: Brookings Institution.

Richardson, S. 1999. Presentation at the annual meeting of the National Academy of Social Insurance, Washington, DC, January.

Riley, T. 1999. "How Will We Know if CHIP Is Working?" *Health Affairs* 18 (2): 64–66.

Scheberle, D. 1997. *Federalism and Environmental Policy: Trust and the Politics of Implementation*. Washington, DC: Georgetown University Press.

Schram, S., and J. Soss. 1998. "Making Something Out of Nothing: Welfare Reform and a New Race to the Bottom." *Publius* 28 (Summer): 67–88.

Selden, T. M., J. S. Banthin, and J. W. Cohen. 1998. "Medicaid's Problem Children: Eligible but Not Enrolled." *Health Affairs* 17 (May/June): 192–200.

———. 1999. "Waiting in the Wings: Eligibility and Enrollment in the State Children's Health Insurance Program." *Health Affairs* 18 (March/April): 126–133.

Starr, P. 1987. "The Sociology of Official Statistics." In *The Politics of Numbers,* ed. W. Alonso and P. Starr, pp. 7–57. New York: Russell Sage Foundation,

Swarns, R. L. 1998. "U.S. Inquiry Asks if City Deprives Poor." *New York Times,* November 8.

———. 1999. "State Investigators Find Medicaid Delays in the City. *New York Times,* February 4.

Thompson, F. J. 1998a. "The Faces of Devolution." In *Medicaid and Devolution: A View from the States,* ed. F. J. Thompson and J. J. DiIulio Jr., pp. 14–55. Washington, DC: Brookings Institution.

———. 1998b. "Federalism and the Medicaid Challenge." In *Medicaid and Devolution: A View from the States,* ed. F. J. Thompson and J. J. DiIulio Jr., pp. 258–296. Washington, DC: Brookings Institution.

Thompson, F. J., and R. P. Nathan. 1999. "The Relationship between Welfare Reform and Medicaid: A Preliminary View." Paper presented at the National Health Policy Forum, George Washington University, February 26, 1999.

Thompson, F. J., and N. M. Riccucci. 1998. "Reinventing Government." In *Annual Review of Political Science,* ed. N. W. Polsby, pp. 231–258. Vol. 1. Palo Alto, CA: Annual Reviews.

Ullman, F., B. Bruen, and J. Holihan. 1998. *The State Children's Health Insurance Program: A Look at the Numbers*. Washington, DC: Urban Institute.

U.S. Department of Health, Education, and Welfare. 1970. *Toward A Social Report.* Ann Arbor: University of Michigan Press.

U.S. Department of Health and Human Services. 1998. *Report to the President: Interagency Task Force on Children's Health Insurance Outreach.* Washington, DC.

U.S. Department of Health and Human Services. 1999a. *Supporting Families in Transition: A Guide to Expanding Health Coverage in the Post-Welfare Reform World.* Washington, DC.

U.S. Department of Health and Human Services, Assistant Secretary for Planning and Evaluation. 1999b. *Understanding Estimates of Uninsured Children: Putting the Differences in Context. http://aspe.os.dhhs.gov/rn/rn21.htm.*

U.S. General Accounting Office. 1999. *Children's Health Insurance Program: State Implementation Approaches Are Evolving.* Pub. no. GAO/HEHS-99-65. Washington, DC.

U.S. Health Care Financing Administration. 1999. *http://www.hcfa.gov* (May).

U.S. Office of Management and Budget. 1998. *Catalogue of Federal Domestic Assistance.* Washington, DC: Government Printing Office.

Waldman, W. 1999. Presentation at the National Health Policy Forum, George Washington University, February 26, 1999.

Walker, D. B. 1981. *Toward a Functioning Federalism.* Cambridge, MA.: Winthrop.

Weingast, B. R. 1995. "The Economic Role of Political Institutions: Market-Preserving Federalism and Economic Development." *Journal of Law, Economics, and Organization* 7 (1): 1–31.

Weiss, J. A., and J. E. Gruber. 1987. "The Managed Irrelevance of Federal Education Statistics." In *The Politics of Numbers,* ed. W. Alonso and P. Starr, pp. 363–391. New York: Russell Sage Foundation.

Weiss, J. A., and M. Tschirhart. 1994. "Public Information Campaigns as Policy Instruments."*Journal of Policy Analysis and Management* 13 (1): 82–119.

Weissert, C. S. 1994. "Beyond the Organization: The Influence of Community and Personal Values on Street-Level Bureaucrats' Responsiveness." *Journal of Public Administration Research and Theory* 4 (April): 225–254.

3

The Governors and Health Policymaking

Michael S. Dukakis

States and their governors have been involved in health issues for decades. Ever since Lemuel Shattuck of Massachusetts went into the Irish slums in the Roxbury section of Boston and exposed the sordid conditions in which Irish immigrants were living, states along with their county and local governments have been deeply involved in what we have generally called "public health."

Minimum standards of fitness for human habitation, regulations governing the quality of drinking water, basic sanitation, and early efforts at environmental cleanup have all been part of the responsibility of state governments for a long time. Increasingly, however, state public health programs were accompanied by some effort to provide medical care for the poor and the indigent. During the early part of this century, that effort often took the form of publicly funded clinics, mandatory immunization, publicly owned and operated hospitals at both the state and local level that provided extensive outpatient and inpatient care to those unable to afford a doctor, targeted programs that focused on tuberculosis, venereal disease, and infectious diseases, and, of course, large state mental hospitals. Moreover, for most of the century, it is the states that have been responsible for the licensing of health providers.

The Progressive movement at the turn of the century also spawned increasing interest in the provision of health insurance generally. Some people know that Theodore Roosevelt endorsed universal health insurance in his third-party Bull Moose campaign of 1912. But few remember that Samuel McCall, the progressive Republican governor of Massachusetts, and his running mate, Calvin Coolidge, proposed universal health insurance for the people of Massachusetts in 1916.

Those early efforts at broader involvement of state government in the provision of primary medical care were unsuccessful, however, and it was not until the 1960s that most governors began to address seriously the challenge of providing comprehensive coverage and services to those unable to pay for them out of their own pockets and unlucky enough to work for an employer that did not provide them. Then, with the passage of Medicaid by Congress in 1965, virtually all states suddenly found themselves confronting a new responsibility—providing, in effect, comprehensive health benefits for hundreds of thousands of their constituents who were either on public assistance or medically indigent under the provisions of the Medicaid law.

For the most part, states and their governors were ill-equipped to take on the Medicaid program. In those days particularly, states were rarely winning blue ribbons for outstanding management. Dedicated but traditional state health bureaucracies often did their jobs well, but none of them had any experience at administering a large and expensive state and federally funded insurance system for the poor. Defining benefits, choosing from among a wide array of optional coverage available under the Medicaid law, setting reimbursement rates, controlling costs, and dealing with fraud and abuse by providers who saw Medicaid as a financial bonanza were all things that most states had never done before.

The result often was administrative chaos, skyrocketing costs, and front-page stories about Medicaid mills that were ripping off their patients and the states that were paying them. It took years for many states to manage their Medicaid programs effectively, and annual double-digit inflation in health costs in the 1980s forced governors and their budget directors to confront directly the challenge of skyrocketing Medicaid budgets. No wonder that most states began turning to managed care and its capitated payments as one important answer to budget-busting Medicaid expenditures.

Today, those efforts appear to have had considerable success. While the inexorable rise in private health costs has slowed at least temporarily, the rate of increase in state Medicaid budgets has slowed even more dramatically. For example, between fiscal years 1998 and 1999, the cost of state Medicaid programs was budgeted to rise by only 3.8%, one of the lowest annual increases since the program began in the 1960s (National Conference of State Legislatures 1998). All states now have fully computerized reimbursement systems. Congress and the Clinton administration have given the states far more authority to require Medicaid-eligible recipients to join managed care plans and greater latitude in setting reimbursement rates. Governors and their Medicaid administrators in most states are far less troubled about the level of Medicaid expenses than they were just a few short years ago.

While the nation's governors were struggling to get the management and expenditures of their Medicaid programs under control, however, more and more state chief executives began addressing the issue of access to health care for low- and moderate-income working people and their families. Hawaii, of course, has been far and away the leader on the health access front (Neubauer 1993). While Congress and Presidents Nixon and Ford were struggling unsuccessfully to win approval of some form of universal health coverage at the national level, Hawaii and its legislature approved the first and only operating universal health plan in the nation in 1974. Hawaii's Prepaid Insurance Act and subsequent expansions of the original law to include the unemployed and part-time workers not covered by the law's employer mandate still serve as one important model for those states seeking to expand coverage to low- and moderate-income working families.*

Nevertheless, by the mid-1980s, expanding Medicaid coverage to include at the very least pregnant mothers and their children became the subject of intense discussion at meetings of the National Governors' Association (NGA) and their chief health officials. Congress, too, got into the act, much to the annoyance of most governors, who genuinely wanted to expand access within their states but did not take kindly to congressionally imposed mandates for expansion of coverage that expected the states to come up with at least half of the cost in most cases. In fact, the annual meeting of the NGA in 1989 virtually exploded into a bipartisan attack on Congress for insisting on approving legislation to expand mandated benefits and eligibility under Medicaid at a time when state Medicaid budgets were increasing at the rate of 15–20% annually.

Nonetheless, the 1980s were a period of intensive activity at the state level. In virtually all states, efforts were made to broaden eligibility for Medicaid to poor working mothers and their children who were making the transition from welfare to work. In states like Massachusetts, Washington, and Oregon, those efforts took the form of Hawaii-type employer mandates, all of which have subsequently been modified or repealed.

In almost every case, however, where states attempted to dramatically expand health coverage, governors played dominant or key roles. That they should do so is not surprising. Expanding access to health care is a tough political issue, which is particularly true if a state attempts to require all or most of its employers to provide such coverage. Groups purporting to represent small business will immediately protest that the added cost of health insurance for their employees will put them out of business. Hospitals will fight any attempt by state regulators to control hospital costs. And those insurance companies that stay profitable by refusing to provide coverage for persons or families with a history of health problems will fight to the death any effort to prohibit the denial of coverage for preexisting conditions, an absolute necessity if a state wants universal coverage through the private market.

Furthermore, opponents of mandated coverage will spend, and spend freely, to defeat any such legislation. State governments, as a practical matter, cannot tap the public treasury to counter such attacks over the airwaves. Under the circumstances, the governor is the one key figure in any state who can attempt to build the kind of political coalition without which efforts to expand access to health care for the uninsured are doomed to failure. He or she, as the case may be, commands "the bully pulpit," as Theodore Roosevelt used to say. The media covers

*Hawaii Revised Statutes § 393-17 (1999); § 431N-1 (1999).

what governors say on a daily basis, and they give them an opportunity to mount a well-conceived communications strategy that may overcome the opposition. Most governors have key legislative allies who are deeply committed to expanding access, and they will be more than willing to join a chief executive who involves them actively and genuinely in that effort. And governors have resources at hand to do the kind of policy analysis and number crunching that are essential, especially in the preparation of the executive budget.

Little wonder, then, that in most states that have attempted to move toward universal or near universal access, it is the governors who have taken the lead. On the other hand, as we shall see, even the most powerful and persuasive chief executive cannot do it on his own. He needs strong and creative legislative allies. He must mobilize and build a broad coalition of enlightened business leaders, health care providers, union officials, and consumer advocates. He must focus laser-like on a press strategy that makes the case for his health care initiative. He must keep his agenda short and make sure that his health care proposals are at the top of the list. Even so, he may not carry the day.

On rare occasions, and Oregon may be the exception to the rule, a key legislative leader may lead the charge. But in Oregon that legislator was the Senate president who carried with him his credibility as an emergency room physician. Such a situation at the state level is rare indeed. In almost every other case, governors were at the forefront of their states' efforts to expand access. Five states in particular and the role their governors played will be the subject of this chapter. Three of those governors were Democrats, two were Republicans. All demonstrated leadership in a variety of important ways.*

MINNESOTA

Minnesota has been in the forefront of many of the state-initiated progressive reforms that have found their way into national policy. Health care is no exception. Beginning in the late 1980s, Minnesota began to expand Medicaid coverage to include the children of the working poor. At the same time, with Governor Rudy Perpich's blessing, the legislature created the Health Care Access Commission, which, in the words of its enabling act, was designed to "develop and recommend to the legislature a plan to provide access to health care for all state residents." Two members of the commission ultimately became part of what came to be known as the "Gang of Seven." They were Senator Linda Berglin and Representative Paul

*Some of what follows is based on cited sources. Fortunately, I was able to personally interview all but one of the governors in preparing this chapter. In addition, I have followed John Kitzhaber's work in Oregon closely over the years. We discussed it when he was Senate president, and I was able to talk at length about the current status of Oregon's health care reform efforts with one of his top policy aides, Barney Speight.

Ogren, both Democratic Farmer Labor Party members, and they were deeply involved in the work of the commission that ultimately served as the basis for what is now known as MinnesotaCare (Leichter 1993).

Minnesota, like most other states at the time, was trying to cope with a national recession and the almost inevitable impact that an economic downturn has on state budgets. The state was running a huge budget deficit; Arne Carlson, the recently elected Republican governor, was struggling to deal with it; and a Democratic legislature not only was not cooperating, but there was also enormous public pressure to expand access to health care even in the face of the state's severe fiscal problems.

The commission's recommendations were detailed and sweeping. It wanted health coverage guaranteed for all Minnesotans up to 275% of the federal poverty line. It proposed tough restrictions on the ability of insurers to deny coverage. It endorsed community rating. It attempted to control costs by proposing the creation of a network of regional health care commissions and the establishment of statewide limits on health care spending.

Unfortunately, it did not propose a funding source for the plan at a time when the state's budget was already in deep trouble. Despite strong public support for the plan and his own low poll ratings, Carlson vetoed the bill on grounds that without a funding source, Minnesota could not possibly afford it. He urged legislators to work on a plan that broadened coverage and was affordable, but he made it clear that he would not support it if it included an increase in the state income tax. At that point, the legislature, not the governor, was facing reelection in 1992. Public support for expanded health access was still strong. Much work had been done by the commission and in the legislature to produce the 1991 bill. The governor himself needed and wanted a political boost.

Seven legislators representing both parties coalesced around a bipartisan effort to find a solution. Governor Carlson was only peripherally involved in the details of the proposals, but two members of his staff, Curt Johnson and Mary Jo O'Brien, were in fairly close touch with the Gang of Seven. The governor's office did, however, lay out in fairly specific terms what he would not accept—an increase in the state income tax and, at least initially, coverage for single adults without children.

Over many weeks of negotiation, the Gang of Seven hammered out a wide-ranging compromise: statewide and regional limits on total health care spending; regional health planning agencies; a prohibition on doctors' balance billing for Medicare; limits on the ability of insurers to deny coverage to small businesses; purchasing pools; standardized health policy provisions; health insurance for all families up to 275% of poverty with sliding scale premiums based on income; and a combination of tobacco and provider taxes to pay for the program.

The proposal for provider taxes caused an uproar in the provider community. Governor Carlson met on a number of occasions with protesting groups of providers. When asked why their opposition was so strong even though they would inevitably pass the tax on in the form of increased charges, he said simply, "People are usually against change when it affects them" (Carlson 1999). Providers over the line in states bordering Minnesota were particularly incensed since the tax was also designed to apply to them in proportion to the number of Minnesotans they treated.

Carlson's eventual support for the bill and what even his critics concede was aggressive and effective implementation of the new plan (Berglin 1999) were deeply rooted in his own personal experience. While he was growing up in New York City, a New York doctor had refused to care for his seriously ill two-year-old brother unless his mother could come up with four hundred dollars in cash at a time when they did not have—and could not afford—health insurance. Carlson still talks about the impact that experience had on him as a motivating force during his governorship.

He also believed that the passage of comprehensive and well-financed health coverage for thousands of uninsured Minnesotans would be a boon to the Minnesota economy at a time when it and most state economies were hurting. A strong and robust health care sector, he reasoned, would lead to strong and robust growth in health-related industries like biotechnology and medical instruments. In short, he saw two important reasons for supporting the bill: it was morally right, and it could make a real contribution to reviving the state's economy.

TENNESSEE

The situation in Tennessee, while it adopted a plan even more expansive than Minnesota's, was a marked contrast to the Minnesota experience. In Tennessee, it was Governor Ned McWherter, a Democrat facing the end of his gubernatorial tenure in his second term as governor, who exercised strong and absolutely dominant leadership in the fashioning and approval of what has come to be known as TennCare.

McWherter was a child of rural western Tennessee. He describes health care in his home region while he was growing up as consisting largely of a single doctor within a fifty-mile radius of his small rural town. The nearest clinic was thirty miles away; the nearest hospital, a hundred miles away. Health insurance was virtually nonexistent, and medical care, such as it was, was provided largely by that single doctor in people's homes (McWherter 1999).

McWherter entered the legislature during the late 1960s and was an early advocate of Tennessee's involvement in the Medicaid program. As Speaker of the House, he continued to provide strong support for the program. Unfortunately, like most other states, Tennessee during the 1980s began to experience double-digit increases in Medicaid costs that drove the percentage of the state budget devoted to Medicaid from 3% to nearly 25% in a matter of a few years.

By the time McWherter was governor, it was clear, as he began saying often, that the state was facing a budgetary "train wreck." At the same time, Tennessee, like a number of states, financed a substantial portion of its share of Medicaid costs with a provider tax. For a while that was tolerable, but as the federal government began clamping down on how and to what extent states were using provider taxes to defray their portion of the cost, the Tennessee provider tax really began to bite, and the provider community made it clear that it would no longer tolerate a tax that by McWherter's second term was producing half a billion dollars a year. Repeal or substantial modification of the tax soon became the number one item on the providers' agenda.

Like many other states, Tennessee was also experiencing runaway inflation in the cost of providing health coverage for its state employees. Accordingly, McWherter began by first seeking to organize a statewide preferred provider organization (PPO) that could provide coverage for all state employees and their families and get the cost of that coverage under control. A statewide PPO under Blue Cross was created, and service districts were established. The new program was not without its stresses and strains, as state employees and providers had to adjust to the reality that all health care for them would have to be obtained through the new PPO. Nevertheless, McWherter persisted; the program went into effect; and after some early difficulties it appeared to meet its two principal goals: comprehensive health benefits for state employees and their families at a cost the state could afford.

Emboldened by that experience—and McWherter now says that his success in dealing with the state employee program was absolutely critical to his resolve to proceed with TennCare—he decided to embark on a dramatic and virtually unprecedented attempt outside of Hawaii and Massachusetts to provide affordable and accessible health care coverage for virtually all Tennesseans while substantially eliminating the provider tax that providers were loudly and effectively protesting (Bureau of National Affairs 1999).

McWherter had always believed that health care was something to which all citizens were entitled. He increasingly came to believe as well that there was something fundamentally unfair about a situation where people on welfare were receiving generous benefits under Medicaid while their next-door neighbors who were working in low-wage jobs got nothing. Accordingly, he designed the program so that all Tennesseans up to 400% of poverty would be eligible. Benefits would be free up to the poverty line. Those with incomes above the poverty line would pay premiums on a sliding scale based on their income.

Insuring nearly half a million uninsured Tennesseans over and above those covered by Medicaid while eliminating a tax that was yielding half a billion dollars a year to pay for the state share of Medicaid was a formidable task, to put it mildly. Encouraged by the success of his statewide managed care effort on behalf of state employees, however, McWherter believed that enrolling all Medicaid-eligible Tennesseans in managed care organizations and requiring managed care for the thousands of additional enrollees in TennCare would more than make up in savings for the loss of the provider tax revenue while dramatically extending coverage to the people of his state who were uninsured or uninsurable.

Unfortunately, because of extended discussions and delays in negotiating a waiver with the U.S. Department of Health and Human Services, McWherter lost valuable time in attempting to put the program into operation. In fact, he finally had to appeal personally to an old friend and neighboring governor, Bill Clinton, and it was the president's intervention that finally won HHS approval. And who can blame HHS? Here was a governor arguing that he could insure hundreds of thousands of previously uninsured people, throw half a billion dollars in revenue away, and come out even.

TennCare continues to be an ongoing story in Tennessee politics. McWherter had only a few months to implement the program after he finally got the administration's approval for his waiver. Tennessee had no established managed care network like those in California, Massachusetts, and Minnesota, and the state literally had to create one out of whole cloth. Tennessee doctors were neither used to nor comfortable with the capitation that accompanies managed care, and they continue to complain loudly and bitterly that they are being woefully undercompensated for TennCare patients. Subsequent state administrations have felt compelled to periodically shut down enrollment in the program because of excessive budgetary costs, even with its low reimbursement rates (Bureau of National Affairs 1999).

There is no question, however, that McWherter's leadership produced a plan that represents an extraordinary expansion in the availability of health care for uninsured residents of any state in the country. Particularly as the kinks have been ironed out of the program, the degree of patient satisfaction has risen significantly (Fox and Lyons 1998, 4). All but one of the managed care organizations that provide coverage under TennCare claim that they are losing money, but health care advocates in Tennessee point out that Blue Cross–Blue Shield continues to make a profit on TennCare business as proof that it can be done. Some doctors are still threatening to pull out of the program, and within the past few months the legislature has appropriated nearly two hundred million additional dollars for TennCare and raised reimbursement rates by a modest percentage.

McWherter considers the program one of his greatest achievements, as well he might. If he had had more time to implement it administratively, he might have been able to avoid some of the difficult problems that plagued its early years and continue to make it one of the state's most difficult challenges. No one, however, including the present Republican governor, has proposed repealing it, and recent evaluations give it high marks for quality and breadth of coverage.

WISCONSIN

On July 1, 1999, Wisconsin began implementation of BadgerCare, a program designed to provide health care coverage for all children and adults with children up to 185% of poverty and, ultimately, its governor hopes, to all working adults. In fact, four-term governor Tommy Thompson has set as his goal the insuring of at least 98% of the state's population in a state that today already has one of the lowest percentages of uninsured residents in the nation (Bartels and Boronlec 1998).

BadgerCare, like MinnesotaCare, represents a logical progression from health care coverage for children to coverage for their families and ultimately for all working adults. Like the other governors that I discuss in this chapter, Thompson had strong personal reasons for pushing the expansion of health care access, two in particular. First, he was a state legislator from small town, rural Wisconsin where the number of uninsured people was unusually high, largely because so many of his constituents were either farmers or small business people. These are two groups that have unusual difficulty finding and affording coverage in the private insurance market, and Thompson was acutely aware of this in his days in the state legislature. In fact, he talks about how he and his state senator, Joe Leean, used to talk for hours in the legislature about what they would do to make health insurance available for so many of their uninsured constituents if they were ever in a position to do so. Thompson is now serving his fourth term as governor, and Leean is his secretary of health and family services. Clearly, they are now in a position to do something (Thompson 1999).

The second powerful influence on Thompson has been his meetings with women on welfare. Wisconsin under Thompson has become known for its tough but well-funded welfare to work program. As he developed the program, Thompson began periodically inviting groups of 10 or 11 welfare mothers for lunch at the executive mansion in Madison to talk about welfare and what it would take to help them and their children become independent and self-sufficient. Not surprisingly, they told him it would take three things: training for real jobs, child care, and some guarantee of health insurance for themselves and their children when they left welfare for work.

Those conversations with welfare recipients had a profound effect on him, and they served to strengthen his conviction that extending Medicaid coverage to working adults as well as their children was an essential part of what it would take to help thousands of families get off and stay off welfare. The result is BadgerCare and the ambitious goal of virtually universal coverage before Thomson leaves office at the end of his fourth and final term.

One of the issues with which he and his staff have had to wrestle is one that can plague any plan that provides government supported health insurance for working adults—the danger of disinsurance by employers who have previously provided coverage for their workers. Thompson and the Wisconsin legislature have included some interesting provisions in their plan designed to block the "crowd out" problem. No one is eligible for BadgerCare who has been insured at any time during the previous three months, and under some circumstances BadgerCare will pay the employee's share of the premium if his or her employer provides comprehensive coverage and pays between 60 and 80% of the monthly premium. Both of these provisions are designed to prevent employers who do insure from transferring their responsibility to the state while encouraging them and their employees to stick with the employer's health insurance plan.

Thompson and his administration have now embarked on an ambitious enrollment effort. He has already begun televised public service announcements encouraging people to enroll. So have members of the legislature. Since coverage initially will be limited to adults with children, every effort will be made to contact adults whose children are already covered by Wisconsin's children's health plan. Not surprisingly, one of the program's informational pieces is targeted specifically to farmers and their families. Thompson and Leean have not forgotten where they came from.

OREGON

Oregon was the subject of extensive press coverage and much public scrutiny as it developed the Oregon Health Plan through a process of public participation. There was also an explicit commitment to making the tough decisions that many of its political leaders believed would be necessary to expand coverage while keeping costs under control. "Rationing" became the operative phrase as the plan was being put together, largely through the leadership of the then Senate president, John Kitzhaber, who today is the governor of his state (Fox and Leichter 1993).

Lawrence Jacobs, Ted Marmor, and Jonathan Oberlander discuss the origins and evolution of the Oregon Health Plan in detail in Chapter 8. The plan began as an effort both to expand coverage and to pay for it by determining in advance what procedures would be covered for those benefiting from the expanded coverage. It included broadened definitions of Medicaid eligibility that provided coverage for both children and adults up to 100% of poverty who were not otherwise eligible for Medicaid. It provided for an employer mandate that would sunset in 1995 if the state was unable to persuade Congress to exempt it from the provisions of the Employee Retirement Income Security Act of 1974 (ERISA). It also tried to define in some detail those procedures that would not be eligible for reimbursement. It was the last part of the plan, however, that won it widespread notoriety and generated the greatest controversy.

In fact, as Jacobs, Marmor, and Oberlander point out, the plan did not—and does not—provide for widespread or dramatic "rationing," the thing that got it so much notice in the first place. Although other states have now gone beyond Oregon in expanding the income limits within which people are eligible, the Oregon Health Plan is responsible for the enrollment of over 200,000 additional people under the Oregon Medicaid program.

John Kitzhaber, the current governor, was the principal moving force behind the original plan when he was Senate president. An emergency room doctor by profession, he obviously took on the challenge of expanding access as somebody who was not only a health professional but also spent so many of his professional hours treating hundreds of uninsured people whose only recourse was the emergency room. As Senate president, he organized an extraordinary outreach effort that sought to involve the citizens of his state actively in the development of the plan. Dozens of health "town meetings" were held. Virtually every group with an interest in health care was invited into the process. What emerged at the time was one of the most expansive proposals in the nation along with the so-called "rationing" scheme.

Kitzhaber was elected governor in 1994 and spent most of his first two years in office overseeing the successful implementation of that part of the plan that substantially expanded Medicaid eligibility. Oregon was unable to obtain a congressional exemption from ERISA, so under the terms of the original legislation, the employer mandate died. However, he successfully pushed small group reforms and guaranteed issue in 1995, and then supported a ballot initiative in 1996 that asked for a 30% per pack increase in the cigarette tax "for the maintenance and expansion of the Oregon Health Plan" (Speight 1999). Kitzhaber did not initiate the proposal, but he gave it his blessing and campaigned for it. It was sponsored by a broad-based coalition of hospitals, doctors, Blue Cross–Blue Shield, Kaiser Permanente, and all of the state's public health groups, and despite fierce tobacco industry opposition, it was approved by the voters by a margin of 10 points.

Kitzhaber then asked the Oregon Health Council, an advisory group appointed by the governor, to come up with a plan for expanding access with the funds made available by the ballot initiative. The council recommended, and the legislature approved, expanding coverage up to 170% of poverty for pregnant women and children up to the age of 12. The federal children's health initiative has now made it possible for Oregon to expand eligibility for all children up to 170% of poverty.

Oregon is currently debating what to do with its tobacco settlement money. The legislature has just approved another ballot initiative that will ask voters to approve the creation of a health trust fund with the settlement money, the interest on which will be used for unspecified health purposes, while the corpus of the trust will be held in anticipation of an economic downturn that may require its use to supplement existing funded health programs.

Kitzhaber has admittedly not taken as prominent a leadership role in the expansion of access to health care as he did as Senate president. Part of that is the result of other obligations that the state is now required to shoulder for the funding of public school education at the local level. In fact, Kitzhaber has proposed unsuccessfully that some portion of the tobacco settlement money be used for K–12 educational funding.

He has three years to go, however, on his second and final term, and he intends to turn once again to health care as a priority. Unfortunately, Oregon, like many states, is beginning to experience double-digit increases in health insurance premiums that presumably will be reflected in major increases in costs for the Oregon Health Plan, most of whose members are now in some form of managed care. Under the circumstances, Kitzhaber is likely to spend most of his time trying to get costs under control while maintaining quality. Further expansion of the plan may have to take second place to these concerns.

MASSACHUSETTS

Massachusetts was the first state after Hawaii to pass and partially implement universal health insurance. It is well worth examining as a case study in the perils and pitfalls of expanding health care reform and the role that governors can play both as proponents and opponents of reform (Goldberger 1990).

I, too, had strong personal reasons for making universal coverage one of my top priorities in my third term as governor. I was the son of a doctor, and my dad was an old-fashioned general practitioner who did his own general surgery, made house calls, delivered about 3,000 babies, and would take care of you whether you could pay or not. In fact, I was his designated successor until I ran into general physics at Swarthmore College with disastrous results.

I was just beginning to come of age politically when Harry Truman in 1945 became the first American president to propose universal health insurance. Given my upbringing and my knowledge of my father's practice, I was personally appalled at the notion that millions of Americans, including elderly Americans, had only one choice if they were lucky: the charity ward of the local public hospital, if there was one.

In short, like so many other governors, it was a combination of strongly held philosophical views and personal experience that served to make health care a major challenge for me. Furthermore, there was a compelling policy reason for acting, and acting decisively, in the mid-1980s. Massachusetts, under my predecessor, Ed King, had created a free care pool by imposing a surcharge on all hospital inpatient bills that was then used to reimburse hospitals for the free care they provided to uninsured patients.

As the cost of health care in the 1980s rose at double-digit rates, the free care surcharge was also rising and was being passed on to premium payers, a large proportion of whom were employers. The Massachusetts business community, and especially the Massachusetts Business Roundtable, became increasingly alarmed. Nelson Gifford, the CEO of the Dennison Corporation and a remarkably farsighted and well-informed member of the roundtable, was sounding the alarm among his business colleagues and at the statehouse. He understood that unless all or a large majority of the state's employers were required to provide health insurance for their employees and their families, the burden of paying for free care would continue to mount and would have to be paid for by those employers who were providing coverage for them.

Of course, like all states we faced the problem of cross-state competition. New Hampshire, in particular, made no bones about pitching its appeal to Massachusetts businesses as a low tax, low regulation state that contrasted sharply with what at least some New Hampshire politicians liked to refer to as "Taxachusetts." Fortunately, the Massachusetts economy was very strong. Unemployment in late 1987 and early 1988 was below 3%. Thousands of New Hampshire residents worked in Massachusetts and would benefit from a plan that required most Massachusetts employers to provide health insurance for their employees. And Nelson Gifford was there to remind the Massachusetts business community that we already had an employer mandate, a mandate imposing a free care surcharge on the substantial majority of Massachusetts employers, including small businesses, that already insured their employees.

We began with a broad-based task force under the chairmanship of my secretary of human services, Phil Johnston, an ardent proponent of universal coverage. It included key legislators as well as representatives of all of the major interest groups. Despite our efforts, however, and my own intensive personal involvement, it was impossible to achieve consensus on the task force. The state's hospitals, in particular, were unhappy with those provisions in our draft plan that attempted to control hospital costs, and many small businesses were opposed to any employer mandate, even one that exempted small businesses with five or fewer employees and start-up companies for the first two years of their existence.

Our efforts were further complicated but ultimately strengthened by my presidential campaign. As the campaign began to make real progress, there was a genuine desire on the part of many members of the overwhelmingly Democratic legislature to approve something that no other mainland state had been able to do. And, as in many states that were attempting major expansion of health care access, key legislators like the chairs of our House and Senate Ways and Means Committees, Representative Richard Voke and Senator Patricia McGovern, played absolutely critical roles in the final passage of a bill that went beyond anything that any state, including Hawaii, had attempted.

Of course, the Massachusetts experience is also a reminder that what one governor attempts to do can be undone by another governor who is neither philosophically nor politically committed to the same course. Bill Weld, my successor, was strongly opposed to the employer mandate portion of the bill that was supposed to take effect on January 1, 1992. Thus, while we were able, before I left office, to implement key provisions of the plan that provided guaranteed coverage for students, the severely disabled, and the unemployed, Weld successfully fought the legislature to a standstill on the broader employer mandate issue; argued that it would make it even more difficult for the state to fight its way out of the recession that gripped the Northeast and much of the rest of the country in the early 1990s; won the support of the business community as Nelson Gifford's company was acquired by a California corporation; and, in a strange turn of events, unintentionally pushed the legislature into agreeing on repeal of the mandate as a way to win business support for a children's health bill that Weld vetoed and on which he was overridden by the legislature.

Today, Massachusetts provides coverage for all children up to 200% of poverty and all working adults up to 133% of poverty. Responsible employers who insure their employees are still paying the bill for free care, however. Before he left office, Weld signed legislation ensuring that they would do so by imposing a 2% tax on all health insurance premiums to pay for free care.

SUMMARY

What, then, can we conclude about the work and leadership of governors on health issues in general and expanding access in particular?

First, governors and their legislatures almost invariably must wait until economic times are good before they try to expand access in any significant way. In fact, recessions are the worst time to try to make progress on the issue even though it is precisely the time when many people in an employer-based system will lose their coverage as they lose their jobs. One can argue that there is a strong case to be made for providing coverage for those laid off from their jobs and eligible for unemployment compensation, and, in fact, the 1988 Massachusetts bill did precisely that, funded by an increase in unemployment taxes of $16.80 per employee per year. But we made this change when unemployment in the state was 2.7% and our unemployment taxes were the third lowest in the country. It would have been politically impossible to take that step three years later in the middle of a recession when the state's unemployment rate was over 8%.

Second, certain legislators normally play a key role in the process. In some cases, of course, they, not the governor, drive the process. That was certainly the case in Oregon where John Kitzhaber provided extraordinary leadership from his position as Senate president. It was also true in Minnesota where the Gang of Seven dominated the process. But, with the possible exception of Tennessee, winning final passage for our proposals requires broad legislative support and, at key junctures, the strong and often courageous efforts of key legislators. That was certainly the case in Massachusetts. Without the support of a handful of important, well-placed legislators who were deeply committed to universal access, we would never have won the battle for the 1988 bill.

Third, no state other than Hawaii has passed and implemented a broad-based employer mandate, and, at least for the foreseeable future, no governor is likely to try. Three states have attempted it—Massachusetts, Oregon, and Washington. All have had to repeal or substantially modify what was originally enacted into law. ERISA remains a key obstacle to state-imposed mandates, and that was particularly true in the case of Oregon. But the fear of cross-border competition from states that are easy on business and have no such mandate is a very tough hurdle to climb. In fact, during the debate over repeal of Washington's employer mandate, one business spokesman referred to it as "the Northern Idaho Development Act." Small business organizations will fiercely oppose any attempt at broad-based employer coverage, even with generous exemptions for small business, and unless there is a Nelson Gifford who understands that a majority of employers are paying the freight for the free care provided in hospital emergency rooms to the employees of their competitors, that opposition is tough to beat.

Fourth, the difficulty in winning support for some form of employer mandate has inevitably moved governors, who want to exercise leadership on the issue, in the direction of broadening Medicaid coverage for low- and moderate-income working families whose employers do not provide health insurance for their workers. That has been the path taken in each of the states discussed in this chapter. It has been encouraged and strengthened by the new federal Children's Health Initiative and those provisions of that legislation which, under some circumstances, will provide additional federal assistance for health coverage for eligible children's working parents. Furthermore, many states are now in a position financially to expand coverage directly with state revenues that have grown dramatically during the current long economic boom and with tobacco settlement money that is an easy and logical source for the money required to expand coverage to working adults.

Fifth, governors who attempt to provide leadership on health issues will find plenty of willing allies. In fact, in my own experience, virtually all of the key interests, with the exception of the small business community, were actively supporting our bill. And why not? Most people believe that working people and their families should be insured. Furthermore, expanding access to health care for those who are uninsured reduces the burden on employers who are paying free care surcharges either explicitly or in the form of increased hospital charges that are passed onto them as premium payers.

Sixth, any governor who wants to expand access or otherwise reform and improve the health care provided to his constituents needs a well-designed and well-executed communications strategy that can build public support and guarantee effective implementation after the bill is signed and the pictures are taken. I spent a great deal of my time after I signed the 1988 Massachusetts bill doing press events all over the state designed to continue to build support and encourage eligible individuals and families to enroll in the new plans. Governor Thompson is currently doing much the same thing as he travels his state and does televised public service announcements urging uninsured Wisconsinites to sign up for BadgerCare.

Even the choice of a name for the new program is crucial. Many working people are not comfortable showing up at welfare offices to sign up for Medicaid. Calling it BadgerCare or MinnesotaCare or TennCare or MassHealth makes it a lot easier for them to take advantage of the program's benefits without the welfare stigma that many of them abhor.

Seventh, no governor can provide leadership on this kind of issue without key staff or cabinet level aides who are absolutely critical to his or her success. For me, it was Cathy Dunham, my senior staff person for human services and health issues, and Phil Johnston, my cabinet secretary for human services. For John Kitzhaber, it was Barney Speight and Mark Gibson when Kitzhaber was Senate president, and it is no accident that he brought Speight with him to the governor's office where he plays a key health care role. For Arne Carlson, it was Mary Jo O'Brien and Curt Johnson, and so it goes. These are the people who make it possible for us to have our share of successes. They must combine a profound commitment to the goal of universal access with impressive political skills if they are going to help governors win passage of major health care initiatives.

Can governors and the states by themselves achieve the goal of universal coverage? Not likely, especially if the economy softens and demands for coverage for the uninsured and unemployed go up as they always do in times of recession while state revenues are plummeting. But if the state of Wisconsin and some of the other states that have taken leadership on this issue can achieve 98% coverage—and that is Governor Thompson's goal—it may well be a sign that a combined federal-state effort that builds on the Children's Health Initiative, enrolls more and more working adults, and uses a combination of budgetary surpluses and tobacco settlement money can finally get us close to the goal that Harry Truman first articulated over a half century ago—basic health security for all Americans.

REFERENCES

Bartels, P., and P. Boronlec. 1998. "BadgerCare: A Case Study of the Elusive New Federalism." *Health Affairs* 17:65–169.

Berglin, L. 1999. Interview by the author, July 20.

Bureau of National Affairs. 1999. "State Lawmakers Considering Future of Underfunded Program for Poor, Uninsured." *Health Care Policy Report,* April 5, p. 14.

Carlson, A. 1999. Interview by the author, July 12.

Fox, D., and H. Leichter, 1993. "The Ups and Downs of Oregon's Rationing Plan." *Health Affairs* 12:66–70.

Fox, W., and W. Lyons. 1998. "The Impact of TennCare: A Survey of Recipients." Center for Business and Economic Research, College of Business Administration, Social Science Research Institute, University of Tennessee, Knoxville.

Goldberger, S. 1990. "The Politics of Universal Access: The Massachusetts Health Security Act of 1988." *Journal of Health Politics, Policy and Law* 15:857–885.

Leichter, H. 1993. "Minnesota: The Trip from Acrimony to Accommodation." *Health Affairs* 12:283–287.

McWherter, N. 1999. Interview by the author, August 6.

National Conference of State Legislatures. 1998. "State Budget Actions 1998." *http://www.ncsl.org/programs/Fiscal/sba98sum.ltm.*

Neubauer, D. 1993. "Hawaii: A Pioneer in Health System Reform." *Health Affairs* 12:31–39.

Speight, B. 1999. Interview by the author, August 17.

Thompson, T. 1999. Interview by the author, July 16.

4

State Legislatures and Health Policy in the Market Era

John E. McDonough and Robert McGrath

In each chapter in this book, state legislatures play a critical and determinative role at some stage in the policymaking process. While the role of legislatures in state health policy and reform is central, the legislative process often appears baffling to those who have neither served nor worked in such an assembly. Added to this difficulty is the varied range of rules, structures, cultures, and norms dispersed over the nation's 99 state legislatures (Nebraska is the only state with a unicameral legislature). Moreover, state legislatures are dynamic institutions, individually and collectively, constantly evolving through their own or citizen action.

Fortunately, a growing body of literature over the past 35 years has increased our understanding of legislatures and legislators. In this chapter, we examine both in the context of the past decade of state health care reform. Understanding the unique role of state legislatures in health policy requires understanding legislatures themselves. We explore legislatures and legislators in this chapter by presenting ten points important to that understanding. Some of these points have always been fundamental to the nature of legislatures, while others are more specific to the recent political era and to the current environment of state health care reform. We label this period as "the market era" in state health policy because of the dominant reliance on market mechanisms to regulate costs and to organize the industry. Most legislative and regulatory initiatives at the state level during this period have sought to enhance market dynamics or to cushion harsher market effects, not to alter the fundamental state/market relationship.

The chapter concludes with two brief case examples that illustrate the dynamics of legislative health care reform during the past decade and summary comments on the future of state health reform.

TEN POINTS TO UNDERSTAND ABOUT
STATE LEGISLATURES AND LEGISLATORS

1. The state legislature is the key institution in all states that advances or thwarts health care reform.

In the market era of health policy that has been broadly prevalent since the early 1990s, state governments play eight distinct and vital roles:

- Provision of public health services
- Regulation of professionals and facilities
- Regulation of insurance and HMOs
- Financing and provision of services for specified populations
- Health workforce education and training
- Cost containment
- Market oversight
- Information dissemination

In each of these eight areas, state action is nearly always authorized and framed in statute, giving legislatures preeminent policymaking power—when they choose to exercise it. Because any statutory change in any one of these eight areas may be characterized as "reform," legislatures thus hold the keys to the vast majority of "health care reform." Indeed, health care reform may be characterized as a core, ongoing responsibility of state legislatures in health policy. In many respects, legislatures' powers exceed that of any state's chief executive. While many legislatures have imposed various health reforms on recalcitrant chief executives, fewer governors have successfully forced reforms on unwilling legislative bodies.

Beaufort Longest (1996, 37) provides a helpful map of the four specific phases of policymaking in the U.S. context: agenda setting; development of legislation; rulemaking; and policy implementation and operation. While the prelegislative phase of agenda-setting involves a wide swath of players (often including but not limited to legislators), and the postlegislative phases of rulemaking and implementation often leave legislators behind, their preeminent lawmaking function makes legislators critical players in most attempts to accomplish health care reform. As noted, nearly every program and policy framed in the eight areas mentioned at the start of this section are embedded in state statute, requiring the assent of legislatures to change.

In addition to making laws—their essential function and responsibility—legislatures and legislators involve themselves in the health sector and health policy in three other substantial ways. First, in all 50 states, review and approval of the state budget is typically the single most important and time-consuming activity for legislative bodies (performed annually in 30 states and biennially in the other 20). The budget is a political document through which state government establishes its priorities and values, determining what it chooses to invest in and what it does not. In every state, the budget is first and foremost a bill subject to each chamber's rules and customs for deliberation. While 43 governors have the authority to reduce legislatively authorized appropriations, this line-item veto power can impose only reductions—not increases—and usually can be overridden by supermajorities in both branches (Rosenthal 1998). Nearly every state health activity—Medicaid, public health, state employee health insurance, state medical schools, boards of registration in medicine, nursing, and other health professions, insurance departments, and so on—comes under the direct scrutiny of legislators no less than every other year. Their budgetary decisions have enormous and direct impact on the success or failure of state health programs and initiatives. For example, the use of the $246 billion that will be paid to states as part of the 1998 master legal settlement with the tobacco industry will be determined principally through the legislative appropriations process—whether all, some, or none of the proceeds are used for health- or tobacco-related purposes or for other governmental activities.

Second, legislatures and legislators monitor the activities of the executive branch, including all health agencies, to ensure that legislative priorities are respected. Each legislature has its own process and structure to enhance executive branch accountability. Disagreement with an agency's activities or policy interpretations can quickly lead to the introduction of legislation or to budget activity to force behavior change. Sometimes, the disagreement may involve a large number of legislators concerned about a particular policy area. At other times, though, the disagreement may only involve a single, influential legislator upset about a policy choice that has a direct impact on his or her legislative district. In either case, legislators employ a variety of techniques to make agencies pay heed, including oversight hearings, budget riders, corrective legislation, or direct intervention.

Third, most legislators spend considerable time performing constituent services. While a large portion of this time is spent providing assistance to individuals who have problems they have been unable to solve, legislators also provide help to institutions (hospitals, community health centers, home health agencies) in ways that may impact broader state health policy. For example, in 1999 and 2000, a group of Massachusetts community hospitals was frustrated by the state Department of Public Health's unwillingness to grant them certificate of need authority to perform certain cardiac surgery procedures. Each hospital's local legislators worked to insert language in the fiscal year 2000 state budget as an outside section or budget rider to compel the health department to grant this authority over the objections of larger academic teaching hospitals that have the sole franchise for this service. The amount of time legislators spend on such services will vary from legislator to legislator and from state to state, although some researchers suggest that the amount of service provided grows with an increase in staff and resources assigned to individual legislators.

2. Enacting health care reforms, as well as most controversial legislation, through state legislatures is difficult because the process was designed to be that way.

The average state legislature considers about 4,000 bills each session, with a range between 600 and 32,000. About 20% of those bills are enacted each session, with a range from 5% in states with high numbers of bills introduced to more than 60% in states with lower numbers of bills filed. A large proportion of bills enacted are routine or noncontroversial, while the numbers of approved bills resulting in substantial changes to state laws are relatively few.

Each state legislature has its own unique process to dispose of legislation. Common features include separate and repeated readings of each bill on the chamber floor and referral to committees. This division of labor created by the committee process is an essential component of legislative deliberations. Unless lobbied by district-based interests or constituents, legislators generally defer to the judgment of committees on most bills, recognizing that chairs and committee members have more specialized information and perspective on issues under their purview. This is also true in matters related to health care and health insurance, which are viewed by many legislators as highly complex. Because much health legislation has a potential financial impact, budget and appropriations committees will also review bills released by health and insurance committees, thus providing another level of oversight. While several states have joint House-Senate committees, most states mimic the U.S. Congress in organizing distinct committees within each branch.

Because 49 states have two legislative branches, conference committees are an important feature of legislative life, bestowing particular power on committee chairs who get a "second bite at the apple" in structuring legislation as members of these committees. Indeed, in a dynamic that largely escapes public view, branches often fashion their respective bills with an eye toward the bargaining that commonly occurs in the conference phase of the legislative process.

State legislatures use different ways to divide responsibility for health policy among various committees. Some combine health with insurance, social services, environment, and/or business affairs, while others make health the sole responsibility of a distinct committee. Many legislative bodies also rely on subcommittees as a further review step, thus providing a broader range of leadership opportunities for rank-and-file members and allowing a greater level of scrutiny of legislative proposals as well as additional opportunities for delay (Francis 1989).

A key—yet counterintuitive—point about legislatures is that their various processes are designed to kill, not to approve, most legislation. Multiple levels of seemingly redundant review by a broad number of players are a deliberate feature to make it as difficult as possible for controversial laws to be passed. Most legislatures have one or several committees or process steps, frequently appropriations committees, understood to be legislative "graveyards" where bills die rather than face defeat on the chamber floor. This reality is not accidental and is consistent with the intentions of the framers of the U.S. Constitution, who sought to establish a governmental structure to inhibit the ability of officials to acquire excessive power (Madison 1961).

Numerous commentators have observed that the legislative process is, among other things, messy, imperfect, and not wholly deliberative. This is not a recent observation and even precedes Bismarck's comparison of the processes of making laws and sausages. More charitably, *Washington Post* columnist David Broder (1996) observed that legislatures are "collecting points for conflicting views," where conflict, debate, and ensuing negotiation/compromise are healthy, not pathological. While governors can speak with a single voice for an entire executive branch, legislatures are structurally composed of differing parties and factions, each with process rights that guarantee a degree of discord and chaos. James Madison's (1961, 321) desire that "ambition must be made to counteract ambition" in the structure of the governmental process is amply demonstrated and fulfilled in every one of the nation's legislative assemblies. Dissension, conflict, and debate are signs of strength, not weakness. In the context of health care change, this means that reformers should expect difficulty in enacting major health reform legislation because the process was designed to be that way.

3. Important similarities exist among all 99 state legislative bodies, including on actions related to health care policy.

The core function of each state legislative body is precisely the same—to make laws. Although a variety of rules, norms, and cultures are developed within each body to carry out its central role, in each state the overriding purpose is the same. And in each state, elections are the ultimate mechanism by which legislators are held accountable. In 5 House branches and 38 Senates, members run for reelection every four years; in all others, two years is the length of a legislator's term. While incumbency is a critically valuable asset for any legislator, members who stray from the expectations of their constituents risk defeat or serious challenge. Additionally, about one-third of the states provide for the electoral recall of legislators. Nonetheless, the huge majority of House and Senate seats across the nation are considered "safe" for individual members or their political party or both (Rosenthal 1998, 168).

An additional element present in every legislature and legislator is an acute awareness of time. Burdett Loomis, who spent one year studying the Kansas legislature, wrote: "In every policy making setting the three elements of political time— trends, cycles, and deadlines—come together to forge a unique situation. . . . Political time emerges as a central element of policy making, even as it appears in multiple forms—in particular, long term trends, different kinds of cycles, and countless deadlines" (1994, 15–23). All legislative sessions—long or short—run according to time deadlines that structure the pace and intensity of the process. Some floor debates are permitted to go on for as long as members choose to argue, while others operate under strict time rules. Some laws continue in perpetuity, while others live under strict sunset provisions. These factors have influence over the fate and shape of legislative proposals, including those affecting the health sector.

In all 99 state legislative chambers, health care policy has been a major preoccupation and priority concern during the 1990s on a wide array of fronts. Health policy controversies rarely stand within one state's borders, but instead travel from one jurisdiction to another, often quite quickly. Legislators watch and learn from each other's successes and often follow suit. For example, in 1995, Maryland became the first state in the nation to require in statute that all health insurers pay to permit new mothers to stay in a hospital for at least 48 hours after giving birth. Within several months, New Jersey's legislature followed suit. Within two years, more than 40 states had passed similar requirements.

The Health Policy Tracking Service of the National Conference of State Legislatures (NCSL) divides health-related legislation into five distinct categories: behavioral health, finance, Medicaid, providers, and pharmaceuticals, with as many as 50 subcategories within each. Table 4.1, shows subcategories in which 25 or more states enacted new laws in 1998 in that area.

Table 4.1 demonstrates the broad range of areas that legislators explore and influence in the health policy arena. The full NCSL list of categories includes more than 200 distinct policy areas. No single legislator can be expert in all of these areas; many health-oriented legislators tend to specialize in a narrower set of health policy domains. Another observation from Table 4.1 is the heavy orientation in legislatures toward provider issues. This tendency should not be surprising, because providers are most likely to have organized into sustainable interest groups and have the capability and resources to monitor and influence legislative activities. Indeed, national surveys of lobby groups have demonstrated the longtime dominance of professional and occupational interests. Another reason for the dominance of provider issues is that it is one of few remaining areas where the state does not share authority with the federal government. The federal role in provider issues is small and limited to reimbursement issues in Medicare and Medicaid, whereas provider licensure is a purely state function.

Why do legislatures in strikingly different states follow similar patterns and seem to imitate each other? There are several reasons. First, the trends shaping the nation's health system, such as managed care and the growth of for-profit medicine, will be felt in numerous, different states in similar ways, leading legislators to propose similar policy responses. For example, with the growth of investor-owned health enterprises in the early 1990s, many nonprofit hospitals and health insurers sought to convert to for-profit ownership, leading legislators in numerous states to propose legislation to establish stricter conversion standards. Often, the proposed conversion of an in-state institution provokes legislative interest. Second, legislators learn from each other through the news media and through special organizations that attract state lawmakers. NCSL and other groups organize meetings, seminars, and other materials to educate lawmakers across the

Table 4.1 1998 State Health Legislation by Category

Category		Number of States Passing New Laws
Behavioral Health	Mental health parity	29
	Tobacco	29
Finance	Appropriations	37
	Commissions	36
	Health insurance	34
	Mandated benefits	33
	Patient records	28
	Uninsured Children	35
Medicaid	Disability	26
	Eligibility	25
	Long-term care	34
	Medicaid administration	33
	Medicaid managed care	25
	Reimbursement rates	28
Pharmaceuticals	Pharmacies	33
Providers	Alternative providers	37
	Assisted living	33
	Dentists	37
	Graduate medical education	30
	Long-term care providers	40
	Malpractice/tort reform	31
	Medical records	27
	Nurses	41
	Optometrists	31
	Physician Assistants	30
	Physicians	40
	Podiatrists	25
	Provider administration	34
	Provider assessments	32
	Provider billing and reimbursement	36
	Rural health	30

Source: NCSL Health Policy Tracking Service, 1999.

nation about emerging trends. Third, national interest groups with local affiliates will advise their state-based branches to seek similar reforms and redress in legislative assemblies. In the case of for-profit medicine, national organizations of nonprofit hospitals and other interests were active in promoting state-based legislative activity. (Actually, the diffusion of policies is not at all limited to health policy; state governments have long copied each other across numerous policy domains.)

4. On other key features, there is striking variety among the nation's state legislative bodies.

Having noted some significant ways that state legislative bodies are alike, it is worth noting several of the many ways they differ. Some examples follow.

Length of sessions. In some state legislative chambers, the sun rarely, if ever, sets as members conduct official business right up until the commencement of the next legislative session. Legislatures in large industrial states such as California, Michigan, Illinois, New York, Pennsylvania, Massachusetts, and Ohio are often described as full time. In most other states, state constitutions mandate that the House and Senate meet for fixed periods of time, often no longer than 30 to 90 days and in some cases only every other year. The Florida legislature meets for 60 days, only 45 of which are working. New Mexico's assembly meets for 60 days in odd-numbered years, but for only 30 in even-numbered (election) years. The Texas legislature convenes only every other year. Legislatures with short sessions will conduct studies and do a substantial amount of preparatory work during interim periods. Some will regularly call members back for special sessions to consider specific priority matters. But in the majority of states, consideration of health reform legislation must wait for members to convene and must fit into a tightly restricted period. For example, while most state legislatures adopted child health insurance programs under the new federal Children's Health Insurance Program (Title XXI) in late 1997 or 1998, action in Texas had to await the convening of the regular legislative session in the spring of 1999.

Professionalization. In some state legislatures, members are paid high salaries (New York and California) and are assisted by generous allowances for the hiring of full-time professional staff. Legislative committees may also have the assistance of permanent staff support. Often, statehouse and district offices are also provided, courtesy of the state treasury. At the other end of the spectrum, members of the New Hampshire House of Representatives are paid $100 per year and have no official offices (district or statehouse) or professional staff. More legislatures veer toward the New Hampshire than to the New York end of the spectrum.

Alan Weil of the Urban Institute, who has worked for many years on national and state health reforms, reflected on his experience as health adviser to former Colorado governor Roy Romer to caution against grand national health reform designs that would stretch the limited capacities of many state legislatures. In most states, legislatures are composed of regular citizens, not experts or full-time professional politicians, meeting for short sessions with limited—if any—staff support. National health reform frameworks that regard all state legislatures as though they had the support capacity of the U.S. Congress are doomed to disappoint.

Some states have moved aggressively to modernize the legislative process and to make legislative documents and information readily available and accessible to citizens. Nearly all state legislative assemblies now provide a wealth of legislative information through the Internet. The quality and detail of information, though, vary substantially from state to state.

Districts. State legislators vary enormously in the size of the constituencies they are elected to represent. California senators and assembly members represent

744,000 and 372,000 constituents respectively, while New Hampshire senators and representatives represent 46,210 and 2,770. It is not just people but also the geographic size of districts that vary within the same state (California's districts range in size from 18 to 28,991 square miles). The ability of legislators to stay in close contact with their constituents varies widely from district to district and state to state.

Constitutional features. States vary widely in the powers and rights granted to legislatures, governors, and the people. For example, in 18 states—all but one with voter initiative powers—the number of terms that elected members can serve is limited (nearly all of these limits were approved during the 1990s through ballot proposals). Term limit requirements have forced from office (in varied states such as Arkansas, Maine, Michigan, and California) many popular and successful legislators who made health care reform their major focus. Health policy is generally regarded as a difficult policy domain to master. One effect of term limit provisions has been to weaken the ability of legislative bodies to retain experienced members and institutional memory in this key area.

In 24 states, voters have the right to place public policy questions on the state ballot to enact laws even if their state legislators refuse to pass them. These privileges were largely created during the Progressive reform era during the early part of the twentieth century. In some states such as California, use of this political option is frequent. Citizens who live in states with these powers have used them, for example, to approve cigarette tax hikes to fund antismoking programs, permit the medical use of marijuana, allow physician assisted suicide, and much more. Citizens have also used this authority to reject important health policy proposals such as the rejection by California voters of a health care employer mandate (1992) and a single-payer, Canadian-style health-financing scheme (1994).

As noted earlier, in 43 states, governors possess line-item veto authority to reduce legislative appropriations, subject to supermajority overrides in both legislative chambers. The line-item veto authority (or lack thereof) often has significant ramifications on budget issues related to health matters. Edward Clynch and Thomas Lauth (1991, 150) suggest that states can be distinguished as executive dominant, legislative dominant, and middle range, depending on constitutional structure, personalities, balance of partisan power, and other attributes. The existence and structure of the line-item veto is an important feature of the executive/legislative relationship.

Legislative process. In no two states is the process for reviewing and acting on bills exactly the same. Each chamber's rules (both formal and informal), procedures, and policies will vary significantly, even within the same state. Alan Rosenthal suggests that legislatures are "prisoners" of their respective pasts, and that each state—and legislative chamber—possesses a unique political culture, with habits transmitted from one successive generation of legislators to the next (1998,

85–86). While each legislature's rules are adopted at the beginning of each biennial session, changes normally are made incrementally, using the prior rules as the foundation.

All of these distinct features will have an impact on the way legislatures address their responsibilities in the health policy arena. Some are predictable and some will surprise; those seeking to influence change in state legislatures need to heed them.

5. State legislatures modernized and evolved significantly between 1960 and 1990.

In 1966, Alexander Heard described state legislatures as poorly organized, technically ill-equipped, crowded, understaffed, and operating with archaic systems, procedures, and committee structures. "State legislatures may be our most extreme example of institutional lag," he argued (Heard 1966, 3). This commonly held view had important policy ramifications as the federal government deliberately crafted health and welfare programs in the 1960s that preempted or minimized state legislative oversight and control. Many war on poverty programs deliberately bypassed state legislatures, sending federal resources directly to local governments and community organizations. Even the federal/state behemoth Medicaid was originally designed to provide state governments with minimal flexibility and discretion in benefit design, financing, and implementation.

But over the course of three decades, between 1960 and 1990, most state legislatures worked hard to reinvent themselves, focusing on capacity building, professionalization, and institutionalization (Rosenthal 1998, 67). The range of changes was impressive: increased staffing and specialization, salaries improved at all organizational levels, sessions lengthened, resources provided to members, technology and communications systems upgraded, and more (Hicock 1992). The result has been vastly enhanced institutional capacity to tackle major health and human services policy challenges. In the late 1980s and early 1990s, legislators in numerous states, including Massachusetts, Oregon, Minnesota, Tennessee, Washington, and Vermont, among others, led the way in enacting far-reaching health system reforms. Most of these complex reforms would have been inconceivable in legislative chambers in the pre-1960s era.

Legislatures have changed in other significant ways over the last four decades. Supreme Court rulings in the early 1960s (*Baker v. Carr,* 1962; *Reynolds v. Sims,* 1964) ended the practice of multimember districts and required more precise and proportionate districting practices. The number of women in legislative assemblies has grown dramatically, from 4% in 1970 to 21.5% in 1997; research has demonstrated that females are more liberal and feminist in their policy priorities than men and are more likely to focus on family, children, and women's concerns such as health care and social services (Reingold 1996). Gains among African Americans have been less substantial, from 3% in 1975 to 6% recently, although the lengthy tenure of many minority legislators provides them with enhanced opportunities to rise within the legislative structure (Patterson 1996).

As these groups and others have grown in representation—along with the number of individuals who identify themselves as "full-time" legislators—the proportion of assemblies dominated by lawyers and businessmen has declined substantially to about one out of six for the former group and one of five for the latter (Gordon 1994).

6. Many state legislatures have undergone a period of deinstitutionalization during the 1990s.

The decade of the 1990s has witnessed a second set of dramatic changes that Rosenthal (1998, 72–73) labels as a period of "deinstitutionalization" because of public pressures for change. The most striking example of this is the adoption of term limits in 18 states, mentioned under the fourth heading, arbitrarily limiting the number of terms that individuals can serve in office. It is a key example of how legislative assemblies have felt a citizen and public opinion backlash that persisted throughout the decade and which began during the deep economic recession of the early 1990s. Another indicator is a rapid increase in legislative turnover: only 28% of senators serving in 1997 also were serving in 1987, while turnover in individual House and Senate chambers in that decade ranged between 46% and 100% (Rosenthal 1998).

An intensified focus on strict interpretations of legislative ethics has undermined a sense of legislative community, a development that has eroded the building of relationships necessary for the negotiation and compromise required for the passage of complex and controversial legislation. Increasingly, political contributions are seen as an inherent evil in the system as pressure has grown for public financing of campaigns (approved in Arizona, Maine, Massachusetts, and Vermont, among others). Ironically, this level of distrust has grown in an era when campaign finance and ethics statutes are more explicit and stringent than in any previous era. The public reporting of campaign finance and ethics statements has created a sense among many segments of the public that the political system is inherently and increasingly corrupt when it is actually more accountable and open than at any other point in the nation's history.

The historic 1994 national election swing to the Republican Party increased interparty rivalry at the state level of government in addition to the changes brought to the U.S. Congress. A more robust interparty competition, defined as the number of legislatures where the balance of power between the parties is close, in state legislatures has also led to increased partisanship and diminished trust. Prior to the 1990s, state legislatures were largely under Democratic Party control (Rosenthal 1998).

Some view these changes as positive, while others see many of them as distinctly negative. No research has been able to document or quantify an impact on the quantity or quality of statutes produced as a result of these changes. However, there is no doubt that these changes have forced interest groups and citizens seeking to influence the legislative process—on health or other policy matters—to change their practices in order to achieve policy change. While legislatures differ enormously from one to the next, it is striking to observe the degree to which these broadscale changes have been felt in one way or another in most legislative chambers across the nation.

7. Most state legislators perform four distinct tasks in their jobs as they respond to a variety of influences in making decisions and casting votes.

Representing a district, whatever its size or makeup, involves significantly more than casting votes on bills that come before a committee or a full chamber. Richard Fenno (1978) lists four key legislator activities: first, *"being one of them,"* i.e., getting around the district to solicit advice and input, relating to the culture and activities of the various communities; second, *providing services* in terms of helping constituents with problems at all levels of government and organizing community initiatives; third, *acquiring resources,* using the prerogatives of the office to obtain budget appropriation and executive branch resources; and fourth, *expressing district policy views and interests.* Citizens often will disagree strongly with many of a legislator's policy views and votes and yet still vote for and support that individual because of the way he or she carries out the first three responsibilities.

The choices facing legislators commonly are posed as bipolar: to represent one's own values and beliefs (the trustee model) or to represent the views and opinions of the electorate (the delegate model). Hannah Pitkin (1967) reframes this duality and poses instead a "continuum theory of representation." Each legislator will position himself or herself at the most comfortable point on a continuum between these two poles, consistent with his or her values. The individual's position on the continuum often will change as the number of terms in office increases (the longer in office, the more a legislator moves toward the trustee end of the spectrum), as electoral and constituent pressures change, as the individual's position in the chamber's leadership hierarchy advances, and more. The legislator's position will also shift from issue to issue, depending on the level of complexity, the volume of citizen feedback, and the nature of the issue.

In terms of their voting behaviors, how obsessed are legislators with the positions of the various interest groups and with their own reelection needs? Douglas Arnold (1993) finds that on any given policy issue, there will be two sets of publics: the "attentive publics" who pay close attention to fine details and process points and who have "expressed preferences" on the matter, and the "inattentive publics" who are largely unaware but who may have "potential preferences" should a future electoral opponent make an issue of the official's position or vote. Legislators will consider the expressed views of the attentive publics but also will heavily weigh the potential preferences of the inattentive publics, judging whether a particular vote will be defensible if made an issue by a future electoral opponent.

Reelection is an important consideration for any legislator, and often the preeminent one, yet it is still only one of many. An important factor in considering any legislator's motivation is to understand the individual's future plans: does he or she want to run for higher office, move up in the legislative hierarchy, move to the private sector, move to an executive or judicial branch position, or more? Every legislator brings his or her own set of principles, behaviors, preferences, political needs, and personal styles to the policy process. The combinations of personalities within a committee, chamber, or statehouse will produce an extraordinary range of results on issues that are starkly similar in all other respects.

Rosenthal notes that legislators have different "decisional modes" that will be brought to bear on any particular issue: these include acquiescence, deflection, bargaining, and fighting it out. Because legislators must address a wide variety of issues that will create constantly shifting coalitions and networks of support, the fourth option—fighting it out—will be least frequently used. To minimize electoral uncertainty and to protect their rank-and-file members, legislative leaders normally will seek to delay and defer controversial votes as often as possible, urging leaders to find compromise and common ground.

8. Interest groups play a vital role in the legislative process, although not as dominant as many assume. Health groups are among the most influential.

A large body of research has focused on the impact of interest groups, lobbying activities, political action committees, and other activities of "interests" that seek to influence legislators and the policy process. There is no doubt that the sheer number of associations, lobbyists, and PACs has ballooned over the past several decades, at both the federal and state levels. Researchers have made progress in understanding the internal dynamics of interest groups, including how groups overcome the dilemmas of mobilization, what their predominant activities involve, and how the broader social environments affect their choices. At the same time, a large volume of conflicting research has been unable to explain the actual, real-life influence of groups, lobbyists, and PACs on legislative decision-making (Baumgartner and Leech 1998).

Recent studies show that lobbying techniques do not differ greatly among associations. While interest groups monitor and take an interest in a large number of legislative proposals in any given session, they are "inactive advocates on the vast majority of bills before the state legislature." Three types of activities seem to predominate in the 1990s: monitoring, PAC giving, and grassroots lobbying. The volume of activity has been on the rise, and "the data indicate that state group politics—even in small, relatively unprofessional state capitals—is now similar to Washington group politics. Groups of all kinds are active, a wide range of techniques is used, and the level of group activity is high" (Nownes and Freeman 1998, 105).

New restrictions on lobbying activities and campaign contributions have encouraged the development of new forms of lobbying activities, especially grassroots organizing, whereby lobbying firms and associations seek to put individual constituents in direct contact with legislators. One example of this activity is called "astro-turf" lobbying where telephone operators will connect constituents sympathetic to an interest's position directly to a legislator's office. Rosenthal

(1998) describes these innovations as changing the legislative lobbying field to less of an insiders' club and more of a permanent campaign.

Health care interests are prominent among the types of associations that lobby at the state level. A ranking of the 25 most influential interest groups active in the states in the early 1990s showed three health-related interests near the top: no. 6, physician and state medical associations; no. 7, general and medical insurance companies; and no. 9, health care organizations (chiefly hospital associations) (Thomas and Hrebnar 1995, 149–150). Given the size of the health sector within the overall national economy, it is not surprising that health interests, at about 14% of U.S. gross domestic product, play such a prominent role.

9. "Policy entrepreneurs" play an important role in the state policy process; "legislative entrepreneurs" hold an especially important role in legislative policy development.

Any meaningful policy change requires at least one key advocate or champion willing to invest personal resources—time, energy, reputation, money, votes—to secure approval. While "policy entrepreneurs" can be found in many settings, both inside and outside of government, any significant change in a state statute requires the commitment of a "legislative entrepreneur" willing to invest his or her limited political capital to attract sufficient support to win approval in a legislative chamber (Kingdon 1995). Experienced legislators know they must focus on a limited number of priority bills in order to be successful. More powerful legislators, such as committee chairs, will be able to focus on a larger, though still limited, number. Entrepreneurial legislators seek those legislative initiatives where they can make the most dramatic impact.

This dynamic has been specifically observed in state health reform activities during the past decade. Pamela Paul-Shaheen (1998), examining six states that adopted major health access reforms in the late 1980s and early 1990s (Massachusetts, Oregon, Florida, Minnesota, Vermont, and Washington), notes two sets of factors critical in explaining the successes in these states. The first set of factors is labeled "contextual conditions" and includes socioeconomic factors such as income and employment levels, political factors such as culture and levels of partisanship, and institutional factors such as resources and prior health reforms. The second set of factors is called "dynamic" and includes leadership, ideas, and power. Paul-Shaheen concludes that the ultimate determinants of a state's capacity for reform are the relative dynamic factors of leadership, ideas, and power. Leadership is needed to recognize opportunities for change and to commit resources to challenge the status quo.

While a variety of institutional actors played the role of entrepreneur in Paul-Shaheen's study, legislators played a key role in each of the six states. She identifies five key tasks and strategies involved in their role: identifying the market opportunity (or opportunities for innovation); designing the innovation by crafting a course of action that meets technical and political feasibility requirements;

attracting political investment, both institutional access and political capital; marketing the innovation by creating a sufficient level of legislative support to defray opposition; and monitoring production and market trends to adapt the innovation to changes in the market. The entire reform process thus becomes one of experiential learning as much as initial planning and development.

10. Increasingly in state health reform activities during the past 15 years, legislators learn from and copy each other's innovations.

Legislators get ideas from a variety of local and state-based sources: news media, interest groups, constituents, relatives and friends, civic groups, and more. Legislators also obtain health reform ideas from a variety of national organizations that specialize in state health policy. Three principal examples are mentioned here (the first author has been closely associated with all three for many years).

The National Conference of State Legislatures. NCSL is the national organization for all state legislatures (as well as for legislative bodies in the District of Columbia and the U.S. territories). With large staffs based in Denver and Washington, D.C., NCSL devotes considerable resources to health policy, and closely monitors and seeks to influence the course of federal health legislation that may have state impacts. NCSL also runs a series of health-specific programs to educate legislators on complex health policy issues, such as the Forum for State Health Policy Leadership, the Health Chairs Project, and a new summer training institute for state legislative health staff. NCSL also produces a bimonthly newsletter, *State Health Notes,* that examines state health policy trends across the nation.

The Reforming States Group. In the early 1990s, as state governments took the lead in a number of states to reform their health systems to expand access and to control costs, the Milbank Memorial Fund, a private philanthropy, organized a network of public sector leaders from these states. Though access reform and universal coverage have diminished as central state health policy objectives, the RSG continues to bring state health leaders together from all 50 states to examine key policy challenges, to nurture and develop new leaders, and to produce highly polished and useful policy reports in diverse areas such as market oversight and regulation, children's health, alternative medicine, end-of-life care, and more.

The National Academy for State Health Policy. NASHP, created in 1987, is a national network of state health policy leaders. Although legislators form a significant subgroup, NASHP attracts a much wider range of state leaders from governors' staffs, Medicaid programs, departments of public health, insurance divisions, attorneys general offices, and more. With offices in Portland, Maine, NASHP conducts educational and policy briefings throughout the year in addition to an active policy consulting practice. NASHP's annual conference, held each

August in a different region of the country, is the largest broad-based state health policy gathering in the nation.

These are three leading examples of the growing level of sophistication and depth now being applied to state health policy networking and analysis that has expanded over the past 15 years. These resources are particularly important in the 18 states with term limits, where members are pushed forward into key leadership posts much more quickly than in states without term limits.

CASE EXAMPLES

Two cases are presented below, each demonstrating different ways that legislators and legislatures have assumed health policy leadership in the past decade.

Legislatures and Health Care Access Reform

Between 1988 and 1993, legislators and governors in six states (Massachusetts, Oregon, Florida, Minnesota, Vermont, and Washington) developed major health access initiatives. The reforms included employer mandates to provide health insurance to workers; single-payer health financing plans; state subsidized health insurance programs to offer coverage to families and individuals below certain income levels; health purchasing cooperatives; health system integration; and more. Some of the reforms created during this period were successful and sustained, while others were not. Thomas Oliver and Pamela Paul-Shaheen (1997) describe three processes in each of these states that led to formal political action: first, the creation of a "policy culture," or an institutional predisposition toward reform; second, the leadership of key legislators committed to advancing the process; and third, the political feasibility of the reform initiative in the context of each state's economic and cultural context.

The road to reform in each state was far from smooth. Although many devised workable plans, technically feasible policy is insufficient to trigger formal legislative action. In Minnesota, Washington, and Florida, initial efforts to create access expansion legislation failed but paved the way for future discussions. Some state leaders observed the development of a "policy culture" as reform issues continued to reappear. Policy cultures contribute to a growing knowledge and sophistication about key issues and potential solutions. In Massachusetts, Minnesota, Oregon, and Vermont, enacted reforms faltered in the implementation stage but set the policy stage for significant—albeit less dramatic—access expansions in later years.

In each of these states, the dynamic factors of leadership and power—more than culture, resources, and capacity—were catalysts for reform efforts. Policy innovation was initiated by politically experienced legislators who were "more concerned with piecing together a set of tangible and politically viable reforms than with engineering an intellectually coherent product" (Oliver and Paul-Shaheen 1997, 746). Because most legislators are not health policy experts, leadership is an invaluable component of program development. While individual legislators were key to success in each of these states, no single policy leader was ever responsible for the entire process (even in Oregon where Senate president—and future governor—John Kitzhaber made the Oregon Health Plan proposal a national issue). Instead, the process involved team collaboration among numerous legislators and outside players. This was most in evidence in Minnesota where a bipartisan team of legislative reformers dubbed the "Gang of Seven" engineered the creation in 1993 of MinnesotaCare, a nationally recognized access expansion.

In each of these successful states, political feasibility took precedence over technical policy considerations. Policy decisions were based on political viability, the structure of the legislative body, the role of the individual legislators, and the conditions that gave rise to the policy innovation. These examples show how legislatures, operating within larger political environments, merge policy analysis with considerations of political feasibility to craft viable and implementable reform.

In the next case, we describe how state legislatures influence policy by sending "policy signals" through the legislative process.

Legislatures and Primary Care Mandates

When state governments began to establish their own medical schools to ensure an adequate local supply of physicians and other medical providers, legislatures generally adopted a hands-off approach to school governance. In the past 15 years, however, many legislatures have begun to involve themselves directly in the business of these schools by passing broad and diverse legislation designed to send policy signals to medical schools to address legislative concerns or else risk more intrusive government intervention.

For years, legislative health policy leaders have felt that medical schools graduate too few primary care physicians, with estimates in the early 1990s of a national shortage of 35,000 generalist physicians by the year 2000 (Weissert and Silberman 1998). In 1995–1996, state and local governments financed 9% of all medical school budgets and up to 17% of public medical school budgets. In at least eleven states (Arizona, Illinois, Kentucky, Minnesota, North Carolina, Nebraska, Oklahoma, Tennessee, Virginia, Washington, and Wisconsin), legislators have directed schools to change curricula, set graduation targets for generalists, address admissions procedures, or initiate planning processes to do so.

For the most part, these state laws contained broad, noncoercive provisions. Some states used public funding as an incentive to encourage medical school cooperation. Many laws, however, were unfunded mandates, or requirements for change without funding to accomplish that provision. Seven states enacted requirements that 50% of graduates from public (and in three states, private) medical schools pursue primary care careers, although only California's statute threatened revocation of state funding if targets were not met. Other statutes addressed admissions requirements, requirements for service to underserved areas, and training protocols. States varied with regard to whether oversight was performed by the medical school (eight states), the board of regents (four), university administration (four), or others (seven). Legislative entrepreneurs played key roles in all of these initiatives. In nearly all of these states, the push for more primary care practitioners came from individual legislators concerned about growing, underserved medical areas. Legislatures viewed their medical schools as public institutions and recognized the link between the public mission of the school and the public funding it receives.

By enacting noncoercive mandates, legislatures sent signals to medical schools to adjust their behavior, much in the way that health market regulation seeks to adjust market performance. "Sending a message"—according to legislators, staff, and lobbyists—was an explicit intent behind the approved legislation. Ironically, after enactment, state medical school officials reported receiving so little feedback from their subsequent reports that they had no idea if any legislators even read them. Thus, even in an issue they generate, legislators continue to exhibit a marked loss of interest in pursuing reforms at the implementation stage.

FUTURE CHALLENGES AND OPPORTUNITIES IN STATE HEALTH CARE REFORM

Assessing the future of state health care reform reaches beyond purely legislative considerations that are the focus of this chapter. But such a discussion is not out of context here because legislators always have been and always will be centrally involved in any significant reform activities. The most accessible way to discuss coming challenges and opportunities is to examine them through the traditional tripartite lenses dividing health policy into issues of access, cost, and quality.

Whatever the issue, reformers will run into numerous obstacles. Two loom particularly large: first, the reality that state governments do not control the major flows of health system financing, thus limiting their ability to implement major systemic changes; and second, federal preemption of much potential state health reform activity because of the 1974 Employee Retirement Income Security Act (ERISA).

Regarding health financing, state governments pay directly for a portion of Medicaid, many public health activities, and state employee health insurance, as well as certain disability systems such as mental health and mental retardation, and have the authority to regulate health insurance. That leaves out a lot: Medicare, employer self-funded insurance plans, military and veterans' health, and more. Even state control of Medicaid is significantly curtailed by federal statute and regulation. To significantly reshape overall health system financing requires effective control over Medicare and elements of the federal tax code allowing tax deductibility of employer health insurance costs. Absent control of these major elements, states can only play at the margins. Changes to either impediment would require congressional approval, an unlikely prospect in spite of rhetorical support for devolution from the federal government to the states.

ERISA was written in 1974 to regulate employer-provided pension plans but amended in conference committee to preempt state regulation of employer-provided health and welfare benefits. This provision has since been interpreted by the courts to prevent states from imposing mandated benefits on employers who self-insure (affecting an estimated 40% of the insured U.S. workforce), to prohibit states from mandating employers to cover their workers, and to stop states from imposing various regulations on employer-sponsored managed care arrangements. ERISA has also been broadly interpreted to prevent states from allowing most liability suits against any employer-related managed care plans. ERISA has been subject to numerous court rulings altering its interpretation over the years; the U.S. Congress made minor changes to it through the 1996 Health Insurance Portability and Accountability Act and other laws. But once again, Congress has proven distinctly unwilling to modify ERISA to provide greater state authority and flexibility regardless of any rhetorical support for devolution.

Access. The financing and ERISA roadblocks are substantial impediments to many potentially far-reaching state efforts to address growing access problems, particularly those affecting more than 44 million uninsured Americans. The ERISA roadblock prevented Oregon in 1995 from implementing its employer mandate. The financing roadblocks also imperil any state initiative to create a single-payer financing scheme. While these obstacles limit the options available to states to address access concerns, they do not leave them without any options.

The major opportunity for states to address access needs is to create and/or expand programs to provide subsidized low-cost insurance to lower-income workers and families. Medicaid and the new federal/state Children's Health Insurance Program provide the keys to understanding how states can move forward. Over the past 15 years, Medicaid has evolved into a program that provides growing numbers of Americans with their only affordable health insurance option. In more and more states, over half of Medicaid enrollees no longer fit into the traditional category of mothers and their children eligible for TANF/AFDC but instead are working families who obtain Medicaid coverage because of their limited income.

From the states' perspective, no other option besides Medicaid comes close to making financial sense because any initiative launched through Medicaid brings federal financial participation paying between 50 to 79% of the program costs (and between 65 and 85% for CHIP expansions). This is why most of the major access expansions of the past decade have all utilized Medicaid to some substantial degree (for example, MinnesotaCare provides subsidized coverage to families with incomes up to 275% of the federal poverty line, TennCare up to 400%, Washington Basic Health Plan up to 200%—all using Medicaid to a significant extent).

When recipients are required to share an affordable portion of the cost, the financial obligation of the state is further reduced.

Countering these advantages is the traditional hostility of state officials to Medicaid expansion for many reasons, particularly the entitlement nature of the program that restricts state budgetary flexibility in times of fiscal stress. But the most aggressive state Medicaid expansions have all utilized the so-called section 1115 waiver authority in federal Medicaid statutes enabling them to expand coverage subject to budgeted appropriations and not on an entitlement basis. States have even sought to address the Medicaid stigma issue by creating new names for their programs (TennCare, MinnesotaCare, MassHealth).

The Children's Health Insurance Program provides a model for how the federal government can support this initiative. The federal government can create a new source of funding to provide enhanced federal financial participation to states to expand existing programs or to create new ones to provide insurance options for lower-income working families. The CHIP experience (plans are now in operation in all 50 states) shows this model to be politically as well as programmatically feasible.

In their examination of access reform movements in the states in the 1988–1993 period, Oliver and Paul-Shaheen demonstrate that the critical ingredient is sustained, pragmatic, and visionary political leadership. With that leadership, much is possible. Without it, it is difficult to see how any progress at all will be achieved.

Cost control. The creation of Medicare and Medicaid in 1965 quickly established a new context for government and the health sector. Prior to the 1960s, government provided financial support to encourage the growth of the health sector in numerous ways, from construction of hospitals to training of physicians to medical research. But when the federal and state governments became major financiers of health services through Medicare and Medicaid, controlling out-of-control costs (which the government itself helped to generate) became an urgent priority. From 1965 until the 1990s, federal and state governments used regulation to address escalating costs and to control system growth. Certificate-of-need rules to control capital and technological expansion, Medicare and state prospective payment programs to regulate hospital budgets, health planning systems to organize employer and consumer interests, and HMO development to instigate new financial incentives are a few examples of how government sought to assert control. By the end of the 1980s, most of these initiatives were judged to be well-intentioned failures as health costs rose at historically unprecedented rates.

In the past decade, particularly since the collapse of 1993–1994 national health reform efforts, federal and state governments have pursued market strategies to determine the distribution of health resources. The payers of health services—employers, unions, and governments at all levels—asserted their financial authority to negotiate with health plans and providers and to demand accountability and value for the services they purchase. Between 1994 and 1998, this strategy appeared to work, as private health insurance premiums experienced record low rates of growth. Recent experience, however, suggests that this low premium growth is over. Economic projections now point to higher annual rates of costs over the coming decade, though not as high as those that occurred during the hyperinflation years of 1987 to 1993.

Coinciding with this higher rate of cost growth are three noteworthy trends. First is a high degree of consolidation among providers and health plans that gives private and public purchasers fewer options when seeking cost-effective and quality-driven partners. This trend is most pronounced among acute hospitals and health plans, though it affects every part of the industry. Second is the withdrawal of interest in much of the health sector by the investor community. Health stocks were the darlings of Wall Street during the heady days of 1994 to 1996, providing a huge infusion of capital that spurred a record number of acquisitions, fast growth, and artificially suppressed premiums. The romance is indisputably over (to cite just one example: Medpartners, the investor-owned physician practice management firm that was a Wall Street favorite in the mid-1990s, was declared by the *Wall Street Journal* in early 1999 as the single worst performing stock of the previous three years), and even traditional favorites such as pharmaceutical stocks are no longer highly favored. The third trend is a sharp antimanaged care backlash, generated by consumer and provider interests with substantial legislative support on the state and federal levels, forcing health plans to pull back from their most aggressive cost-control practices.

Because government surrendered its most potent regulatory cost control tools to the market, it is not in a strong position to react effectively to a resurgence in health care cost inflation in the near term. A reduction in the number of HMO plans willing to participate in the Medicaid and Medicare markets has thwarted hopes that managed care would be the financial savior of these programs. Indeed, while overall participation in Medicaid managed care continues to grow, several state governments in recent years have returned to fee-for-service Medicaid in the face of plan withdrawals.

These developments are of concern for many reasons, prominent among them the clear and compelling connection between cost and access. The Lewin Group, a highly regarded health consulting firm, has calculated that every 1% increase above inflation in health insurance premiums nationally leads to an increase in the uninsured by about 300,000 individuals. Reignition of health care inflation will have other consequences, including the encouragement of employers to move to defined contribution instead of defined benefit plans, leaving workers at risk for future health premium increases.

Thus far, few have focused on identifying practical solutions for a new era of destructive cost increases, which may be because the answers are not easily apparent. Hard choices and tradeoffs will be the order of the day. Only one development is certain—the public will press their legislators, state and federal, for solutions. Those officials, however, will be hard-pressed to respond effectively.

Quality. In the past decade, reference to "health care quality" has most typically evoked images of managed care plans denying benefits or services to their enrollees, triggering a response by legislators and other public officials seeking to protect consumers. While these practices have been documented sufficiently to demonstrate their validity, no empirical evidence has indicated excess morbidity or mortality resulting from them. At the same time, a large volume of quantitative evidence has emerged that points to other forms of pervasive and persistent poor quality in the U.S. health care system completely unrelated to whether one's health plan is managed care or fee for service.

The overriding quality problems in the U.S. health care system are fourfold: underuse of necessary medical services, overuse of unnecessary services, inexplicable variation in the provision of services, and error in medical practice. The Institute of Medicine has estimated that between 48,000 and 98,000 deaths each year are attributed to medical errors alone in areas such as the administration of prescription medications. It has been estimated that if the U.S. airline industry had the safety record of the health sector, we would see at least three jumbo jet crashes every two days at U.S. airports (Leape 1994). Whatever the sins of managed care and HMOs, little compares in severity with the burden of fatal errors in medical practice.

Because deaths due to medical errors happen in a dispersed and random fashion, the public has been slow to pick up on the scope of the problem. Policymakers and regulators have been hard-pressed to respond because "magic bullet" solutions are not appropriate to these problems. Legislators and other public officials are also disadvantaged in addressing these quality problems because the standard regulatory response to errors is first to assign blame, to determine fault, and to assign penalties. The lessons from the aviation industry, though, demonstrate that the vast proportion of errors can be assigned to faulty systems rather than errant individuals, and further that a culture of blame leads individuals to avoid reporting systemic problems. The public regulatory "command-and-control" response is inappropriate in addressing these pervasive problems.

The stakes in moving the health care industry in the quality direction taken by other sectors are potentially high and rewarding. One of the lessons gleaned from the burgeoning U.S. quality industry is that the cost of poor quality is much higher than the cost of doing things right the first time. Every identified defect is an opportunity that can open doors to improvements in quality as well as to reductions in costs. And reduction/stabilization of costs is one of the key dynamics necessary to prevent further erosions in health care access in the coming years.

What is the appropriate role for legislators and other public officials in addressing the genuine quality problems in the U.S. health care system? An effective response calls for new models of lawmaking and regulation that create positive incentives for all levels of the system to respond to the quality challenge. Public officials should demand evidence that plans and providers continuously and aggressively seek to identify errors and to improve quality, although prescriptive regulatory formulas can do more harm than good and can stifle innovation in a fast-changing environment. All levels of the system must be engaged beyond pro forma activities. Government can best help by providing incentives and resources to help identify sources of error and poor quality. The rewards for society will be considerable.

CONCLUSION

Legislatures and legislators have vitally important roles to play in advancing progressive and humane health policy. Legislators often are key individuals who spotlight emerging problems and potential solutions. They are the citizens' voice holding bureaucrats responsive to citizen needs. They have the platform and the ability to advance new ideas that can lead to effective and important improvements in policy. On the other hand, they also can be agents for change that considerably worsen the status quo, inadvertent advocates for alterations that can diminish quality, harm access, and worsen costs. One thing they should never be is ignored.

REFERENCES

Arnold, D. 1993. "Can Inattentive Citizens Control Their Elected Representatives?" In *Congress Reconsidered,* 5th ed., ed. L. C. Dodd and B. I. Oppenheimer, pp. 401–416. Washington, DC: CQ Press.

Baumgartner, F., and B. Leech. 1998. *Basic Interests: The Importance of Groups in Politics and in Political Science.* Princeton, NJ: Princeton University Press.

Broder, D. 1996. Address at Collins Center, Florida Legislative Project, St. Petersburg, January 11.

Clynch, E. J., and T. P. Lauth. 1991. "Conclusion: Budgeting in the American States—Conflict and Diversity." In *Governors, Legislators, and Budgets,* ed. E. J. Clynch and T. P. Lauth, pp. 149–155. Westport, CT: Greenwood.

Fenno, R. 1978. *Home Style.* Boston: Little Brown.

Francis, W. L. 1989. *The Legislative Committee Game: A Comparative Analysis of Fifty States.* Columbus: Ohio State University Press.

Gordon, D. 1994. "Citizen Legislators—Alive and Well." *State Legislatures* (January): 24–27.

Heard, A. 1966. *State Legislatures in American Politics.* Englewood Cliffs, NJ: Prentice Hall.

Hicock, E. 1992. *The Reform of State Legislatures.* Latham, MD: University Press of America.

Kingdon, J. 1995. *Agendas, Alternatives, and Public Policies.* 2d ed. New York: HarperCollins.

Leape, L. 1994. "Error in Medicine." *Journal of the American Medical Association* 272 (23):1851–1857.

Longest, B. 1996. *Seeking Strategic Advantage through Health Policy Analysis.* Chicago: Health Administration Press.

Loomis, B. 1994. *Time, Politics, and Policies.* Lawrence: University Press of Kansas.

Madison, J. 1961. *The Federalist Papers.* No. 51, pp. 320–325. New York: New American Library.

Nownes, A., and P. Freeman. 1998. "Interest Group Activity in the States." *Journal of Politics* 60 (1): 86–112.

Oliver, T. R., and P. Paul-Shaheen. 1997. "Translating Ideas into Actions: Entrepreneurial Leadership in State Health Care Reforms." *Journal of Health Politics, Policy and Law* 22 (June): 721–788.

Patterson, S. C. 1996. "Legislative Politics in the States." In *Politics in the American States,* 6th ed., ed. V. Gray and H. Jacob, pp. 177–178. Washington, DC: CQ Press.

Paul-Shaheen, P. 1998. "The States and Health Care Reform: The Road Traveled and Lessons Learned from Seven that Took the Lead." *Journal of Health Politics, Policy and Law* 23 (2): 319–361.

Pitkin, H. 1967. *The Concept of Representation.* Berkeley: University of California Press.

Reingold, B. 1996. "Conflict and Cooperation: Legislative Strategies and Concepts of Power among Female and Male State Legislators." *Journal of Politics* 58 (May): 464–485.

Rosenthal, A. 1998. *The Decline of Representative Democracy.* Washington, DC: CQ Press.

Thomas, C., and R. Hrebnar. 1995. "Interest Groups in the States." In *Politics in the American States,* 6th ed., ed. V. Gray and H. Jacob, pp. 149–150. Washington, DC: CQ Press.

Weissert, C., and S. Silberman. 1998. "Sending a Policy Signal: Legislatures, Medical Schools, and Primary Care Mandates." *Journal of Health Politics, Policy and Law* 23 (5): 743–770.

PART II
Current Controversies

5

The Backlash against Managed Care

David A. Rochefort

Speaking before a conference at Harvard University in May 1999, Dr. Paul Ellwood startled his audience by calling for stiff government regulation to improve the quality of American medical care (Knox 1999). Considered the "father of the HMO movement," Ellwood has long argued for the ability of managed care to remedy the nation's health care ills through economic competition and the voluntary efforts of physicians and health plans. Ellwood abandoned this position, however, after a series of perilous medical errors were made when he was receiving treatment for an equestrian accident. Although this health policy conversion experience was triggered by an episode that took place in a for-profit, fee-for-service setting, the HMO proponent believes that quality problems also abound in HMOs and other managed care organizations. "We've been talking about quality improvements for 30 or 40 years without much to show for it," Ellwood stated. "I'm mad— in part because I've learned that terrible care can happen to anyone. . . . We've got to build a consumer movement here" (Knox 1999, A1).

Ellwood's declarations mark a threshold of sorts in the backlash against managed care, a sign both of how far the sea change of opinion has carried and how fundamental the rethinking of public/private relations in the health care market is. In fact, the states are already well advanced in a legislative campaign to expand control over the managed care industry (Pear 1998). All 50 have enacted laws guaranteeing at least basic grievance and appeal procedures for patients of health maintenance organizations, and some have gone much farther than that. In New York, for example, lawmakers enacted a measure increasing the access of managed care patients to experimental treatments.

On the federal level, regulating managed care has also developed into a pivotal, if unresolved, issue. Following the report of a special presidential advisory panel, the Democrats submitted patients' protection legislation in March 1998. In July, after having convinced themselves of the political popularity of the antimanaged care theme, Republicans countered with a plan of their own (Alvarez 1998). By late fall 1999, the Senate and House each had passed patients' rights bills (Pear 1999). However, the House version, which President Clinton favored, was much stronger, its provisions applying to 161 million Americans compared to just 48 million under the Senate measure. It also proposed giving consumers new rights to bring suit against HMOs, unlike the Senate plan. Following an extraordinary maneuver in which Republican House leaders stacked the House-Senate conference committee with opponents of the House regulatory plan, the year ended with congressional inaction on the legislation (Rosenbaum 1999). At the time of this writing, a last-ditch effort by Senate Democratic leaders in the summer of 2000 to break the logjam by using the leverage of election year politics also appears headed for failure (Gullo 2000; Pear 2000).

For the time being, then, the states remain in firm control of this issue, and the odds are against any sweeping federal action that would dislodge them from the lead role they have claimed in this area. Moreover, a decision by the U.S. Supreme Court in a June 2000 ruling against the liability of HMOs in federal court for their cost-containment practices has redirected attention to state courts as a possible venue for such action (Greenhouse 2000). As Rodwin (1999, 1123) has commented, "A national regulatory authority could be more efficient and systematic [than a patchwork system of state regulation], but it is unlikely to be tried before alternatives are exhausted."

There is more than a little irony to this series of events. In 1994, even as the majority of citizens believed the U.S. health care system to be in "crisis," government was firmly rebuffed from intervening in the private medical marketplace. Now, just a few short years later, public policymakers at all levels are being implored to charge into that arena brandishing new rules and threatened penalties. Indeed, some of the most plaintive rescue cries are coming from groups—such as physicians—who earlier had fought to defeat national health care reform.

In this chapter, I will attempt to answer several questions about this backlash against managed care. How and why has the movement come into being? What types of regulatory strategies has it spawned? What are the prospects for the states' effective implementation of new bureaucratic protections in the health care sector?

CONTEMPORARY MANAGED CARE TRENDS

Precise causes may be hard to pin down, but the sequence of the backlash against managed care is unmistakable, following as it has the precipitous expansion of managed care from a peripheral practice to the nation's most prevalent form of health insurance coverage. Underlying this transformation, and contributing to it, has also been a growing diversification of managed care plans and changing sources of organizational control. It is impossible to understand the social and

political currents of the managed care regulatory movement without first reviewing this revolution with the managed care industry.

The basic concept of managed care refers to controlling the use of medical
services by confining patients to a specified group of providers or reviewing providers' treatment decisions or both. Originating with the prepaid health plans of
the 1930s and 1940s, the earliest and most well-known form of managed care is
the health maintenance organization (HMO) (Starr 1982). HMOs simultaneously
act as service providers and insurers of health care that operate on the basis of a
fixed capitated fee for each enrolled member. The first HMOs owned their own
facilities and hired physicians as salaried employees. Subsequently, other HMO
types developed in which physician services were provided on a contract basis
(group model) or by arrangement with networks of independent hospitals and
physicians (independent practice association).

HMOs initially gained strong favor with the health policy community because of their reputation for controlling costs while emphasizing primary care
and continuity of services. Attracted by these advantages, the Nixon administration succeeded in passing legislation in 1973 promoting the growth of HMOs
among employee groups. Even with this stimulus, however, HMO enrollments
climbed sluggishly, reaching a level of only 4% of the U.S. population by the start
of the 1980s (Brown 1983).

Over the 1980s and 1990s, the relatively precise concept of the HMO as
the prototypic alternative health care delivery system gave way to a much broader
set of organizational and financial innovations within the health insurance field
(Starr 1994). For example, one important variation on the HMO model is the
preferred provider organization (PPO), in which an insurer directs enrollees to
an affiliated list of doctors and hospitals who agree to abide by the insurer's
rules for lowered fees, utilization review, and gatekeeping procedures. More and
more, both HMOs and PPOs are also developing point-of-service (POS) plans
that give members the option to use services outside of their own health plan,
but with a penalty of higher premiums or higher copayments and deductibles or
both. Still another form of managed care is fee for service with benefits management. This hybrid combines the traditional health insurance model giving
patients freedom of choice in regard to health care providers while employing
potentially aggressive controls in the form of preadmission approvals, second
opinions, and treatment plan reviews.

Offered this diversified collection of insurance products and backed by strong
political support for the philosophy of market competition, corporate managers
nationwide have seized on managed care as the main vehicle for fighting health care
cost inflation in the 1990s. Statistics on the number of Americans covered by managed health care plans tell the story: in 1995, 73% of all Americans insured through
an employer were enrolled in HMOs, PPOs, or POS plans (Jensen et al. 1997). This
was an increase of 22 points over the comparable figure in 1993. POS plans, although still the least common of the three types of managed care, are by far the fast-

est growing and more than doubled over this time period. Add to such figures the number of people covered by managed fee-for-service plans and the resulting estimate is 95% of the U.S. group insurance market in managed care (Starr 1994, 38).

Hoping to trim budgets and improve service delivery, government has also jumped on the managed care bandwagon. In Medicaid, managed care enrollments soared from 9.5% of the program in 1991 to 40.1% in 1996 to 53.6% in 1998 (HCFA 1999b; Rowland and Hanson 1996). Growth of Medicare managed care has lagged behind Medicaid but now is also on the upswing. About 16% of Medicare recipients belonged to managed care plans by the start of 1998, an increase of 156% in the program's managed care enrollment since 1992 (HCFA 1999a).

Finally, a different kind of change in the health care marketplace has drawn much attention during recent years. Over a brief period, the dominant segment of the managed care market has shifted dramatically from not-for-profit status to for-profit (Gabel 1997). From 1988 to 1994, the membership of for-profit HMOs increased approximately 92% or nearly four times the rate of nonprofit enrollees. Aggressive pursuit of growth has been a hallmark of for-profit managed care organizations, which have easier access to capital than their nonprofit counterparts. This trend toward consolidation of the managed care market though mergers and acquisitions, combined with rampant profit-taking, has been identified as a new stage in the corporatization of American medicine (Light 1997).

GAUGING THE REACTION

"Managed care has lost its luster as an industry and as the answer to the nation's health care needs." So concluded the *New York Times* in assessing the new hegemony of managed care on the American medical scene (Kilborn 1998). Spreading discontent with managed care can be traced by means of a variety of indicators. Here I focus on the mass media, public opinion, and popular culture representations, which all supply strong evidence of the trend.

Mass Media

The media play a key part in the agenda standing of any political issue (Alger 1996). Media coverage determines, to a great extent, the notoriety of an issue. It helps to frame the way an issue is perceived, including the specific facets that are to be taken as most important. Moreover, the media provide a battleground for competing interests seeking to expand or limit the audience for a conflict. In all of these ways, changing media coverage has contributed to the emergence of managed care as a political issue.

For a previous study I extracted all items discussing the topics of HMOs and managed care appearing in the *Reader's Guide to Periodical Literature* over the period 1987 to 1996 (first quarter) (Rochefort 1996). Included in the *Reader's*

Guide are abstracts for articles published in most major newspapers and popular newsmagazines. Based on a methodology developed by Baumgartner and Jones (1993), I coded each story as "positive," "neutral," or "negative" in its tone of coverage for managed care and then calculated the percentage of each type of story by year.

The amount of coverage given to managed care rose substantially over this period, from only 20 articles in 1987 to 83 in 1995. (The peak year was 1993, when the Clinton administration announced its national health proposal featuring a central role for managed care.) Although negative articles represented a small percentage of all articles on managed care in the late 1980s, this segment gained rapidly in the 1990s, topping 65% in the early part of 1996. As negative articles climbed, positive stories plummeted, to a level below 10%.

Brodie, Brady, and Altman (1998) examined trends in media coverage of managed care for the period January 1980 to June 1997. Selected for this study were approximately 2,100 stories taken primarily from a limited group of national and regional newspapers and the magazines *Time, Forbes,* and *Business Week.* Researchers also analyzed the content of 65 broadcast news stories on managed care from *ABC World News Tonight, CBS Evening News, and NBC Nightly News.* Although the majority of news coverage on managed care was characterized as neutral in this study, the authors identified a definite shift for the remaining coverage so that, by 1997, 28% of all news stories were critical of managed care, while only 4% were positive. The most negative treatments tended to occur when managed care was the subject of a special newspaper series. In addition, more than one-half of all broadcast news stories on the subject fell into the negative category. Whether a managed care story was positive or negative also reflected the focus of coverage. Positive stories tended to delve into economic themes, such as employers' health care cost-cutting through managed care or corporate developments. Negative stories, by contrast, centered on patient care or the phenomenon of backlash itself. Thus, not only the tone but also the content of coverage has altered over time.

In a similar vein, Peterson (1999) described a shift in major newspaper treatment of health care issues. An earlier period of coverage centering on the problem of health care costs and the proposed solution of health care reform gave way in the mid-1990s to a period concerned with the problem of managed care and the proposed solution of a patients' bill of rights.

Public Opinion

One of the earliest large-scale studies to gather opinion data on managed care was carried out in the mid-1980s (Rubin et al. 1993). Researchers asked more than 1,700 adult outpatients belonging to different kinds of prepaid and fee-for-service medical practices in Boston, Chicago, and Los Angeles to fill out a questionnaire after completing an office visit. Of all practice types and payment methods considered, patients of solo fee-for-service practitioners rated their episodes of care most favorably, while HMO patients rated them the worst. This pattern applied both to overall satisfaction and to a set of eight specific items related to technical, interpersonal, and convenience aspects of care.

In the decade since this pioneering research, numerous additional studies have sought to gauge public reaction to managed care. Despite inconsistencies in some of the results, the overall finding from a mass of opinion items is one of substantial public negativity, as summarized in a recent review of more than 20 national surveys by Blendon et al. (1998). For example, a majority of Americans currently say they are unsure if managed care patients will receive the services they need when very sick. As compared to 34% of respondents with traditional health insurance, 55% of managed care enrollees suspect that if they were ill, their health plan would care more about saving money than providing them with the best medical treatment. In a poll by the *New York Times* in July 1998, nearly 60% said that "HMOs had impeded doctors' ability to control treatment" (Kilborn 1998).

Opinions about managed care clearly have been worsening over the past few years. As reported by the *New York Times,* between 1995 and 1998 the proportion of Americans saying managed care would improve the quality of medical care rather than harm it reversed from the majority to the minority. In a survey conducted with CNN, *Time* magazine found that 42% of those with managed care, but only 25% of those with traditional coverage, felt that over the past five years it had "become more of a hassle to deal with your health-care plan" (Tumulty 1998). Jacobs and Shapiro (1999) tracked changes for several managed care opinion items that were repeated in four Louis Harris surveys between 1995 and 1998. Increasing public negativity was found in regard to managed care's impact on quality as well as its cost-containment potential. One question asked, "On the whole do you think this trend away from traditional fee-for-service coverage and toward managed care is a good thing or a bad thing?" Those saying "a good thing" dropped from 59% to 40%, while the opposite position rose from 28% to 47%.

Many specific complaints appear to be contributing to public disaffection with managed care. In a 1994 survey of adults with employer health coverage in Boston, Los Angeles, and Miami, managed care enrollees were more satisfied than fee-for-service enrollees in the areas of out-of-pocket costs, paperwork, and preventive care (Davis et al. 1995). This satisfaction was outweighed, however, by respondents' greater unhappiness with the issues of physician choice, access to specialty care, availability of emergency care, and waiting times for appointments. In a 1997 national poll, 72% said they believed that "the money saved by HMOs and other managed care plans helps health insurance companies to earn more profits." This figure was more than 20 points higher than the number who felt the savings "makes health care more affordable for people like you" (Blendon et al. 1998, 88). Asked by pollsters in a 1999 Discovery/*Newsweek* survey "which restriction is reasonable if it keeps health-care costs low for most Americans," only

37% of those insured and 31% of the uninsured approved of "restricting choice of treatment plans." Similar low percentages were willing to back "requiring authorization for hospital care, even in emergencies" (Cowley and Turque 1999).

Reflecting this mix of fears, frustrations, and resentments, there is now widespread support for increased government regulation of the managed care industry. In a 1997 national survey, 52% agreed that, even if it increases costs, "government needs to protect consumers from being treated unfairly and not getting the care they should from managed care plans" (Blendon et al. 1998, 86). In the *Time/CNN* poll, majorities of between 63 and 79% favored government regulation of managed care to protect consumers by allowing patients to select their doctor; requiring payment for emergency care even when not preapproved; requiring payment for treatment by a specialist recommended by a primary care doctor even if not approved by the managed care provider; allowing patients to appeal treatment denials to a neutral third party; and allowing patients to sue their managed care provider (Tumulty 1998). In April 1999, 74% in a Kaiser/Harvard survey said they supported strong federal patients' rights legislation after its provisions were described to them. When a prospective annual cost increase of $200 per family was attributed to the legislation, support fell to 46%, but this response was still the most frequent (Kaiser/Harvard, 1999). Thus, as Jacobs and Shapiro (1999) have written, although public support for managed care regulation is weakened by the public's philosophical reservations about government intervention and the possibility of higher costs due to regulation, even with such factors noted the public tends to give broad support to most regulatory reforms.

Based on their review of the myriad survey data that have been collected, Blendon et al. (1998) tersely conclude that the public backlash against managed care is real in its depth and its breadth, and they predict that "debate about regulation of the managed care industry is likely to be a permanent fixture on the health care agenda for years to come" (92).

Popular Culture

Political scientists have generally ignored the relevance of popular culture for the public policymaking process, yet this oversight is unfortunate. The messages of popular culture are both aimed at and depend upon a receptive mass audience. For this reason, they provide a key indicator of an issue's perception in society. When the representations of popular culture coincide with the broadly held views of citizens, policy advocates, and elected officials, the result can be irresistible pressure for a redirection of public policy (Rochefort 1986).

In recent years, HMOs and managed care generally have met with harsh criticism in the worlds of cinema and television drama. One of the most notable such moments occurred in the popular movie, *As Good As It Gets,* as the character played by Helen Hunt railed in exasperation against an HMO for not giving better care to her asthmatic son. The managed care industry was sufficiently threatened by that scene to produce a defensive ad for showing in movie theaters (Gorman 1998). Fans of the number one television series *ER* have witnessed a variety of dramatic situations in which managed care was conflicting with clinicians' judgments of good quality care, such as the time that Nurse Hathaway stormed off the job in frustration over HMO limits on how long patients could be kept in the hospital. In the short-lived series *Michael Hayes,* a New York district attorney prosecuted an HMO because of administrative misdeeds affecting a young boy stricken with cancer: the HMO had first denied a timely diagnostic test ordered by the boy's physician, then it destroyed all records of the act and tried to shift the blame for malpractice onto the treating physician. In the fall of 1998, a new television series named *LA Doctors* centered on a group of young physicians devoted to the practice of nonbureaucratic medicine based on unhurried, caring, personalized doctor-patient relationships. The story line of one episode culminated with a member of the practice invading the headquarters of a health insurer to chase down and throttle an uncooperative claims processer.

Newspaper cartoons have been another venue for frequent lampooning of managed care. "Mother Goose & Grimm," by Mike Peters, modernized the fabled encounter between a lion with a thorn in its paw and a little mouse. In this version, however, the mouse, having sent the lion limping back into the jungle with no more assistance than a harsh pep talk, goes on to start his own HMO. Two other examples of HMO cartoon humor are reprinted here from the widely circulated strips of Mike Luckovich and Jack McPherson. With absolutely no attempt at subtlety, these and countless other such representations press the point that many standard aspects of managed care—from gatekeeping to efficiency standards to conservative practice styles—become absurd when carried too far.

On late-night TV, at cocktail parties, and (most likely of all) around the water coolers of America's medical care establishments, other professional and amateur humorists are also taking aim at "mangled care." Repeated by the *Economist* (1998):

Q: How can you tell that a death certificate was filled out by an HMO doctor?
A: He signs his name under "cause of death."

In another joke related on the Garrison Keillor public radio program, Saint Peter meets a recently deceased nurse who had worked in utilization review for a managed care company; after some intense figuring with a calculator, Saint Peter grants her five days in heaven. The "Preferred Providers" is a managed care blues band formed by a retired physician in Florida (Manning 1997). Their recent CD consists entirely of parodies of well-known blues numbers rewritten to express anti–managed care themes (e.g., "You Picked a Fine Time to Leave Me Blue Shield"). And in the novel *Mount Misery* by Samuel Shem (1997), a pseudonym for psychiatrist-writer Steven Bergman, managed mental health care practices are skewered with black humor. According to Freud, humor often serves as a release

CLOSE TO HOME   JOHN M^cPHERSON

"I'm sorry, Mrs. Morris, but to prevent office visits from dragging on, the HMO requires that I answer only 'yes' or 'no' questions."

for deeply held feelings. In fact, little psychoanalytic skill is required to uncover the hostile sentiments in these varied illustrations.

A Broad-Based Convergence

Some in the managed care industry have blamed the backlash on a biased media manipulated by organized opponents of the managed care revolution (Ignagni 1998). To be sure, the health care sector includes powerful interests determined to resist the encroachments of managed care on existing privileges and benefits. Specialist physicians, for example, have become very active in lobbying for weakened gatekeeping and quicker referrals (Kilborn 1997). Nonphysician health care workers and consumer advocates have also mounted vigorous anti–managed care legislative efforts (Enthoven and Singer 1998). Depending on idiosyncrasies of the legislative process and local leadership factors, in some states these groups have formed powerful, if unusual, coalitions (Langdon 1997).

However, a narrow interest-group explanation of the managed care backlash is unsatisfactory. Publicity campaigns have been launched by the managed care industry as well as its opponents (*Providence Journal-Bulletin* 1998; Walsh 1998). Additionally, among citizens who are most negative toward managed care, the majority claim their impressions are based on direct personal experiences or those of family and friends (Blendon et al. 1998). Media "horror stories" may intensify, but they do not seem to create, managed care antagonisms for most people. The remarkable scope of public mobilization on the issue has been revealed in California, where the legislature created a special task force in 1997 to respond to managed care concerns. In this state, "an estimated 202,000 Californians contacted an elected official about a problem with their health plan in the past year" (Enthoven and Singer 1998, 106).

Yet it would be unfounded to generalize that the managed care backlash necessarily results from a low quality of medical care by managed care organizations. In fact, despite complaints, most survey respondents are satisfied with their existing health plans (Blendon et al. 1998; Enthoven and Singer 1998). Research studies on quality of care within managed care plans have also been inconclusive in their findings. Based on a review of 37 studies comparing HMO and non-HMO care, Miller and Luft (1997) found that half the time HMOs performed better, half the time worse. To some extent, results depended on population group, such as patients with or without chronic illnesses (Ware et al. 1996). Other complexities have been found in outcome studies for different groups under managed mental health care (Callahan et al. 1995).

A collection of organized and unorganized groups exhibiting diverse concerns is involved in the backlash against managed care. Large-scale change is disruptive, and no one should have expected a warm welcome for the limits, rules, and penalties that managed care has brought to American medicine. It does not help that such changes have occurred with astounding rapidity, or that most people fail to recognize the existence of accompanying benefits. Promising better quality, lower costs, and the choice of numerous competing plans, the managed care movement has been a betrayal in the eyes of many consumers (Swartz 1999). Mechanic (1996, 1997) writes that managed care has struck at one of medicine's most precious assets, public trust. The growth of for-profit ownership, an emphasis on production efficiencies, and the encouragement of price-sensitive consumption all have tended to commodify medicine under managed care, forcing the public into the role of prudent purchaser. A strong reaction to this "buyer beware" atmosphere is not surprising, nor is the self-protective demand for government to play a multifaceted new role as referee, intermediary, and policeman in the health care arena.

THE TRANSFORMATIONAL POLITICS OF MANAGED CARE

Baumgartner and Jones (1993) have traced how issue areas having long-term stability in their structure of decision-making, policymaking participants, and distributive benefits can suddenly be disrupted. According to their thesis, volatile
political change is typically a function of the introduction of new policy ideas
"which can be communicated directly and simply through image and rhetoric"
(p. 7). New ideas, in turn, mobilize elites and the mass public to become involved
in the policy process. In effect, an issue is redefined so that a particular problematic condition or set of conditions is highlighted and associated with a cause. One
of the principal indicators that this sequence is under way is a surge and shift in
media interest on the topic.

   This scenario closely describes what has occurred with the evolution of managed care as a public issue. From the time that prepaid health plans first gained a
foothold in the U.S. health care system decades ago, managed care has met with
a degree of skepticism, wariness, and even hostility from organized medicine.
However, the HMO movement also once had a "populist flavor to it" (DeLeon,
Bulatao, and VandenBos 1994, 16), and many health policy experts praised such
organizations for their ability to outperform fee-for-service medicine. It was in
this context that the Nixon administration sought to expand HMO coverage in the
1970s. HMO performance measures were also often seized upon for use as a standard in health system planning under the National Health Planning and Resource
Development Act of 1974 (Brown 1983). Culminating this approach to managed
care as the embodiment of "best practices" in the health insurance field was President Clinton's 1993 reform proposal, which provided incentives for a massive
movement of Americans into managed care plans.

   Yet, as we have seen, by the early 1990s there already were signs of great
disquiet over the expansion of managed care. Increasingly, managed care was being
defined less as a promising innovation and more as a rigid organizational system
suspected of placing other interests ahead of patient care. The media actively
participated in this change through their expanded coverage of managed care, their
increasingly negative tone of coverage, and their redirection of focus, from cost-
cutting successes and managed care corporate achievements on the one hand to
provider and patient complaints and unsatisfactory medical outcomes on the other.
Applying Baumgartner's and Jones's model to these circumstances, we would
predict a large-scale disruption in public policy toward managed care, one shaped
by the demands of new policy participants and aimed at the industry's most controversial practices.

   This is just what has occurred in health policymaking—and in striking fashion—over the past few years. Since 1996 on the federal level, all of the following
have taken place: legislation has been passed guaranteeing minimum hospital stays
for mothers and newborns; President Clinton appointed an executive commission

to respond to reports of managed care abuses; the president mandated new requirements for managed care organizations serving Medicare and Medicaid enrollees; and Congress has taken up omnibus patients' rights legislation. Such actions, however, are a pale shadow of developments on the state level. In 1996, more than 1,000 managed care regulatory bills were introduced, and legislation subsequently was enacted by 33 states (Families USA Foundation 1996). In 1997, 17 states adopted comprehensive patient-protection measures; in 1998, another 10 did the same (Pear 1998). Again at the start of 1999, every state legislature in the country reported plans to consider new managed care regulations (Sorian and Feder 1999). Marking the policy process on this issue in many states has been a high degree of bipartisanship.

One might well wonder why, with all the financial and political resources of the insurance industry and its allies, this regulatory legislative response has proceeded so far. Why, as managed care organizations have become pervasive within the health system, including government's increasing reliance on managed care for its own health plans, has control of the politics of health care seemingly shifted so decisively into the hands of managed care opponents? A relevant concept to draw upon here is Huntington's (1981) "politics of creedal passion," which describes the recurrent American tendency to attack social institutions seen as conflicting with basic national values that are individualistic, libertarian, anticoercive, and antiauthoritarian. In this sense, not only has managed care interfered practically with Americans' habitual ways of receiving medical treatment, but it also has sparked an intense cultural dissonance, a "disharmony" to use Huntington's term, that is capable of overriding typical interest-group politics. At the same time, however, the difficulty with a politics fueled by popular protest, outrage, and moralism is the improbability of sustaining its fervor as well as the lack of political means to support the effective implementation of enacted reforms. I will return to an analysis of these problems in a later section of this chapter.

DESCRIBING THE REGULATORY INTERVENTIONS

Managed care regulatory measures adopted on the state level take varied forms—broad and narrow, focusing on different patient groups, medical concerns, or administrative issues, and embodying different philosophies of regulatory authority. As Hyman (1999) puts it, the regulatory onslaught ranges from obvious antimanaged care initiatives to "direct regulation by body part" to more complete regulatory frameworks. Following is a description of major managed care regulatory approaches, categorized according to their strategic character. Examples are also provided of specific state actions. For the most part, these laws have resulted from a remarkable burst of legislative activity since 1995, and most states now have in place one or more of the measures described. (This information is culled form reports in Dallek, Jimenez, and Schwartz [1995], Families USA Foundation [1996, 1998], Pear [1998], Rochefort [1996], Rodwin [1996a, 1996b], Serafini [1996], and Tumulty [1998]).

Disclosure Requirements

The purpose of disclosure requirements is to ensure that managed care enrollees have sufficient information in regard to such matters as the benefits offered by their health plan, the administrative and service procedures under which a plan operates, cost-sharing arrangements, the qualifications of providers, and performance outcomes. The premise is that such information is instrumental both for consumers selecting between competing insurance plans and for existing plan members to gain access to services and make use of available rights and protections.

Examples. In nearly every state, the range and types of information managed care plans must provide to members and prospective enrollees are addressed under law, although broad variation exists in the nature of the requirements. An Oregon law requires managed care organizations to disclose information about the financial incentives given to physicians to control costs. New Jersey publishes HMO report cards based on data the HMOs are required to supply to state government. Many states compel HMOs to make available to their members information on the financial status of the plan.

Consumer Protections

In addition to information disclosure, several other kinds of consumer protection provisions have been formulated as part of managed care regulatory legislation. Their common purpose is to provide standards, procedural safeguards, and guarantees of fair treatment and privacy not to be infringed upon by health plans' economic incentives and market behaviors.

Examples. The criteria employed in utilization review processes have received detailed attention within several state statutes. All states have grievance and appeal procedures offering managed care patients the right to appeal denials of treatment. An increasing number of states—including Hawaii, Maryland, New York, Pennsylvania, Tennessee, and Vermont—are enacting laws that give patients recourse to an independent external review panel for appeals. Florida and Vermont have established independent consumer assistance programs to aid health plan members with appeals and other consumer issues. Most states have put in place rules against abuses in managed care marketing and enrollment practices, such as the requirement for licensure of marketing agents. One of the latest areas to become the focus of state regulation is the confidentiality of medical records. For example, in the area of mental health care, Massachusetts passed a law in 1996 prohibiting health plans from requiring any personal information beyond name, diagnosis, and date and type of service until the first $500 of benefits is exceeded.

Mandated Benefits

Regulatory requirements in the area of mandated benefits seek to specify the particular types or conditions of care that managed care enrollees will have available to them. Issues of both access and financial protection are involved.

Examples. One of the most common managed care regulations is to require health plans to pay for emergency room services whenever usage meets a "prudent layperson" standard. A growing number of states give patients the right to access OB/GYN specialists without referral from a primary care doctor or permit patients to choose OB/GYNs as their primary care practitioner. Under some state legislative acts, enrollees with chronic or life-threatening conditions are permitted to use specialists as primary care providers. Provisions against "drive-through" deliveries that guarantee minimum maternity stays of 48 hours were an early focal point of managed care regulation. Other state laws mandate coverage of particular procedures or conditions, such as the New York law that facilitates access to experimental treatments and clinical trials for patients whose illnesses are life-threatening. An unsuccessful regulatory proposal in Connecticut in 1996 sought to define the essential components of treatment for children with mental health problems. An Arkansas law offers an example of regulation giving members access to prescription drugs not on their plan's established formulary.

Administrative Monitoring

Regulations concerned with managed care administration are meant generally to provide for mechanisms of quality control and accountability in the operation of health plans. Some oversight devices are internal to the regulated organization, others are external, and in the latter situation they may be under public or private auspices.

Examples. HMOs in all states are required to have their own systems of quality assurance, and several states are working at strengthening and elaborating this provision. The participation of plan members in areas of policy and operations has sometimes been provided for through state rules for enrollee representation on governing boards of health plans. State laws have also given important new oversight powers to state agencies, such as a Rhode Island law granting the Department of Health authority to certify qualified health plans. Certain states allow HMOs to satisfy the requirement for an external examination of quality of care through a private agency, such as the National Committee on Quality Assurance (NCQA).

Provider Protections

A last category of regulatory legislation addresses provider interests. Each of these approaches seeks to strengthen the position of providers within an economic marketplace where buying power lies in the hands of large organizations able to determine who is eligible to offer services, under what conditions, and for what levels of payment.

Examples. Two leading examples of restrictions on selective contracting are any-willing-provider (AWP) and mandatory point-of-service (MPOS) laws. AWP legislation requires managed care networks to include any provider who has appropriate credentials and meets other terms and conditions of the plan. MPOS laws give managed care members the right to seek care from providers not affiliated with their health plan. Other states have established in law the rules and guidelines by which health plans may choose participating providers. Managed care restrictions on physicians' ability to inform patients about all of their treatment options have also been struck down in nearly all states with the banning of "gag rules."

Summary

The popularity of all of the above regulatory interventions continues to grow, as state legislatures around the nation with each new session receive hundreds of bills focusing on managed care plans. Yet extensive variation does exist among the forms of regulation currently in place. According to a 1999 tabulation by the National Conference of State Legislatures (1999), 47 states had bans on gag clauses, whereas only 2 states allowed consumers to sue their HMOs for malpractice. In general, states have acted most quickly on narrow, (seemingly) uncomplicated, service-specific issues, such as access to emergency care and minimum maternity stays. Regulations advantaged by strong backing from health care providers or by a combination of provider-consumer support, such as information disclosure requirements, have also fared well. By contrast, state lawmakers have been more reluctant to enact measures that interfere with managed care as a system of health care delivery either by limiting practices fundamental to the character of the industry or by undermining its legal position. Despite the frenzy of legislation in this area, most states still have not established comprehensive frameworks of managed care supervision of a kind that would meet the standards of health care consumer advocates (Families USA Foundation 1999). Beyond these observations, however, it is difficult to analyze the pattern of diffusion in managed care policymaking, which reflects both political and health care market idiosyncrasies that vary from state to state.

AN ASSESSMENT OF REGULATORY BARRIERS

Are there hidden pitfalls capable of undoing the purpose of managed care regulatory reforms? What issues will merit attention in future waves of managed health care policymaking? To answer such questions requires a consideration of many political, organizational, and administrative forces at play on the health policy scene. As a policy instrument, regulation can assume a wide range of forms, from weak to strong. In addition, any specific regulatory intervention may be applied with differing levels of coercion. Legislative design, the process of policy implementation, and the responses of regulated groups all figure into a critical assessment of the managed care regulatory movement. (The following discussion draws, in part, on Rochefort [1996].)

The Danger of "Capture"

Bolstered by a very supportive public opinion, regulatory proponents have won surprising legislative victories against powerful managed care industry interests in state legislatures around the country. With the passage of new statutes, however, the political process of regulatory policymaking has not ended; it has merely entered a new phase (Meier 1985). As Huntington (1981) has pointed out, American history holds many examples of reforms produced by the "politics of creedal passion" that failed at the phase of implementation, instances where the intended functions and purposes of new public requirements were "trusted, perverted, or corrupted." Indeed, according to Huntington, "There seems to be a certain inevitability and invisibility to the process" (p. 118). Unlike the ad hoc coalitions that have frequently provided the impetus for new regulations, well-organized and well-financed managed care industry groups are not likely to dissipate after legislation has been enacted. Rather, they have a panoply of means at their disposal to continue to seek success on issues decided against them in the legislative arena. They may simply drag their feet on tasks requiring industry cooperation. Or, benefiting from good access to bureaucratic officials, such groups may alternate between pressure tactics and cultivation of relationships to delay program implementation, weaken the stringency of operational standards, and influence those aspects of regulation selected for attention or neglect. They may also use the courts to challenge legislative requirements, attacking in whole or in part the legal premises of a new regulatory framework.

Far from idle speculation, these dynamics already are being seen in the post-legislative stage of managed care regulation. For example, under a 1990 federal law requiring disclosure of provider incentives by HMOs enrolling Medicare and Medicaid patients, the U.S. Department of Health and Human Services did not issue detailed rules until March 1996. Then, in July, the department quietly suspended these rules to a future date due to "a torrent of criticism" from regulated organizations (Pear 1996). In Massachusetts, which passed the law constraining insurers from seeking detailed personal information before supplying $500 of state-mandated mental health benefits, regulators reported that many MCOs were evading or simply ignoring the law (Bass 1996). (Subsequently, this same privacy measure was repealed as part of a legislative deal expanding mental health insurance coverage in the state [Hsu 1999].) In Vermont, the managed care industry continued to "complain bitterly" after the passage of regulatory legislation in 1994, shifting its lobbying effort to the governor's office (Rochefort 1996). In part owing to such political resistance, it took state regulators there roughly two years to establish the licensing and appeals procedures mandated by law. A similar pattern of resistance or evasion to managed care regulatory activity has surfaced elsewhere. In Rhode Island, in April 2000, the Department of Health fined an HMO subsidiary of Blue Cross and Blue Shield for violating state law governing grievance and appeals processes. Regulators noted a pattern of "repeat deficiencies" and "continued noncomplicance" by the health plan, which included the backdating of correspondence to make it appear as if the insurer was responding to consumer complaints within the required time period (Freyer 2000, 1998).

The role permitted to regulated interests within the administrative process will differ from state to state depending on the stance of public officials as well as the ability of regulation advocates to adapt from legislative to bureaucratic politicking. Given their resource advantages, however, it is not uncommon for industry groups to dominate at this juncture, a phenomenon of "capture" that has often been described in the regulatory literature. "Agencies that regulate a single industry have tended to become advocates of their industries, rather than impartial protectors of the public interest," writes Peters. "Capture results from the agencies' needs to maintain political support . . . when the only logical support is the regulated industry itself. The public is usually too amorphous a body to offer the specific support an agency may need in defending its budget, or its very existence" (1996, 90).

Strained Regulatory Capacity

One way that regulatory practices are sure to fall short of objectives is if responsibilities exceed the capacity of public bureaucracies to carry them out. The new regulatory burdens being created by managed care legislation are unprecedented in some ways, and undoubtedly enough so to strain existing agency manpower and expertise. Within some states, regulatory agencies already are very overburdened by other commitments. Yet it is questionable whether the capacity issue is being taken seriously enough by legislators.

In Vermont, for example, legislators did not increase funding at all for the Department of Banking, Insurance, and Securities when charging it with licensing all mental health utilization review agents in the state and setting up an independent managed care board of appeals. Together with the political factors previously noted, insufficient agency capacity and lack of technical knowledge accounted for departmental delays in issuing necessary rules and procedures under the bill. In Rhode Island, legislation did specify that managed care organizations would pay a processing fee for certification of qualified health plans. Whether this means adequate administrative resources for the Department of Health, hard-pressed on other fronts, is uncertain nonetheless. Just one month before the managed care legislation was signed, the *Providence Journal-Bulletin* cast a spotlight on 175 uninvestigated nursing home complaints lodged with the department concerning possible neglect and verbal or physical abuse of patients (Tooher 1996). Acknowledging the backlog as a chronic problem, the department cited its lack of staff, and it proposed stepping down the intensity of inspection procedures as a coping measure. Once again, nearly one year later, while plans for implementing managed care regulations lagged, the department went public with its inability to maintain scheduled inspections of nursing homes, restaurants, schools, and day-care facilities (Gregg 1997). Reportedly, the situation continued into 1999, shortly before a second phase of managed care legislation in the state added to the department's regulatory responsibilities (Gregg 1999; Freyer 1999).

Thompson (1997) has identified agency capacity as one of the most important factors shaping successful health policy implementation. Such capacity depends on a combination of adequate resources, skilled leadership, and supportive institutional arrangements. In general, state bureaucracies have made advances in all these ways over recent decades with the devolution of programs from the national government under various "new federalism" initiatives. However, states vary enormously in their capacity for specific areas of responsibility such as health policy, and managed care has brought with it unique demands. Salaries and career paths in state government also continue to trail behind opportunities in the private sector, limiting the potential for recruiting personnel in new specialized fields (Fox 1999).

For effective monitoring of managed care regulation, officials will need continuous empirical feedback on compliance behavior, service delivery impacts, and organizational development of private health plans, all within a very complex health care environment. Yet comprehensive systems of data collection and regulatory evaluation have received little attention to date. One study of the states' oversight of managed care under Medicaid found that "doing Medicaid managed care 'right' may be beyond the managerial and political reach of more than a few states" and that most states neither collected reliable, good-quality data nor had the capacity to make use of such data administratively (Fossett et al. 1999, 56). How well the states manage such tasks in the long run remains to be seen, but, as Thompson (1997) points out, the low status of public administration within our society virtually ensures chronic difficulties with bureaucratic capacity-building.

Consumer Protections as Symbolic Politics

The realities of pressure-group politics combined with administrative overload accentuate the possibility of managed care regulation that proves more symbolic than real. Political scientists have long noted the mismatch between stated goals and actual results under many regulatory regimes. Legislative language that gives strong pledges of protecting the public interest and promoting values like fairness and quality is capable of attracting much positive publicity (Edelman 1964). Preambles to regulatory bills are ritually devoted to such themes. However, analysts have observed a marked discrepancy between the labeling and content of many managed care regulatory bills. Under the banner of "consumer protection" and "patients' rights," some new laws are quite narrowly focused on physician concerns (Kilborn 1998). Moreover, where consumers and providers are in direct conflict—for example, on the issue of patients' access to doctors' complaint records—consumers often lose out in the lawmaking process.

What matters most in regulatory policymaking is not abstract assurances and stirring mottos, but rather the operational powers established by a law combined with faithful execution. Experience from a variety of policy domains shows that the practice of regulation often does not live up to high-flying legislative rhetoric. Not only is there frequently a lapse in the delivery of promised public benefits, but "the deprived groups often display little tendency to protest or to assert their awareness of the deprivation" (Edelman 1964, 24–25). Significantly, consumer-oriented groups that have tried to carry out early tracking of the implementation of managed care laws have found uneven enforcement across states as well as a lack of consistency in the criteria used by different states for triggering regulatory penalties on health plans (Families USA Foundation 1996; Dallek, Jimenez, and Schwartz 1995). In general, level of effort is one of the most elusive dimensions of regulatory performance for regulators and other watchdog groups to capture in any systematic way. Under these circumstances, there is the danger that managed care regulation may simply be repeating the timeworn political pattern in which political decisionmakers, according to Stone, "give the material victory to the strong and the symbolic victory to the weak" (1999, 1215).

The Challenges of Consumer Empowerment

Information disclosure is one of the main regulatory methods being applied to managed care, reflecting both its appeal as a mildly coercive intervention and the belief that better information will improve the operation of health insurance as an economic market. However, for consumer choice genuinely to be strengthened, transforming it into an estimable force for quality improvement, regulators will have to amplify current legislative provisions. According to the Center for Health Care Rights, "States' HMO statutes and regulations generally provide little guidance on how much detail HMOs should provide enrollees on their benefit structure, benefit limits or how to obtain benefits" (Dallek, Jimenez, and Schwartz 1995, 127). More concrete requirements are now coming to the fore in some legislation, but the clarity of information provided as well as the means by which managed care plans disseminate information to consumers remain problematic.

Consumers are prone to focus on immediate tangible concerns like waiting times and freedom to choose a provider, even though a health plan's quality assurance mechanisms have more to do with the overall health care experience provided (Conniff 1996). Accordingly, consumers need to become much more familiar with the broad array of plan performance indicators that reflect on their interests. For this to happen, both regulators and health plans will have to develop innovative strategies in this area. In general, it is easy to underestimate the superiority of MCOs in regard to information access, including their ability to manipulate this advantage strategically in relation to different consumers and buyers of care (Frankford 1999).

As already described, legislative actions are being taken to broaden consumer participation in upper-level MCO governance. Consumer involvement is a potentially important internal monitoring tool and a natural supplement to the external regulatory efforts of public officials and private accrediting and rating groups. To be effective, however, it requires genuine organizational commitment. The most comprehensive study on this topic concluded that "although over half of the states provide for some enrollee participation in HMO policy, the laws in this area are so vague they may not result in a meaningful participatory role for enrollees" (Dallek, Jimenez, and Schwartz 1995, 146). Neither has consumer involvement so far received a great deal of attention from private groups like NCQA. It remains the case that government is the most reliable ally consumers have, and only government can institutionalize consumer participation as a public policy goal.

In general, the risks of purely symbolic regulatory action resulting from public inattentiveness make consumer empowerment crucial for the regulatory enterprise. Further, as explained by Rodwin (1996b), for available consumer protections such as grievance procedures to be used to best advantage, they must be backed up by a well-organized consumer presence. Regulatory support is one kind of leverage that consumers need to strengthen their position vis-à-vis the management of HMOs and other MCOs to achieve inclusion in plan decision-making and to guard against tokenism and showcasing (Steckler and Herzog 1979). However, consumers may also need to find ways to mobilize collectively and to create alliances with other groups, such as employee purchasing groups, in order to establish their role in the process of regulatory administration (Rodwin 1996b). Such consumer activism, coupled with expanded public controls, could provide for much greater oversight and consumer protection than ever existed under our previous system of fee-for-service medicine, but this supposition is still more theory than practice.

Specialty Care Issues

A major quandary in the regulation of managed care is how best to handle specialty care areas characterized by care-giving patterns, facilities, consumer concerns, and service cultures that are distinctive. How well will the general model of public oversight work for these sectors? Of primary interest in this regard is mental health care, which has been subject to some of the most intensive applications of managed care techniques leading to explosive controversy.

Exceptionalism is a familiar dilemma in mental health policymaking (Rochefort 1997). Proponents of managed mental health care regulation have been faced with a hard tactical choice over whether to seek their own specialized regulatory mechanisms or to subsume the mentally ill under one broad framework of health care protections. Both methods are seen in existing legislative enactments as well as pending proposals. At this stage, it is impossible to know a priori what will work best as standard policy. There may well be more than a single answer, depending on the precise regulatory issue or population group concerned. One area deserving careful monitoring by regulators will be appeals process alternatives and, in particular, how review boards dominated by health care generalists as opposed to mental health specialists make their decisions.

Approximately three-quarters of all privately and publicly insured Americans receive their mental health coverage through some type of "carve-out" arrangement in which a specialty organization either provides the services directly or conducts utilization review and patient management for the enrollee's general health plan (Findlay 1999). Between 1993 and 1999, these enrollment figures have doubled. The preeminent role of specialty entities in managed mental health care is likely to continue for the foreseeable future, especially as Medicaid changes and state mental health policy initiatives lead more seriously mentally ill into managed care. Carve-out competition is also expected to increase, as mental health and substance abuse providers organize specialty networks to vie for public and private contracts (Manderscheid and Henderson 1995). Thus, for an area like mental health, it is essential that the regulatory function pay particular heed to the process as well as the content of contract development.

The many organizational forms that specialty mental health contracting can take are just now coming to light and will proliferate further. Also, purchase of service often takes on a layered character, as a primary organization contracts to a secondary organization, which in turn contracts to a series of tertiary organizations, each specialists for particular users or forms of care. At each organizational intersection, it is contract terms that create incentives for performance and set the rules for reporting. Use of regulation to prohibit financial arrangements that flagrantly reward or induce providers to limit services merely scratches the surface of important risk-sharing issues and the operation of contracted networks. State departments will have to build specialized technical and legal contracting expertise among their staffs to delve into this topic, reinforcing an earlier point about capacity-building (Portz, Reidy, and Rochefort 1999). Emerging contract approaches will require documentation and their relationship tracked to service development, benefit flexibility, and treatment outcomes (Frank, McGuire, and Newhouse 1995).

Coordinating the Regulatory Effort

The movement for managed care legislation has struck pell-mell across the states, a reflection of national currents, indigenous political pressures, and state policy style all at once. Little effort has been made in the process to rationalize the overall regulatory environment in which managed care organizations operate.

At the same time, much legal ambiguity exists about the applicable scope of new regulatory authority. A chief issue, for example, concerns the Employee Retirement Income Security Act (ERISA), which preempts state laws regulating employee benefit plans when it comes to so-called self-insuring businesses. ERISA plans are exempt from state benefit mandates. Courts have been more divided as to whether any-willing-provider statutes apply under ERISA. Also unclear at present is the relevance of state third-party administrator laws for self-insuring plans. And several courts have decided that ERISA plans have no liability under state utilization laws (Brennan and Berwick 1996). When managed health care plans include self-insured enrollees as one part of their membership, as many of them do, it creates a morass for managers to assess when they must—and when they need not—abide by different regulatory standards (Bass 1996).

Parallel uncertainty surrounds the application of regulations when public and private managed care enrollees are being served by the same organizations. Federal regulations applying to Medicare and Medicaid populations may or may not be in force for privately insured enrollees of the same health plan. Even for specific categories of federally insured patients, such as those in waiver programs, required patient protections differ (U.S. GAO 1999). Depending on the nature of the statute, a comprehensive new federal enactment could go far toward standardizing this situation. However, substantial variation inevitably will occur in how the states implement such a law, and some states would still choose to exceed federal policy in their regulatory requirements. If new federal legislation acted to lift current ERISA restrictions on the states, this change could actually open the door to new kinds of regulatory variation around the country.

These observations point to a critical need for greater coordination of evolving regulatory actions in managed care. A number of useful steps to make the regulatory process more efficient while still being supportive of industry innovation have been outlined by Brennan and Berwick (1996). These authors call for regulation that is simultaneously responsive to the organizational needs of regulated health care plans and collaborative in its orientation without sacrificing the basic aim of protecting the public interest. Specific items they recommend include:

- Developing a common set of measurable objectives to which all regulatory authorities agree to give priority
- Reconceiving the regulatory strategy to make it more population-based, community-oriented, and focused on the relationships among different organizations rather than the independent operation of organizational fragments

- Eliminating unnecessary excess in the overlap, duplication, and contradictions among rules in place or under development by all public and private regulating parties
- Helping to promote positive innovations in care and quality improvement systems, with regulators fashioning a new role as "quality consultants"

CONCLUSION

In retrospect, the national debate over health care reform during the past decade remains a curious episode in U.S. public policymaking, no less for its aftermath than for the nature of that struggle itself. Many opponents of the kind of system overhaul put forward by the Clinton administration feared the widespread changes it would encourage, including a tremendous expansion of managed care. Yet the defeat of the Clinton proposal appears only to have accelerated the movement into managed care. Today, enrollment in one or another of its forms is fast approaching universality among the insured population. What government could not prescribe, the market has accomplished with rapidity and relative ease.

The price of this remarkable transformation has been a public and professional backlash unprecedented in U.S. health policymaking. Ironically, it is this backlash that has given government an important new role to play in supervising the operation of the private medical market. For the moment, that responsibility is being taken up principally on the state level with a confusing swirl of legislation and regulatory activity.

Unsurprisingly, the managed care regulatory movement is marked by great inconsistencies and gaps across the states. As noted, some states have adopted isolated protections; others, a broader regulatory package. The right to sue HMOs in state courts is still a rarity. And only a portion of a given state's managed care population—those not in "self-insured" plans—fully benefits from state regulation. Latest developments in the health care marketplace also challenge public regulators to expand the scope of their scrutiny over managed care. The financial upheaval that has led such highly respected managed care organizations as Harvard Pilgrim Health Care and Tufts Health Plan to retreat hastily from large areas of New England underscores that health plan quality and stability are hardly the same thing, and having one without the other is not very meaningful (Jones 1999; Brelis 1999). Thus, one can predict that the next wave of regulation by the states will involve greater financial oversight over managed care to complement the current focus on patient and provider safeguards.

Critics of public regulation have often denounced it as reactive, unfair, and ineffective, among other faults. These views were very influential in the movement away from earlier regulatory interventions in the health field, such as health system planning and certificate of need controls. The contemporary revival of regulatory policy instruments in health care is at once a momentous political crusade and an intriguing public policy experiment. As we have seen, there are many conceptual ambiguities to resolve and practical obstacles to be overcome with this approach. For better or worse, the dynamics of this process will be the focus of U.S. health care reform for years to come, its results setting the stage for continued incremental adjustment of the system or the next attempt at more fundamental repairs.

REFERENCES

Alger, D. 1996. *The Media and Politics.* 2d ed. Belmont, CA: Wadsworth.
Alvarez, L. 1998. "After Polling, G.O.P. Offers A Patients' Bill." *New York Times,* July 16.
Bass, A. 1996. "Health Insurers Allegedly Snub Law." *Boston Globe,* May 7.
Baumgartner, B., and B. Jones. 1993. *Agendas and Instability in American Politics.* Chicago: University of Chicago Press.
Blendon, R. J., M. Brodie, J. M. Benson, D. E. Altman, L. Levitt, T. Hoff, and L. Hugick. 1998. "Understanding the Managed Care Backlash." *Health Affairs* 17 (July/August): 80–94.
Brelis, M. 1999. "Tufts Health to Quit N.H., R.I., Maine." *Providence Journal-Bulletin,* November 23.
Brennan, T., and D. Berwick. 1996. *New Rules: Regulation, Markets, and the Quality of American Health Care.* San Francisco: Jossey-Bass.
Brodie, M., L. A. Brady, and D. E. Altman. 1998. "Media Coverage of Managed Care: Is There a Negative Bias?" *Health Affairs* 17 (January/February): 9–25.
Brown, L. 1983. *Politics and Health Care Organization: HMOs as Federal Policy.* Washington, DC: Brookings Institution.
Callahan, J., D. Shepard, R. Beinecke, M. Larson, and D. Cavanaugh, 1995. "Mental Health/Substance Abuse Treatment in Managed Care: The Massachusetts Medicaid Experience." *Health Affairs* 14 (Fall): 175–184.
Conniff, J. 1996. Presentation at panel on "State and Federal Regulation," 7th Annual Managed Care Law Conference, American Association of Health Plans, Washington, DC, April 24.
Cowley, G., and B. Turque. 1999. "Critical Condition." *Newsweek* (November 8): 58–61.
Dallek, G., C. Jimenez, and M. Schwartz. 1995. *Consumer Protections in State HMO Laws, Volume I: Analysis and Recommendations.* Los Angeles: Center for Health Care Rights.
Davis, K., K. S. Collins, C. Schoen, and M. Morris. 1995. "Choice Matters for Consumers." *Health Affairs* 14 (Summer): 100–112.
DeLeon, P., E. Bulatao, and G. VandenBos. 1994. "Federal Government Initiatives in Managed Health Care." In *Managed Behavioral Health Care: An Industry Perspective,* ed. S. A. Shueman, W. G. Troy, and S. L. Mayhugh, pp. 97–112. Springfield, IL: Charles C. Thomas.
Economist. 1998. "Health Care in America: Your Money or Your Life." (March 7): 23–26.

Edelman, M. 1964. *The Symbolic Uses of Politics.* Urbana: University of Illinois Press.

Enthoven, A. C., and S. J. Singer. 1998. "The Managed Care Backlash and the Task Force in California." *Health Affairs* 17 (July/August): 95–110.

Families USA Foundation. 1996. *HMO Consumers at Risk: States to the Rescue.* Washington, DC.

———. 1998. *Hit and Miss: State Managed Care Laws.* Washington, DC.

———. 1999. "State Managed Care Patient Protections." *http://www.familiesusa.org/hitmisup.htm* (October).

Findlay, S. 1999. "Managed Behavioral Health Care in 1999: An Industry at a Crossroads." *Health Affairs* 18 (September/October): 116–124.

Fossett, J. W., M. Goggin, J. S. Hall, J. Johnston, C. Plein, R. Roper, and C. Weissert. 1999. *Managing Accountability in Medicaid Managed Care: The Politics of Public Management.* Albany, NY: Nelson A. Rockefeller Institute of Government.

Fox, D. M. 1999. "Strengthening State Government through Managed Care Oversight." *Journal of Health Politics, Policy and Law* 24 (October): 1185–1190.

Frank, R., T. McGuire, and J. Newhouse. 1995. "Risk Contracts in Managed Mental Health Care." *Health Affairs* 14 (3): 50–64.

Frankford, D. M. 1999. "Regulating Managed Care: Pulling the Tails to Wag the Dogs." *Journal of Health Politics, Policy and Law* 24 (October): 1191–1200.

Freyer, F. J. 1998. "State Fines Health-Care Insurer for Consumer Violations." *Providence Journal-Bulletin,* June 13.

———. 1999. "RI in Lead on Rights of Patients." *Providence Journal-Bulletin,* August 2.

———. 2000. "Blue ChiP Pays $10,000 Fine for Back-Dating Correspondence." *Providence Journal-Bulletin,* April 15.

Gabel, J. 1997. "Ten Ways HMOs Have Changed During the 1990s." *Health Affairs* 16 (May/June): 134–145.

Gorman, C. 1998. "Playing the HMO Game." *Time* (July 13): 22–28.

Greenhouse, L. 2000. "H.M.O.'s Win Crucial Ruling on Liability for Doctors' Acts." *New York Times,* June 13.

Gregg, K. 1997. "State Health Department Mired in Backlogs." *Providence Journal-Bulletin,* March 13.

———. 1999. "Shortages Still Plague Department of Health." *Providence Journal-Bulletin,* February 23.

Gullo, K. 2000. "Kennedy May Offer Patients' Rights Bill." *Boston Globe,* June 7.

Health Care Financing Administration. 1999a. "Managed Care in Medicare and Medicaid." *http://www.hcfa.gov/facts/f980220.htm.*

———. 1999b. "National Summary of Medicaid Managed Care Programs and Enrollment." *http://www.hcfa.gov/medicaid/trends98.htm.*

Hsu, K. 1999. "Bill to Expand Mental Health Coverage Sparks Privacy Concerns." *Boston Globe,* October 30.

Huntington, S. P. 1981. *American Politics: The Promise of Disharmony.* Cambridge, MA: Harvard University Press.

Hyman, D. A. 1999. "Managed Care at the Millennium: Scenes from a Maul." *Journal of Health Politics, Policy and Law* 24 (October): 1061–1070.

Ignagni, K. 1998. "Covering a Breaking Revolution: The Media and Managed Care." *Health Affairs* 17 (January/February): 26–34.

Jacobs, L. R., and R. Y. Shapiro. 1999. "The American Public's Pragmatic Liberalism Meets Its Philosophical Conservatism." *Journal of Health Politics, Policy and Law* 24 (October): 1021–1032.

Jensen, G. A., M. A. Morrisey, S. Gaffney, and D. K. Liston. 1997. "The New Dominance of Managed Care: Insurance Trends in the 1990s." *Health Affairs* 16 (January/February): 125–136.

Jones, B. 1999. "Harvard Pilgrim Collapse: How Did It Happen?" *Providence Sunday Journal,* December 19.

Kaiser Family Foundation/Harvard University School of Public Health. 1999. *Update on Americans' Views on Consumer Protections in Managed Care.* Menlo Park, CA.

Kilborn, P. T. 1997. "In Managed Care, 'Consumer' Laws Benefit Doctors." *New York Times,* February 16.

———. 1998. "Reality of the H.M.O. System Doesn't Live Up to the Dream." *New York Times,* October 5.

Knox, R. A. 1999. "HMOs' Creator Urges Reform in Quality of Care." *Boston Globe,* May 2.

Langdon, S. 1997. "Critics Want More 'Management' of Managed Care Industry." *Congressional Quarterly,* (March 15): 633–640.

Light, D. W. 1997. "The Restructuring of the American Health Care System." In *Health Politics and Policy,* 3d ed., ed. T. J. Litman and L. S. Robins, pp. 46–63. Albany, NY: Delmar.

Manderscheid, R., and M. Henderson. 1995. *Federal and State Legislative Program Directions for Managed Care: Implications for Case Management.* Rockville, MD: Center for Mental Health Services.

Manning, A. 1997. "Singin' the Managed Health-Care Blues." *USA Today,* September 3.

Mechanic, D. 1996. "Changing Medical Organization and the Erosion of Trust." *Milbank Quarterly* 74 (2): 171–189.

———. 1997. "Managed Care as a Target of Distrust." *Journal of the American Medical Association* 277 (June 11): 1810–1811.

Meier, K. J. 1985. *Regulation: Politics, Bureaucracy, and Economics.* New York: St. Martin's Press.

Miller, R. H., and H. S. Luft. 1997. "Does Managed Care Lead to Better or Worse Quality of Care?" *Health Affairs* 16 (September/October): 7–25.

National Conference of State Legislatures. 1999. "New Report Shows States Making Strides to Protect Consumers in Managed Care Plans." *http://www.ncsl.org/programs/press/1999/MANGCARE.HTM* (July 26).

Pear, R. 1996. "U.S. Shelves Plan to Limit Rewards to H.M.O. Doctors." *New York Times,* July 8.

———. 1998. "States Take Lead in Health Legislation." *New York Times,* September 14.

———. 1999. "House Passes Bill to Expand Rights on Medical Care." *New York Times,* October 8.

———. 2000. "Ruling Sends Call for Action to Congress and the States." *New York Times,* June 13.

Peters, B. G. 1996. *American Public Policy: Promise and Performance.* 4th ed. Chatham, NJ: Chatham House.

Peterson, M. A. 1999. "Introduction: Politics, Misperception, or Apropos?" *Journal of Health Politics, Policy and Law* 24 (October): 873–886.

Portz, J. H., M. Reidy, and D. A. Rochefort. 1999. "How Managed Care Is Reinventing Medicaid and Other Public Health-Care Bureaucracies." *Public Administration Review* 59 (September/October): 400–409.

Providence Journal-Bulletin. 1998. "HMO Refuses to Treat Aneurysm," August 24.

Rochefort, D. A. 1986. *American Social Welfare Policy: Dynamics of Formulation and Change.* Boulder, CO: Westview.

————. 1996. *Regulating Managed Mental Health Care: A Policy Analysis and Discussion of the Role of Evaluation.* Cambridge, MA: Human Services Research Institute.

————. 1997. *From Poorhouses to Homelessness: Policy Analysis and Mental Health Care.* 2d ed. Westport, CT: Auburn House.

Rodwin, M. A. 1996a. "Consumer Protection and Managed Care: Issues, Reform Proposals, and Trade-Offs." *Houston Law Review* 32:1319–1381.

————. 1996b. "Consumer Protection and Managed Care: The Need for Organized Consumers." *Health Affairs* 15 (Fall): 110–123.

————. 1999. "Backlash as Prelude to Managing Managed Care." *Journal of Health Politics, Policy and Law* 24 (October): 1115–1126.

Rosenbaum, D. E. 1999. Not Quite Business as Usual in House on Managed Care." *New York Times.* November 4.

Rowland, D., and K. Hanson. 1996. "Medicaid: Moving to Managed Care." *Health Affairs* 15 (Fall): 150–152.

Rubin, H. R., B. Gandek, W. H. Rogers, M. Kosinski, C. A. McHorney, and J. E. Ware Jr. 1993. *Journal of the American Medical Association* 270 (August 18): 835–840.

Serafini, M. W. 1996. "Reigning in the HMOs." *National Journal* (October 26): 2280–2283.

Shem, S. 1997. *Mount Misery.* New York: Ballantine.

Sorian, R., and J. Feder. 1999. "Why We Need a Patients' Bill of Rights." *Journal of Health Politics, Policy and Law* 24 (October): 1137–1144.

Starr, P. 1982. *The Social Transformation of American Medicine.* New York: Basic Books.

————. 1994. *The Logic of Health Care Reform.* New York: Penguin Books.

Steckler, A. B., and W. T. Herzog. 1979. "How to Keep Your Mandated Citizen Board Out of Your Hair and Off Your Back: A Guide for Executive Directors." *American Journal of Public Health* 69 (August): 809–812.

Stone, D. 1999. "Managed Care and the Second Great Transformation." *Journal of Health Politics, Policy and Law* 24 (October): 1213–1218.

Swartz, K. 1999. "The Death of Managed Care As We Know It." *Journal of Health Politics, Policy and Law* 24 (October): 1201–1206.

Thompson, F. J. 1997. "The Evolving Challenge of Health Policy Implementation." In *Health Politics and Policy,* 3d ed., ed. T. J. Litman and L. S. Robins, pp. 155–175. Albany, NY: Delmar.

Tooher, N. 1996. "Nursing Home Complaints Overwhelm Health Department." *Providence Sunday Journal,* June 2.

Tumulty, K. 1998. "Let's Play Doctor." *Time* (July 13): 28–32.

U.S. General Accounting Office. 1999. *Medicaid Managed Care: Four States' Experiences with Mental Health Carve-Out Programs.* Pub. No. GAO/HEHS-99-118. Washington, DC.

Walsh, B. 1998. "HMO War to Hit Airwaves this Fall." *Seattle Times Picayune,* September 21.

Ware, J. E., M. S. Bayliss, W. H. Rogers, M. Kosinski, and A. R. Tarlov. 1996. "Differences in Four-Year Health Outcomes for Elderly and Poor, Chronically Ill Patients Treated in HMO and Fee-for-Service Systems: Results from the Medicaid Outcomes Study." *Journal of the American Medical Association* 276 (13): 1039–1047.

6

Launching SCHIP: The States and Children's Health Insurance

William P. Brandon, Rosemary V. Chaudry, and Alice Sardell

Amidst the ostensibly deficit-reducing provisions of the Balanced Budget Act of 1997 (P.L. 105-33) is a noteworthy expansion of government responsibility to provide health care for the poor. The State Child Health Insurance Program (SCHIP, or CHIP as it is more commonly abbreviated in state contexts*) is a new entitlement program, albeit a very peculiar entitlement that is formally limited to 10 years and caps federal expenditures.† SCHIP was codified as Title XXI of the Social Security Act. The Reforming States Group, which believes that CHIP is a "major step toward coverage of all children," has called its creation "the single largest

The authors gratefully acknowledge financial support for this research from the Metrolina Medical Foundation Research Fund (WPB), the City University of New York PSC-CUNY Research Award Program (AS), and the Robert Wood Johnson Foundation (AS). We would like to thank all of those interviewed for taking time from busy schedules to share their very valuable insights into the policy processes described here. We also appreciate the help of Dr. Reginald Obi on aspects of this research.
*The authors adopt this convention, using SCHIP when we are speaking of the federal program and CHIP for the generic state program. Because our case-study states give proper names to their separate programs, we also often use those names in the appropriate context.
†Rosenbaum et al. (1998) argue that it is states rather than individual children who are "entitled" (p. 77), although later (p. 82) they imply that Medicaid expansion may constitute an individual entitlement. It is reasonable to ask how there can be an entitlement if the federal funds earmarked to fulfill the promise are limited. The answer is provided by researchers at the Urban Institute (Ullman, Bruen, and Holahan 1998), who calculate that the federal funds allocated are sufficient to cover 5.8 million children. Their analyses of the Current Population Survey and other data demonstrate that only about 2.9 million uninsured children are eligible for CHIP. Thus, the real issue is whether the states can use all of their allocation (unless an extraordinary amount of crowding out of private insurance should expand the number of CHIP eligibles).

federal commitment to child health since the enactment of Medicaid" in 1965 (Johnson and McDonough 1998).

The passage of any government expansion by the 105th Congress, whose leaders pilloried entitlements and preached deficit reduction and tax-slashing, could hardly have been expected when that Congress convened. The previous Congress, the high tide of the Gingrich "Contract with America," had shut down the government in a budget battle that included efforts by the Republican-dominated Congress to transform Medicaid into a block grant and to initiate privatization of Medicare (Sardell and Johnson 1998; Brandon and Bradley 1997). Clinton's effort to provide universal access to health care had clearly failed by September 1994 (Marmor and Barer 1997). The last entitlement to become law, the ill-fated Medicare Catastrophic Coverage Act of 1988, was largely repealed before it was implemented. Significantly, the important sections in the Catastrophic Coverage Act that gave the federal government more responsibility were repealed; some provisions relating to Medicaid and state responsibilities were implemented (Thompson 1998; Brandon 1991, 344–347).

In the case of SCHIP, the legislation gives states extraordinary freedom in policy decisions that extends even to the choice of expanding Medicaid or starting an entirely new program for children in low-income families. This chapter, then, explores the states' responses to this federal legislation. It begins with a brief section enumerating the federal themes that set the context for state deliberations about the type of program to adopt. Another brief section presents information on the outcomes of the deliberations in the states and the District of Columbia about adopting CHIP programs. Then case studies of three states—New York, Ohio, and North Carolina—highlight the very different dynamics that occurred in each state. This chapter closes with a concluding discussion that uses Theodore Lowi's (1964, 1972) classification of policies—with emphasis on the redistributive type— to organize the results of the case-study material and to generate low-level hypotheses that guide the broader inquiry.

This collaboration had to focus on state adoption of CHIP programs, because the research and writing were completed before many states had even a year of experience with an operational program. Many of the most interesting and important political and policy issues in implementing federal programs at the state level arise in the decisions regarding policy adoption by the states (Miller and Byrne 1977; Beamer 1998, 1999). Where relevant, we do provide information about states' program implementation. Each of the authors conducted interviews with key informants in the case-study states and examined relevant documents and contemporaneous accounts of the decision-making process. National electronic databases developed by the Health Care Financing Administration (HCFA) and national interest groups as well as studies by other scholars provide information about developments outside of the case-study states. In addition, this chapter is enriched by an extensive study of the federal adoption of SCHIP that Alice Sardell is completing.

THE FEDERAL THEMES

The federal SCHIP legislation reflects both the political environment of the 105th Congress, referred to above, and the specific concerns of key policy actors involved in its creation. The policy process that produced SCHIP was filled with both interparty and intraparty conflict, and it is remarkable that, in spite of this conflict, significant legislation was produced. Conflict was negotiated and ultimately resolved because Democratic senator Edward Kennedy and his partner in policy entrepreneurship, Republican senator Orrin Hatch, pushed their carefully framed children's health insurance proposal to the center of policy consideration and then worked in alliance with a grassroots coalition to give it national attention. As framed by this coalition, legislators found the program "hard to refuse."

Three themes underlying the SCHIP legislative process are relevant here:

- Policy conflict about the extent of appropriate federal authority versus state autonomy in children's health policy
- The central role of state level actors in this federal level process
- The importance of ideology in framing the children's health legislation at the federal level

The first two themes will be explicated briefly in summarizing the legislative history of SCHIP and then related to significant provisions of the legislation. The third will be discussed as an important characteristic of the politics of legislative enactment.

During the 1980s, as children's issues became salient, a policy community concerned about children's health status raised the issue of financial barriers to access to health services and ultimately won major Medicaid expansions for low-income pregnant women and children (Sardell 1991). After the failure of President Clinton's Health Security Plan in 1994, congressional liberals and health activists viewed children's health insurance as the next incremental step that could be taken to increase health care access (Pear 1994). By 1997, the problem of an increasing number of uninsured children, partly caused by major structural changes in the economy, was widely discussed. At the beginning of the 105th Congress, the Senate Democratic minority leader announced that children's health insurance was number one on the Democrats' health policy agenda (Nather and Simendinger 1997). Momentum grew for action on children's health insurance.

Given the dominant ideology of policy devolution to the states, almost all of the legislative proposals introduced into Congress during the first four months of 1997 used mechanisms for establishing state-administered programs to enroll uninsured children in private health insurance. Favorite policies were tax credits, voucher plans, or block grants to the states (Johnson et al. 1997).

All but six states had taken some action to reduce the number of uninsured children in the years before congressional action on children's health insurance. The major efforts were either expansions of Medicaid eligibility beyond federally mandated levels or the establishment of state-funded children's insurance programs (Gauthier and Schrodel 1997). It was in the context of this evolution that Senator Kennedy, a liberal from Massachusetts, joined with Senator Hatch, a conservative representing Utah, in introducing a bill that provided federal grants to the states to help families purchase health insurance. Both men had long histories of activism on health and children's issues. States would contribute 40% of their share of Medicaid; the federal portion of the program's funding would be financed by a 43-cent increase in the tax on tobacco products (Johnson et al. 1997). The Kennedy/Hatch bill was developed after a long series of negotiations that included policy compromises by both sides (Republican and Democratic Senate staff interviews November 1998).

Senator John Chafee, a Rhode Island Republican, and Senator John D. Rockefeller IV, a Democrat from West Virginia, were concerned about preserving individual entitlements to health insurance. They therefore joined in introducing a bill into the Senate that provided an enhanced federal matching grant to states that expanded Medicaid coverage for certain groups of pregnant women and children. The competing Kennedy/Hatch and Chafee/Rockefeller proposals became the focus of debate in the Senate Finance Committee. The debate involved the extent of state autonomy in decisions about benefits and eligibility. Many governors were opposed to the Chafee/Rockefeller bill and pressured Republican members of the committee to vote against it. After much conflict in the Senate Finance Committee, a compromise was crafted that allowed states to choose whether to expand Medicaid, establish a new children's health program, or combine the two approaches (Democratic Senate staff interview February 1999).

The spending portion of the Balanced Budget Act of 1997 (BBA 1997) allocated almost $40 billion for grants to states for health assistance for children during the 10 years of program authorization. Eligible children are those in families with incomes below 200% of the federal poverty level, about $32,000 for a family of four in 1997, or 150% of a state's Medicaid eligibility level if this amount is higher. States must contribute toward program costs no matter which type of program is chosen. The required state match is 70% of the state's Medicaid contribution. States are prohibited from using provider taxes to finance their contribution to CHIP (Rosenbaum et al. 1998).

The legislation includes several maintenance of effort provisions strongly supported by members of the Senate Finance Committee who were concerned that states would use the new federal dollars to reduce their own contribution to providing health insurance coverage for children (Republican Senate staff interview February 1999). States cannot reduce their Medicaid eligibility levels below the cutoff existing on June 1, 1997, and cannot spend less than the 1996 expenditures for state-funded health programs for children (Families USA Foundation 1997). In addition, the legislation requires that states engage in outreach and enrollment for SCHIP-funded programs and that all children found to be Medicaid-eligible during this process be enrolled in Medicaid (Rosenbaum et al. 1998).

The demand for state autonomy continued as a theme throughout the SCHIP legislative process, particularly on the issue of the scope of benefits that would be required. Representatives of the National Governors' Association (NGA) argued the case for "flexibility" in state actions.* The key role played by the NGA, part of the "intergovernmental lobby" (Beer 1976), in the process of crafting SCHIP was due to the access it enjoyed to the Republican Party leadership, which controlled a Congress that was committed to devolution in social policy. In this respect, the SCHIP policy process continued the NGA's opposition to federal Medicaid mandates, which had been the driving force behind the 1995–1996 effort to make Medicaid a block grant (Sardell and Johnson 1998).

The Senate bill, then, was the result of policy compromise, but the House enacted a bill based on NGA policy. It was drafted by the House Commerce Committee staff, which worked closely with the staff of the NGA (former NGA staff interview November 1998). The House bill required only basic services (i.e., inpatient hospitalization, well-baby care, x-ray services) in its benefit package, but it also exempted group plans from these requirements if the children in a state's CHIP program received the same benefits as other children covered by the plan (Rosenbaum et al. 1998). (This provision allows managed care plans to cover CHIP children for the same benefits that they provide to commercial or other enrolled groups, if the state agrees.) Governors were very active during the deliberations of the House-Senate Conference Committee (Nather 1997a); not surprisingly, the benefits required by the SCHIP legislation give states greater "flexibility" than they had in the Senate bill (Nather 1997b). Benefits under a separate state program must be the same as one of several "benchmark plans" (the Blue Cross/Blue Shield PPO option under the Federal Employees Health Benefits Plan, the main state employee plan, or the HMO having the largest share of commercially insured people in the state) or the "actuarial equivalent of these packages, including certain basic services" (K. Johnson 1998).

In the antientitlement climate of the 105th Congress, adding another group of children to a government program was problematic. The strategy to make additional government coverage acceptable involved presenting the program as advancing a set of traditional American values, which was accomplished in at least two ways. First, the group of children given the opportunity to have health insurance coverage was "constructed" (Schneider and Ingram 1993) as a "worthy"

---

*State governors have been organized as a group since 1908. The NGA has had a Washington, D.C., office since the late 1960s, which serves as its base for promoting the interests of the states in the federal policy process (Cigler 1995, 135).

group. The sponsors and supporters of the Kennedy/Hatch bill framed the proposal as a benefit for working families and clearly distinguished it from a "welfare benefit." A press release from the office of Representative Nancy Johnson, one of the sponsors of a House bill similar to the Kennedy/Hatch bill, nicely illustrates this positioning: "We are moving forward in our fight to improve the health of our children. . . . There are millions of families with uninsured children who are working hard, paying taxes and playing by the rules. They need and deserve our help" (N. Johnson 1997).

Second, the Children's Defense Fund was able to build a coalition to support the Kennedy/Hatch bill based on antismoking sentiments, because the program was to be partially financed by a tax on tobacco products. The coalition, which included antitobacco groups such as the American Cancer Society, emphasized the message that cigarette companies that advertised to young people were evil and that health care for children was good. The ads sponsored by the coalition featured a picture of a young boy and the icon of "Joe Camel" with the words underneath, "Joey vs. Joe Camel." Legislators not initially supportive of the legislation felt that this very effective public relations campaign made it politically impossible to continue in opposition (Republican Senate staff interview February 1999).

In the end, perhaps, the most striking characteristic of the new federal legislation was the success of those who wished to ensure that great flexibility could be exercised at the state level in designing and implementing legislation establishing CHIP in each jurisdiction. Heretofore, HCFA's regulatory structure had ensured that considerable national uniformity was maintained despite the formal role of the states in most of the health programs for low-income Americans. We now will examine first broadly and then narrowly—in three case studies—how the states used their new autonomy.

OVERVIEW OF STATE RESPONSES

According to testimony by Nancy-Ann Min DeParle, HCFA administrator, before the Senate Finance Committee at the end of April 1999, 52 CHIP programs have received federal approval. At that time, 26 states or territories chose to expand Medicaid; 14 established or expanded a CHIP program that is separate from Medicaid; and 12 adopted a combined approach (DeParle 1999). By early May 2000, HCFA reported receiving 27 amendments to expand and change states' original programs; 12 such requests remained under review (see Table 6.1).

For each state and the District of Columbia, Table 6.1 gives the type of program (Medicaid expansion, separate program, or a combined program), date of implementation of the original program, number of amendments to CHIP that each state has submitted and the status of the most recent state amendment to its program (through May 25, 2000), proportion of Medicaid expenditures paid by the federal

Table 6.1 CHIP and Medical Program Characteristics by State, 1999

State	Type Program[a]	Date Original Program Implemented[a]	Plan Amendment Status[b]	Medicaid Rate FY 1999 (%)[c]	Enhanced CHIP FY 1999 (%)[c]	CHIP Eligibility Ceiling (% of FPL)[a,d]
Alabama	Combined	2/1/98	2nd approved 9/28/99	69.27	78.49	200
Alaska	Medicaid	3/1/99		59.8	71.86	200
Arizona	Separate	11/1/98	3rd approved 12/1/99	65.5	75.85	200
Arkansas	Medicaid	10/1/98	1st submitted 12/4/98	72.96	81.07	100
California	Combined	3/1/98	5th submitted 4/17/00	51.55	66.09	250
Colorado	Separate	4/22/98	1st approved 9/21/99	50.59	65.42	185
Connecticut	Combined	7/1/98	1st submitted 1/27/00	50	65	300
Delaware	Separate	2/1/99	1st approved 11/23/99	50	65	200
DC	Medicaid	10/1/98		70	79	200
Florida	Combined	4/1/98	3rd approved 3/21/00	55.82	69.07	200
Georgia	Separate	11/1/98	1st approved 4/20/00	60.47	72.33	200
Hawaii	Medicaid	7/1/00	1st submitted 1/11/00	50	65	185
Idaho	Medicaid	10/1/97	2nd submitted 3/14/00	69.85	78.89	150
Illinois	Medicaid	1/5/98	1st approved 3/30/00	50	65	133
Indiana	Combined	10/1/97	1st approved 12/22/99	61.01	72.71	200
Iowa	Combined	7/1/98	3rd submitted 3/16/00	63.32	74.32	185
Kansas	Separate	1/1/99	1st approved 4/20/00	60.05	72.03	200
Kentucky	Combined	7/1/98	1st approved 9/3/99	70.53	79.37	200
Louisana	Medicaid	11/1/98	1st approved 8/27/99	70.37	79.26	150
Maine	Combined	7/1/98	1st submitted 1/5/00	66.4	76.48	185
Maryland	Medicaid	7/1/98		50	65	200
Massachusetts	Combined	10/1/97		50	65	200
Michigan	Combined	5/1/98	1st approved 6/26/98	52.72	66.91	200
Minnesota	Medicaid	10/1/98		51.5	66.05	280
Mississippi	Combined	7/1/98	2nd approved 12/17/99	76.78	83.75	200
Missouri	Medicaid	9/1/98	1st approved 9/11/98	60.24	72.17	300
Montana	Separate	1/1/99	1st submitted 12/27/99	71.73	80.21	150
Nebraska	Medicaid	5/1/98	1st approved 10/13/98	61.46	73.02	185
Nevada	Separate	10/1/98	1st submitted 5/3/00	50	65	200
New Hampshire	Combined	5/1/98	1st approved 3/25/99	50	65	300
New Jersey	Combined	3/1/98	4th approved 3/16/00	50	65	350
New Mexico	Medicaid	3/31/99	1st disapproved 7/8/99	72.98	81.09	235
New York	Combined	4/15/98	2nd approved 12/24/99	50	65	192
North Carolina	Separate	10/1/98	3rd approved 9/30/99	63.07	74.15	200
North Dakota	Combined	10/1/98	1st approved 11/12/99	69.94	78.96	140
Ohio	Medicaid	1/1/98	1st submitted 4/11/00	58.26	70.78	150
Oklahoma	Medicaid	12/1/97	1st approved 3/25/99	70.84	79.59	185
Oregon	Separate	7/1/98	1st submitted 8/16/99	60.55	72.38	170
Pennsylvania	Separate	5/28/98	3rd approved 3/7/00	53.77	67.64	200
Rhode Island	Medicaid	10/1/97	2nd submitted 11/29/99	54.04	67.83	300
South Carolina	Medicaid	10/1/97		69.85	78.89	150
South Dakota	Medicaid	7/1/98	1st approved 10/29/99	68.16	77.71	140
Tennessee	Medicaid	10/1/97		63.09	74.16	100
Texas	Combined	7/1/98	1st approved 11/8/99	62.45	73.72	200
Utah	Separate	8/3/98	1st disapproved 11/29/99	71.78	80.25	200
Vermont	Separate	10/1/98	2nd approved 2/28/00	61.97	73.38	300
Virginia	Separate	10/22/98		51.6	66.12	185
Washington	Separate	2/1/00		52.5	66.75	250
West Virginia	Combined	7/1/98	1st approved 3/19/99	74.47	82.13	150
Wisconsin	Medicaid	4/1/99	1st approved 1/22/99	58.85	71.2	185
Wyoming	Separate	12/1/99		64.08	74.86	133

[a]Type program, date implemented, and CHIP eligibility ceiling from HCFA web site (www.hcfa.gov/init/enroll99.pdf), 5/25/00.
[b]Plan amendment status from HCFA web site (www.hcfa.gov/init/statepln.htm), 5/25/00.
[c]Medicaid rate and enhanced rate from Families USA web site (www.familiesusa.org/allocst.htm), 5/25/00.
[d]CHIP eligibility ceiling defined as % of federal poverty level (FPL). In 1998, FPL was $16,450 for a family of four.

government, proportion of CHIP expenditures paid by the federal government, and the CHIP eligibility ceiling as a percent of the federal poverty level (FPL).

Table 6.1 shows that New York and Ohio were quick off the mark, implementing their largely uncontentious programs by the end of March 1998, less than a year after the BBA 1997 was approved. North Carolina, which became mired in legislative gridlock, was not able to submit its application until the legislature could agree on compromise legislation. Therefore, its separate CHIP was not implemented before October of that same year.

Beamer (1999) points out that states like Texas that use CHIP to raise Medicaid to 100% of the poverty level are only accelerating their compliance with a federal mandate that must be met by 2002 in any event. How states make such decisions can only be learned by examining the debates in particular states (Miller and Byrne 1977). Thus, the next section examines in detail the policy-making process in three states that were chosen to represent the different types of CHIP programs.

For some states, information on estimated enrollment is difficult to determine, because it includes both Medicaid and CHIP enrollment numbers for those states with combined programs. Table 6.2 presents states' estimated enrollment for the fiscal year by September 2000. It also contains estimates of projections for the year 2000 of the numbers of U.S. children through age 18 who are uninsured, Medicaid-eligible, and CHIP-eligible.

The larger question is what difference SCHIP will make. The Center for Studying Health System Change tracks change in health insurance coverage by surveying large representative samples of U.S. families. It reported that overall coverage of children in families with incomes below 200% of FPL did not change between 1996–1997 and 1998–1999, but that state-sponsored health insurance (including CHIP) had increased and employer-sponsored insurance had decreased by 1998–1999 (Cunningham and Park 2000). Most of the changes occurred in families with incomes from 100% to 199% of FPL, the intended beneficiaries of SCHIP. Although this finding is consonant with "crowding out," no causal connection could be established. Moreover, the second survey was conducted before the full impact of CHIP implementation in most states could be achieved.

The authors chose to study New York, Ohio, and North Carolina both because they each represent a different type of CHIP program and because the authors had access to the health policy networks in these three states. New York's program is one of three preexisting programs that provided a model for the federal legislation. Ohio repackaged a simple Medicaid expansion to produce its first CHIP legislation, thereby earning 12.5% higher federal reimbursement for actions that it would have taken without CHIP. North Carolina chose to establish a separate program administered by the agency that runs the state employees' health plan. Thus, Ohio is one of the states that chose to expand Medicaid, North Carolina created a separate program, and New York, whose existing program was grandfathered in by the federal legislation, did both.

Table 6.2 Uninsured and Medicaid-Eligible Youth and Projected Enrollment by State, 1999

State	Uninsured[a]	Medicaid-Eligible[a]	CHIP-Eligible[a]	Estimated Enrollment by Sept. 2000[b]
Alabama	200,200	77,428	50,166*	36,000
Alaska	15,336	9,236	NA	5,000
Arizona	355,570	186,971	107,408	50,000
Arkansas	133,468	101,946	NA	3,600
California	2,026,688	1,019,228	673,431	500,000
Colorado	130,976	55,368*	17,541*	23,000
Connecticut	96,014	62,017*	24,640*	15,000
Delaware	35,413	17,789	8,440*	10,500
DC	19,593	17,121	NA	8,400
Florida	675,593	326,566	116,701	175,000
Georgia	417,722	241,487	27,202*	58,000
Hawaii	31,230	4,377*	NA	<1,000
Idaho	62,692	37,441	NA	5,000
Illinois	448,984	216,120	64,975	40,000
Indiana	218,499	114,294	20,959*	58,000
Iowa	53,648	39,869*	1,892*	55,000
Kansas	57,090	17,195*	14,975*	30,000
Kentucky	125,542	90,491	7,721*	50,000
Louisana	215,994	129,321	NA	39,000
Maine	33,429	17,912*	2,242*	10,400
Maryland	223,184	145,241	NA	15,500
Massachusetts	123,298	48,855	15,503*	37,000
Michigan	262,236	131,118	47,641	133,000
Minnesota	124,205	90,246	NA	<1,000
Mississippi	165,522	100,256	45,085	45,000
Missouri	109,726	80,753*	NA	90,000
Montana	43,727	16,847	1,404*	9,000
Nebraska	20,032*	15,420*	NA	17,000
Nevada	105,227	47,871	13,410	44,000
New Hampshire	32,743	19,551*	3,557*	4,000
New Jersey	271,833	114,765	98,438	102,000
New Mexico	82,148	63,037	NA	5,000
New York	681,064	354,345	145,025	360,000
North Carolina	285,435	156,663	59,185	35,000
North Dakota	20,754	12,154	3,012*	<1,000
Ohio	252,673	133,430	NA	133,000
Oklahoma	150,447	74,819	NA	71,000
Oregon	103,077	48,023*	24,190*	17,000
Pennsylvania	272,948	118,469	77,719	109,000
Rhode Island	17,946*	15,324*	NA	4,000
South Carolina	138,173	97,010	NA	75,000
South Dakota	25,385	8,230*	NA	7,400
Tennessee	150,293	141,510	NA	10,000
Texas	1,506,475	734,129	407,938	58,000
Utah	86,691	40,354	17,615*	21,000
Vermont	11,266*	6,898*	0*	1,000
Virginia	226,815	94,128	55,498*	54,000
Washington	148,283	64,248*	18,258*	3,700
West Virginia	45,397	27,796*	3,763*	11,000
Wisconsin	113,809	43,138*	NA	18,000
Wyoming	25,092	11,243	1,155*	<1,000

*Standard error is greater than 20% of estimate; interpret with caution.

NA = Not applicable, since state had a combined program at the time the table was compiled.

[a]Number uninsured, Medicaid-eligible, and CHIP-eligible from American Academy of Pediatrics web site (www.aap.org/advocacy/usEligibility2KGraph.pdf), 5/25/00.

[b]Total estimated enrollment reflects all approved plans and amendments. Numbers based on states' unrevised estimates of enrollment by September 2000 and estimated enrollment from HCFA web site (www.hcfa.gov/init/chstatus.htm), 9/16/99.

Key actors in the policy processes resulting in each state's decisions about how to respond to federal SCHIP were identified through a review of archival materials and by preliminary interviews. Each author then conducted qualitative, in-depth interviews about these policy processes, adding interviews with additional policy actors in each state via a snowball sampling strategy.

In all three cases, interest groups, particularly children's advocates, managed care plans, and the insurance industry, were important policy actors, although the extent of their influence varied across the states. In each case, governors (two of them Republicans) positioned themselves as champions of children and framed their CHIP programs as the SCHIP legislation had been framed at the federal level: as state subsidies to hardworking, tax-paying families. All three states responded to federal mandates on Medicaid and CHIP enrollments by designing new enrollment strategies. Differences in the political cultures of these states do appear to have been linked to the differences in their pre-SCHIP arrangements for children's health coverage and the nature of their policy debates—including the degree of compromise and negotiation—on their CHIP programs. These topics will be discussed in detail below.

CASE STUDIES: NEW YORK, OHIO, AND NORTH CAROLINA

New York: Child Health Plus—A Grandfathered Plan

New York State has had a state-funded children's health insurance program, Child Health Plus (CHP), since 1991. Initiated by a Democratic governor in response to policy entrepreneurship by a coalition of children's advocates and pediatricians, the program was embraced and expanded by a Republican governor. It was, in fact, a model for the federal SCHIP legislation. When the federal SCHIP was created in 1997, New York had an ongoing program with 135,000 children enrolled, an administrative and provider infrastructure, and, significantly, a political infrastructure. The political infrastructure was a policy community that had worked together over a number of years to fashion a program that now enjoys broad bipartisan support from elected officials.

The large infusion of federal SCHIP money ($257 million per year for the first three years) along with certain federal requirements have moved New York on a path to large-scale community-based outreach and enrollment efforts for children's health insurance programs and toward the integration of the Medicaid and CHP programs. This is a political irony, because one of the reasons for CHP's widespread political support was that it was viewed as having characteristics that were very different from those of the Medicaid program. The two major themes that emerge from this New York State case are the importance of the framing of the issue and the construction of the program in a way that attracted broad bipartisan support during its history; and the challenges that faced the state in implementing a new system of outreach and enrollment for CHP and Medicaid, programs that in New York have become more similar to each other.

New York's policy system. New York is a large and very diverse state. Its economic, social, and ethnic heterogeneity result in diverse policy interests. Constitutionally, it has a comparatively strong governor and historically New York's governors have exercised their considerable powers (Benjamin and Lawton 2001). However, over the last 40 years, the legislature has become professionalized and has become an independent policy actor. Today, state policy is made via negotiations between the governor and the two houses of the legislature, the Senate and the Assembly.

The legislature is divided by party. For the past 25 years, the Assembly has had a Democratic majority and the Senate, a Republican majority. Strong party leadership in each house is maintained by building consensus around the diverse interests and policy concerns of the party's members (Petersen and Stonecash 2001). There are broad ideological differences between Republican and Democratic parties on the role of government in society, in their attitudes toward business and toward social programs funded by government (Brewer and Stonecash 2001). Policymaking in New York involves these differences, but also the differences in the perceived interests of urban, suburban, and rural voters. The result is often policy conflict. One of the interesting characteristics of the politics of the CHP program has been the generally consensual nature of the issue as compared to many other issues at the state level.

Another aspect of the general policy context is New York's historical liberalism. While the parties differ ideologically, their differences operate within a general landscape in which government activity for the purpose of improving the lives of New York's residents, particularly the economically disadvantaged, is legitimate. New York's initial Medicaid eligibility provisions were extremely generous; the state's all-payer hospital reimbursement system established in the early 1980s gave the state a major regulatory role in health care financing (Hackey 1998).

Children's health insurance on the policy agenda. At the end of the 1980s, policymakers in the state health department and Democratic legislators were discussing proposals for a universal state health insurance program (Hackey 1998, 69). Within this policy context, Statewide Youth Advocacy, a children's advocacy group founded in 1976, and the New York State chapter of the American Academy of Pediatrics initiated the Campaign for Healthy Children and suggested to policymakers in the governor's office and the legislature that children's health insurance would be a politically viable first step (Campaign for Healthy Children cochair interview September 1999). In his 1990 State of the State Address at the beginning of a gubernatorial election year, Democratic governor Mario Cuomo proposed a children's health insurance program. At the end of that legislative session the New York State legislature enacted such a program for children not eligible for Medicaid.

The program. Child Health Plus was enacted as part of New York's hospital reimbursement legislation and financed by hospital and insurance company surcharges that were paid into the state's bad debt and charity care pool* (Sardell 1994). In subsequent years, CHP continued to be financed from the bad debt and charity care pool, even after the system of state-set inpatient hospital rates was changed by the New York State Health Care Reform Act of 1996 to a market-driven system in which hospital reimbursement rates were negotiated by the players (Bureau of National Affairs 1996b).

The original program subsidized health insurance for children up to age 13 in families with net incomes up to 185% of FPL. Families whose net incomes were between 133% and 185% of FPL paid annual premiums of $25 per child up to $100; families with higher incomes could buy into the program for about $500 per year per child. The benefits provided to children enrolled were primary care, laboratory tests, and all kinds of outpatient treatment, including outpatient surgery and kidney dialysis. It did not include inpatient care. The only mental health services covered were drug and alcohol abuse counseling. The program was administered by insurance companies and managed care plans under a contract with the state; Citizen Action, an advocacy group, was awarded a contract for outreach and enrollment activities. Twenty million dollars annually for three years was allocated for the program; the health department estimated that this sum would cover premiums for 35,000 of the 168,000 children believed to be eligible.

The exclusion of adolescents from the CHP program in its early years was related to the politics of reproductive health issues, or the "politics of morality" (Morone 1996). The state's Catholic Conference had expressed concern that the program might be used to fund abortions. Between 1991 and a major expansion in 1996, the age for program eligibility was incrementally increased as children already in the program reached age 13 and additional funding was added by the legislature (N.Y. Health Department official and N.Y. Assembly staff interviews September 1999).

New York was the first state to establish a state-only funded children's health insurance program. However, unlike 26 other states, it did not raise Medicaid eligibility for pregnant women and children beyond the levels mandated by the federal government prior to the enactment of federal SCHIP (Gauthier and Schrodel 1997). A major reason for this unwillingness to expand Medicaid was that local governments in New York paid one-half of the state's share of Medicaid spending (Johnson and McDonough 1998). New York's local governments paid a much

---

*One of the original arguments for using this source of funds was that providing primary care to uninsured children would result in a reduction in hospitalizations (Johnson and McDonough 1998, 27).

higher percentage of the nonfederal cost of Medicaid than did the local governments in the handful of other states that required local cost-sharing (National
Association of Counties 1999).

Bipartisan support. During CHP's first few years, the Republican Senate was less
supportive than the Democratic Assembly, but by 1993 or 1994 there was bipartisan "ownership" of Child Health Plus. In 1995, when George A. Pataki became
governor, he and his health commissioner, Dr. Barbara De Buono, embraced the
program (Campaign for Healthy Children cochair and managed care association
official interviews September 1999).

The New York State Health Care Reform Act of 1996 allocated $109 million
for CHP in 1997, $150 million in 1998, and $207 million in 1999 (Bruno 1998).
The number of children covered was expected to increase from 104,000 to 250,000
(Bureau of National Affairs 1996a). Eligibility for the program was expanded in
terms of both age and family income; benefits were also increased. Children
through age 18 living in families with incomes up to 220% of FPL ($34,632 for a
family of four) became eligible for state subsidies; children in families up to 120%
of FPL were fully subsidized (*Albany Times Union* 1997). The benefit package
was improved by adding hospital inpatient services. Children's advocates and the
Assembly and Senate wanted to include dental and vision benefits but lost these
benefits in negotiations with the governor (*Albany Times Union* 1996).

The bipartisan popularity of the CHP program has been based on several factors. First, of course, is the perception, which polling data support, that the public
likes programs for children. And policy for children is often framed in terms that
resonate with deeply held cultural values (Sardell 1991). In New York, as nationally, CHP's beneficiaries were children of "working parents," beneficiaries who
were imagined to be different from the beneficiaries of other public programs. In
speaking of a Republican from a "very conservative district," one children's advocate noted that this state senator was supportive of the CHP program because it
was "always seen as a working families' benefit, not a welfare benefit."

Second, the policy entrepreneurs who initiated Child Health Plus engaged in
coalition-building very early in the process, bringing together a wide range of
interested parties in designing the original program. Representatives of both the
New York State Business Council and managed care plans attended the first meetings with state officials along with children's advocates and pediatricians. "We
knew that if we didn't have the private sector with us, it wouldn't work" (Campaign for Healthy Children cochair interview September 1999).

The CHP structure is constituted so that it can be supported by policymakers
who believe that health care services are best managed through market arrangements. It is a program in which the state contracts with private managed care plans
to enroll patients and deliver services. Thus, it is a partnership of the public and
the private sectors that Republican governor Pataki can philosophically support

(governor's staff interview October 1999). "CHP has never been seen as a government entitlement, but rather as a commercially sold health insurance" (managed care association official interview September 1999).

In addition, Child Health Plus had historically paid much higher rates to providers than did Medicaid. It was initially a much smaller program than Medicaid and paid higher premiums in order to give health plans an incentive to participate in the program (N.Y. Health Department official interview September 1999). Its rates were set as an insurance product by a bureau of the Department of Health working with the Department of Insurance in a different process than that used to set Medicaid rates (managed care association official interview September 1999).

Finally, the financing of CHP from the bad debt and charity care pool is indirect and therefore *appears* not to come from taxpayer dollars. Elected officials concerned about the cost of government programs can say to their constituents, "Here's a great program for kids and it's not costing you anything" (managed care association official interview September 1999).

Several of the key actors in the CHP policy community described the program as now "institutionalized" in New York State politics, a program that "everyone wants to take credit for." In fact, CHP is such a popular program that members of the policy community and other elected officials have an unspoken agreement not to raise issues that would threaten the consensus that surrounds it. Two of the areas of potential conflict are reproductive health issues and issues related to the enrollment of certain categories of immigrants in the program.

New York's response to SCHIP. Child Health Plus was one of the models for the federal SCHIP legislation. Both New York's commissioner of health and the deputy commissioner overseeing the CHP program testified at Senate Finance Committee hearings on children's health insurance in 1997. The CHP benefits package along with those of Pennsylvania and Florida were grandfathered in by BBA 1997, but these states were required to maintain the level of state program funding that existed in 1996 (Bureau of National Affairs 1997a). Children's advocates in New York State had lobbied federal policymakers to include such a state maintenance-of-effort provision in the federal legislation (Campaign for Healthy Children cochair interview September 1999).

A major state expansion of CHP had occurred in 1996, a year before the federal enactment of SCHIP. In that year, the state had allocated far more money to the program than would be required as a state match for the federal funds in 1998 (N.Y. Health Department official interview September 1999). The federal legislation and money presented state policymakers with an opportunity to expand CHP still further. In the view of children's advocates, however, SCHIP was more significant as an opportunity to expand Medicaid eligibility. Federal SCHIP also required some policy changes in New York: the major mandate was to screen all potential CHP applicants for Medicaid eligibility and enroll the child in Medicaid if eligible.

Improved eligibility and benefits. The Pataki administration initially responded to federal SCHIP legislation with a plan to eliminate copayments for those in families with incomes up to 160% of FPL (which was required by BBA 1997) and to reduce copayments paid by those with incomes between 160% and 222% of FPL. In his State of the State Address in January 1998 (ten months before he was to stand for reelection), Governor Pataki said that he would sponsor an expansion of Child Health Plus that "would guarantee access to comprehensive health coverage 'for every single child of New York through the age of 18'" (Ayres 1998). Responding to children's advocates and other critics who called for an expanded program, in February he proposed a more generous plan for both CHP and Medicaid expansion. He wished to add dental, eye, and hearing services, inpatient mental health services, substance abuse treatment, and medical equipment to the CHP benefits package (Perez-Pena 1998) and expand Medicaid eligibility to include adolescents between the ages of 15 and 18 in families with incomes below the poverty level (which would accelerate a federally mandated phase-in of these children). Moreover, he proposed to guarantee Medicaid coverage to all eligible children for one year (Bureau of National Affairs 1998b), a feature that greatly facilitates coverage by capitated managed care.

In May 1998 the Democratic Assembly passed legislation that expanded the CHP benefit package, raised eligibility for CHP to families with incomes up to 300% of FPL, expanded Medicaid eligibility for all children through age 18 in families with incomes below 185% of FPL, and combined the administrative structures of CHP and Medicaid (Bureau of National Affairs 1998a).

As discussed earlier, legislative agreements in New York are negotiated by the governor and the Senate and Assembly leadership. In the policy debate over how New York would use the new federal funding, the Assembly generally agreed with the positions of the advocacy community, while the Republican-dominated Senate generally supported the positions taken by the governor. The most contentious issue was the advocates' proposal to expand Medicaid eligibility, an issue of great importance to the advocates, although it was not initially on the governor's agenda. The Child Health Now! Coalition proposed that new federal money be used to pay for the local government (county) share of a Medicaid expansion, a proposal that was ultimately accepted and led to agreement on the expansion of Medicaid eligibility (children's advocate interview November 1999).

The agreement made by the governor and the Senate and Assembly leadership on the final day of the 1998 legislative session expanded both Child Health Plus and Medicaid eligibility and improved CHP benefits. It did not formally create a single program for children, but it made the two health programs for children more similar to one another. Premiums paid by some families to participate in CHP were reduced, and several administrative changes were made in Medicaid eligibility. It mandated a new process for enrollment of children in both Medicaid and CHP.

Eligibility for the CHP program (as of January 1, 1999) was expanded to include children in families whose gross income was up to 230% of FPL. On July 1,

2000, this ceiling was raised to 250% of FPL, or $41,059 for a family of four. No premiums are required for children in families with gross incomes below 160% of FPL, or $25,620 for a family of four. The law reduced monthly premiums and eliminated all copayments.

Enrollment. One of the most important policy issues and implementation problems in relation to children's health services has been enrollment in both the Medicaid and separate state children's health insurance programs. There has been much policy discussion about this issue at both federal and state levels. New York, with its relatively long experience with a child health insurance program, a strong advocacy community committed to an effective outreach effort, and one of the largest and most diverse foreign-born populations in the country, is an important place to examine the issues and activities related to program enrollment.

Enrollment in Child Health Plus has always been substantially lower than policymakers' projections of the number of children who should be enrolled. An evaluation of the early years of CHP found that in 1993 only 37% of eligible children statewide were enrolled. Enrollment varied by region: only 29% of eligible children in New York City were enrolled, whereas 50% of eligible kids in the rest of the state had signed up. African-American and Hispanic kids and children in the lowest income group were slightly underrepresented in the enrolled population. The evaluators suggested that enrollment could be improved by developing strategies to better reach special populations (University of Rochester 1996).

CHP enrollment has always been done by the health insurance plans operating in the area where the applicant lived. Two organizations ran information hot lines about the program. Citizen Action and, beginning in 1997, the New York Health Plan Association, which represented managed care plans, referred callers to insurance plans for actual enrollment. Each plan had its own application form, which the family could mail back to the insurance company. Some Medicaid-eligible children were enrolled in Child Health Plus, but before SCHIP, state policy did not require that these children be dropped from CHP (N.Y. Health Department official interview September 1999).

In contrast, Medicaid enrollment in New York State was done by Department of Social Services (DSS) case workers and required a face-to-face interview in a DSS office. Money was never allocated for outreach to encourage Medicaid enrollment (Storey 1998). The Medicaid application itself was long and complicated, requiring far more information than CHP application forms did. It was estimated that DSS workers required at least two hours to make eligibility determinations in simple Medicaid cases and four hours in more complex ones.

To the general barriers in enrollment must be added the further complications caused by the immigrant status of a large number of CHP-eligible children in New York. New York has the second largest immigrant population in the United States and immigrants are much less likely than nonimmigrants to have health insurance. This disparity increases with poverty: poor immigrants are twice as likely (51.7%

vs. 26.4%) as poor native-born Americans to be uninsured. Barriers to enrollment of immigrants in publicly funded health programs include language, culture, lack of familiarity with the U.S. health care system, and fear related to immigration status. In addition to Spanish, New York State has recognized the need for information written in Hebrew, Russian, Chinese, Korean, Farsi, and Haitian-Creole, but materials are not yet available (New York Task Force on Immigrant Health 1999). Policymakers and advocates hope that the use of community outreach workers as part of the new enrollment process will reduce these barriers.

The requirement in the federal BBA 1997 that all Medicaid-eligible children must be enrolled in the program has meant that CHP enrollment now involves screening for Medicaid-eligible children as well as efforts to enroll those who are eligible. The issue of children who are eligible for but not enrolled in Medicaid has become much more visible. The Office of the State Comptroller reported in June 1998 that 70% of New York's 663,000 uninsured children were eligible for either Medicaid or CHP but were not enrolled. Moreover, many children enrolled in CHP were Medicaid-eligible (McCall 1998).

One of the positive outcomes of the deliberations over expanding Child Health Plus in response to the federal SCHIP has been an agreement on new enrollment methods in both Medicaid and CHP. The new "facilitated enrollment program" was designed through an informal collaborative process that involved key members of the policy community—advocacy organizations, health plans, and state health department officials (Campaign for Healthy Children cochair interview September 1999). Its purpose is to make the enrollment process more user-friendly and thus more effective; facilitated enrollment is regarded as part of the process of bringing the Medicaid and CHP programs closer together. Although many other states have mail-in applications for Medicaid and this change was supported by the state Assembly (Assembly staff interview September 1999), the Pataki administration has insisted on maintaining face-to-face interviews. It argues that interviews prevent fraud and require Medicaid applicants to take responsibility for appearing at an interview (governor's staff interview September 1999; Storey 1998, 51). Under the new enrollment system, however, the face-to face interviews take place with "multi-lingual, community-based workers" in schools, child-care centers, and other sites in the community rather than in DSS offices. It is hoped that such a change will reduce some of the enrollment barriers in immigrant as well as other communities. These community outreach workers, who come from existing community-based organizations, will be trained in enrollment procedures and regulations by a training organization under state contract to insure statewide uniformity.

The Department of Health has an annual budget of $3 million for advertising CHP and the new facilitated enrollment process, $10 million to implement the enrollment process itself, and $1 million for training the community-based workers. Beginning in early 2000, a simplified, shortened application for Medicaid, CHP, and the Women, Infants, and Children (WIC) programs will be used by all health plans as part of the facilitated enrollment process (N.Y Health Department official interview September 1999). Children's advocates used the opportunity presented by the federal SCHIP legislation to argue for and get significant changes in New York in the process of enrolling children in both Medicaid and CHP. Implementing this policy of facilitated enrollment faces many challenges because the eligibility requirements for the two programs remain distinct. For example, children found to be eligible for Medicaid when they are recertified for CHP will now be removed from the CHP program (N.Y. Health Department official interview September 1999). Their enrollment in Medicaid may be problematic, federal officials believe, because some local governments have not been eager to enroll Medicaid beneficiaries (Hernandez 1999). Some observers in the policy community also argue that the stigma associated with Medicaid will continue to inhibit people from enrolling. During 1999 and 2000, enrollment in CHP increased rapidly. By September 2000, approximaltely 539,000 children were enrolled. After initially declining from 1998 to 1999, the enrollment of children in Medicaid also increased. By July 2000, about 1.2 million children under age 19 had enrolled.

Summary. New York's response to the enactment of a national program for children's health insurance differs from most other states because New York had a relatively large program for almost 10 years. Yet there are several aspects of the New York experience that permit informative comparisons. The children's advocacy community played a central role as policy entrepreneur in initiating New York's Child Health Plus program and in arguing that the money made available by SCHIP presented an opportunity to cover more children and expand benefits without spending additional state funds. A conservative Republican governor embraced the program, both because children's issues appear to be an arena in which all elected officials hope to demonstrate their humanity and compassion and because child health insurance in New York reached the policy agenda framed as a government subsidy of a market good rather than as a government program. The earlier history of CHP also illustrates variables that make bipartisan consensus on children's programs possible. CHP was defined as a program for children in working families and it used state subsidies to pay private insurance companies to cover these children. Indeed, CHP was developed with the participation of the business community, insurers, health plans, and physicians as well as children's advocates.

Ohio: Expanded Medicaid

The Ohio Child Health Insurance Program had its roots as an expansion of the state's Medicaid program for children and pregnant women. Thus, the Ohio CHIP differed from both the North Carolina CHIP, which emerged from a special legislative session as a separate program, and the New York CHIP, which expanded an existing public/private partnership for children not eligible for Medicaid. This discussion of policymaking for Ohio's program begins with an overview of CHIP Phase I, the Medicaid expansion, and CHIP Phase II, the amended model that was authorized in the state budget for the 2000–2001 fiscal biennium and was implemented on July 1, 2000. The following sections describe the roles of the state's governor and legislature in Ohio's policy process, particularly in the emergence of CHIP as a governor's budget initiative, and compare the roles of the policy community in the policy process that generated CHIP Phase I and CHIP Phase II.

The proposal for an expansion of Healthy Start, Ohio's Medicaid program for children and pregnant women, was included in the budget submitted by the state's governor on February 3, 1997, for the coming 1998–1999 fiscal biennium. Following passage of federal SCHIP legislation in August 1997 and secured funding authorization in the forthcoming budget, the Ohio Department of Human Services (ODHS) drafted a proposal for the first phase of the state's CHIP that simply built on existing arrangements for administering Healthy Start. Thus, Ohio was able to leverage federal dollars at an enhanced CHIP matching rate ($72 federal/$28 state, compared to its Medicaid rate of $58 federal/$42 state) to fund part of a Medicaid expansion for children that was in the works before the passage of federal SCHIP legislation.

The combined CHIP Phase I/Medicaid expansion was implemented by ODHS on January 1, 1998, with retroactive approval secured from HCFA on March 23, 1998. The expansion raised the eligibility threshold from previous levels of 133% of the federal poverty level (FPL) for children up to age 6 and 100% of FPL for children ages 6 through 14 to 150% of FPL for children from birth through age 18. A CHIP eligibility level of 150% of FPL placed Ohio in a category (with 12 other states) of having a low eligibility level of 100–175% of FPL compared to a high eligibility level of over 220% of FPL (9 states) and a modal eligibility level of 175–215% of FPL (23 states) (Beamer 1999, 6).

There are two basic differences between Ohio's Healthy Start program and its CHIP Phase I: the federal/state matching rates for the two programs and the requirement that children enrolled in CHIP not have any other existing health care coverage. Unlike CHIP, underinsured children who have another source of coverage may enroll in Healthy Start for wraparound coverage. Both programs are under the direction of ODHS, which uses existing administrative structures to administer CHIP. The benefit package is identical for CHIP Phase I and for Healthy Start. Health services are provided through the fee-for-service delivery system in all 88 counties and through managed care plans in 16 counties (as of February 2000). Basic eligibility requirements for Medicaid and CHIP are established by ODHS.

The Medicaid expansion that became Ohio's first CHIP (CHIP Phase I) emerged as incremental policymaking through the budget process. The formulation of a second version of the program in Ohio, CHIP Phase II, differed somewhat from the first by the creation of a 17-member advisory task force charged with making recommendations for its structure. In contrast to the legislative history behind the New York and North Carolina programs, the policymaking processes for both phases of the Ohio CHIP were not characterized by the give-and-take of political compromise among the legislative bodies and the executive branch. The story of CHIP in Ohio depicts incremental policymaking through the budgeting process and the importance of political ideology in shaping CHIP as a policy outcome in an era of devolution to the states.

The Political Stream and Ohio CHIP. Ohio has been characterized as a middle-of-the-road state that is often somewhat slow in adopting most national trends (former state legislator interview August 1999). The legislature in Ohio generally is considered to be a professional one, with salaries that allow for full-time commitment as legislators, a personal staff, and availability to leadership at any time during the two-year legislative tenure for session or committee work. Ohio's governor enjoys a strong role in budget authority with full responsibility for preparation of the state budget and therefore is central to policymaking (Gargan 1994). Health care policymaking often entails a great deal of compromise, given the presence of several strong lobbies including the insurance and nursing home industries. In general, however, legislators, who are often unfamiliar with the programmatic issues of Medicaid, tend to focus on the bottom-line costs when considering welfare policies (hospital association representative interview July 1999). Thus, both the enactment of the Medicaid expansion that became CHIP Phase I and the executive branch's creation of a task force to structure CHIP Phase II illustrate the importance of the incumbent governor's political role and ideology in the policymaking for both phases of the program.

CHIP Phase I began as a relatively small incremental expansion in a slow-growth Medicaid budget proposed by a fiscally conservative moderate Republican governor who pledged to improve the health and education of children, the efficiency of government, and the self-sufficiency of Ohioans during his tenure as governor. Republican George Voinovich began the first of two terms as Ohio's governor in 1991, succeeding Democrat Richard Celeste, whose chief legacy as governor was regarded by many to be a 90% increase in the state income tax rate (Miller 1994). George Voinovich's ascent to the governorship of Ohio was based largely on the reputation he gained as a skillful manager with financial expertise during his tenure as mayor of Cleveland. He raised the city's income tax, presided over a revitalization of the downtown, and helped earn Cleveland the reputation of a "comeback city" (Curtin 1996); he also was credited with resurrecting that city from financial default during a declining economic period (Suddes 1994).

Voinovich made the health and education of Ohio children his top priorities when he became governor. The state initiated a major review of its Medicaid program during Voinovich's governorship, given the changes brought about by the success of welfare reform in decreasing the general assistance rolls, the growing numbers of uninsured children, and the move to streamline state government. ODHS with the assistance of the Lewin Group conducted five public forums across the state in 1996. Over 1,500 participants, representing advocacy, provider, and administrative groups, attended the forums. The major theme that emerged most strongly, frequently, and consistently across every forum was the need to expand Medicaid eligibility, especially by providing coverage for the working poor to ease their transition to independence (Lewin Group 1996). This theme was a direct indictment of existing state policy, since Ohio's Medicaid eligibility levels had never gone beyond what was federally mandated.

Like many other states, the budgeting process is often the route for enacting major policy initiatives in Ohio. The state constitution requires a balanced budget, and the budget proposal is based on projected state revenues with new initiatives being funded by known revenue streams. The amount of money available to the legislature outside of the budget process is in reality much smaller than that available to the governor. Given the decrease in the welfare rolls, the sustained period of low growth in the Medicaid budget, and an avowed commitment to children, the inclusion of a modest Medicaid expansion in the governor's budget proposal provided a relatively simple way to move forward to improve the health of Ohio's children.

The proposed Medicaid expansion was a relatively small part of a huge but low growth Medicaid budget in a stable economic period (*Ohio Report* 1997b). It was seen as an affordable program for poor children, with a sizable share of financial support from the federal government. There was no observable opposition regarding CHIP among legislators, and there were no comments or debates worth mention about the proposed expansion during the legislative budget authorization process (former Ohio state legislator and ODHS official interviews August, June 1999). In June 1997, the governor's Office of Budget and Management announced the availability of an additional $200 to $400 million for 1998–1999 spending, due in part to overall decreases in Medicaid spending. The Office of Budget and Management also announced its intention to target these funds to education, child care, the Medicaid expansion, and the state food bank (*Ohio Report* 1997b).

The ability to reconceptualize problems in a different way is a major political achievement (Kingdon 1995), and the various characterizations assigned to a program can give it the "right features to pass through ideological filters" (Weissert and Weissert 1996, 257). In Ohio, policymaking for health care often includes a great deal of compromise, with a strong presence among such lobbying groups as the insurance and nursing home industries. As a former state legislator noted, because both the Ohio executive and legislature are reluctant to raise taxes, social programs must be "sold" to the public and to legislators if they are to be funded.

According to a representative of the state children's hospital association, Republican politicians in Ohio saw CHIP as a way to support the state's small business sector and its employees. In a state where the Supreme Court has decreed the present system of funding education unconstitutional, linking CHIP to education was politically prudent. The governor, who made the education and health care of children his top priority, portrayed CHIP as a solution to both needs, because "healthy children will be more ready to learn and better able to perform in school" (Rowland 1998b).

Fiscal authorization for the Medicaid expansion was included in the budget for the fiscal year beginning July 1, 1997. Thus, with funding authorization secured for the forthcoming biennium, Ohio was well positioned to act quickly after the passage of federal SCHIP legislation in August 1997 to prepare a CHIP application, thereby taking advantage of a windfall by funding a portion of its Medicaid expansion—which only brought the state up to what many other states were already doing—at the enhanced federal SCHIP matching rate.

The policy community and Ohio CHIP. The children's lobby in Ohio has assumed increasing importance due to the growing salience of children's issues and in part due to the presence of an office of the nationally recognized Children's Defense Fund in the state's capital city, Columbus. According to a state hospital association representative, there has been a general ongoing and regular communication between state Medicaid officials and children's advocates. Despite this communication, however, there was little visibility of advocates or outside agencies—and little publicity—in drafting the proposed Medicaid expansion that became the state's CHIP Phase I (minority health commission and state children's hospital association representatives interviews July 1999).

When Governor Voinovich created a task force on January 14, 1998, charged with making recommendations for expanding CHIP Phase I (covering children up to 150% of FPL) to CHIP Phase II (covering children up to 200% of FPL), it provided an opportunity for an enhanced, more formal role for the policy community than they had in the first phase. The task force included 17 individuals representing a variety of interest groups (health care providers, child and consumer advocates, the insurance industry, business, state and public health agencies, and health plans). Despite the "great concern [regarding] how to successfully get potentially eligible children to participate in the CHIP" and the goal of maximizing participation by consumers (Ryan 1998, i, 15), there were no parents of children enrolled in CHIP Phase I on the task force, and some task force members believed that the process did not include a full understanding of the perspectives of program users themselves (minority health commission representatives interviews July 1999).

Although all parties basically agreed that the expansion should be done, there were philosophical differences among members from the beginning about the way it should be structured. When the creation of the task force was announced publicly, the chairperson (also the state health director and former director of the state's Medicaid program) acknowledged the need to reinforce the state's strong private insurance market and expressed doubt that a Medicaid expansion was the only solution (Rowland 1998a). The health insurance industry, the most powerful and active interest group in Ohio state government (Funderburk and Adams 1994), considered it of foremost importance that CHIP Phase II not be an entitlement and not undermine the integrity of employer-based plans (health insurance representative interview August 1999). Advocates for children pressed for a CHIP Phase

II that would build on the current Medicaid expansion rather than a separate program and would provide the same benefit package (Ohio Child Health Coalition 1998). Nonetheless, at the task force's first meeting the conveners clearly communicated to the members that, unlike CHIP Phase I, CHIP Phase II would not be an entitlement program (children's health advocate interview June 1999).

Meanwhile, the print media noted that the state's efforts to provide coverage for uninsured children stacked up poorly against other states, pointing out that of the 28 states with CHIP plans, only 2 were less generous than Ohio, and one of those—Alabama—was preparing to expand its program (Rowland 1998b). The director of Children's Defense Fund–Ohio noted that expanding CHIP to cover children at or below 200% of poverty would "put Ohio in a real leadership position" (Rowland 1998b).

In its final recommendations, the task force called for the implementation of CHIP Phase II subject to available funding, rather than as an entitlement program, and with specific features to "discourage crowd-out and encourage family responsibility" (Ryan 1998). These features included a 90-day waiting period from the date of application and the imposition of cost-sharing through an annual premium and copayments for selected services. Recommendations also included providing a modest fee to certified representatives of community agencies and health care providers and to certified licensed private health and accident insurance agents for assisting consumers who completed an approved application (Ryan 1998, iv).

Final task force recommendations were supported by the governor and by both 1998 major gubernatorial candidates. There were no specific plans to earmark forthcoming tobacco settlement dollars for CHIP Phase II, although the governor-elect did indicate in November 1998 that he would target some of those monies toward expanding Medicaid coverage for uninsured children (A. Johnson 1998). Authorization for CHIP Phase II, covering children up to 200% of FPL, was included in the state budget that was passed in July 1999. There was essentially no debate on the program during the budget process, and it was authorized basically unchanged from the original proposal (ODHS official interview June 1999). CHIP Phase II was implemented July 1, 2000 (*Ohio Report* 2000).

Enrollment. Analyses performed by the Lewin Group in 1997 using data from the Current Population Survey indicated that by June 1999, a maximum of 133,000 children would be eligible for Healthy Start and CHIP Phase I (ODHS 1999). For the month of September 1998, 46% of children who were potentially eligible were being served by CHIP; this number represented 32% of the caseload expected by June 1999. In the 22 months between January 1998, when the Healthy Start Medicaid expansion/CHIP began, and October 1999, 151,863 children enrolled in the program. Of these, 26% (39,727) moved to another Medicaid category and 31% (47,216) left the rolls completely due to failure to reapply or income ineligibility (Children's Defense Fund–Ohio 2000).

According to a senior official with ODHS, families may decide not to apply for redetermination or renewal of coverage if they do not perceive a need or have not used any services, or if they perceive that the procedural barriers to redetermination are not worth the effort. In addition, some cases may be improperly closed when their eligibility is assessed for other programs. ODHS is working to minimize the problem with improper case closures; however, a senior ODHS official noted that complete explication of reasons for the large number of children who leave the program each month is constrained by a lack of credible data for analyses. Although program policy regarding eligibility is set at the state level, determination of eligibility for CHIP or Medicaid has been established at the county level, and counties have had some latitude in setting documentation requirements. A simplified two-page common application form is used to determine eligibility for Medicaid or CHIP as well as for WIC, Child and Family Health Service programs, and the program for children with special health care needs administered by the state's Bureau for Children with Medical Handicaps (ODHS 1999). Enrollment and retention figures should get a boost from two program changes that became effective July 1, 2000: the coverage period is extended from six months to one year and the documentation required for eligibility verification has been reduced.

Summary. The story of CHIP in Ohio reaffirms previous findings (Beamer 1999) that political ideology is a key determinant of the scope of the program as a policy outcome. Phase I and Phase II of Ohio's CHIP were governor's policy initiatives enacted through successive biennial budgeting processes in a state where the governor, who enjoys strong budget-making authority, pursued an agenda as an advocate for children's health and remained true to a fiscally conservative, moderate Republican political ideology. These incremental policymaking processes that culminated in Ohio's CHIP enabled the executive branch to shape a policy outcome that was consistent with a pro-children agenda, minimized the need to negotiate with advocates, interest groups, or legislators, and did not compromise a cultural aversion to big government.

Beamer (1999) notes that states with Republican-led governments are likely to enact separate children's health insurance programs rather than combined CHIP/Medicaid expansion programs. The serendipitous passage of federal SCHIP legislation in August 1997 allowed the state to convert the governor's proposal for expanding the state's Medicaid program for children (which only brought Ohio's Medicaid program closer to the pre-CHIP levels of many other states and lower than levels allowed by federal law) into a proposal for the first phase of the state's CHIP. Within two weeks of the implementation of the state's CHIP Phase I, the governor announced the task force that would modify the program into a separate CHIP Phase II. The move to limit the expansion of CHIP as a publicly funded insurance program is not uncommon, given the concern that future declines in federal funding will mean financial burdens for states and the trend toward limited government (Iglehart 1999). With the implementation of CHIP Phase II in

July 2000, Ohio joined other states with Republican-led governments that enacted CHIP programs that are separate from their Medicaid programs. The case study of children's health policymaking in Ohio supports previous findings that federal legislative initiatives do not necessarily bring about fundamental shifts in states' goals or policies (Miller and Byrne 1997, 101), particularly in an era of devolution to the states.

North Carolina: Health Choice—A Separate Plan

North Carolina's CHIP program, named Health Choice, is instructive for at least three reasons. First, it appears to show how federal programs exercise their greatest impact when the potential federal dollars are relevant to the political agendas of significant groups and stakeholders within a state (Miller and Byrne 1977). Second, it exemplifies at the state level how the passion for large political-philosophical issues can affect the political process in the modern post–civil rights South (Beamer 1998, 1999). Finally, the organizational structure that emerged from the legislative process surprised the executive branch that had to implement it, seemed fraught with potential interagency rivalries, and yet has produced a program that places North Carolina among the most successful states in objective measures of CHIP implementation.

The legislation. Health Choice (the Act to Establish the Health Insurance Program for Children and to Authorize a Tax Credit for Certain Purchasers of Dependent Health Insurance) differs from Ohio's law in that the state established a separate program rather than expanding Medicaid. Its benefits are essentially those of Medicaid, but the reimbursement rates follow those established for the North Carolina Teachers' and State Employees' Comprehensive Major Medical Plan. That medical plan is also charged with paying providers and tracking the copayments required from families with incomes above 150% of poverty. Copayments specified in the legislation are $5 for most visits to providers or outpatient hospital visits, $6 for each outpatient prescription drug, and $20 for hospital emergency room visits that do not lead to hospitalization (unless other appropriate care is unavailable). An annual enrollment fee of $50 for one child and $100 for two or more children is collected for families with incomes above 150% of poverty; it is kept by the county departments of social services to help defray the costs of determining eligibility. Thus, children who are not eligible for Medicaid in families with incomes of 150% of poverty or below have no cost-sharing, while those above 150% of poverty have limited cost-sharing. When kids enrolled in Health Choice become ineligible because their family income rises above 200% of poverty, families with incomes not exceeding 225% of poverty may purchase continued coverage for up to one year at "full premium cost" (N.C. Senate Bill 2, para. 108A-70.21, 70.24).

In order to make the teachers' and state employees' health plan fundamentally equivalent to Medicaid, the legislation specified that vision, hearing, and some dental benefits (preventive care and "routine" fillings) would be added for children enrolled in Health Choice. Advocates were also concerned that children with special needs (including but not limited to behavioral and mental health needs) would require special funding that would kick in when the teachers' and state employees' health plan refused to reimburse for a service. They were able to include a special provision in the act to provide services for children with special needs (N.C. Senate Bill 2, para. 108A-70.23).

Although the teachers' and state employees' health plan is "responsible for the administration and processing of claims for benefits under the program" (N.C. Senate Bill 2, para. 108A-70.24[a]), the North Carolina Department of Health and Human Services (NCDHHS) has broad responsibilities for developing a state plan that meets the federal requirements for funding under Title XXI of the Social Security Act and submitting the plan to HCFA. NCDHHS has taken responsibility for evaluation—including quality of care—and enrollment. Both federal and state officials view CHIP as an opportunity to find children who qualify for Medicaid but are not enrolled and get them on the Medicaid rolls. In North Carolina, the Division of Medical Assistance in DHHS has designed a seamless enrollment process that puts those who inquire about Health Choice but are eligible for Medicaid into the latter program. For the first time, applications can be mailed in, but those qualifying for Medicaid must still have a face-to-face interview with a county social services intake worker.

In addition to dividing responsibility for the plan between the teachers' and state employees' health plan and NCDHHS, the act (N.C. Senate Bill 2, para. 105-151.27) also created a major tax expenditure that is administered though the state's Department of Revenue. This provision establishes North Carolina's first refundable tax credit, which provides $300 to families at or below 225% of poverty who purchase private health insurance for kids without the benefit of employer support or other sources of pretax dollars. For families with adjusted gross incomes over 225% of poverty and under $100,000 (married, filing jointly) or $60,000 (single), the tax credit is $100. The refundable tax credit was added over the objections of children's advocates and their legislative supporters during the six-week special session of the state legislature that was devoted to the single issue of CHIP.

This subsidy for the purchase of private insurance became operational for the 1999 tax year, so revenue losses could not be calculated when this chapter was written. Because revenue officials had no experience with refundable tax credits, they refused to estimate the number of claims or their value. However, the figure of $64 million annually for tax credits to 405,000 families was reported at the time the act passed (Wagner 1998a). (An earlier, more generous version was estimated to cost more than $200 million [Wagner 1998g; *Raleigh News & Observer* 1998a.])

How North Carolina came to have a separate non-Medicaid program that is administered by the teachers' and state employees' health plan and a refundable tax credit to subsidize the purchase of private health insurance for kids in families with incomes up to $100,000 is an interesting story that illuminates much about modern state policymaking in the era of divided government.

State policymaking. The BBA 1997 provisions for SCHIP fell on fertile North Carolina soil that had been well plowed. North Carolina had exercised the options to expand Medicaid eligibility that federal legislation in the Reagan and Bush administrations permitted. More recently, the state became habituated to issues of social responsibility for children by Governor James B. Hunt Jr.'s signature Smart Start program, which focuses on early childhood education. Although not itself a health program, some of the networks established by that program, which reached all of North Carolina's 100 counties, proved to be very important in the successful implementation of Health Choice. A number of child health advocates, academics, and officials of the NCDHHS formed the Children's Health Insurance Task Force convened by the North Carolina Institute of Medicine* in July 1997 at the behest of NCDHHS secretary David Bruton. This task force, which was open to anyone interested in the issues and included representatives of the insurance industry, met monthly from July through October; a draft plan was delivered to Secretary Bruton in November 1997. The final report of the task force consisted of policy alternatives rather than a developed list of recommendations.

At first the task force surveyed a number of modest incremental changes, for there was considerable skepticism about the state's ability to fund a major new program. Background documents prepared for the first meeting on July 14 suggested that Congress would pass a significant appropriation for children's health insurance coverage but recognized the large gaps between Senate and House versions. Before the August meeting the state sent an analysis of the federal SCHIP legislation to the task force members (Vitaglione 1997). SCHIP provided a secure funding source. Indeed, the formula is more generous to the states than existing Medicaid (where North Carolina has to pay about a third of the costs as compared with a quarter for SCHIP). The larger proportion of federal funds made it easier for the legislation that ultimately emerged to forgo the county match of 5% that is required in North Carolina's Medicaid program. The child health advocates and sympathetic state officials who dominated the task force agreed that North Carolina should have a Medicaid expansion plan that would achieve the aims outlined in the task force report.

---

*The North Carolina Institute of Medicine (NC-IOM), which was chartered as an independent nonprofit organization by the North Carolina General Assembly in 1983, is intended to be a forum for quasi-public inquiry into health policy issues like the national institution for which it is named. Dr. David Bruton, a pediatrician who served as secretary of the NCDHHS during the adoption of CHIP, was influential in establishing NC-IOM when he was president of the state organization of pediatricians. By the time CHIP reached the state agenda, NC-IOM was housed at the Sheps Center, a nationally known institute for health services research at the University of North Carolina–Chapel Hill.

In November 1997, John Hood, president of the John Locke Foundation, a conservative think tank, distributed a briefing paper titled "The Worst Option: Lawmakers Should Not Expand Medicaid," which argued that Medicaid expansion would "encourage tens of thousands of North Carolinians to become dependent on government for their health insurance." The briefing paper then suggested the creation of a tax credit to correct the unfair bias in the tax code that allows health insurance to be purchased with untaxed dollars, thereby favoring those who are affluent or are fortunate to work for employers who provide health insurance. According to child advocates and other proponents of the plan, the argument that Medicaid was perceived as stigmatizing led them to yield on their preference for expanded Medicaid.

In December 1997, following the work of the NC-IOM Task Force, NCDHHS secretary Bruton won Governor Hunt's acceptance for the general outline of what became Health Choice. In a bid to obtain Republican support in the House, the administration proposed a separate plan instead of the expanded Medicaid that advocates and Medicaid officials (including Dr. Bruton) favored (Wagner 1997; *Raleigh News & Observer* 1997).

Another task force—this time a bipartisan legislative task force composed of members from each chamber and headed by Lieutenant Governor Dennis Wicker—worked out the details of the administration's legislative proposal in January and February 1998. With only a mild suggestion from House Republican Lanier Cansler that the state was moving too quickly to establish a new program, it adopted the consensus Democratic plan for a separate Medicaid look-alike program (Wagner 1998e).

The easy interaction of state officials, advocates, and academics suggests the existence of an issues network. As momentum grew, the insurance companies and chief conservative think tanks became involved, but they were not driving the legislation. As one of the conservative strategists explained, North Carolina always takes federal program dollars when they are offered. In retrospect, it appears that conservatives set out to make the resulting legislation more to their liking without risking the loss of federal funds. Because legislators appear not to have played a key role until after the outlines of the initial policy proposal had been accepted, political scientists might describe the policy structure as a traditional iron triangle. However, the fluid interactions of an issues network seem more apt to describe the interactions leading to Health Choice for two reasons. The best funded lobby groups—the health insurance and managed care industries—played a watching game rather than attempting to fashion the legislation. Yet they did secure language in the bill permitting managed care plans to be offered to Health Choice enrollees along with the teachers' and state employees' health plan, so long as managed care plans delivered the same benefits for the same premium. (In any event, no insurer or managed care company actually decided to compete against the state's indemnity plan.) The unusual forum of a special session following the ad hoc bipartisan legislative commission chaired by the lieutenant governor also does not suggest backroom politics as implied by the metaphor of the iron triangle.

The most visible advocates for CHIP legislation favored Medicaid expansion and no copays or other impediments to the receipt of services. Yet the North Carolina Health Access Coalition (NCHAC) and the Covenant with North Carolina's Children loyally supported the administration's proposal for a separate plan and the inevitable compromises that the Democrats were forced to accept during the legislative process. NCHAC represents the liberal position on health issues; the Covenant advocates for children on all types of issues. Because health and children's interests often overlap, these two coalitions—and the central lobbyist identified with each—often collaborate. Both are umbrella organizations. In March 1999 the Covenant claimed over 90 member organizations, which represented more than 500,000 individuals across the state (National Association of Child Advocates 1999). NCHAC, which in 1998–1999 claimed about 40 organizational members and many individual memberships, is a project of the North Carolina Justice and Community Development Center, an advocacy organization that works for a broad range of progressive causes in the state (North Carolina Health Access Coalition 1999).

The North Carolina Child Advocacy Institute (NCCAI), a member of the National Association of Child Advocates, the North Carolina Council of Churches, and the North Carolina Justice and Community Development Center, decided to collaborate in creating the Covenant in 1995. Its supporters claim that the Covenant has fundamentally changed advocacy for children by uniting the many voices of organizations that sometimes worked at cross-purposes and by leading them to support a more comprehensive agenda. The NCCAI provides—but does not direct or supervise—the one-person staff of the Covenant: Paula Wolf, whose title is chief lobbyist (National Association of Child Advocates 1999).

Proponents of the bill decided to consider it in a special session of the legislature, a costly procedure that focuses attention on a single item. The special session convened on March 24, 1998, with the expectation that it would last perhaps a week. Although the governor can call special sessions and define the area for legislation, the legislature was not in the hip pocket of the governor. On the contrary, divided government had returned to North Carolina in 1995 for the first time in almost 100 years. While the Democrats had retained control of the Senate, North Carolina Republicans, who ran in fall 1994 on a conservative platform similar to the "Contract with America" that made Newt Gingrich Speaker of the U.S. House of Representatives, achieved a majority in the House. The 1997–1998 General Assembly also was divided, with a slim Republican majority organizing the House and Democrats in control of the Senate.

State officials and child advocates explain that the rigid deadline set by the federal legislation for state action necessitated legislative endorsement of North Carolina's response in a special session; they reject the suggestion that considerations of symbolism or drama influenced the decision to call this session. Conservatives objected to the special session, arguing that the perceived federal deadline for submitting state CHIP plans to HCFA could be evaded, thereby allowing CHIP to be considered in the upcoming second, or short, session (Hood 1998c). The legislature's regularly scheduled short session was set to convene in early May. These CHIP proponents felt that trying to push through a bill in the opening weeks of the short session—especially if Health Choice might be sidetracked by other business—was too risky given the apparently rigid timetable that HCFA had adopted.

Proponents believed that the legislative ways had been thoroughly greased to launch the North Carolina version of SCHIP. Almost immediately after the special session convened, the Democratic Senate passed its bill, which had low copayments and no premium-sharing by recipients or the application fee that emerged in the compromise bill (Wagner 1998g). To the surprise of the proponents, the House Republicans substituted their own bill for the Senate version. In addition to larger copays and premium-sharing, the Republicans wanted stringent waiting periods to discourage "crowd out"—the temptation to drop private health insurance to go on government-subsidized health coverage with its typically more comprehensive benefits.

The Republican bill was also the source of the idea that the teachers' and state employees' health plan would administer the program. The position in the state government of the North Carolina Teachers' and State Employees' Comprehensive Major Medical Plan is anomalous. It does not report to the governor and functions autonomously. Presumably, part of the attraction for the Republicans in the House was the fact that this health plan is tied more closely to the legislature and is in an entirely different hierarchy of administrative accountability from that governing the Medicaid program and NCDHHS. It should also be noted that Blue Cross–Blue Shield of North Carolina, the state's largest health insurer, provides the claims processing and other administrative services for the state. (Medicaid, in contrast, contracts for claims processing and other services with EDS, Ross Perot's first data processing company.)

The most unusual aspect of the Republican House bill was the refundable tax credit that promised to return one-third of the cost of private insurance purchased for children with pretax dollars to the family. (A refundable tax credit requires the Department of Revenue to send refund checks to those who do not earn enough to pay taxes.) As originally introduced, the refundable tax credit had no income cap; its cost was estimated to be $219 million (Hood 1998b; Wagner 1998g; *Raleigh News & Observer* 1998a), more than twice the cost of the federal-state funding for Health Choice. Thus, it was an open-ended tax expenditure entitlement designed to support individual purchase of health insurance. Moreover, no federal dollars were available to offset the program costs to the state. Hood emphasized the importance of equity for those denied access to the tax subsidies enjoyed by North Carolinians whose employers provide health insurance. Although mentioning that such a refund constitutes a tax cut, he did not emphasize this interpretation of the policy (Hood 1998b, 1998c, 1997).

North Carolina had no refundable tax credit, but the federal government has the earned income tax credit. Normally, one does not identify refundable tax credits as a conservative Republican policy mechanism, although they are acknowledged to be a very efficient mechanism for redistributing income and do have the advantage of accomplishing a policy objective without any increase in government bureaucracy. Conservative proponents of the tax refund justified the large expenditure of state funds on the grounds that it would encourage self-reliance rather than dependence upon state subsidies and that it was an equitable measure that extended the benefits already enjoyed by those in the private market whose insurance is purchased with pretax dollars (Hood 1998a).

The special session that was supposed to be over in a week dragged on for six weeks, leading one newsletter to calculate that it cost taxpayers $1.5 million, or enough to insure 3,846 children for a year. Many of the legislators went home while their leaders and the health specialists among the lawmakers wrangled. (Demonstrating their allegiance to true North Carolina values, some key lawmakers interrupted their negotiations to follow UNC–Chapel Hill's Tar Heels to San Antonio for the NCAA Final Four basketball tournament [Wagner 1998d]). Finally, compromise was reached. In general, the tenacious House Republicans managed to force the Democrats to give them much of what they wanted. Their biggest victory was in securing the passage of North Carolina's first refundable tax credit, although the compromise restricted it to families with adjusted gross incomes under $100,000 and the House negotiators agreed to a limited and means-tested tax credit of $300 for low-income families and $100 for the middle class and the affluent. The Republicans surrendered on the issue of augmenting the benefits of the state teachers' and employees' health plan to make coverage equivalent to the more comprehensive Medicaid benefits (Wagner 1998c). The compromise bill passed the Senate 45 to 1 and the House 99 to 12 on April 30, 1998 (*Raleigh News & Observer* 1998b).

Implementation. Secretary Bruton gave responsibility in NCDHHS for implementing Health Choice to June Milby, a senior official appointed to coordinate NCDHHS's part of the program, and Tom Vitaglione, an official in what used to be called the Division of Maternal and Child Health (an entity that had recently rejoined NCDHHS and was charged with responsibility for social services and Medicaid). Milby worked on alternative plans during the legislative process in order to be prepared to rush a final plan to the HCFA (which required submission of plans at least three months prior to its October 1, 1998, "drop dead" deadline). She was also responsible for evaluation and quality, program areas where she could draw on the strengths of the division that has administered Medicaid. Vitaglione, building on his public health experience, developed the outreach component of Health Choice. He was also responsible for the smooth functioning of the provision of the act that covers children with special needs when the care that they require exceeds the standards established by the teachers' and state employees' health plan.

To state Medicaid officials, perhaps the biggest surprise in the legislation that passed was the provision that charged the teachers' and state employees' health plan with its administration. Paul Sebo, director of plan services for the state health program, became responsible for its involvement in Health Choice. In particular, he played the key interface role between the claims processors at Blue Cross–Blue Shield and the patient advocates and outreach specialists in Vitaglione's division or the county social services networks. (These networks are maintained by the Division of Medical Assistance, which also has the state's medical care and quality expertise.) Vitaglione and Milby had not worked with Sebo prior to the enactment of Health Choice. Initially, some at NCDHHS suspected that officials from the teachers' and state employees' health plan may have had conversations with Republicans in the legislature about playing a major role in administering Health Choice, but in interviews, Sebo and Milby maintained that this outcome was as much of a surprise to officials there as to others in government. In any case, the three responsible officials began meeting on a weekly basis and consulting with each other even more often to make the program successful.

The conventional wisdom in public administration suggests that interagency collaboration, especially when significant action must be accomplished on abbreviated timetables, is likely to lead to turf battles and delay. Moreover, North Carolina added no additional staff (with the possible exception of Milby's position as coordinator).* Thus, the organizational structure seemed to be a pretty slim reed on which to build an ambitious program in a short period of time.

The triumvirate were also tested by implied criticism of their decision to pursue a grassroots strategy in enrolling eligible children. The *Raleigh News & Observer,* North Carolina's newspaper of record, appeared to draw invidious comparisons in reporting that other states planned major media campaigns to reach the public with details of the program. It also quoted Adam Searing, director of the North Carolina Health Access Coalition, as saying, "If I were running the thing, I'd have full-page ads in every newspaper in the State" (Wagner 1998b).

Enrollment received an early boost when Blue Cross, which had been administering and largely funding a nonprofit program for some 8,000 uninsured low-income kids called the Caring Program for Children, terminated the program and suggested that its clients should seek coverage from Health Choice. Unfortunately, because federal law precludes SCHIP coverage of children of immigrant parents, an unknown number of low-income children in the Caring Program were not eligible for Health Choice (Wagner 1998f, 1998b). Despite controversy about the subject in the legislative debates and negotiations regarding waiting periods, none of the published materials or interviews used for this chapter pointed to the termi-

---

*The legislation called for the next legislature to fund 10 auditors and 2 clerical positions for the Department of Revenue to guard against fraudulent claims for tax credits (Senate Bill 2, para. 105-151.27 [c]), but the new legislature reneged on the promise.

nation of the Caring Program as a large-scale example of crowding out, the replacement of private (in this case nonprofit charity) arrangements for public subsidies.

Aside from the influx from the Caring Program, North Carolina, almost alone among the states, based its enrollment strategy on the conviction that Milby explained this way: "The people who know how to reach people are the people who live there, out in each county. Word of mouth sells the program" (Wagner 1998b). Interviews with Milby, Sebo, and Vitaglione, the three program administrators, confirm that although they were fully aware that other states were investing heavily in media, they were firmly convinced that a media strategy would not work in North Carolina. In retrospect, their administrative decision is likely to be viewed as displaying both foresight and considerable bravery. But several important background conditions shed light on it. First, the legislature had appropriated only $500,000 to publicize Health Choice. In a large and very diverse state with many media markets, half a million dollars will not buy much of a media campaign.

Moreover, with a target audience of eligible children that was estimated to be 71,000 (out of a North Carolina population of over 7.5 million in mid-1998), large media expenditures do not appear to be a very efficient way to reach children, especially low-income families who may live in isolated rural areas. Because the act establishing Health Choice required that enrollment be conducted through social services departments in each of the state's 100 counties, any media campaign had to be coordinated with the relevant county agencies. After years of working together, Medicaid program managers naturally used the well-established working relationships with social service and Medicaid officials at the local level. The networks of nonprofit organizations, some of which are state-funded, that implemented the Smart Start program have already been mentioned. More generally, the grassroots enrollment strategy is evidence of the maturation of collaboration throughout the state by nonprofit advocacy groups and county social services agencies.*

The result of this strategy to use a grassroots local outreach program and streamlined enrollment on a two-page form that can be mailed in proved to be highly successful. In early July 1999, less than a year after the program began, enrollment had reached 45,245 children, or 64% of the projected target of 71,000 children (Medlin 1999). Ironically, as the end of the first year of full operations came to a close, the triumvirate were planning a modest media campaign timed to coincide with the end of the first year. They were concerned that as enrollments expired, total enrollment would drop off because families might fail to reapply.

Lessons of the North Carolina experience. This brief account of North Carolina's implementation of the federal SCHIP program has some rich implications. Several points are worth noting here.

---

*A statewide umbrella agency, the Center for Nonprofits, Duke University–sponsored training programs across the state, and the Hunt administration itself have fostered the growth of the nonprofit sector and its engagement in attempts to solve social problems.

First, child health would have reached the political agenda without the federal program, but the availability of federal funding from SCHIP determined a number of program choices (e.g., failure to cover the children of immigrants). Thus, the findings of Miller and Byrne (1977) seem reaffirmed as to the effects that can be expected when the federal government tries to secure cooperation by involving the states in new health programs.

Second, ideology or disagreement about basic values played a large part in determining the outcome. This observation confirms the general findings of Beamer (1998, 1999). Of course, the existence of a bill in this area depends on the value-driven pro-child advocates. But the Republicans in the House advanced ideas developed by the John Locke Foundation, a conservative think tank based in Raleigh, that seem at odds with the pragmatic, fiscally responsible, tax-cutting Republican stereotype. Their willingness to secure a refundable tax credit costing more than $200 million at a time when the state faced severe budget shortfalls is defended by John Hood in abstract terms of equity (Hood interview 1999; Hood 1997, 1998a, 1998b, 1998c).

Other value issues also intruded in the deliberations about Health Choice. For example, explicit language prohibiting payment for any services delivered by school-based health clinics contradicted an established state commitment to foster school-based clinics as an effective way to reach kids. This prohibition was reportedly added to the Health Choice bill because pro-life conservatives have targeted these clinics, alleging that they spread knowledge about abortions and birth control (*Raleigh News & Observer* 1998c). Repealing this provision was given top priority when the newly elected General Assembly with a thin Democratic majority in the House arrived in Raleigh at the beginning of 1999 (Andrew D. McBride, personal communication). The prohibition was repealed.

Finally, the administration of the program has succeeded well in enrolling low-income kids, sorting out and signing up those eligible for Medicaid, streamlining the application form with a two-page questionnaire that can be mailed in to the local county social services agencies, and establishing a seamless reimbursement system that automatically supplements the teachers' and state employees' health plan for children with special needs without threatening their families with the news that Blue Cross–Blue Shield has rejected the claim.

The success of this unlikely administrative structure appears to a considerable degree to be due to the program leaders' individual expertise, commitment, and ability to work together. But Sapolsky, Aisenberg, and Morone (1987), in a provocative article about the first use of diagnosis-related groups in New Jersey caution that it is difficult to maintain innovative state programs. They argue that the creative administrative cadre who are necessary to implement innovative programs will move on to new jobs, propelled in part by their reputation for success with new programs. When they leave, an important element in the success of an interaction is lost.

REDISTRIBUTIVE POLICY IN THE ERA OF DEVOLUTION

From the perspective of state policymakers, SCHIP was an opportunity to distribute a new good that is largely subsidized by federal taxpayers. In Lowi's noted policy typology, both SCHIP at the federal level and CHIP in each state are "'welfare state' programs" and therefore are "redistributive." Thus, Lowi's analysis (1964, 1972) leads one to expect greater than average conflict, a primary political role for associations, stable government and political structures where executives and peak associations make primary decisions, and implementation left to centralized agencies.

Review of Case-Study Results

New York added the new federal financing program to the existing program that liberal policy entrepreneurs had established when welfare expansion and regulation were in ascendancy in the state. Child Health Plus became so popular that by 1993 or 1994, it was a bipartisan program. It depends on a public-private partnership based on participation by commercial health insurers and is funded by the bad debt and charity pool rather than taxes. Thus, it is consonant with a market regime, an important consideration in light of Governor Pataki's commitment to a market approach for controlling costs and the strong position of New York's governor in determining health policy outcomes (Hackey 1998). The unspoken agreement not to raise ideological issues of reproductive health and enrollment of immigrants demonstrates that Child Health Plus is a program that is beyond both ideological and political bickering. Thus, New York's adoption of CHIP can be seen as a model of nonideological, nonpolitical incremental expansion, even though advocates may have disputed details regarding the use of the new federal funding.

Unlike New York, Ohio had no preexisting program. Moreover, the state manifested limited interest in expanding health care for low-income children, as demonstrated by its unwillingness to take advantage of federal support for Medicaid expansion. Yet Governor Voinovich had already decided to raise Medicaid eligibility levels when Congress passed SCHIP. Ohio's governor was in an even stronger position than the chief executive in New York, for he had the full panoply of executive powers but did not have to contend with an independent and strongly entrenched legislature where each party controlled one house. Thus, Ohio CHIP Phase I was determined largely by a second-term Republican governor, a moderate and fiscal conservative who had risen to prominence when, as the mayor of Cleveland, he guided the city through a recovery from financial default.

At the time SCHIP was enacted, Governor Voinovich was planning a run for the U.S. Senate. (Ohio's governor is limited to two terms.) SCHIP presented him with the enviable prospect of enhanced federal payment to make good on one of his first pledges upon assuming office in 1991—to promote children's health. To cap his good fortune, the federal SCHIP program could even be presented as federal devolution of decision-making to the states, if anyone was interested in challenging the conservative governor about expanding a welfare program. CHIP could be spun to attract political support from a number of quarters, but that was unnecessary. Its fit with the governor's political agenda, and publicly stated policy goals virtually assured its formulation and enactment as part of a routine budget package.

Ohio's CHIP Phase II involved decisions that raised issues that typically have divided conservatives and liberals in terms of political aims and ideology: a separate, nonentitlement program, waiting periods to guard against crowd out, and premiums and copays. Liberal child advocates objected, but political consensus behind the establishment proposal to recommend a separate program prevailed. Both Democratic and Republican gubernatorial candidates endorsed CHIP II as it progressed from task force report to a law that contained many of the features favored by conservatives.

Only in North Carolina did the availability of federal SCHIP funds become an occasion for a political donnybrook that fully meets the expectations for ideological and class conflict predicted by Lowi's typology. Miller and Byrne (1977) suggest (in much more staid language) that the outcome of state responses in such federal-state partnerships can best be read as a sort of political Rorschach test that displays a state's political culture. Unlike Ohio, the liberal position in North Carolina was represented by the administration, although it began making compromises even before legislation was drafted. The Republicans had recently wrested control of the lower house of the legislature from the hands of Democrats who had monopolized legislative power for almost 100 years.* Moreover, that victory had been driven by the North Carolina equivalent of the national Republican Party's hard-edged, right-wing Contract with America. Even given this political context, there appears to have been no question of refusing the federal largess.

Instead, Republicans worked to enhance the private aspects of the opportunity that SCHIP represented and reduce its entitlement features. In addition to their effort to naturalize CHIP—to make North Carolina's version of CHIP into a Republican kind of program—they also connected it with the genuinely creative idea of a refundable tax credit for the purchase of health insurance with taxable dollars. It is revealing that the conservatives did not blanch at the high cost of that program, despite the fact that it had to be entirely state-funded. In the end, conservatives were able to obtain most of the basic features that they wanted to see included in the final legislation, although they had to settle for smaller amounts of continuous variables like premiums and copayments than they had originally demanded. It should be noted that the liberal advocates claimed victory, seeming subtly to suggest that the Republicans had intended to defeat the program.

In contrast to the orderly progress of CHIP legislation in New York and Ohio, North Carolina's debate resulted in legislative gridlock lasting for six weeks. Yet

*Several Republican moderates had served as governor in recent years, however.

this policy debate fostered a clash of ideas. The liberals argued for the utility and social justice of the program. In retrospect, it seems clear that conservative Republican legislators would not have permitted North Carolina to lose its allotment of federal money. And they certainly did not want to see North Carolinians go without needed health care. Yet the debate was over more than the means for achieving a common end. At least the ideological leaders among the conservatives used the issue to raise questions of the proper nature of the helping hand extended by government, of the fundamental injustice perpetrated by the hidden tax subsidies for the purchase of health care with tax-free dollars, and of the appropriate role of government. The two sides largely talked past each other. A cynic might argue that the debate was irrelevant, for it was the conservative votes and their party discipline that gave them most of what they wanted (albeit in reduced quantities) rather than the power of their ideas. But political talk can serve other purposes, such as raising the consciousness and morale of one's supporters and evangelizing for conservative ideas among the unengaged.

SCHIP as Redistributive Policy

In general, the three case studies have probably exposed more similarities than dissimilarities even with the North Carolina policy process. Lowi (1972) counted such similarities and dissimilarities, indicating that he would be satisfied to create a policy framework that allowed inferences that would be accurate in two-thirds of the cases. It would be false precision to attempt such quantification here. But a brief comparative recapitulation of the cases in light of the Lowi framework will provide a useful summary.

CHIP did not generate political or ideological battles in two states. In New York, a strongly supported bipartisan program expanded incrementally: despite a policy regime in transition (Hackey 1998), Child Health Plus appealed to all sides. In Ohio, the governor essentially dictated both phases of CHIP. In North Carolina, however, a fierce ideological battle emerged, perhaps because of recent changes in voting patterns in the state. The administration, with the support of liberal advocates, finally achieved passage of a program that it has successfully implemented, but leading advocates and administrators would have preferred to be operating a Medicaid expansion.

Lowi's typology (1964, 1972) associates the adoption of redistributive policy with high levels of conflict (Ripley and Franklin 1987). It therefore leads to the question of why CHIP was not contentious in two of the three states. Part of the explanation may simply be that CHIP was perceived in those states as an incremental expansion of long accepted federal-state health programs for children. Yet the historical account of the origin of New York's Child Health Plus does not disclose intense conflict in its origins, so a wider slice of policy history would not disclose missing conflict in New York or Ohio. The fact that children are currently regarded as sympathetic targets of redistributive programs might also explain the comparative lack of controversy.

Another consideration is that at the state level those paying the largest share of program costs—federal taxpayers—have no representation. In this respect, the politics of CHIP may differ from the redistributive programs that generated Lowi's typology, where those who are losing from a policy proposal have greater opportunities to resist the "re" in redistribution. It is possible to test this proposition with CHIP. New York's Child Health Plus and North Carolina's Health Choice both lack a provision that causes state Medicaid costs to register clearly on a payer within the state that has a significant voice. New York and North Carolina are both among the small number of states that force local jurisdictions to pay a share of Medicaid costs. In establishing separate CHIP programs, local contributions were not required. (The local share in both states is more than made up by the difference between the enhanced federal CHIP share and what the federal government pays for Medicaid.) If local contributions had been proposed, local governments are likely to have protested.

This last speculation about the lack of conflict over CHIP in two of our case-study states is tantamount to asking whether the absence of an identifiable payer with a voice in state policy deliberations may "fuzz over" the redistributive characteristics of the policy. Although welfare policy is by definition redistributive, a useful way to enact new welfare policies is by camouflaging their more redistributive aspects as distributive (Ripley and Franklin 1987, esp. 164–175). In North Carolina, the John Locke Foundation did not let the administration and its child health advocate allies frame the issue in such a benign manner. Indeed, the refundable tax credit—an overtly redistributive proposal paid for entirely by state taxpayers and defended in terms of equity—may have served the function of framing the child health issue in terms of competing redistributive plans.

In terms of locus of decision-making, the Lowi taxonomy is only partly predictive. The Ohio governor determined the policy adopted. In North Carolina, the administration drove the agenda, but the final legislation was the result of compromise. The other significant players in both cases were associations that represented advocates (except for the role of a conservative think tank in North Carolina). In New York, the child advocates both framed the issue and secured the gradual evolution in the positions of the Republican governor and Senate that produced their desired policy. That outcome, of course, is in keeping with the liberal political culture of New York. Stable policy structures over the years in the three states—also consonant with Lowi's list of characteristics of redistributive policy—had led to collaboration in responding to SCHIP (National Association of Child Advocates 1999).

Finally, implementation in Ohio and New York can be described as centralized (as suggested by Lowi's taxonomy). However, in North Carolina the distribution of responsibility among two components of NCDHHS and the teachers' and state employees' health plan is highly unusual. The triumvirate responsible for the North Carolina program are all high-level civil servants, as is typical with the implementation of redistributive policies.*

An explanation of the adoption of Lowi's framework in this conclusion is needed. How useful is a framework if one's findings seem to raise a number of disparities between the empirical case-study material and the expected character-istics based on the taxonomy? Moreover, Lowi developed his typology using fed-eral level case studies in order to enhance understanding of federal policymaking. Therefore, in applying this conceptual framework to state responses to SCHIP, the authors are extending the taxonomy beyond its genesis. We are also aware that some disparage his classification as largely ignored and not useful for research (Sabatier 1999, 10–11).

The Lowi approach has guided us in organizing the diverse materials in our case studies so that they bear on common political categories that continue to be of interest to most students of politics. In addition, it generated expectations about what we would find, i.e., essentially providing us with low-level hypotheses. In particular, the typology suggested that relatively high levels of conflict typically occur when redistributive policy is considered. The fact that the CHIP policy pro-cess in Ohio and New York exhibited little conflict may indeed show the irrele-vance of Lowi's conceptual framework to the state level—or the idiosyncratic nature of our cases. On the other hand, it may reveal something important about this kind of devolution of redistributive programs from the federal government to the states.

Could devolution, a kind of political handoff from the federal government to the states, be an innovative political strategy for attaining new redistributive pro-grams? Because those favoring progressive legislation have preferred national solutions when they could get them, a sea change would be required for liberals to embrace what has heretofore largely been the conservative mantra of devolu-tion. New redistributive programs of any magnitude were unthinkable until the budget deficits turned into surpluses on the eve of the millennium. Now, with well-organized progressive advocacy groups in the states and the costs largely paid by those who have a voice in national politics but have limited ability to stop legisla-tion at the state level, perhaps other redistributive programs can be enacted. Fed-eral SCHIP might be the harbinger of a new type of "devolved" redistributive programs. From another point of view, it could also be seen as the beginning of the end of entitlements to social benefits. It will therefore be crucial to evaluate the future of CHIP in the states in making this judgment.

---

*This summary has largely ignored North Carolina's refundable tax credit, which is ad-ministered by the Department of Revenue. It might well serve as a textbook example of controversial redistributive policy, and its passage even involved rhetoric suggesting class conflict. Of course, it was forced on the Democratic governor by the Republican House supported by an influential conservative association.

REFERENCES

Albany Times Union. 1996. "Pataki Pressed to Broaden Kids' Health Coverage." July 11.
————. 1997. "Ads to Tout Health Plan for Kids of Working Poor." June 5.
Ayres, B. D., Jr. 1998. "Pataki Proposing Health Care Plan for Young People." *New York Times,* January 8.
Beamer, G. 1998. "Creating a Public Good: State Enactment of the Children's Health Insurance Program." Paper presented at the 1998 Annual Meeting of the American Political Science Association, Boston.
————. 1999. "Ideology, Partisan Control, and the Politics of the Children's Health Insurance Program." Paper presented at the 1999 Annual Meeting of the American Political Science Association, Atlanta.
Beer, S. H. 1976. "The Adoption of General Revenue Sharing: A Case Study in Public Sector Politics." *Public Policy* 24:127–195.
Benjamin, G., and R. C. Lawton. 2001. "New York's Governorship: Back to the Future?" In *Governing New York State,* 4th ed., ed. J. Stonecash. Albany: State University of New York Press.
Brandon, W. P. 1991. "Politics, Health, and the Elderly: Inventing the Next Century—The Age of Aging." In *Health Politics and Policy,* 2d ed., ed. T. J. Litman and L. S. Robins. Albany: Delmar.
Brandon, W. P., and D. B. Bradley. 1997. "The Elderly and Health Politics: The 'Coming of Age' of Aging." In *Health Politics and Policy,* 3d ed., ed. T. J. Litman and L. S. Robins. Albany: Delmar.
Brewer, M. D., and J. M. Stonecash. 2001. "Political Parties and Elections." In *Governing New York State,* 4th ed., ed. J. Stonecash. Albany: State University of New York Press.
Bruno, J. L. 1998. *The Child Health Plus Insurance Plan and Selected Related Program Provisions.* Albany, NY: Majority Council Program Office, Council on Health Care Finance, New York State Senate.
Bureau of National Affairs. 1996a. "New York: Health Care Industry Prepares for Big Changes in Rate-Setting System." *Health Care Policy Report,* December 6, pp. 1939–1940.
————. 1996b. "New York: Lawmakers Approve Bill to Overhaul State's Hospital Rate-Setting System." *Health Care Policy Report,* July 22, p. 1197.
————. 1997a. "Children's Health: HCFA Releases More Guidelines on Law as State, Federal Officials Wrap Up Talks." *Health Care Policy Report,* September 22, pp. 1439–1441.
————. 1997b. "New York: Health Commissioner Outlines Children's Health Insurance Plan." *Health Care Policy Report,* December 15, p. 1860.
————. 1998a. "New York: Assembly Passes Legislation to Expand Children's Health Insurance Program." *Health Care Policy Report,* May 25, p. 870–871.
————. 1998b. "New York: Gov. Pataki Proposes Expansion of State's Children's Health Program." *Health Care Policy Report,* February 16, p. 300.
Children's Defense Fund–Ohio. 2000. *New Faces, Working Families: Child Health Insurance Works for Ohio Families.* Columbus, OH.
Cigler, B. 1995. " Not Just Another Special Interest: Intergovernmental Representation." In *Interest Group Politics,* 4th ed., ed. A. J. Cigler and B. A. Loomis. Washington, DC: CQ Press.

Cunningham, P. J., and M. H. Park. 2000. *Recent Trends in Children's Health Insurance Coverage: No Gains for Low-Income Children.* Issue brief from HSC, no. 29. Washington DC: Center for Studying Health System Change.

Curtin, M. F. 1996. *The Ohio Politics Almanac.* Kent, OH: Kent State University Press.

Dao, J. 1997. "Pataki Plan Seeks U.S. Funds to Cover Uninsured Children." *New York Times,* October 4.

DeParle, N-A. M. 1999. Testimony of Nancy-Ann DeParle, administrator, Health Care Financing Administration, on the Children's Health Insurance Program before the Senate Finance Committee, April 29 (HCFA web page: *www.hcfa.gov/init/testm429 .htm*).

Dutton, M. 1998. *New York's Child Health Insurance Expansion: Summary of S.7843/ A.10767B.* New York: Children's Defense Fund–New York.

Families USA Foundation. 1997. *Field Report.* August, pp. 1–6.

Funderburk, C., and R. W. Adams. 1994. "Interest Groups in Ohio Politics." In *Ohio Politics,* ed. A. P. Lamais, pp. 303–330. Kent, OH: Kent State University Press.

Gargan, J. J. 1994. "The Ohio Executive Branch." In *Ohio Politics,* ed. A. P. Lamais, pp. 258–282. Kent, OH: Kent State University Press.

Gauthier, A. K., and S. P. Schrodel. 1997. *Expanding Children's Coverage: Lessons from State Initiatives in Health Care Reform.* Washington, DC: Alpha Center.

Hackey, R. B. 1998. *Rethinking Health Care Policy: The New Politics of State Regulation.* Washington, DC: Georgetown University Press.

Hernandez, R. 1999. "Inquiry Grows as Rolls Fall for Medicaid." *New York Times,* June 8.

Hood, J. 1997. "The Worst Option: Lawmakers Should Not Expand Medicaid." Briefing paper, November 20. Raleigh, NC: John Locke Foudation.

———. 1998a. ". . . House's Plan Is Better." *Raleigh News & Observer.* Letter to the editor, March 27.

———. 1998b. "The RITE CHIP: Comparing House and Senate Kid Care Plans." Briefing paper, March 27. Raleigh, NC: John Locke Foundation.

———. 1998c. "Stacking the CHIPs: Myths Surround Child Health Care Debate." Briefing paper, April 1. Raleigh, NC: John Locke Foundation.

Iglehart, J. K. 1999. "The American Health Care System—Medicaid." *New England Journal of Medicine* 340 (November 5): 403–408.

Johnson, A. 1998. "Ohio to Sign Multistate Tobacco Pact." *Columbus Dispatch,* November 19.

Johnson, K. A. 1998. Presentation on CHIP to the National Conference of State Legislatures, May.

Johnson, K. A , C. DeGraw, C. Sonosky, A. Markus, and S. Rosenbaum. 1997. *Children's Health Insurance: A Comparison of Major Federal Legislation.* Washington, DC: Center for Health Policy Research, George Washington University Medical Center.

Johnson, K. A., and J. E. McDonough. 1998. *Expanding Health Coverage for Children: Matching Federal Policies and State Strategies.* New York: Reforming States Group and the Milbank Memorial Fund.

Johnson, N. 1997. Press release, Office of Congresswoman Nancy Johnson, May 1.

Kingdon, J. W. 1995. *Agendas, Alternatives, and Public Policies.* 2d ed. New York: HarperCollins.

Lewin Group. 1996. *Ohio Department of Human Services Regional Community Forum Summary Report.* Columbus: Ohio Department of Human Services.

Lowi, T. J. 1964. "American Business, Public Policy, Case-Studies, and Political Theory." *World Politics* 16:677–715.

———. 1972. "Four Systems of Policy, Politics, and Choice." *Public Administration Review* 33:298–310.

Marmor, T. R., and M. L Barer. 1997. "The Politics of Universal Health Insurance: Lessons for and from the 1990s." In *Health Politics and Policy,* 3d ed., ed. T. R. Litman and L. S. Robins. Albany, NY: Delmar.

McCall, C. 1998. *Child Health Insurance: Current Issues and Policy Options.* Office of the New York State Comptroller, Albany.

Medlin, D. 1999. Memo to G. Daughtry regarding North Carolina Health Choice, July 15.

Miller, T. 1994. "The Celeste Era, 1983–1991." In *Ohio Politics,* ed. A. P. Lamais, pp. 136–150. Kent, OH: Kent State University Press.

Miller and Byrne, Inc. 1977. *Final Report: The Evaluation of the Impact of PHS Programs on State Health Goals and Activities.* Pub. no. (HRA) 77-604, U.S. Department of Health, Education, and Welfare, Health Resources Administration.

Morone, J. A. 1996. "Universal Health Insurance for Children: The Political Prospects." Draft prepared for the Conference on First Steps for Children: Strategies for Universal Health Insurance for Our Nation's Youth, cosponsored by the Robert Wood Johnson Foundation and the Columbia University School of Public Health, October 3–4.

Nather, D. 1997a. "U.S. Budget: GOP Divided over Kid Care Benefits; Choice of Seven Plans Under Discussion." *BNA's Health Care Policy Report,* July 21, pp. 1126–1128.

———. 1997b. "White House, Republicans at Odds over Kids' Care, Medicaid Proposals." *BNA's Health Care Policy Report,* July 28, pp. 1165–1167.

Nather, D., and A. Simendinger. 1997. "Children's Health: Daschle to Introduce Tax Subsidy Plan, Will Allow Debate on Other Approaches." *BNA's Health Care Policy Report,* January 13, pp. 74–76.

National Association of Child Advocates. 1999. *Child Advocates: Making a Difference.* Washington, DC.

New York Task Force on Immigrant Health. 1999. *Child Health Insurance for Immigrants: Overcoming the Barriers.* New York: U.S. Public Health Service, Region 2.

North Carolina Health Access Coalition. 1999. From web site *http://www.ncjusticeorg/health/description.html* (July 12).

North Carolina Senate Bill 2, An Act to Establish the Health Insurance Program for Children and to Authorize a Tax Credit for Certain Purchasers of Dependent Health Insurance. 1998. Ratified bill, General Assembly of North Carolina, extra session. Telefacsimile obtained from the State Library of North Carolina, June 22, 1999.

Ohio Child Health Coalition. 1998. *Consensus Document on the State Children's Health Insurance Program (CHIP).* Columbus, OH.

Ohio Department of Human Services. 1999. *Ohio Annual CHIP Report for Fiscal Year 1998.* Columbus, OH.

Ohio Report. 1997a. "Budget Bill Conferees Told They Have $200 Million to $400 Million More Available." Columbus, OH: Gongwer News Service. June 9, 1–3.

———. 1997b. "Government Budget, While Termed Low-Growth, Will Create High Interest." Columbus, OH: Gongwer News Service. February 3, pp. 1–6.

———. 2000. "Taft Announces Simplified Healthy Start Sign-Up; Program Expansion." Columbus, OH: Gongwer News Service. March 14, p. 2.

Pear, R. 1994. "Clintons Should Address Health Care One Issue at a Time, Experts Suggest." *New York Times,* October 10.

Perez-Pena, R. 1998. "Pataki Broadens Health Plan for Children." *New York Times,* February 11.

Petersen, R. E., and J. M. Stonecash. 2001. "The Legislature, Parties, and Resolving Conflict." In *Governing New York State,* 4th ed., ed. J. Stonecash. Albany: State University of New York Press.

Raleigh News & Observer. 1997. "Healthy Start for Kids." Editorial, December 20.

———. 1998a. "Kids Are Waiting." Editorial, April 17.

———. 1998b. "Legislative Tally." May 4.

———. 1998c. "Listening Post." May 10.

Ripley, R. B., and G. A. Franklin. 1987. *Congress, the Bureaucracy, and Public Policy,* 4th ed. Chicago: Dorsey.

Rosenbaum, S., et al. 1998. "The Children's Hour: The State Children's Health Insurance Program." *Health Affairs* 17 (January/February): 75–89.

Rowland, D. 1998a. "Governor Seeking Ways to Expand Child Health Care." *Columbus Dispatch,* January 15.

———. 1998b. "Kids' Coverage May Get a Booster Shot." *Columbus Dispatch,* January 14.

Ryan, W. T. 1998. *Report of the Children's Health Insurance Program Advisory Task Force.* Columbus, OH: Ohio Department of Health.

Sabatier, P. A. 1999. Introduction to *Theories of the Policy Process,* ed. P. A. Sabatier. Boulder, CO: Westview.

Sapolsky, H. M., J. Aisenberg, and J. A. Morone. 1987. "The Call to Rome and Other Obstacles to State-Level Innovation." *Public Administration Review* 47:135–142.

Sardell, A. 1991. "Child Health Policy in the U.S.: The Paradox of Consensus." In *Health Policy and the Disadvantaged,* ed. L. D. Brown. Durham, NC: Duke University Press.

———. 1994. "Health Policy in New York State: Health Care Needs and System Reform." In *Governing New York State,* 3d ed., ed. J. M. Stonecash, J. K. White, and P. W. Colby. Albany: State University of New York Press.

Sardell, A., and K. Johnson, 1998. "The Politics of EPSDT Policy in the 1990s: Policy Entrepreneurs, Political Streams, and Children's Health Benefits." *Milbank Quarterly* 76 (2): 175–205.

Schneider, A., and H. Ingram. 1993. "Social Construction of Target Populations: Implications for Politics and Policy." *American Political Science Review* 87 (2): 334–347.

Sparer, M. S., and L. D. Brown. 1999. "Nothing Exceeds Like Success: Managed Care Comes to Medicaid in New York City." *Milbank Quarterly* 77:205–223.

Storey, J. 1998. "Lip Service: Getting Out the Word on Public Health Programs." *Empire State Report* (May 1998): 50–53.

Suddes, T. 1994. "Panorama of Ohio Politics in the Voinovich Era, 1991–." In *Ohio Politics,* ed. A. P. Lamais, pp. 157–180. Kent, OH: Kent State University Press.

Thompson, C. R. 1998. "A Presidential Transition and Public Policy: The Repeal of Medicare Catastrophic Coverage." In *George Bush: Leading in a New World,* ed. W. F. Levantrosser. Westport, CT: Greenwood.

Ullman, F., B. Bruen, and J. Holahan. 1998. *The State Children's Health Insurance Program: A Look at the Numbers.* Occasional paper no. 4, "Assessing the New Federalism: An Urban Institute Program to Assess Changing Social Policies." Washington, DC: Urban Institute.

University of Rochester. 1996. *Evaluation of Child Health Plus in New York State.* The Rochester Child Health Studies Group, Department of Pediatrics, University of Rochester School of Medicine.

Vitaglione, Tom. 1997. Memoranda of August 8 and September 3 and other documents (including agenda for meetings on July 17, August 14, September 9, and October 8) pertaining to the Children's Health Insurance Task Force. From the files of Vice President Pam Silberman, North Carolina Institute of Medicine.

Wagner, J. 1997. "Hunt Plan Could Raise Health Tab." *Raleigh News & Observer,* December 18.

———. 1998a. "Child Health Measure Goes to Hunt." *Raleigh News & Observer,* May 1.

———. 1998b. "Coverage for Kids Offered Quietly." *Raleigh News & Observer,* October 1.

———. 1998c. "Deal Reached to Insure Children." *Raleigh News & Observer,* April 29.

———. 1998d. "Health Bill Faces Legislative Gridlock." *Raleigh News & Observer,* April 18.

———. 1998e. "Panel Backs Health Plan for Children." *Raleigh News & Observer,* February 6.

———. 1998f. "Program for Uninsured Children Ending As State Effort Gets Started." *Raleigh News & Observer,* September 25.

———. 1998g. "Talk, No Action on Child Health." *Raleigh News & Observer,* April 1.

Weissert, C. S., and W. G. Weissert. 1996. *Governing Health—The Politics of Health Policy.* Baltimore, MD: Johns Hopkins University Press.

7

Managed Care in Public Mental Health Systems

Chris Koyanagi and Joseph J. Bevilacqua

This chapter addresses state-level reforms for the inclusion of people with serious mental disorders in public-sector managed care arrangements. It describes the history of these reforms and their impact and assesses the roles and motivations of key actors.

The history of recent mental health reforms is briefly reviewed, beginning with the community mental health movement of the 1960s and 1970s and the community support system initiatives of the 1980s. The introduction, through these reforms, of a systems approach to mental health care that included rehabilitation and supportive services such as housing, employment, and income maintenance is related to the current managed care reform movement. The important implications of Medicaid resources in these reforms are identified and their relationship to managed mental health care is analytically reviewed. The emergence of managed care and its use as a vehicle for reform by states is explained and its energizing impact on the mental health constituencies is explored. The larger theme of accountability is reviewed against the different interests of the state and its various authorities (i.e., the mental health and Medicaid agencies), private companies, and the various constituencies of providers, consumers, family members, and advocates. The chapter concludes with a discussion of the impact that managed mental health care has had on the public system and with an update on the current status of these reforms.

PUBLIC MENTAL HEALTH POLICY POSTDEINSTITUTIONALIZATION

Medicaid reforms, including mental health managed care arrangements, were given significant impetus by the failure of national health care reform in 1994. Managed mental health care in the public sector also has roots in earlier policy reform movements.

Unlike other categories of health care, mental health has long been a public responsibility. In 1998, the nation spent nearly $80 billion on direct treatment of mental illness, 54% of it government funds for the public mental health system (McCusick et al. 1996, 147–157). The history of the public mental health system can be viewed as a series of attempts at reform (Goldman 1999), of which managed mental health care is the latest round. Recent relevant public-sector reforms include the community mental health movement (deinstitutionalization) of the 1960s and 1970s and the community support system initiatives that occurred during the 1980s to assist individuals with severe and persistent mental illnesses (Goldman 1999).

Public systems were slow to respond to the complex needs of individuals with serious mental illness who, following deinstitutionalization, found themselves in the community without adequate supports. However, by the early 1980s, federal and state mental health policy began to focus on community support services for those who, in a previous era, would have resided in state hospitals. These reforms went beyond just mental health treatment to endorse a systems approach to care, including important rehabilitation and supportive services along with basic medical and mental health clinical treatments. Importantly, the need for other supports, such as housing, job training, and income maintenance, was also addressed.

To find the resources for such a broad service array in a politically conservative time, state mental health agencies devised new expansions of Medicaid. These Medicaid expansions were funded at the state level by state mental health authorities, which contributed the Medicaid match. As a result, community mental health services could be significantly increased using federal Medicaid resources, sometimes without increasing the mental health agency's budget very much either, as state mental health appropriations were redirected to serve as the Medicaid match. This was a "win-win" situation for state officials, but it had the effect of making it harder for individuals who were not Medicaid-eligible to access the public mental health system.

The states' financing strategy was so effective that today Medicaid contributes over half of all public-sector community mental health care spending. However, the expansion greatly increased the overall costs of Medicaid, and this approach, used by other agencies as well as mental health, helped fuel the overall escalation of Medicaid spending in the early 1990s.

PUBLIC-SECTOR MANAGED CARE FOR PEOPLE WITH MENTAL ILLNESS

With the failure of national health care reform in 1994, states were left to deal with the problem of Medicaid expenditures that had doubled from 1987 to 1992 and then doubled again between 1992 and 1994. To control this rapid rise, states, as had private purchasers before them, turned to managed care as a means to cut costs and rein in utilization.

Managed care for the Medicaid population initially involved placing low-income women and children in health maintenance organizations and similar group health care arrangements. Meanwhile, people with severe disorders and disabilities remained in the fee-for-service Medicaid system. But states could not control Medicaid spending without addressing the public mental health delivery system, now heavily funded by Medicaid. Moreover, decisions on when and how to shift to managed mental health care were being made by Medicaid agencies and state budget officers, not by state mental health authorities. As a result, individuals who rely on the public mental health system became the first group of people with disabilities to be included in Medicaid managed care approaches as public mental health systems were swept up in states' Medicaid managed care reform.

As states developed their policies for these reforms, two broad patterns of Medicaid managed care arrangements for mental health service delivery have emerged, often coexisting in the same state. The most prevalent approach is inclusion of basic mental health benefits in the benefit packages of health maintenance organizations (HMOs) or other managed care organizations (MCOs). The most significant arrangement for individuals served through public mental health systems is the carve-out managed behavioral health care approach. In these specialized carve-outs, all of the care for individuals who depend on the public mental health system is managed, including acute and long-term care.

These two approaches to managed mental health care reflect the different histories and different goals of the public mental health system and the Medicaid program. The public mental health system serves individuals with severe disorders, most of whom are also poor; in contrast, Medicaid acts as a health care purchaser for low-income individuals and families, some of whom need mental health services. The carve-out managed mental health care plans should thus be viewed in the context of state mental health public policy, as discussed above, while the HMO/MCO managed care arrangements represent part of the evolution of health care insurance and health policy for low-income people.

For low-income women and children, states found managed care a significant cost-control device, and between 1993 and 1998, Medicaid managed care enrollment grew dramatically. The percentage of the Medicaid population enrolled in managed care was less than 15% in 1993, but over 53% by 1998 (Health Care Financing Administration 1999). In addition, managed care provided a single medical home for a population that had little or no access to routine care. Unfortunately, mental health services are a poor stepchild compared to medical services under health maintenance organizations, as well as a relatively new aspect of HMO benefit packages (Durham 1995). As a result, the mental health benefits in HMO/MCO Medicaid contracts are limited in the array of services covered and have strict limits on the duration of treatment.

This is clearly not good policy for those who rely on the public mental health system, most of whom have serious and persistent mental illness. States have therefore adopted an approach used by private-sector purchasers to separate, or carve out, mental health benefits for this population. Many have also adopted the same delivery mechanism as the private purchasers, contracting with managed behavioral health care corporations.

In the private sector, these companies had shown an ability to significantly reduce escalating mental health inpatient costs. States sought similar results (Essock and Goldman 1995). Although perceived as more qualified than HMOs/ MCOs, these corporations turned out to have limited experience in managing care for people with the most serious mental disorders. To compensate, many hired public mental health officials (often former state commissioners) to design their new public-sector plans.

HISTORY OF MANAGED MENTAL HEALTH CARE IN THE PUBLIC SECTOR

The first Medicaid managed care carve-out program began operation, using non-profit entities, in 1990 in Arizona. In 1991, Utah adopted managed care in its public mental health system by shifting its traditional community mental health providers into managed care contracts. Then, in 1992, Massachusetts became the first state to contract with a private, for-profit company to manage care for individuals with serious mental illness in the public system.* This move by Massachusetts stimulated other states' interest, and Iowa, Tennessee, and Nebraska soon also contracted with managed behavioral health care plans.

Managed care reforms for public mental health systems really took off, however, only after federal health care reform stalled. Between 1995 and 1997, virtually all states entered into discussions about how and when to implement Medicaid managed mental health care. A review of the status of managed mental health care under Medicaid undertaken in 1995 found that 17 states had statewide (or nearly statewide) federally approved managed care arrangements for people in the public mental health system. Eight of the 17 had carve-out contracts with private managed behavioral health care corporations. More than 20 additional states had submitted waiver requests for managed mental health care to the federal government or were planning to do so (Bazelon Center for Mental Health Law 1996).

By 1999, however, this momentum had slowed significantly. Although 97 managed care programs in 47 states were providing some form of mental health and/or addiction services (Substance Abuse and Mental Health Services Administration 1998), most were HMOs/MCOs providing a limited acute-care mental

---

*The Massachusetts carve-out is unique in that it does not cover all individuals in the state. Those in HMOs receive their mental health benefit from the HMO, while only those in primary care case management receive their mental health care through the carve-out.

health benefit. In such cases, some other Medicaid financing mechanism (such as fee-for-service or a mental health carve-out plan) exists for public mental health system clients. Only about 20 states had operational managed mental health care carve-out programs that covered people with serious mental illness in the public system; most of these were restricted to certain areas of the state, and some only covered a specific population, such as children (Substance Abuse and Mental Health Services Administration 1998).

Medicaid managed care for clients of the public mental health system is very idiosyncratic, and each state's arrangement is unique, reflecting the historic organization of mental health care delivery in the state as well as various political factors. Thus, while contracts with private firms are still important, states have explored various other approaches. For example, many states (including California, Pennsylvania, Michigan, and Washington) have used county or regional public or quasi-public bodies as the lead contract entity. Others have become their own system managers (Delaware) or have limited private companies to administrative services only (Maryland). New Mexico rejected the carve-out approach for individuals with serious mental illness and developed contracts with three HMOs/MCOs for all mental health services previously delivered in the public sector. In several states, various approaches coexist, particularly where responsibility has devolved down to the county level (California, Pennsylvania, and Texas).

Clearly some significant change has occurred since 1995, when the vast majority of states seemed poised to shift the public mental health system into statewide managed care using private for-profit contractors. To explore the reasons for this change, it is necessary to understand the motivations of the key players—Medicaid agencies, mental health agencies, and stakeholder groups of advocates and providers.

MOTIVATIONS FOR MANAGED MENTAL HEALTH CARE

The use of managed care contracting for public mental health services has been explained as an effort to control costs, minimize risks, and contract out what state mental health authorities do poorly themselves (Essock and Goldman 1995). While these were certainly significant motivators, the picture is more complex.

When Massachusetts contracted management of a substantial portion of its mental health system to a private corporation, it was rejecting the incremental approach to mental health reforms in the 1980s (see earlier discussion) and adopting Medicaid's privatization reform approach. This led to drastic change both in service delivery and in financing and to the introduction of market issues and competition in the previously isolated public mental health system. Over time, as other states moved to adopt managed care, there was an increased emphasis on trying to control Medicaid costs and privatize the mental health system to achieve efficiency. At the same time, state mental health officials were attempting to incorporate the long-standing public policy goal of organized systems of care that provide continuity of care and an essential safety net.

For the states, the primary motivation has always been restraining costs. State officials were concerned about overall public mental health spending, the costs to Medicaid, the high rate of cost increases, and their need to be able to predict future expenditures (Bazelon Center for Mental Health Law 2000c). This was especially true during the early 1990s, when Medicaid costs escalated. During those years, Medicaid agencies often made many of the most critical decisions on managed care contracting for mental health services. State mental health officials, when they were involved at all, shared or had imposed on them the cost-saving goal of senior state policymakers. However, many also sought to use managed care to continue the goal of restructuring their mental health systems into more organized and rational systems of care. Undoubtedly, they understood that efficiencies could be realized by providing more appropriate care. Cutting inpatient and residential costs and reducing reliance on more expensive providers of care could enable state mental health agencies (Iowa is an example) to slow the rise in spending, expand community services, and increase the quality of care, all at the same time (Rohland 1998).

Several events made it possible for states to combine these goals of cost-saving and improved quality. First, the escalation of Medicaid costs had decreased significantly since 1994, which reduced the pressure for extreme cuts. Second, stakeholder groups organized and demanded more attention to quality of care issues. Finally, the federal government's failure to enact national health reform left a void for states to fill with respect to providing access to mental health services.

Moreover, controlling costs over the long term requires having a system that is efficient and at the same time grants reasonable access to those in need. Mental health policymakers believed that organized systems of care would reduce fragmentation and overlapping, conflicting, or redundant services and could thus ensure appropriate utilization and prove the most efficient (Dixon and Croze 1997). In many states, the goals of the community support system reform had not yet been realized due to inertia and resistance among traditional providers. State officials wanted to focus on the needs of the individual, not to fund agency programs that would then attempt to fit consumers into the services the agency wanted to provide (Bachrach 1996; Day and Cohen 1993). Managed care contracts could bypass these pockets of resistance. Mental health administrators wanted the plans to do what they themselves had not been able to successfully accomplish—rapidly redirect resources from expensive 24-hour services into rehabilitation and other community supports. State mental health officials focused on the fact that many aspects of managed care, such as a flexible benefit package, individualized care, case management, and limiting of access to residential settings, are highly compatible with goals in the public mental health system (Essock and Goldman 1995).

Stakeholder groups were motivated by a desire to improve quality of care. A major fear of all constituent groups was that the private vendors would focus on maximizing profits and reducing costs rather than on meeting the needs of people with severe mental illnesses (Sullivan 1995; Hoge et al. 1994). Consumer groups viewed with alarm the level of cost savings being proposed in public mental health systems that, in their view, were already grossly underfunded. Yet the family and advocacy groups were also sympathetic to reforming the system, so their goals did not entirely conflict with those of state officials (Ross 1999). They also saw some advantages to contracting with private plans. For example, they saw how states could make good use of the managed care vendors' expertise in providing cost-effective treatment and could benefit from their billing and information systems. Nonetheless, they wanted the state to retain control over the shape of the contract and to insist on detailed program requirements for plans.

Providers, while sharing some of the advocates' concerns, were more focused on the competitive aspect of contracting and its impact on their programs.

CONSTITUENCY GROUPS ORGANIZE

Individuals with serious mental illness in the public sector have strong, organized constituencies that are often very active politically. Caught off guard at first, these constituencies—including family, advocacy, and community provider groups—organized to oppose what they saw as unseemly haste in states' shift to managed public mental health care approaches. Groups such as state alliances for the mentally ill, mental health associations, and others pressed for inclusion in the process of reform. As a result, after Massachusetts, Tennessee, and Nebraska changed their systems very rapidly, other states spent years discussing and redesigning their approach through processes that have given stakeholders a considerable voice.

Mental health stakeholder groups had a history of collaboration at the state level. However, with respect to managed care issues there were some significantly different points of view. Professional associations, representing the interests of their members who are primarily in private practice, generally sought greater regulation of private-sector managed care. For the most part, these groups were not very active in the public-sector managed care debate, and those that were tended to bring their negative experiences in the private sector to the discussions. Public-sector provider agencies were not inherently opposed to managed care but were vehemently opposed to the introduction of private, for-profit companies, which they saw as usurping their own role. Groups representing consumers, families, and advocates, which all had long-standing concerns about the public mental health system, were far more open-minded. They wanted reform, and if they could achieve it by shifting to managed care, then they would support that change. For the purposes of this chapter, the term stakeholder group, if not more explicitly defined, refers to these consumer, family, and advocacy groups.

While the consumer-oriented stakeholder groups were not able, and did not want, to prevent the shift to managed care, they demanded a voice in how the system was to be redesigned. These groups wanted consumer protections because they viewed managed care with suspicion. In particular, they sought more specific contracting requirements to protect vulnerable consumers from profit-driven plans. The advocacy groups often aligned themselves with state mental health authorities, with whom they had working relationships of long standing, and supported those agencies as they sought increased involvement in Medicaid managed care planning. Given their long history of involvement in mental health policy issues, these groups knew how to make their voices heard at the state level through grassroots advocacy and key contacts with government officials and legislators.

Initially, however, stakeholder involvement was more token than real. At the outset, advocacy groups of consumers, families, and citizens had difficulty gaining access to the planning process and, when they were permitted to participate, felt their input was not taken seriously (Stevenson, Bevilacqua, and Koyanagi 1997). Later, stakeholder groups were able to exert more influence. And once state mental health agencies had a larger role, they often began to promote significant involvement by consumers and other stakeholders (American Managed Behavioral Healthcare Association and National Association of State Mental Health Program Directors 1995), as they realized the importance of these groups' political influence and the similarity of some of their goals.

Stakeholder groups called for more thorough planning during the changeover to managed care. They pressed for a top-to-bottom review of the state mental health system and for clear articulation of the goals and objectives of managed care reform. They wanted to know how and by whom services would be delivered. They wanted to be sure the most effective services were required. They wanted clear statements in the contract regarding the role of consumer and family choice, protections to ensure meaningful appeals, and the manner in which medical-necessity decisions would be made.

Both stakeholders and state mental health authorities were concerned that if costs were controlled merely by limiting access, then the population in need would be cost-shifted to other systems, such as jails. If inpatient utilization were drastically reduced without alternative services, a series of crises could result and long-term savings would not be achieved.

Planning groups to address these systemic issues formed in all the states that were shifting toward managed care. These groups now struggled with how to write a Request for Proposals (RFP), which would delineate in a single document all aspects of a mental health system—a monumental task. Slowing the process even more was the fact that these discussions often force public debate on important, long-standing, and unresolved policy issues. For example, as efficiency became the goal, states grappled with the need to define priorities and determine how to strike the balance between the needs of a few high users, whose care is very expensive, and the needs of the majority (Rosenheck 1999). States also wrestled with how to delineate the roles and responsibilities of other agencies in meeting the needs of mental health consumers and how to prevent cost-shifting either into or out of the mental health managed care system.

Stakeholders demanded more protections, and states became more cautious and concerned that they needed to stipulate in the contract all the factors they wanted addressed. Detailed concept papers, requests for information, and draft RFPs were issued and often revised several times before a final RFP was released. State mental health planners attended numerous meetings, receiving advice from each other and from the cadre of consultants who were available to help them. States' planners sought to become "intelligent purchasers" who could reduce regulation while maintaining the values of their public system and who could provide incentives and demand outcomes from managed care vendors (Croze 1995).

The combination of stakeholder demands and hard-learned lessons from certain states resulted in RFPs becoming far more specific, very lengthy, and more difficult for the bidders to meet. Iowa, for example, gradually increased the specificity of each of its contract renewals, placing greater emphasis on preventing denials, premature discharge, and inappropriate medical-necessity decisions; on addressing the problems of children; and on improving reporting from the plan on significant performance indicators (Rohland 1998; Nardini 1999).

National advocacy groups also sought to influence the process, producing manuals and guides to managed care contracting for local advocacy groups (Malloy 1995; Bazelon Center for Mental Health Law 1995). Several national groups, such as the National Mental Health Association, organized training sessions around the country to help their affiliates understand managed care. They also hired staff to work with their affiliates' leaders. Manuals on what should be included in managed care contracts gradually gave way to reports on what were considered good examples of contracting language (Huskamp 1996; Rosenbaum et al. 1998; Bazelon Center for Mental Health Law and Legal Action Center 1998). The National Alliance for the Mentally Ill issued an assessment of the major firms doing business with the public sector, grading most of them as failing on several important indices (Hall, Edgar, and Flynn 1997).

Public-sector providers became better organized too. They spoke loudly about how well suited they were to comply with the new, more stringent contract demands. Community mental health providers organized themselves, first to obtain subcontracts from the carve-out companies, then to partner with them, and finally to become the contracting entities themselves.

In time, then, while Medicaid and senior state officials still set the overall direction for managed mental health care (cost-saving), the important specifics were designed by those who had traditionally influenced public mental health policy. These forces included family groups, advocates, consumers and providers, and state mental health officials.

THE ROLE OF PRIVATE COMPANIES

Advocates were greatly concerned about the companies states were using to manage their systems. They believed that these plans did not have the knowledge to manage a public mental health system (Dixon and Croze 1997). The private market, where the plans had their prior experience, serves a population significantly different from the group served by public mental health care. Private-sector managed care techniques also differ in important ways from public-sector management (Essock and Goldman 1995). For example, cost savings from provider payments will be hard to achieve in the public sector, and short-term savings from limiting access may result in significant future costs or cost-shifting to other public systems.

The service array is also different. The working population covered under private insurance generally requires medical care, clinical treatment, and medications. These are provided through traditional systems, such as hospitals and office-based practice. In contrast, the public sector requires a far broader, more sustained set of services because its population has much more serious disorders. These services include crisis and other residential services (including group homes and supported living programs), intensive community services (such as psychiatric rehabilitation), specialized services for children (such as in-home family support services and day treatment programs in schools), peer-run and peer-support services, and more. Stakeholders were afraid that their states' fragile systems of care, especially the less traditional services, would crumble as private companies emphasized inpatient hospital care, medications, and psychotherapy. Anecdotes from the first states to institute managed care fueled this concern. For instance, Massachusetts' design left nonacute community support services in the fee-for-service category, creating significant problems with continuity of care for individuals with serious mental illnesses and leading to underutilization of community services and concern about poor outcomes.

The failure to deal promptly with problems that arose in several states heightened advocates' concerns. They viewed with alarm, for example, a number of difficulties with the Tennessee managed care program, TennCare. Yet not until 1996 were these concerns finally recognized by officials in the state and federal governments. Then the Health Care Financing Administration cited TennCare's mental health carve-out program as having significant problems in the areas of access, funding, quality of care, assessment of data, contract issues, and state mental hospital utilization (Health Care Financing Administration 1998).

Advocates' concerns about the private plan's experiences were valid, but the public sector also benefited from the plan's expertise, and the transfer of knowledge flowed in both directions. Company executives handling public-sector contracts admitted that they learned a lot from the public sector about which services work for whom. Public officials, providers, and other stakeholders acknowledged the significant improvement offered by the companies. These improvements included their data infrastructure, their capacity to monitor and direct utilization of various services, and their attention to early access to services (Ross 1999).

States generally credited by stakeholders with having achieved significant reforms through the use of managed care for their public mental health systems include Iowa, Colorado, Utah, Florida, Maryland, and Delaware (for children). In a number of these states, formal evaluations also found positive results.

STATE CAPACITY TO MANAGE

Another concern of stakeholders was that contractors would not be held accountable by the states. State mental health authorities have considerable experience working in a bureaucratic environment of limited resources and have developed significant capacity in terms of policy expertise and system development. Thus they were skilled at the no longer relevant bureaucratic tasks required to run grant-in-aid programs and manage a network of state hospitals, but they were not prepared for the shift to managed care. State agencies were practiced at organizing a system of services to deliver necessary care, but the shift to managed care contracting placed a number of decisions in the hands of vendors who were likely to deliver only what they were specifically required to and who would make their own decisions on any issues left open by vague contract language. These new challenges were not initially appreciated, and even once recognized, they were not easy to meet.

Managed care contracting required state mental health authorities to acquire new skills in a hurry, such as the ability to structure and monitor purchasing agreements. But they lacked experience with incentive contracting and fee negotiation (Essock and Goldman 1995). These agencies were also hampered by a lack of the tools private vendors of managed mental health services have perfected over the past decade, such as management information systems. State data systems were so inadequate that mistakes in the number of individuals a plan would have to serve and the level of service they would require led to miscalculation of needed resources. Several contracts had difficult start-up periods due to these kinds of problems.*

State mental health authorities felt sufficiently insecure about their new responsibilities to develop a white paper (in conjunction with the national organization for managed behavioral health care plans) defining their appropriate role. According to the white paper, an "effective state mental health agency" is one that is involved in the procurement process, has access to information, provides advocacy on behalf of the clients, sets standards, and provides leadership (American Managed Behavioral Healthcare Association and National Association of State

---

*For example, San Diego, where efforts to include 10,000 new enrollees in the managed care plan resulted in significant problems in the United Behavioral Health data system and delayed payment of claims.

Mental Health Program Directors 1995). The paper urged state officials to ensure that RFPs were clear and specific and developed by individuals who were "competent." In a second version of this paper, state officials and managed care plan executives acknowledged the need for new definitions of medical necessity and new models of physical and behavioral health integration for public-sector, as contrasted with private-sector (employer), contracts.

The changeover to contracting had other effects as well. State mental health authorities found others taking over their responsibilities. Medicaid agencies assumed some of their policy responsibilities, and managed care organizations established clinical practice guidelines and medical-necessity criteria for public mental health services (American Managed Behavioral Healthcare Association and National Association of State Mental Health Program Directors 1995). It soon became apparent that the shift to contracting for management of public mental health services meant the state mental health authorities must rise to meet new challenges or risk disappearing. Stakeholders wanted the mental health authority, not the Medicaid agency, to make the critical decisions in contracting for managed mental health care, feeling that these agencies were more familiar with the needs of people who use the public sector (Essock and Goldman 1995). They were alarmed when contracting either precipitated or followed a consolidation and reorganization of state executive agencies to give the mental health authority lower status.

Although initially many of the contracts for carve-out managed mental health care were designed and controlled through the state Medicaid agencies, state mental health authorities did reassert themselves and enter into partnerships with Medicaid in many states (Stevenson, Bevilacqua, and Koyanagi 1997). By 1998, their role in relationship to Medicaid agencies had changed. By this time, with approximately 20 active mental health managed care carve-outs, 19 state mental health authorities shared responsibility with their Medicaid agency for the design and/or writing of the section 1115 or 1915(b) waiver. However, they were still not the agency primarily responsible for managing the contracts. Only 10 mental health authorities jointly shared responsibility for contracting with the Medicaid agency, and only 12 jointly shared responsibility for monitoring and evaluation (National Association of State Mental Health Program Directors 1999). The importance of state mental health authority engagement was underscored in an evaluation of the Massachusetts experience, where researchers attributed the mental health agency's intense engagement with the contractor as an important ingredient linked to the program's success (Callahan et al. 1995). In states where mental health officials were not engaged with Medicaid staff in the reform, they believed the two agencies often worked at cross-purposes.

State mental health officials therefore worked to develop an effective state mental health agency strategy (American Managed Behavioral Healthcare Association and National Association of State Mental Health Program Directors 1995). They struggled to find the appropriate role for the plans while retaining authority to set detailed requirements for their public system. Concern about clients being underserviced and dumped into other systems led to specific requirements that plans report on their performance and assess consumer outcomes. As a result, the managed care vendors have been able to report, for the first time, the real costs and actual utilization of public mental health services. The value of this data is significantly reduced, however, by the poor information systems of state mental health authorities (Essock and Goldman 1995), which lack both historical data to compare with the new information and the sophisticated systems needed to analyze important trends.

THE RESULTS

Evaluations and anecdotal reports show that managed mental health care in the public system has had mixed results. In a few states, the concern expressed by some stakeholders about unwise, drastic cost-cutting has proved valid. But in other states, managed mental health care is credited with significant reform and is now strongly endorsed by stakeholder groups.

Data from the health sector indicate that state Medicaid managed care payment rates vary greatly (Holahan, Rangarajan, and Schirmer 1999; Urban Institute 1999). Although fewer data are available for it, the same pattern appears to be true for carve-out mental health managed care arrangements (Rosenheck 1999). Some states, overly concerned with cost-cutting, underfunded their new managed care systems so much that access was significantly delayed, essential services in the community were not available, prescription drugs were tightly managed, and inpatient care was drastically reduced. In these states, the shift of the public mental health system into managed care was a disaster. The clearest examples are Tennessee, Arizona, and Montana. Tennessee was forced to recalculate its rates and commit to significantly higher expenditures (Health Care Financing Administration 1998). Arizona's largest managed care entity went bankrupt, and continuing fiscal problems led to the resignation in frustration of the Arizona Department of Health Services director (*Mental Health Weekly* 1999). Montana's state legislature stepped in and prohibited renewal of the contract, while its managed care contractor reported losses of $1 million per month.

On the other hand, many state officials and consumer advocacy groups found that managed care made states better able to deal with long-standing problems. One such problem is resistance to change among public-sector providers. Despite improved understanding of how to effectively treat the most severe mental illnesses, state systems have been slow to implement the necessary changes.

Part of the difficulty state mental health authorities have faced has been the resistance of entrenched providers. States have frequently been forced to develop new delivery mechanisms separate from the traditional provider network. Innovations, such as psychiatric rehabilitation programs, were therefore layered on old systems. Meanwhile, the old systems still demanded— and received— resources from the legislature. The opportunity to fund newer service approaches with Medicaid, which states adopted during the era of community service system reform, alleviated some of these difficulties. However, it did not create an efficient system. Partly as a result of this phenomenon, a major study of public-sector treatment for individuals with schizophrenia (Lehman and Steinwachs 1998) found that more than half did not receive the needed array of effective services. Particularly lacking was access to newer antipsychotic medications and assertive community treatment. Under managed care, stakeholders believe access to these services may be expanding.

Unfortunately, there have been few formal evaluations of public-sector managed mental health care, even though such systems should lend themselves to assessment and evaluation because they collect and report a good range of data. In this respect, managed care systems can be far more accountable than the traditional grant-in-aid approach they replace.

Studies of the Massachusetts and Utah systems found early cost savings, generally achieved by decreasing use of inpatient services (Callahan et al. 1995). There was also evidence of increased access, as measured by penetration rates. Cost reductions were significant (22% in Massachusetts) but, surprisingly, did not appear to result in any overall reduction in access or relative quality (Callahan et al. 1995; Dickey et al. 1995; Christianson et al. 1995). Savings in Massachusetts came from decreased use of inpatient care and from the rates negotiated with providers. In this early study, the plan received generally favorable reports on quality from providers (other than providers of children's services), and based on the data the authors did not "believe that costs were shifted to the alternative payers" (Callahan et al. 1995).

In Colorado, capitation was initiated through two different options: contracts with community mental health centers and a contract involving a private, for-profit vendor in another area. An evaluation of these two approaches did not find significant differences between the two. Both reduced costs without significant change in clinical status (Bloom et al. 1998).

Nonetheless, concern continued to be expressed about managed care's impact on people with the most severe disorders. The very few studies of this population that exist show conflicting results. Several studies find that cost reductions have been achieved without significant negative clinical effects, even for people with serious mental illnesses.* One study, however, did find evidence of prob-

*A study in Massachusetts conducted for the federal Health Care Financing Administration found a substantial decline in expenditures (37%) for persons with disabilities, including persons with severe mental illness, below projections for a non–managed care environment. A subsequent study found evidence that this reduced use was accompanied by increased referrals to lower-intensity treatment settings that substituted for inpatient hospitalization, and that there was no increase in treatment denials for this group (Stroup and Dorwart 1995). A study of child services under managed care in Massachusetts questioned the decline in hospital use but pointed out that only more focused research on outcomes could ascertain if this led to poorer quality of care (Nicholson et al. 1996)

lems with the quality of care for individuals with schizophrenia. In Utah, there was significant reliance on medication management in the prepaid health plan compared with the situation before managed care. A substantial number of individuals were found to have been prescribed suboptimal dosages of psychotropic medication and had increased attrition from treatment. On the other hand, numerous other measures of care management showed no change, and the managed care clients received more case management, experienced fewer crisis visits, and had fewer changes in primary therapist (Popkin et al. 1998).

An evaluation conducted by the National Alliance for the Mentally Ill (NAMI) collected information from nine major private plans doing business with the public mental health system. NAMI assessed these plans on nine specific issues related to the needs of people with serious mental illnesses (Hall, Edgar, and Flynn 1997). The plans failed on all measures. NAMI charged that the most effective services and medications were not available, that the plans had inadequate responses to the needs of individuals with severe mental illnesses, and that they failed to expand services to include rehabilitation, assertive community treatment, and housing. According to NAMI, the industry as a whole "failed to exert leadership in . . . helping to create a public mental health system that is systematically expanding . . . supports in the community . . . promote(s) recovery and form(s) the basis of a true system of care." Although the plans retorted that NAMI had out-of-date information and misrepresented their policies, the overall conclusions continue to fuel stakeholder discomfort with managed care delivered through private plans.

An interesting evaluation that compared the operation of integrated health maintenance organizations (many of which subcontracted for managed care with specialized behavioral health carve-out companies) and a pilot prepaid mental health carve-out managed care plan in another area of the state found significant problems with the HMOs, including several that specifically affected persons with serious mental illness (Shern 1998). In terms of access, it was significantly more difficult to obtain needed mental health services, especially for adults on supplemental security income, than to obtain services through the carve-out, and even easier to obtain access in a comparison fee-for-service site. The evaluators conducted 15 detailed case studies of children and consistently found that care and outcomes in the carve-out plan were better. This was true even when the services were delivered by the same provider agencies, thus confirming that it was the *management* of the benefit, not the delivery of clinical care, which led to this result.

As experience has grown and stakeholders have asserted themselves more aggressively, new trends in managed care contracting have emerged. It may be that the experiment of privatizing the mental health system is drawing to a close. More than one contract with a private corporation has ended. Twenty states have county-level mental health authorities, and many of them are now delegating the implementation and management of their managed Medicaid program to individual counties or groups of counties (e.g., Pennsylvania, California, Michigan, and Ohio). A number of states have recently developed managed care programs utilizing their established public-sector systems. Many states have not embraced the concept of using fully integrated health plans (responsible for both general medical services and mental health care) for consumers in the public mental health system. States that have utilized health maintenance organizations have had problems; consequently, stakeholder groups in those states (especially in New Mexico) have been vocal in their complaints of insufficient service and inappropriate cost-cutting (Flynn and Bernstein 1998; Washburn 1998; Bazelon Center for Mental Health Law 2000 a, b). In fact, only in a state with an integrated plan, New Mexico, has HCFA found such serious deficiencies that it refused to renew the Medicaid waiver.

STATE MANAGED MENTAL HEALTH CARE REFORM TODAY

The trend away from private companies reflects several realities. Medicaid costs are no longer out of control, therefore the financial crisis has passed. The number of plans competing for business has dropped considerably, as consolidation in the industry has left only a handful of major national companies. State planners may be realizing, as the Florida evaluation emphasized, that new financing and organizational strategies are not enough on their own to improve mental health care delivery (Shern 1998). Finally, managed care is no longer considered a revolutionary approach requiring outside expertise; it is viewed instead as just another tool for organizing the public system and providing accountability.

As managed care becomes more a tool than a crusade, policymakers seek to use capitation thoughtfully and allow managed care to evolve at a reasonable pace. There is now a significant emphasis on creating more accountability. Initiatives are under way to develop appropriate performance and outcome measures. The American Managed Behavioral Healthcare Association (1998) has its own performance measures (PERMS), which gauge nonfinancial aspects of managed care plans with the goal of creating a single, industry-level database. The association does not report on individual plan performance but develops aggregate data on access to care, quality measures, and consumer satisfaction. In the first year, however, few of the companies had adequate data systems to fully report such information. The association remains focused on this measurement tool, however, and has expanded it in PERMS.2 to include substance abuse services, specific measures for special populations, and additional elements of care concerning individuals with severe and persistent mental illness.

Another accountability initiative is a federally subsidized collaborative effort led by the American College of Mental Health Administration (1997),which produced a core set of outcome and performance measures for mental health and substance abuse care. This effort, known as the Santa Fe Summit on Behavioral Health, involved the leading accreditation groups, mental health administrators, providers, family and advocate stakeholder groups, and federal government representatives. The core measures cover prevention, access, process/performance, outcomes, and structure, with separate measures regarding children and adolescents. The accreditation groups participating in annual gatherings of the Summit, all held in Santa Fe, New Mexico, were the Joint Commission on the Accreditation of Healthcare Organizations, Rehabilitation Accreditation Commission, Council on Accreditation of Services for Families and Children, Council on Quality and Leadership in Supports for People with Disabilities, and National Committee for Quality Assurance. The goal was to influence these organizations to adopt some or all of the core measures in their own accreditation standards for mental health organizations so as to bring some uniformity to data measurement.

These two activities reflect concern that standard measures are needed to assess whether services are effective, and that the criteria and level of care standards used to assess mental health treatment and to make decisions on medical necessity are appropriate (Dixon and Croze 1997).

CONCLUSION

Some aspects of the recent state reform efforts might in time influence the relationship between mental health and other health care. The trend in public mental health systems to follow the same pattern of health care financing and delivery as in Medicaid and the private health sector is important. The segregation of mental health from general health care has been criticized as impeding continuity of care, resulting in poor treatment of mental illness for those who do not seek specialized care and poor recognition of medical needs for those in the public mental health system. The two-tired system of public and private mental health care also results in underfunded and inadequate services to those in the public system and less effective care for those with severe disorders who use a private system unaccustomed to their needs. Greater integration of financing and delivery systems seems desirable but will not be possible unless there are similarities in the organization of the public and private mental health systems and greater similarity in management approaches between health and mental health.

However, the recent round of reforms has also highlighted a fundamental issue in public mental health policy: the continuing and growing lack of appropriate access to effective services and the lack of resources to ensure such access. The shift to capitated arrangements, particularly those using for-profit corporations, has highlighted how little the states expect to have to pay for the responsibility of running the public mental health system. While more careful management can redirect a certain level of resources from more costly services to less costly alternatives, the total level of resources remains minimal. States that tried to make significant reductions as they shifted to managed care have run into great difficulties. Even where managed care appears to work without causing harm in terms of patient outcomes, the public system is now rarely serving those not eligible for Medicaid because it does not have resources. This trend is illustrated by a recent audit of Arizona's mental health system and by growing concern expressed by state mental health authorities.* The inclusion in certain states of the non-Medicaid population in managed mental health care carve-out plans is also a reflection of this need and an attempt to address it.†

Other data confirm how low a priority mental health systems are within state government. They are at the bottom of the list for funding growth compared to other human service systems (Bevilacqua 1999). State mental health spending is now one-third less than it would have been had the spending levels for the institutional system of 1955 (when institutional populations peaked) been maintained and adjusted for inflation and population growth (Bazelon Center for Mental Health Law 1999, 20–21). While the policy of relying on Medicaid has kept mental health systems financially afloat and enabled expansion of certain community services, it has reduced access to public mental health care for those not on Medicaid.

The problems of the public mental health system, therefore, go much beyond the appropriate organization of the system and the decisions on who should manage it and how it should be paid for. The continuing fear and ignorance in the general public concerning mental illness translates into low priority for public spending on community mental health services. To be prioritized by policymakers, social issues must have general support within society; furthermore, there must be agreement over the problems, implications, and urgency (Rochefort and Cobb 1994). Mental health services, under a cloud from the stigma surrounding these disorders, do not generate support. This situation is reflected in the unwillingness of various public and private institutions to pay for mental health treatment. So, in the end, the public will get what the public is willing to pay for. Continued erosion of resources for the mental health system will inevitably lead to various bad outcomes, including tragic and highly publicized violence involving innocent bystanders—events precipitated by lack of access to treatment—and jail, homelessness, and wasted lives for many men and women with serious mental illness.

REFERENCES

American College of Mental Health Administration. 1997. "The Santa Fe Summit on Behavioral Health: Preserving Quality and Value in the Managed Care Equation." Pittsburgh, PA.
American Managed Behavioral Healthcare Association 1998. Performance Measures for Managed Behavioral Healthcare Programs, PERMS 2.0 Washington, DC.

*At least one state (Rhode Island) has specifically requested funds for the non-Medicaid population in its budget proposal.
†Statewide plans in Maryland, Tennessee, and Montana and in Philadelphia, Pennsylvania.

American Managed Behavioral Healthcare Association and National Association of State Mental Health Program Directors. 1995. "Public Mental Health Systems, Medicaid Re-Structuring and Managed Behavioral Healthcare: A White Paper in Progress." *Behavioral Healthcare Tomorrow* (September/October): 63–69.

Bachrach, L. 1996. "Managed Care: Some 'Latent Functions.'" *Psychiatric Services* 47 (3): 243–244.

Bazelon Center for Mental Health Law. 1995. *Managing Managed Care for Publicly Financed Mental Health Services.* Washington, DC.

———. 1996. *Mental Health Managed Care: Survey of the States.* May. Washington, DC.

———. 1999. *Under Court Order: What the Community Integration Mandate Means for People with Mental Illnesses.* October. Washington, DC.

———. 2000a. *Documented Problems with New Mexico's Medicaid Behavioral Healthcare.* March. Washington, DC.

———. 2000b. *New Mexico Information Sheet No. 2: HEDIS Data and Additional Member Survery Data.* March.Washington, DC.

———. 2000c. *Effective Public Management of Mental Health Care: Views from States on Medicaid Reforms That Exchance Service Integration and Accountability.* Available from Millbank Memorial Fund, New York, NY.

Bazelon Center for Mental Health Law and Legal Action Center. 1998. *Partners in Planning.* Rockville, MD: Substance Abuse and Mental Health Services Administration (SAMHSA).

Bevilacqua, J. 1999. Conversation with Ted Lutterman, National Association of State Mental Health Program Directors, June.

Bloom, J., T. Hu, N. Wallace, B. Cuffel, J. Hausman, and R. Scheffler. 1998. "Mental Health Costs and Outcomes Under Alternative Capitation Systems in Colorado: Early Results." *Journal of Mental Health Policy and Economics* 1 (December) : 3–13.

Callahan, J. J., D. S. Shepard, R. Beinecke, M. J. Larson, and D. Cavanaugh. 1995. "Mental Health/Substance Abuse Treatment in Managed Care: The Massachusetts Medicaid Experience." *Health Affairs* 14 (Fall): 173–184.

Christianson, J. B., W. Manning, N. Lurie, T. J. Stoner, D. Z. Gray, M. Pophin, and S. Marriott. 1995. "Utah's Prepaid Mental Health Plan: The First Year." *Health Affairs* 14 (Fall): 160–172.

Croze, C. 1995. "Health Care Reform, State Mental Health Agencies and Managed Behavioral Healthcare." Presentation at National Association of State Mental Health Program Directors.

Day, S., and M. Cohen. 1993. "Leading the Charge: A Guide for New State Mental Health Program Directors." In *Harvard-NASMHPD Program for Executive Leadership in State Mental Health Administration.* 2d ed. Alexandria, VA: National Association of State Mental Health Program Directors (NASMHPD).

Dickey, B., et al. 1995. "Massachusetts Medicaid Managed Health Care Reform: Treatment for the Psychiatrically Disabled." *Advances in Health Economics and Health Research* 15 (99): 116.

Dixon, K., and C. Croze. 1997. "Improving Public/Private Partnerships in Managed Behavioral Healthcare." *Behavioral Healthcare Tomorrow* (February): 67–75.

Durham, M. 1995. "Commentary: Can HMOs Manage the Mental Health Benefit?" *Health Affairs* 14 (Fall): 116–123.

Essock, S., and H. Goldman. 1995. "States' Embrace of Managed Mental Health Care." *Health Affairs* 14 (Fall): 34–44.

Flynn, L., and R. Bernstein. 1998. Letters to Sally Richardson, director, Center for Medicaid and State Operations, Health Care Financing Administration, from Laurie Flynn, National Alliance for the Mentally Ill, and Robert Bernstein, Bazelon Center for Mental Health Law, November 16.

Goldman, H. H. 1999. "The Obligation of Mental Health Services to the Least Well Off." *Psychiatric Services* 50 (5): 659–663.

Hall, L. L., E. Edgar, and L. Flynn. 1997. *Stand and Deliver: Action Call to a Failing Industry.* Arlington, VA: National Alliance for the Mentally Ill.

Health Care Financing Administration. 1998. Final report of the Health Care Financing Administration to Governor Sundquist on TennCare Partners Program.

———. 1999. *Summary of Medicaid Managed Care Programs and Enrollment. www. cfa.gov* (June 30).

Hoge, M. A., L. Davidson, E. E. H. Griffith, W. H. Sledge, and R. A. Howenstine. 1994. "Defining Managed Care in Public-Sector Psychiatry." *Hospital and Community Psychiatry* 45:1085–1089.

Holahan, J., S. Rangarajan, and M. Schirmer. 1999. "Medicaid Managed Care Payment Rates in 1998." *Health Affairs* 18 (May/June): 217–227.

Huskamp, H. 1996. *State Requirements for Managed Behavioral Health Care Carve-Outs and What They Mean for People with Severe Mental Illness.* Arlington, VA: National Alliance for the Mentally Ill.

Lehman, A. F., and D. M. Steinwachs. 1998. "Patterns of Usual Care for Schizophrenia: Initial Results from the Schizophrenia Patient Outcomes Team (PORT) Client Survey." *Schizophrenia Bulletin* 24 (1) 11–32.

Malloy, M. 1995. *Mental Illness and Managed Care: A Primer for Families and Consumers.* Arlington, VA: National Alliance for the Mentally Ill.

McCusick, D., M. Tami, E. King, R. Harwood, J. Buck, J. Dilonardo, and J. Genuardi. 1996. "Spending on Mental Health and Substance Abuse Treatment." *Health Affairs* 17 (5): 147–157.

Mental Health Weekly August 23, 1999 issue. Providence, RI: Manisses Communications Group.

Nardini, C. 1999. "Keys to Successful Implementation of Public Managed Mental Health Programs: Iowa Program Success Borne of 'Hands On' Learning." *Open Minds* (May): 4–5.

National Association of State Mental Health Program Directors. 1999. Alexandria, VA. *www.nasmhpd.org.*

Nicholson, J., S. Dine Young, L. Simon, A. Bateman, and W. Fisher. 1996. "Impact of Medicaid Managed Care on Child and Adolescent Emergency Mental Health Screening in Massachusetts." *Psychiatric Services* 47 (12): 1344–1350.

Popkin, M., N. Lurie, W. Manning, J. Harman, A. Callies, D. Gray, and J. Christianson. 1998. "Changes in the Process of Care for Medicaid Patients with Schizophrenia in Utah's Prepaid Mental Health Plan." *Psychiatric Services* 49 (4): 518–523.

Rochefort, D. A., and R. W. Cobb, eds. 1994. *The Politics of Problem Definition: Shaping the Policy Agenda.* Lawrence: University Press of Kansas.

Rohland, B. 1998. "Implementation of Medicaid Managed Mental Health Care in Iowa:

Problems and Solutions. *Journal of Behavioral Health Services and Research* 25 (3): 293–299.

Rosenbaum, S., et al. 1998. *Negotiating the New Health System: A Nationwide Study of Medicaid Managed Care Contracts, Second Edition; Special Report: Mental Illness and Addiction Disorder Treatment and Prevention.* Washington, DC: George Washington University, Center for Health Policy Research.

Rosenheck, R. 1999. "Principles for Priority Setting in Mental Health Services and Their Implications for the Least Well Off." *Psychiatric Services* 50 (5): 653–658.

Ross, E. C. 1999. "Regulating Managed Care: Interest Group Competition for Control and Behavioral Health Care." *Journal of Health Politics, Policy and Law* 24 (3): 599–625.

Shern, D. L. 1998. *Evaluation of Florida's Prepaid Mental Health Plan: Integrative Summary.* Tampa: University of South Florida, Louis de la Parte Florida Mental Health Institute.

Stevenson, J., J. Bevilacqua, and C. Koyanagi. 1997. *Behavioral Health Managed Care Survey of the States (II).* Washington, DC: Bazelon Center for Mental Health Law.

Stroup, T. S., and R. Dorwart. 1995. "Impact of a Managed Mental Health Program on Medicaid Recipients with Severe Mental Illness." *Psychiatric Services* (September): 885–889.

Substance Abuse and Mental Health Services Administration, Managed Care Tracking System. 1998. *State Profiles on Public Sector Managed Behavioral Healthcare and Other Reforms.* Rockville, MD.

Sullivan, M. J. 1995. "Medicaid's Quiet Revolution: Merging the Public and Private Sectors of Care." *Professional Psychology: Research and Practice* 26: 229–234.

The Urban Institute. 1999. "Assessing the New Federalism." Washington, DC. *http:// newfederalism.urban.org/html/occa26.html.*

Washburn, J. 1998. Letters to Sally Richardson, director, Center for Medicaid and State Operations, Health Care Financing Administration from Jeanmarie Washburn, president, New Mexico Alliance for the Mentally Ill, December 11.

8

The Politics of Health Care Rationing: Lessons from Oregon

Jonathan Oberlander, Lawrence R. Jacobs, and Theodore R. Marmor

Of all the innovations that have marked state health policy in the United States over the past decade, the Oregon Health Plan (OHP) has attracted the most controversy. The notoriety of health care reform in Oregon is a product of the state's decision to confront head-on what no other state has dared attempt: the explicit rationing of medical care services for Medicaid recipients.

Oregon's pioneering model of prioritizing funding for health care through systematically ranking medical services has been widely heralded as an important innovation in American health policy. The Oregon reforms have drawn an extraordinary amount of attention from both national and state policymakers. The state's claim to policy fame is its apparent willingness to make the hard choices and unavoidable trade-offs raised by the inflationary and technological pressures of modern medicine. From the late 1980s on, the state sought through unusual means to expand access to health insurance for uninsured Oregonians. The price for expanded coverage was to be paid by rationing medical care services provided to Oregon's low-income Medicaid population.

The rationing of services ostensibly rested on an elaborate system that merged the promise of technological progress through cost-benefit analysis and medical outcomes research with the democratic wish of public participation in policymaking. The Oregon approach—budget control through explicit rationing of services— was indisputably innovative. It represented a striking contrast to the established practice of implicitly rationing medical care in the United States by income and insurance coverage and, at the time of its inception, to the conventional practice

Unless otherwise indicated, all uncited quotes are from interviews conducted during 1996–1997 with OHP administrators and elected officials in Salem, Oregon. We gratefully acknowledge the support of the Harvard Innovations in Government Project, the research assistance of Laura Sutton and Eric Ostermeier, and the cooperation of all our interin other states that sought to control Medicaid spending by dropping coverage for low-income enrollees.

From the beginning, OHP ignited substantial controversy. What appeared as brave innovation to some was viewed by others as a dangerous and morally dubious experiment of federalism run amok. Positions on the Oregon plan—whether favorable or critical—were formed early on, during the heated debate over its enactment in the late 1980s, and those positions still largely define contemporary understandings of rationing in Oregon.

That reaction is unfortunate, because the operation and results of OHP have in crucial respects very little to do with the original proposals or with the debate over its enactment. The worst fears of Oregon's critics and the tough choices promised by its advocates both failed to materialize. Consequently, the lessons that the Oregon experience holds for state health policymaking and medical care rationing have been widely misinterpreted.

Our aim here is to reevaluate the status of OHP as an innovation in state policymaking and to analyze the overlooked political dynamics of health care rationing. In particular, we address an important puzzle: why, despite the widespread interest in the Oregon rationing experiment, has no other American state followed the Oregon trail by adopting the OHP model? The answer, we argue, lies in the wide gap between the expectations and perceptions of rationing in Oregon and the strikingly different reality of its implementation; misconceptions about what constitutes the real policy innovation in Oregon; and the distinctive nature of politics and public policymaking in the state.

The chapter proceeds in three sections. First, we review the original proposals and ensuing debate over rationing in Oregon. Next, we explore how the politics of rationing unfolded in Oregon from the enactment of OHP to its implementation and how its performance has defied expectations. Finally, we consider the character of Oregon's health policy innovation and the broader lessons it holds for reform efforts in other states. Our analysis is based predominantly on field research in Oregon, including interviews with government officials and other key participants in health politics in the state, as well as primary source materials, including state government documents and data.

THE OREGON EXPERIMENT: CONTEXT AND CONTROVERSY

During the 1980s, Medicaid spending increased dramatically, and the program consumed a growing share of state budgets. In response, many states lowered eligibility standards for Medicaid to an income level well below the federal pov-

viewees, especially Bob DePrete. A previous version of this chapter was published in the *Journal of Health Politics, Policy and Law* 24 (1): 161–180.

erty line (FPL) and cut coverage for optional enrollee categories such as the medically needy. By the end of the decade, the health insurance program for poor Americans covered only 42% of the poor; in order to qualify for Medicaid, AFDC recipients typically needed to live on incomes that were only 50% of the FPL (OTA 1992, 76–77). In addition, those who were not "categorically eligible," such as low-income adults without children, were excluded from Medicaid in most states. Eroding access to Medicaid added to the growing ranks of America's uninsured.

Oregon's reformers promised an alternative to the practice of denying coverage to the insufficiently poor. At a time when most states were ratcheting down income eligibility for medical assistance, Oregon proposed to extend Medicaid coverage to *all* persons living below the poverty line, regardless of traditional eligibility categories. Indeed, Oregon's longer-term goal was universal coverage; the expansion of Medicaid was to be followed by an employer mandate to cover all of Oregon's workers and their families.

However, it was the state's proposed financing mechanism for Medicaid expansion that drew the most attention. Put simply, Oregon said it intended to pay for enlarged Medicaid enrollment by covering fewer services. Expanded coverage for the poor would be made affordable by offering recipients "a basic set of health benefits more limited than those currently offered by Medicaid" (OMAP 1991, ES3). Services would be explicitly prioritized according to their medical benefit and contribution to the population's overall health status. The state legislature could not respond to funding shortfalls, as it had done in the past—and as was common practice in other states—by cutting eligibility for Medicaid. Instead, they would have to reduce program coverage of services according to guidelines established in the prioritization process. In other words, expanded access to health insurance for the poor was to be purchased by rationing their medical care, though advocates understandably preferred the less incendiary language of "prioritization" and "resource allocation."

In its requests for waivers from the federal government's Health Care Financing Administration (HCFA), Oregon argued that its plan "would make the rationing of care—a phenomenon that already exists—more explicit and reasoned" (OMAP 1991, ES4). The stated aim of the "prioritization" process was to allocate Medicaid-covered funds in a more sensible, systematic, and utilitarian manner—benefiting the greatest number of recipients possible within limited resources—than existing program policies and federal regulations allowed. Systematic prioritization would enable the state to identify less valuable and effective services where funding could be cut, thereby making expanded coverage affordable. In the eyes of the plan's advocates, rationing meant not simply limiting services, but also rationalizing medical care priorities.

Oregon's rationing plan rested on an elaborate technical analysis that merged cost-benefit data and medical outcomes research with public preferences. A health services commission was given the job of scientifically compiling clinical information from physicians, treatment costs and benefit data, and community values from the public. Their task was to reduce over 10,000 medical services to a prioritized list that, in its first incarnation, ranked 709 so-called "condition and treatment pairs" that matched particular medical conditions with a range of likely treatments by physicians. The legislature's decision on how much to fund Medicaid literally "drew a line" in this list, with beneficiaries provided all services for conditions ranked above the line and denied all services below it. Advocates of Oregon's plan, such as senior administrator Jean Thorne, trumpeted the state's "painful and explicit choices" as necessary to "allow government to buy more health for the health care dollar" (Wiener 1992). Oregon justified its rationing scheme to HCFA as "recognizing that society cannot afford to pay for everything that is medically possible" (OTA 1992, 76–77).

Oregon's case for denying coverage to low-ranked services for Medicaid recipients touched off a firestorm of protest from outside the state. Since OHP reforms required changes in the basic Medicaid package mandated by federal law, under section 1115 of the Social Security Act the state was compelled to obtain a demonstration waiver from the federal government before implementing the plan. The waiver process nationalized the politics of health care reform in Oregon, turning what had been a relatively uncontroversial and quiescent story within the state into a visceral national debate over rationing. The vicissitudes of the Medicaid waiver process required not only HCFA approval but also the support of the Bush administration. In addition, influential congressional health policymakers and consumer advocates—including Representative Henry Waxman, Senator Al Gore, and Sara Rosenbaum of the Children's Defense Fund—set their sights on Oregon, with the intention of preventing OHP's implementation (Brown 1991a).

Critics assailed the plan as unfair for singling out the poor, and especially women and children, for rationing. Services for the most vulnerable would be cut, it was charged, while the benefits enjoyed by those more able to absorb reductions—the insured middle class—would be left intact. Sara Rosenbaum alleged that the "Oregon plan is not an experiment that can be justified legally, scientifically, programmatically or ethically"; it is "only one more in a long series of proposals to reduce benefits to the very poor" (1992, 103–104). Fears that the state was unjustly singling out the poor for rationing were fueled by reports that low-income Oregonians were underrepresented among attendees at community meetings to discuss the priorities of OHP (OTA 1992, 76–77).

Critics maintained that OHP's promise to ration care was not only unfair but unnecessary. Eliminating administrative waste, squeezing drug companies and providers, and spending more represented, they claimed, proven alternatives. Brookings Institution economist Joshua Wiener argued, for instance, that it was "troubling to ration medically effective procedures before we have truly exhausted other routes to cost containment" (1992, 110). The methodology of Oregon's rationing plan drew fire. The attempt to conflate thousands of complex diagnoses and treatment scenarios into 709 homogenous categories appeared to defy human and organizational ability—and common sense. Even proponents of the inevitability of rationing, such as Henry Aaron, contended that OHP was problematic. Oregon's approach of covering all services above the line and no services below the line regardless of an individual patient's medical condition or treatment prognosis meant that "patients who stood to benefit greatly were denied care, while others, who benefited slightly, received it" (Aaron 1992, 110).* In the eyes of outside critics, OHP confirmed the worst dangers of administrative science. Moral and professional judgment would be replaced by the detached logic of cost-benefit analysis and a flawed methodology (Brown 1991a; Garland, Levit, and DiPrete 1991; Fox and Leichter 1993; Rosenbaum 1992).

Medicaid advocates also worried about the so-called "Mississippi" problem. Even if the Oregon reforms turned out to be benign, what would happen to Medicaid recipients in a rationing system unleashed in a state with fewer fiscal resources and more hostile attitudes toward the poor? Moreover, Oregon's reformers asked for their waiver at precisely the moment when key congressional policymakers, such as Henry Waxman, were attempting to nationalize Medicaid policy. Their goal was to ensure generous and equitable Medicaid standards across all states. Oregon's radical departure from standard Medicaid policy implied a precedent of decentralization that ran directly against that trend and thus provoked the opposition of lawmakers and consumer advocates who favored nationalizing Medicaid.

The firestorm of protest against rationing stalled the introduction of OHP, and in the midst of a presidential election campaign in 1991, the Bush administration turned down the state's controversial waiver application. In rejecting Oregon's request, Secretary of Health and Human Services Louis Sullivan cited potential conflicts between the criteria for ranking medical procedures in OHP—which were partly based on citizens' perceptions of how medical care would impact quality of life—and the newly enacted Americans with Disabilities Act (ADA). However, Bill Clinton's victory in the 1992 campaign changed Oregon's fortunes. After Oregon administrators revised their list to meet the concerns that had been raised concerning the ADA and compromised the initial rankings to satisfy HCFA officials, the Clinton administration approved the Oregon Health Plan Medicaid demonstration project in 1993 (Leichter 1997).

Yet approval of the waiver did not end the controversy over Oregon's reforms. Most observers outside the state have not followed the implementation

*Here as elsewhere we do not deal with the validity of specific criticisms of OHP's conception of rationing or its methodology for doing so. But one should note that its moral posture did in fact seem undermined by the restriction of rationing to the poor. And one should note as well that its method was indeed flawed in quite obvious ways. For example, if a procedure was hugely helpful in just 5% of cases and had *on average* a lower ratio of benefits to costs than the procedure one line higher on the list, that advantage gave no reasonable grounds for funding the latter but not the former. Critics rightly ridiculed the proposal on such grounds, but we cannot separate our own recognition of this problem from those cited by others.

of the plan since 1994, and the health policy community remains bitterly divided over the desirability of the Oregon rationing experiment. Depending on one's perspective, the initial debate still defines either the serious limitations or the courageous virtue of OHP. Largely missed, however, in the decade since controversy first enveloped the Oregon plan is how it has actually operated. The reality is that developments during the implementation of OHP were nearly opposite of those feared by critics and yet were less than what was promised by advocates.

THE MYTHS AND THE REALITY OF THE OREGON HEALTH PLAN

Critics and defenders of OHP from outside Oregon would both be surprised by four developments during its implementation. These developments reveal a persistent gap between conventional understandings of OHP—which amount, we argue, to myths—and the realities of OHP's operation.

The Rationing That Never Was

OHP did not generate substantial savings—as its initial rhetoric promised—by rationing Medicaid services. Setting priorities and drawing a line were never implemented as a formulaic mechanism. Some savings were realized by limiting services and using managed care. But the legislature financed the expansion of Medicaid enrollment and subsidies to those above the poverty line largely through general revenues and the imposition of a tobacco tax. In 1993, the initial expansion of Medicaid coverage was funded primarily through a 17% increase in state general funds and a 10-cent cigarette tax (OMAP 1997). OHP saved additional funds by pushing more Medicaid recipients into managed care plans. By 1997, 87% of all Medicaid recipients were in managed care plans as compared with 33% before enactment of OHP. Administrators estimate that the increased reliance on managed care accounts for a 6% savings off the total costs of the program (OMAP 1997).

In striking contrast to their initial claim that prioritization would finance Medicaid expansion, OHP administrators estimate that the list saved the state only 2% on total costs for the program over its first five years of operation (OMAP 1997, ES3). The failure to cut costs through prioritization resulted from the rules imposed by the federal government and HCFA as well as the political dynamics within the state, which we will discuss later in the chapter. During the budget crisis in 1996, for instance, HCFA pared back the state's attempt to reduce the number of covered benefits, though it did fully approve Oregon's reduction the previous year.

Far from representing a radical new step toward systematic rationing of medical care, OHP has been funded the old-fashioned and familiar way: by raising revenues and contracting with managed care plans in the hope of lowering per capita spending for Medicaid recipients. Oregon, no doubt, was well positioned to use these familiar approaches because of its growing economy and its comparatively low level of expenditures on Medicaid. For example, prior to OHP's enactment, Oregon ranked forty-sixth among all states in spending on Medicaid as a proportion of the state budget.

Not only did rationing fail to produce significant reductions in services, but the process of drawing up the list actually generated a more generous package of benefits than what Medicaid or even the private sector had offered prior to OHP's implementation. Mental health services, for instance, which government and private insurers have resisted covering, are not only included but are subject to no limitations on the duration of care. HIV carriers—an especially expensive, vulnerable, and stigmatized set of patients—have found that legislators are unwilling to cut off their coverage, which extends far beyond basic services (Conviser, Retondo, and Loveless 1994, 1995). Despite the fears of national critics, then, the rationing did not prove to be a significant cost-containment device. Indeed, the list has functioned much more as a mechanism for defining a benefits package than as a strict rationing instrument.

In a further departure from the paradigm of strict rationing, doctors, hospitals, and private insurance companies delivering health services to OHP beneficiaries have not consistently rationed care, as anticipated in the original presentation of the Oregon reform. Doctors and hospitals regularly provide (and insurers pay for) services below the line that they consider appropriate or medically necessary. One major health plan contracting with the state found that 5% of its total costs for OHP were actually below the line. Below-the-line treatment is in fact inevitable since many OHP patients are not diagnosed with only one condition on the list but with comorbidities that are difficult to treat separately. In addition, all diagnostic services are above the line and are often required to diagnose conditions not covered by the list. The point is that OHP's list has not been strictly enforced by medical providers, nor is it possible to do so.

OHP's limited rationing and external misunderstandings of that are vividly illustrated by the case of organ transplantation. OHP caught national attention when the media focused in 1987 on the death of Coby Howard, a seven-year-old boy with leukemia who had been denied a bone marrow transplant. The Howard case seemed to confirm fears that rationing in Oregon would literally kill patients who were denied high-cost, low-benefit services. Indeed, some transplants are understandable targets for rationing because they may require high costs for a few patients and deliver uncertain benefits. In fact, the main proponent of OHP—John Kitzhaber—targeted cuts in transplant coverage during the initial debate as a means to generate the savings to expand access. Oregon, he argued, should "save as many people as we can, because we can't save them all" (Fox and Leichter 1991, 15).

The rhetoric about rationing transplants during the debate over the enactment of the Oregon plan, however, stands in stark contrast to the program's reality. Coverage of transplants actually became more generous under OHP than under the previous Oregon Medicaid system or under many commercial plans. In part, the expanded coverage resulted from new federal guidelines in the 1988 catastrophic health insurance legislation that required states to cover transplants for children. Yet OHP exceeds the new federal requirements. For a number of conditions, including bone marrow, heart, and lung transplants, the state voluntarily expanded coverage of transplants from children (as mandated by the federal government) to include adults. Moreover, in contrast to the initial rhetoric, the state's internal process for ranking health services consistently ranked transplants high on the list.

Expanding Access

OHP's architects promised from the outset to expand access to Medicaid to all the poor as the payoff from rationing. On that count, OHP has more than delivered. Oregon's Medicaid program now covers all residents below the poverty line. The number of beneficiaries has increased by almost 50%, with a total of 320,000 new beneficiaries covered over the plan's first four years. At any given time, over 100,000 newly eligible Oregonians enroll in the expanded Medicaid program.

National and international attention has focused mostly on the techniques of OHP's Medicaid reform. Oregon's reformers, on the other hand, actually saw Medicaid expansion as but one step toward their broader goal of universal access. They proposed to reduce the number of uninsured by pursuing a self-described pincer movement that combined expansion of Medicaid with a range of policies to help those above the poverty line. These policies included requiring an employer mandate, establishing insurance pools for high-risk groups, reforming insurance practices to allow portability and to prohibit exclusions based on preexisting conditions, and offering subsidies to individuals above the poverty line to purchase commercial health insurance. Reforms for those above the poverty line have produced significant but mixed results. The efforts to implement an employer mandate and to move toward universal coverage were blocked by opposition from segments of the business community and by federal reluctance to grant exemption from the Employee Retirement Income Security Act (ERISA). On the other hand, Oregon did establish insurance pools for small businesses and high-risk groups. By 1998, there was also no evidence that the expansion of Medicaid had crowded out employer-based coverage, a concern raised by critics early on. Work-related health insurance coverage rates have remained essentially stable since 1994.

In 1996, 340,000 Oregon residents remained uninsured as a result of the failure of the employer mandate and other reform proposals (OHP 1997). Nonetheless, the number of uninsured Oregonians fell dramatically after OHP's implementation in 1994. In 1993, for instance, 17% lacked health insurance; that proportion dropped to 11% in 1996 (OHP 1997). In the same year, 1996, the national rate of noncoverage for health insurance was 15%. The percentage of Oregonian children without health insurance fell from 21% in 1990 to 8% in 1996, while nationally it rose from 14% to 15% during that period (OHP 1997).

From Technocratic Analysis to Administrative Reality

Oregon did not implement the purely scientific model of rationing health care it seemed to have promised. Resource allocation decisions remained largely adaptations to political and administrative realities. This is nicely illustrated by how the prioritization list was revised. Originally, planners envisioned that medical treatments would be moved up or down (or in the case of new procedures, onto) the list on the basis of a cost-benefit formula that yielded precise quantitative values for specific medical procedures. Scientific and objective methodologies, not political pressures or other considerations, were to determine the state's health spending priorities.

In practice, however, this technocratic vision failed. Adjustments to the list have been determined not by scientific formula, but "by hand" on the basis of judgments by the Health Services Commission (HSC). Federal requirements and opposition within Oregon over the rankings in the initial list also compromised the original rationing methodology. In fact, an analysis by the Office of Technology Assessment (OTA) found that quantitative cost-benefit data, when compared to the considerable influence of subjective judgments by the health service commissioners, had "surprisingly little effect" on the ordering of health services in the list (OTA 1992, 76–77). Once the list of medical treatments was altered to reflect political pressures and administrative judgments, it became much harder if not impossible to base future ranking of services on a formulaic basis. Absent a self-regulating formula, there was no choice for the HSC but to literally reorder the list by hand according to their preferences and understandings of new medical developments and evidence.

Growing Political Support

Many analysts predicted that OHP would be swept away (or at least stalled) by a tidal wave of opposition within the state (Fox and Leichter 1993; Aaron 1992). After all, health reform efforts in Massachusetts, Vermont, Kentucky, Washington State, and elsewhere had collapsed. In the 1990s, the added burden of an untested, and inherently controversial, rationing plan only seemed to increase the odds against the program's survival. Denying services, critics reasoned, could only spark anger and countermobilization by advocates of the poor and other vulnerable populations, as well as by providers resenting interference in their clinical judgments. Commentators warned that adopting OHP would touch off explosive media stories of patients going without care and predicted an unraveling of support by legislators (Aaron 1992).

However, the predictions of imminent doom turned out to be unfounded. OHP became what some observers inside the state now term the "third rail" of state politics. By the time its founding legislation passed in 1989, OHP had ample support from the general public, the Oregon Medical Association, large business organizations, and the AFL-CIO. Members of the Oregon House and Senate gave the legislation nearly unanimously approval. Despite intense tobacco industry opposition, there was a 54% to 46% vote in favor of a 1994 referendum to impose a 30-cent cigarette tax to finance OHP. Nor did the national Republican electoral tidal wave of 1994 undermine this popular support within Oregon.

Perhaps most telling, advocacy groups for the aged and disabled converted from skeptics to supporters. Their initial fears that OHP would systematically deny necessary medical care to vulnerable populations were calmed. They came to appreciate that OHP offered better benefits (especially for mental illness and disability) than many private insurers. The same advocates who once denounced OHP later supported expanding the program to encompass an even larger share of the state's population.

Years after authorizing the program, the legislature continued to reward OHP with new infusions of funds. For example, attempts to divert funds from the cigarette tax earmarked for the program in 1994 were defeated, and the expansion of coverage has consistently won popular support and broad, bipartisan majorities in the legislature. Politicians from both parties frequently claim credit for the success of OHP. The program emerged relatively unscathed from a 1995 state budget crisis, which did result in the imposition of an assets test, a slight reduction in benefits, and a sliding-scale premium for those eligible for OHP as a result of the Medicaid demonstration project.

THE POLITICAL SOURCES OF OREGON'S SURPRISE

National and international observers of OHP seem to have missed the story of its increased political support, its generous benefits, and the absence of systematic rationing.* In part, they misjudged the Oregon case because of the initial rationing rhetoric used by OHP advocates and critics alike. Reformers now concede that they overemphasized the scientific grounding of rationing, repeatedly compromised what was presented as a scientific process, and oversold the extent to which services would be cut. These facts about OHP are only reluctantly (and quietly) acknowledged by program architects and have not reached outside observers whose impressions of the Oregon plan were seared by the original rationing rhetoric.

Yet the main reason the Oregon story has been misread, we believe, is that most analysts have overlooked or misunderstood the political dynamics of rationing in Oregon. As we have argued, rationing did not function as a key technical in-

*The work of Thomas Bodenheimer (1997) and Howard Leichter (1999) are notable exceptions. However, while we are largely in agreement with them on the empirical outcomes of the Oregon case, our analysis focuses on the political explanations for these outcomes.

strument for reallocating resources. The focus on the technical dimension of rationing has obscured its political value: namely, the extent to which the *rhetoric and process* of rationing (as opposed to its programmatic application) were crucial in mobilizing support for OHP.

Mobilizing Support in an Inhospitable Environment

The policy entrepreneurs who formulated and promoted OHP shared an unwavering devotion to expanding health insurance, a commitment that would sustain them through a decade of setbacks and harsh external criticism. Their motto was: "We keep coming back." Priority setting was never the ultimate objective of Oregon's reformers; it was celebrated as the pragmatic means to widen access to health insurance.

Oregon's policy entrepreneurs possessed a talent for interacting with a multiplicity of players and for adjusting to changes in the political environment. John Kitzhaber, who led the reform effort and is currently governor, combined the political sensitivity of a veteran state legislator with both considerable rhetorical skills and a strong commitment to fighting for health reform. Others committed to reform (within and outside government) possessed similar blends of policy expertise and broad political experience in working with legislators and the executive branch in the health policy arena.

From the beginning, reformers drew on these political skills in tailoring policy proposals to what they saw as significant political challenges, though they did not appreciate just how daunting these would be. The political situation during the second half of the 1980s was hardly propitious for health reforms. Republicans hostile to government activism had controlled the White House for three consecutive terms. They had significant influence in Oregon's government—controlling the governor's seat from 1981 to 1985 and cutting Democratic majorities in the statehouse to razor-thin margins.

Reformers designed their proposal on the premise that OHP needed bipartisan support to carry it through the natural vagaries of electoral politics. They also worried about state business interests. In the end, they were successful in winning the backing of Oregon's larger firms, or at least neutralizing them, while tempering the damage from the expected opposition of small businesses.

In short, the process of implementing OHP arose less from a technocratic vision than from a realistic assessment of the obvious political barriers to reform.

The Political Strategy of Oregon's Policy Entrepreneurs

Oregon's health leaders designed their strategy to mitigate the anticipated resistance of interest groups and to mobilize the state's potentially fractious political community behind a broad vision of health reform. They latched onto the language and procedures of policy science and rationing as the centerpiece of a strategy to build and manage political momentum. Their strategy had four central components.

The first was to capitalize on Oregon's participatory culture. As noted earlier, the prioritized list was to be shaped by cost-benefit analysis and by public judgments about basic values solicited through professionally conducted town hall meetings and public opinion surveys. These meetings and the activities of the Health Services Commission attracted sustained media coverage and public attention.

While external critics mostly focused on the final priority list produced by the commission and its alleged shortcomings, Oregonians championed the process that produced it. Within the state, the process of discussing and prioritizing health services was viewed as a welcome continuation of Oregon's participatory political culture. Land use planning and other policy issues in Oregon have long generated community involvement and corporatist bargaining through commissions, Oregon's traditional way of bringing together government, interest groups, and citizens in the "democratic wish" (Morone 1990).

The state's political culture thus offered reformers a political opportunity. Instead of experts designing OHP in a closed room, policy entrepreneurs chose a process that methodically sought out the attention of everyday Oregonians and sparked a very public debate across the state. Reformers solicited public participation as a part of a genuine effort to incorporate the public's "substantive input on the relative importance of health care services." But they also recognized the political benefits of public participation. Oregon's reformers and their external critics (Brown 1991b) appreciated the technical limitations of obtaining a representative measure of public preferences (Daniels 1992, 70). They hoped that soliciting some public discussion would induce what was termed a "public buy-in" into OHP and a sense that it was "their" process.

Reformers welcomed public debate partly to avert two damaging reactions to Oregon's efforts to help the uninsured. First, in the conservative, antiwelfare national political environment of the 1980s, they worried about a backlash against creating a new health program for the poor. Proposals to expand benefits to poor residents ran the real risk of alienating Oregonians.* The second fear of reformers was that apathy, disinterest, and rampant public distrust of government would undermine OHP. Pursuing reform without considerable public support, OHP advocates believed, would set up the process to fail.

Inviting debate in public forums was a carefully designed tactic, its advocates explained, to "break out of the alienation from government" and to avert a welfare backlash. Indeed, OHP administrators look back and credit public participation and the prioritization discussion for restoring some confidence in Oregon

---

*After all, it was precisely this fear of the politically damaging consequences of targeting the uninsured that prompted President Clinton to frame his health reform plan as offering "security for all."

government and for creating a higher level of "trust" and a "reservoir of good-will." As one administrator explained to us, "The public input process was effective at building . . . consensus . . . precisely because [policymakers] said that [the public's views were] being taken seriously and reflected in policy decisions."

Critics of the design of the public forums and their admittedly skewed representation miss their political significance.* The primary value of public discussions was not in accurately representing or measuring citizen attitudes, but in building support for controversial reform by opening up the consultative process to them. By contrast, the Clinton administration's closed health reform process in 1993 invited mistrust and fueled damaging speculation about secret deals.

The second strategy was to transform the legislative politics that had previously dominated health policy. In particular, reformers organized the process of prioritization to change the "political paradigm" and make legislators politically accountable for explicit decisions to cut benefits. Although the stated purpose of rationing was to cut unnecessary services, the architects of OHP viewed it as largely a mechanism to "put legislators on the hook and force them to make the commitment to expanding access." They astutely calculated that explicit discussion of rationing particular services would be politically difficult. In fact, they believed it would pressure legislators to expand access without significantly reducing covered services.

Following the script of reformers, independent actuaries are first to estimate the cost of each treatment ranked by the Health Services Commission and to present the legislature with the list carrying a price tag assigned to each of the ranked services. Legislators then decide how much of the list Oregon can afford. The idea, a longtime administrator explained, was to replace "quiet decisions" over cutting the number of people eligible for Medicaid with "very public decisions to change the benefit package according to very explicit guidelines." John Kitzhaber put it bluntly: "Let legislators make explicit decisions so that they can be held accountable for them" (Mahar 1993, 24).

The result was to put legislators in the position of reaching decisions on funding that have direct and visible cause-and-effect consequences for reducing (or expanding) the number of services offered. Under OHP, withholding treatment for specific services would be easily traceable to a specific legislative decision not to provide funding. Legislators are therefore in the politically uncomfortable position of facing voters' scrutiny over very public, explicit decisions to deny payment for specific health services to program beneficiaries. Legislators in both political parties face the clear prospect that constituents may recoil at such cuts in actual coverage and punish them in the next election.

*Misunderstanding the political significance of these public meetings does not mean that critics were mistaken about their representatives. There is no question that civic participation in Oregon's great rationing debate was dominated numerically by those working in medical care. On the other hand, the views of Oregonians were solicited in a variety of ways, which meant within the state that the external critics seemed like nitpickers.

Paradoxically, then, the use of rationing rhetoric made the actual rationing of medical care for poor Oregonians *less* rather than more likely—just as reformers hoped.

The third strategy was to define their target population expansively to encompass a broad rather than restricted set of beneficiaries. National observers riveted their attention on Oregon's changes in Medicaid, but the state's reformers persistently presented their proposals within Oregon as encompassing a population much broader than Medicaid recipients. Their specific proposals for an employer mandate, insurance pools, and private insurance reforms were all aimed at dispelling the perception that health reform was a poor people's program providing handouts to a stigmatized target population.

In addition to supporting programs reaching beyond the poor, Oregon's reformers explicitly presented rationing as an effort to define the care of the entire population. Participants in its design were warned against singling out the Medicaid population. "The concept of OHP," one longtime OHP administrator emphasized, rested on "making the prioritized benefit package the floor for all Oregonians' coverage, not just Medicaid."

Reformers also used the process of prioritization to transcend formal boundaries between government and private individuals and groups in order to organize continuous negotiations among doctors, hospitals, insurance companies, employers, and labor. This was the fourth strategic element. As one administrator explained, "[Rationing] provided a nexus for the discussions about how limited resources would be allocated" and kept the different stakeholders "directly engaged" for a protracted period.

Hospitals supported reform from the start as a means to reduce the financial drain of handling uncompensated care and inappropriate visits to the emergency room. More telling, though, was the conversion of physicians from initial skeptics to loyal supporters. According to administrators, doctors "didn't particularly take to the idea of public input about what is important in health and health care." They were persuaded of its political importance as a tactic to induce Oregonians' support in a period when the public was in no mood to defer to experts. Physicians had a second concern: the "absence of sound, scientific, longitudinal studies" on the costs and benefits of health services prevented the Health Services Commission from devising a list based on objective as opposed to subjective evaluations. But physicians working on the commission and reformers led by fellow physician Kitzhaber persuaded doctors that they would in fact continue to make "medical decisions every day based on their best clinical judgment." After the implementation of OHP, physicians indeed continued to exercise their judgment, providing services that were at times not covered by the list. Physician support for OHP was also cultivated with the promise that Oregon would provide generous payments for covered services. That promise has held; Oregon's capitation payments for OHP enrollees are comparatively high (Bodenheimer 1997). After physicians' reservations were addressed, they rallied behind OHP's goal of expanding access to the uninsured and funding more of the cost of treating Medicaid patients.

Organizing ongoing bargaining over OHP's priorities was especially important in managing political relations with business representatives. Large and small business concerns, for example, were sharply divided over OHP reforms and the employer mandate. Small businesses were steadfast opponents; larger firms favored the mandate because it would compel small firms to contribute to their employees' health costs and thereby reduce the costs shifted to large employers. While large business initially backed an employer mandate, the election of a Republican state legislature in 1994, vociferous small business opposition, and the near certainty that the Gingrich-controlled Congress would not grant an exemption from ERISA weakened their support for the employer mandate. The result, as some reformers anticipated, was the excision of the employer mandate from OHP reforms in 1995. The prioritization process, though, kept big business engaged in the coalition that supported OHP as a whole even as some of OHP's components—like the employer mandate—became targets of vocal opposition and were dropped.

CONCLUSION

Intended and Unanticipated Consequences

The operational Oregon Health Plan bears little resemblance to the program envisioned either by promoters or by critics during the national debate over its adoption. The political strategies of reformers were crucial in shaping the Oregon surprises. Reformers used the rhetoric and public discussion of rationing to mobilize citizen support, involve medical providers and other interest groups in the process, and establish a new mechanism for political accountability. Ultimately, this approach helped maintain a broad political coalition that has paradoxically made it harder for politicians to ration medical care and easier to raise funds for the state's poor.

Much of what has happened in Oregon, then, was intended but was simply not well understood outside the state. Still, political strategy alone cannot explain what has transpired in Oregon. Unanticipated developments and fortuitous conditions also played a critical role in the development of OHP.

Clearly, Oregon's reformers never fully controlled or anticipated their destiny. They were blindsided by unexpected political troubles, especially the protracted battle for a Medicaid waiver and the chorus of national criticism. Ironically, the same political strategies and processes crafted to produce consensus within the state produced controversy outside it. These largely unanticipated developments had important feedback effects on the formulation of OHP. For instance, the national outcry over the Howard case and incongruities in the initial list intensified HCFA's scrutiny and constrained the state's ability to place services such as transplants lower on the list and to cut funding for other services (ironically aiding forces both within and outside Oregon government who sought to ensure a generous benefit package). Similarly, federal opposition to the plan helped erode the scientific foundation of the prioritization process and guarantee that subsequent reordering of the list could not be done on a formulaic basis.

Paradoxically, these external challenges may have enhanced the public appeal, operational success, and, perhaps, the political longevity of OHP. As a result of pressure from federal agencies and officials, Congress, and citizens groups, Oregon's reformers were forced to compromise their initial plan. While sacrificing the technical integrity mentioned above, that compromise produced a plan that made more sense in its rankings of medical procedures and thereby created a politically more defensible product. External pressures also forced Oregon's reformers to satisfy a broad spectrum of national critics, an unanticipated but ultimately beneficial process that may have contributed to their subsequent success in shielding the OHP from political attacks within the state.

Oregon's health reformers also benefited from several favorable contingencies that raised the probability of success but could not have been predicted. The program was implemented during a period when the state economy prospered, national medical inflation moderated, and OHP's most prominent sponsor was elected governor. Indeed, it is hard to imagine a more favorable environment for implementing the plan. Absent these favorable conditions, the politics of rationing in the state may have had (and may well have in future years) a much different character. With higher rates of health care inflation and a slower economy, fiscal pressures might have forced Oregon to make harder choices about spending priorities, including tougher pressures to implement strong doses of rationing. And without the critical patronage of John Kitzhaber, who played a unique role as legislator, architect, and defender of OHP, it is unclear if the plan would have survived pressures for cutbacks from the legislature as relatively unscathed as it did.

Oregon's Innovation

The formal appeal of the Oregon plan was largely technocratic. The state promised to develop a rational, scientific instrument—the list—to define medical care priorities. The reputed technical power of this administrative instrument has drawn many visitors from other states to Oregon eager to learn its precise formulas and acquire an innovative rationing tool to negotiate the technological, political, and financial dilemmas of modern medicine. Indeed, Medicaid administrators in other states have called the OHP administration asking for the state's famous list in the hope that it could be used to constrain health spending in their own Medicaid programs. Yet, the technical power of Oregon's innovation has proven largely to be an illusion.

Systematic rationing simply has not arrived in Oregon. Based on the rather small and relatively insignificant set of medical services now excluded from OHP (as well as its generous benefits package), observers will be hard-pressed to discover any evidence in Oregon of the tough decisions reformers promised. Nor has OHP operated as an objective, scientific vessel of resource prioritization, as the process of updating the list by hand according to subjective judgments has vividly demonstrated. Reformers have, in fact, repeatedly compromised the much heralded scientific rigor of their rationing decisions in order to gain political support.

In short, the actual implementation of rationing in Oregon has failed to demonstrate the successful application of quantitative cost-benefit analysis to resource allocation in medicine. Instead, OHP's operation confirms the prediction of the OTA that Oregon's "outcome and cost-effectiveness data . . . are inadequate for use as the building blocks of a ranking system for all services" (OTA 1992, 76–77).

The innovation in Oregon is consequently more political than technical. State reformers used the rhetoric of priorities to build a durable political coalition in favor of expanded access for the uninsured. Remarkably, Oregon used a method—rationing—thought to be dangerous to the uninsured in a successful effort to help them. The real innovation in Oregon, then, was developing a coherent political strategy to accomplish reform in a national environment hostile to social reform and Medicaid expansion. The political success of OHP is all the more noteworthy given its troubled beginnings. Ironically, the Oregon plan, which started under a cloud of national controversy and predictions of imminent demise, has proven far more politically durable than health reform efforts by other states that were heralded as promising alternative routes to change.

Lessons for Other States

Given this durability, why, then, have other states not emulated the Oregon model? The answer is that what other policymakers had thought to be the key to Oregon's success—the technical prowess of the prioritization list—had, in actuality, nothing to do with the success of OHP. And the real key to Oregon's success—the political strategies of coalition-building for Medicaid expansion—was not exportable, for it rested not on technical formulas that could simply be duplicated by health service researchers in other states, but on the singular political talents of Oregon's reformers and the liberal, participatory political culture of the state. In short, what other states thought could be copied from Oregon—a system of cost-benefit rankings that would produce large savings and a scientific cover to avoid tough political decisions about Medicaid funding—could not be exported because it did not exist. And what really made the Oregon experiment work—political innovation and a deliberative policymaking process that was inherently controversial and largely a by-product of a unique environment—could not be exported.

It is therefore not surprising that other states have failed to follow Oregon's lead. Oregon's experience does, though, offer some basis for reconsidering the traditional reticence of health reformers to publicly discuss rationing. In Oregon, the rhetoric of rationing pulled into the open the decisions that privately occur every day and that deny services to uninsured or underinsured Americans. OHP's experience points to an unanticipated but possible political benefit of rationing rhetoric: it reconfigured debate toward openly acknowledging, as a society, what medical services Americans—even the politically eviscerated poor—should receive or go without. And it put politicians in the vulnerable position of pulling the plug on particular medical services. Paradoxically, a process ostensibly aimed at saying no might force the voters and politicians—as it did in Oregon—to recoil in horror and say yes.

In other states, however, the political dynamics of rationing rhetoric could produce quite different—and less benign—results. In a less liberal state, without Oregon's tradition of public involvement in policymaking, history of progressive health care reform, and strong involvement from consumer groups, it is easy to envision a system that would produce stringent rationing of needed health care services and abet a political coalition that would have a new and powerful tool ("the list") for justifying even more draconian cutbacks in Medicaid. In these states, politicians and voters might not recoil in horror as Oregonians did and instead say no, with devastating results for the health of Medicaid recipients. Put simply, what has turned out to be a virtue of federalism in Oregon—the freedom to innovate—could quickly become a vice in a different state.

Indeed, given the favorable conditions mentioned above, we cannot confidently generalize the politics of (non)rationing in the Oregon Health Plan from 1994 to 1998 to future years in Oregon, let alone another state. In 1999, OHP endured its strongest political challenge when, in the context of rising program costs, the state legislature passed a sunset provision that potentially could have rolled back the plan by requiring its reauthorization in 2002. Governor Kitzhaber ultimately vetoed the bill, but pressures for reducing OHP expenditures remain, and in the spring of 2000, the state reconvened a series of community meetings for the first time since OHP's enactment to discuss the plan's future. Although OHP remains programmatically stable at this time, it is unclear to what extent these new political and fiscal pressures will erode its success in expanding health coverage and public support, underlining the dangers inherent in extrapolating OHP's experience during 1994–1998 to other states.

Ultimately, then, it is not simply a question of can other states follow the Oregon model, but do we *want* other states to try? OHP has succeeded as a consequence of the political talents of its sponsors, unexpected favorable contingencies, and the welcome political environment of Oregon, where there was widespread support for expanding access to health insurance, a tradition of citizen participation in policymaking, and a somewhat less hostile posture toward the poor. These conditions simply do not exist nor can they be easily replicated in other state laboratories; few, if any, states are in a position to copy Oregon's politics and policymaking process.

In the end, there are two major lessons from the Oregon experience for state policymaking and health care reform. The first is that with the right combination of political skill, fiscal resources, and administrative commitment, states can adopt reforms that dramatically enhance—as Oregon has—coverage for their uninsured and vulnerable populations. The second, and more sobering lesson, is that Oregon offers no magic formula for controlling Medicaid costs while simultaneously expanding access, and therefore its experience cannot be generalized to other states. Far from representing a radical new innovation in systematic rationing of medical care, Oregon's Medicaid expansion was in fact funded the old-fashioned and familiar way: by raising revenues and implementing cost-saving contracts with medical providers.

Without the fiscal and political commitments mentioned above, states will not be able to emulate Oregon's progress in funding coverage for the uninsured. The experience of health care rationing in Oregon, then, highlights at once the remarkable achievements and innovation of that state as well as the formidable barriers to interstate borrowing of health care reform.

REFERENCES

Aaron, H. J. 1992. "The Oregon Experiment." In *Rationing America's Medical Care: The Oregon Plan and Beyond,* ed. M. Strosberg, J. Wiener, and R. Baker, with I. A. Fein, pp. 107–114. Washington, DC: Brookings Institution.

Bodenheimer, T. 1997. "The Oregon Health Plan—Lessons for the Nation." *New England Journal of Medicine* 337 (9): 651–655.

Brown, L. D. 1991a. "Letter: Settling the Score on Oregon." *Health Affairs* 10 (4): 310–312.

———. 1991b. "The National Politics of Oregon's Rationing Plan." *Health Affairs* 10 (2): 28–51.

Conviser, R., M. J. Retondo, and M. O. Loveless. 1994. "Predicting the Effect of the Oregon Health Plan on Medicaid Coverage for Outpatients with HIV." *American Journal of Public Health* 84 (2): 1994–1996.

———. 1995. "Universal Health Coverage, Rationing, and HIV Care: Lessons from the Oregon Health Plan Medicaid Reform." *AIDS and Public Policy Journal* 10 (2): 75–82.

Daniels, N. 1992. "Justice and Health Care Rationing: Lessons from Oregon." In *Rationing America's Medical Care: The Oregon Plan and Beyond,* ed. M. Strosberg, J. Wiener, and R. Baker, with I. A. Fein, pp. 185–195. Washington, DC: Brookings Institution.

Fox, D., and H. Leichter. 1991. "Rationing Care in Oregon: The New Accountability." *Health Affairs* 10 (2): 7–27.

———. 1993. "The Ups and Downs of Oregon's Rationing Plan." *Health Affairs* 12 (2): 66–70.

Garland, M., H. Levit, and R. DiPrete. 1991. "Letter: Policy Analysis or Polemic on Oregon's Rationing Plan?" *Health Affairs* 10 (4): 307–311.

Klein, R., P. Day, and S. Redmayne. 1996. *Managing Scarcity.* Philadelphia: Open University Press.

Leichter, H. 1997. *Health Policy Reform in America.* 2d ed. New York: M. E. Sharpe.

Mahar, M. 1993. "Memo to Hillary: Here's How to Cure What Ails Our Health Care System." *Barron's,* March 1.

Morone, J. A. 1990. *The Democratic Wish.* New York: Basic Books.

Office of Medical Assistance Programs (OMAP). 1991. "The Oregon Medicaid Demonstration: Waiver Cost Estimate." Prepared for HCFA and submitted by the Office of Medical Assistance Programs, Oregon Department of Human Resources, April 15.

————. 1997. Unpublished data provided to the authors by the Oregon Department of Human Resources, 15 April.

Office of Technology Assessment (OTA). 1992. *Evaluation of the Oregon Medicaid Proposal.* Washington, DC: Government Printing Office.

Oregon Health Plan. *The Uninsured in Oregon, 1997.* Salem: Office for Oregon Health Plan Research.

Rosenbaum, S. 1992. "Poor Women, Poor Children, Poor Policy: The Oregon Medicaid Experiment." In *Rationing America's Medical Care: The Oregon Plan and Beyond,* ed. M. Strosberg, J. Wiener, and R. Baker, with I. A. Fein, pp. 91–106. Washington, DC: Brookings Institution.

Wiener, J. 1992. "Rationing in America: Overt and Covert." In *Rationing America's Medical Care: The Oregon Plan and Beyond,* ed. M. Strosberg, J. Wiener, and R. Baker, with I. A. Fein, pp. 12–23. Washington, DC: Brookings Institution.

9

Shifting Frames, Enduring Foe: Tobacco as a State Health Policy Problem

Suzann R. Thomas-Buckle and Leonard G. Buckle

The overall focus of this book is on the role of states in ensuring health care delivery with at least minimal quality, equity, efficiency, and political acceptance, subject to the vagaries of technical change, shifting constellations of power among participants, and an ever-evolving set of ideas about how the U.S. health system ought to be organized. This chapter takes a different cut at the role of the states in the maintenance of health, i.e., the health regulation function that justifies such interventions in peoples' lives as mandatory vaccination, quarantine, and the condemnation of buildings and commercial practices judged to pose a threat to health. As we will argue below, this distinction makes some difference in the way that the state and its municipal creatures approach tobacco control when compared with the management of health care delivery. Our main contention is that the existence of a politically powerful and organized industry cartel establishes tobacco control as a unique policy arena, one with far-reaching implications for the population's health and the broader health policy debate.

Tobacco is a wicked problem for the health care policy community. Like most health care issues, the use of tobacco products is subject to shifting definitions by the formation and recombination of coalitions seeking sufficient political strength to dominate policy discourse about the topic. And just as is true in other arenas of contested problem definition, the outcome of policy debates is strongly influenced by the ability of advocates to create a broadly convincing image of the problem that meets the material and professional needs of major interests. Just as in the case of AIDS (Rochefort and Cobb 1994), however, tobacco is a topic offering much more difficulty than average to would-be problem definers. Both "problems" are capable of being framed in terms of lifestyle, morality, or civil rights as well

Research for this chapter was supported in part by grant no. 031610 from the Robert Wood Johnson Foundation through the Substance Abuse Policy Research Program.

as health. When seen as a health problem, the substance of both AIDS and to-bacco control politics is controversial, in part, because both issues appeared in public health circles more or less full-blown at their outset, carrying a set of pre-existing nonhealth-related definitions.

As we will attempt to explain in this chapter, framing tobacco use as a matter of health policy takes place in a unique sociopolitical setting. First, as the object of health policy definition, tobacco use is sui generis and its consequences are multi-faceted. Far from being simply a matter of public regulation of a product that can be harmful to the user's health and longevity, or a problem of health care delivery to tobacco users, tobacco defeats easy classification. It is deadly not only to its users (Kluger 1997, 412) but also to other members of the public in their vicinity (National Institute for Occupational Safety and Health [NIOSH] 1991). Further, tobacco is known to be an addictive substance and the most certain gateway to abuse of other, legally controlled or proscribed addictive substances (Johnson, O'Malley, and Bachman 1987; Substance Abuse and Mental Health Services Administration 1999). Oddly enough in view of these facts, tobacco has been routinely excepted from most statements of law (Givelber 1998). Finally, tobacco use is generally accepted as the leading preventable cause of morbidity and mortality through a host of dis-ease processes, although it is not linked directly to any one diagnosis (Rabin and Sugarman 1992, 3). The scientific evidence for these negative characterizations of tobacco tends to be grounded in inferential statistics partly because it takes tobacco up to 60 years to do its harm and partly because, as yet, no heart disease, lung cancer, stroke, prenatal and neonatal problem, or other diagnosable illness from which people suffer and die has been connected exclusively to tobacco use (Ndubisi 1999).

A second condition making tobacco use a unique problem for health policy definition is the fact that tobacco is also the product of one of the largest, richest, longest standing, best organized, and most single-mindedly consistent interest groups in world history (Hilts 1996, chaps. 1–2). This interest group is determined to see tobacco defined as anything but a health problem. It spends over $6 billion annually (Hilts 1996, 78) to promote its product as being a part of a young, ath-letic, independent, sexually attractive—even healthy—lifestyle. It has also devised the most recognized cartoon character in history (eclipsing Mickey Mouse), Joe Camel (DiFranza et al. 1991), and it has offered children paraphernalia with which to advertise their identification with that cool character (Hilts 1996, 75ff; University of California–San Francisco 1999).

Such advertising has paid off handsomely, especially over the past decade in which smoking by people younger than 18—despite industry assurances that they are not targeting this audience—has risen by 73%, from 708,000 in 1988 to 1.226 million in 1996. There has been an increase from nearly 2,000 to more than 3,000 persons under the age of 18 who become smokers each day (Borio 1999). These youthful smokers have very small odds of ever quitting. (Of those who smoke but think that they will not smoke in five years, nearly 75% are still smoking five to six years later [CDC 1999c)]. Thus, with each youngster who lights up, the tobacco industry has succeeded in controlling, for at least that person, the issue definition and in framing smoking as anything but a health problem. On the contrary, the new smoker sees tobacco not only as pleasurable and attractive but also as a symbol of adulthood and autonomy, if not outright rejection or defiance of parental authority (CDC 1999d).

This intense advertising campaign is one aspect of the influence of the tobacco industry in the United States, and it is complemented by a wide array of tactics dictated by a strategy adopted as long ago as 1953 (Hilts 1996, 4; Tobacco Control Resource Center 1999). This strategy, besides intensive advertising, has included a carefully orchestrated plan of scientific disinformation and misdirection, concealment of the industry's knowledge that nicotine is addictive and tobacco is dangerous to people, vigorous lobbying before Congress, and a massive, proactive defense against any lawsuit opposing the industry. To illustrate the scope of this strategy, in 1998 British-American Tobacco Company spent over $25.1 million in lobbying before Congress, thus placing tobacco producers ahead of the American Medical Association as the largest lobbying group in the nation (Public Citizen 1998).

In effect, the tobacco companies' strategy can be likened to a conspiracy (Hilts 1996, 3). As has been discovered, thanks to a lengthy battle to reveal the documents needed to prove it (House Committee on Government Reform and Oversight 1997), all of these efforts were organized and carried out by a committee of lawyers who reported to yet another committee of lawyers who represented the tobacco companies and their interests. This bizarre multilayered and complex arrangement permitted the industry to cover up its conspiracy by claiming it as part of the work product of its attorneys, which would be shielded from disclosure by the attorney-client privilege (Glantz et al. 1996).

A great deal of wealth and other resources enhances the political strength of the industry. For example, Philip Morris, the largest tobacco company, had $74.4 billion in sales in 1998, roughly half ($37 billion) of this from tobacco sales, with gross profits on sales of tobacco over 63% (Philip Morris 1999). The manufacture of tobacco is also a business run by a cartel quite effective in its self-defense. Except for a single incident in which the Liggett Group, one of the weakest of the seven major producers, disclosed cartel documents and paid a civil settlement in a case tried in Florida in 1997, the industry has never broken ranks under attack and until 1997 had not paid a penny in damages in civil lawsuits (Stauber and Rampton 1996). As a result of the strength of this cartel, resolving disputes about tobacco use inevitably involves political compromise.

THE UNIQUE HISTORY OF TOBACCO IN AMERICA

This current state of affairs is best understood as the culmination of a long and curious history of tobacco in the United States. Strictly speaking, this history goes back well before the existence of the United States as such (Borio 1999). In colonial times, the economy of British America was firmly based on the export of tobacco (Middleton 1953). In fact, the Virginia and Carolina colonies were primarily producers of tobacco, while the northern colonies were influential in its export to the Old World. The substance was even used as currency (for example, Church of England parish clergy were paid in tobacco in colonial times, and both the Revolutionary War and the Civil War were funded primarily through taxation on tobacco) and as collateral for loans and bank notes (Scharf 1967). While many observers were concerned in colonial times about tobacco as a hazard to good health (Borio 1999), the overwhelming response of the state, whether colonial or independent, to the presence of tobacco was first to tax it and second to regulate it, both as to quantity and quality produced, in order to assure an orderly and reliable market for its sale and export (Borio 1999). Thus, tobacco use was well established as a way of life for much of colonial America, and complaints about its aesthetic or unhealthy properties were muted at best.

Efforts by states to control—rather than promote or tax—the use, sale, and possession of tobacco, however, do go back at least to 1632 in Massachusetts and 1647 in Connecticut. Overwhelmingly, however, most colonial laws regarding tobacco concerned its nature as an item of agriculture and commerce. In 1730, Virginia passed the Inspection Act that standardized and regulated tobacco sales and exports as to quantity and quality. With regulation for quality, there naturally came taxation, since tax stamps served both as evidence of revenue for the state and as proof of governmental quality control for the buyer. Following independence and ratification of the U.S. Constitution, both the federal and state governments got into the taxation process, and in 1794 the U.S. Congress passed its first tax on tobacco. The tax of eight cents applied only to snuff, not the more plebeian—and less used—smoking tobacco. The tax represented 60% of snuff's usual selling price (Borio 1999).

Hence, from 1607 through the mid-1800s, tobacco was framed as a commodity to regulate and tax. The mid-1800s saw a major redefinition of the nature of tobacco, but still the context did not convert tobacco into a health policy issue. This second phase of state action to control the use of tobacco began not as a health matter, but as part of a general crusade of the mid- to late-1800s to improve the morals of an industrializing and urbanizing United States (Borio 1999). Tobacco was viewed less as a commercial product, fit to tax and control, and more as a moral risk. The reform movements of the 1800s varied widely in intensity and impact from place to place, but the core of their strength was in nonconformist religious communities to which tobacco was one of the temptations that led men (both syntactically and biologically defined here) to sin.

States reacted in widely varying and often contrary ways to the rhetoric of the reformers. An extreme case probably was North Dakota, which banned tobacco entirely from 1890 (the year it achieved statehood) through 1941. This complete prohibition, while not typical, was in response to a growing grassroots antitobacco sentiment in the country. By 1890, as a result of rising intolerance of tobacco, 26 states and territories had outlawed the sale of cigarettes to minors (the age of majority in a particular state could be anything from 14 to 24) (Borio 1999). An additional 14 states imposed total prohibition against tobacco. Thus, 40 states had adopted some form of tobacco control measures. Frequently, these restrictions on the use of tobacco came in lockstep with similar measures directed at alcohol. By 1901, there was strong anticigarette activity in 43 of the 45 states: "Only Wyoming and Louisiana had paid no attention to the cigarette controversy, while the other forty-three states either already had anti-cigarette laws on the books, were considering new or tougher anti-cigarette laws, or were the scenes of heavy anti-cigarette activity" (Dillow 1981, 10).

The prohibition movement, however, began to make a distinction between alcohol and tobacco in its later manifestations (Kluger 1997). This differentiation in the framing of tobacco and alcohol was again not primarily associated with a health-related redefinition of the role and nature of tobacco. Rather, beginning in the second decade of the twentieth century, two nearly simultaneous shifts in the public classification of tobacco promoted this redefinition of tobacco politics. First, World War I gave tobacco a major new meaning when General Pershing stated that he would rather have tobacco than ammunition for his troops in the trenches (Borio 1999). What was seen as an evil habit in the context of industrialization and rampant immigration came to be seen as the best way of maintaining morale in the face of horrific battlefield conditions. In a four-year period, tobacco went from moral pariah to savior of our doughboys in the trenches. Simultaneously, the suffrage movement, seeking visible ways of asserting the rights of women, embraced public smoking by women as a token of their liberation, again changing tobacco from a demon to a symbol of patriotism and progress.

The rising acceptability of tobacco use and the decline of the moral opprobrium against it can be explained not so much as a spontaneous response to these two major social trends as by the way that organized interest groups reacted to them. First, the prohibition movement encountered a major, unanticipated bad outcome: far from ceasing to drink, a large portion of the population, especially in urban areas, simply began to drink illegally (Kluger 1997, 64–67). A bigger market for an illegal product led to unprecedented lawlessness and the emergence of a solid consensus for the repeal of the prohibition of alcohol and, arguably, a disenchantment with governmental regulation of private behavior.

Second, and more important, the tobacco industry became much more effective at promotion and marketing of its products. In this effort, they capitalized on—and manipulated—the advantage that came from wartime consumption of tobacco and the universal suffrage movement (Kluger 1997). These early apparent successes in public relations, orchestrated in part by the founder and father of public relations, Edward L. Bernays, were to become the foundation of one of the best image management processes in history.

Thus, in the first half of the twentieth century, the states repealed most of their tobacco prohibitions and once again reverted primarily to taxation of tobacco products. The major difference this time was that they not only taxed the tobacco growers at the front end of the process but also taxed the consumers at the back end (Kluger 1997). It should be noted that some residual restrictions, usually penal, on the access of tobacco products by minors remained continuously in effect. These, however, were moral prohibitions based on the age of the offender—smoking joined a list of objectionable behaviors including stubbornness, truancy, and running away from home—and in no legal way related to health. Thus, it is reasonable to assert that by the 1930s tobacco was still not defined as a health policy issue, whether on the federal or state level. Ironically, the only governmental health-based activity concerning tobacco came from the U.S. Food and Drug Administration, which occasionally reprimanded tobacco companies for making curative claims for their products (Kagan and Vogel 1992, 34).

There things lay until 1964, when the surgeon general began the next phase of the tobacco story by publishing a report articulating the health costs of smoking to those who smoked cigarettes (U.S. DHEW 1964). Spurred by a growing awareness of the strong link between the use of tobacco and a litany of ways of dying early and unpleasantly, including elevated incidences of morbidity and mortality from cancer, heart disease, obstructive lung disease, and stroke, the surgeon general in 1964 made the first definitive statement about the health consequences of tobacco use based on the results of hundreds of clinical experiments.

Upon release of the surgeon general's report, two trends were unleashed. First, Congress was compelled to take some action that would persuade the nation that it was doing something to control tobacco as a potential health hazard. At the same time, it could not alienate the powerful lobby for the tobacco industry, which in the 1960s was still a major influence based both on its historical role as a producer of wealth and tax revenues and on its generous donations to the most powerful members of Congress. Among the latter were many conservative southern Democrats who benefited from long tenure and who represented precisely the states that had the greatest interest in maintaining the tobacco industry. The resulting legislation, enacted in 1965, was the Cigarette Labeling and Advertising Act (P. L. 89-92), and it required warning labels on the side of tobacco packs and on tobacco advertisements in exchange for virtual immunity of tobacco products from federal or, by explicit preemption, state regulation as to content, standards, or, at that point, even most forms of advertising. In effect, the federal government nearly gutted the ability of states to regulate tobacco as a hazardous product in the ways used for other health hazards, notwithstanding the traditional dominance of states in this arena.

In this process, the tobacco companies strengthened the unique status of their product—persuading the U.S. Congress to treat tobacco neither as a food nor as a drink nor as a drug nor as a hazardous substance, thus creating a handy vacuum within which tobacco products were protected from any particular health-related regulation, be it state or federal. At the same time, the tobacco industry was successful in diverting what regulations already existed toward controlling the consumption of tobacco by minors. This diversion gave tobacco a status superior even to that of alcohol—a protected oligopoly operating with minimal federal oversight. What is more, unlike alcohol, which was mandated by the Twenty-First Amendment to be controlled in main part by the states, tobacco gained a reasonable assurance against state intervention or even limitations on civil suit by an individual. (For a fuller description of this latter process from the view of the smoker as plaintiff, see Rabin [1992] and Schwartz [1992].)

In attaining this privileged status, then, manufacturers have diverted attention from tobacco as a health problem and focused instead on tobacco, first, as an advertising and commercial "free speech" problem; and second, as an agricultural product in need of price supports. The most recent achievement of the tobacco industry has been the production of the 1992 Synar Amendment (P.L. 102-321) requiring that all states restrict minors from having access to tobacco and imposing federal mandates for state regulation of tobacco sales to minors along with provisions that states must monitor compliance with the federal law (U.S. DHHS 1996). In effect, while written to ensure that states would prohibit the sale or distribution of cigarettes to minors, the regulation also shut down any future efforts of state or municipal governments to pass or enforce more stringent regulation of tobacco sales to minors (SAMHSA 1998).

CURRENT CONTROVERSIES IN TOBACCO-RELATED HEALTH POLICY IN THE STATES

These events have set the stage for current tobacco-related health policy activities in the states. Given the limitations imposed by the federal government and the wide divergence of public opinion on tobacco in the country, what has followed this evolution of tobacco from revenue source to health menace has been a meandering path of state, municipal, and private efforts toward the development of a regulatory regime, on the one hand, and strategies with which to reduce chronic illness resulting from the use of tobacco products, on the other (Daynard 1988; Rabin 1992). To suggest that this development consists of a series of stages or waves of activity would impose too much clarity on what is even now an evolving situation. With that note, we will, for the sake of analytic effort and in recognition of a general consensus, suggest that roughly three separate but sometimes overlapping health policy campaigns have been going on in the states (Rabin 1992; Daynard 1988; Cupp 1998).

First, as the level of government with primary police power for maintenance of the public health but with very limited and restricted federal funding for control of tobacco as a health hazard, the states have been conducting campaigns of varying seriousness and impact to reduce the sale, use, and health consequences of tobacco. These campaigns, beginning in 1913 when West Virginia prohibited smoking in public schools but predominantly in the past 20 years, have taken place particularly around three health-related aspects of the sale and use of tobacco products: smoking in places where enclosed public activity makes one person's smoke another person's health problem; use of tobacco by minors, both because minors are presumed not to understand the risks of smoking and because a large portion of all smokers begin as teenagers or even younger children; and sales of cigarettes by means that do not offer barriers to access by minors, including vending machines, self-service counters, or unattended displays of cigarettes. As public health interventions, these activities are all important because tobacco's environmental consequences are extremely hazardous and because so much smoking starts by the ease of access that enables children to obtain cigarettes at an age before they are necessarily capable of evaluating the consequences of smoking (Rabin and Sugarman 1992).

Second, because tort liability suits are tried before state courts, the states have become participants in shaping tobacco control through their judicial branches as a result of trials of lawsuits by individuals or classes of individuals who claim to have been made ill as a result of smoking cigarettes. While this judicial role did not constitute a strategic health policy activity of the states toward tobacco until 1994, it has been crucially influential in honing application of the law to this issue on a case-by-case basis (Daynard 1988; Rabin 1992; Cupp 1988), so that the terms under which tobacco companies operate have become slightly more constrained. This activity, more importantly, has succeeded in keeping the topic of the health consequences of tobacco in the press and in bringing to light a mass of documentation revealing the tobacco companies as conspirators as well as a cartel (Glantz et al. 1996).

Third, at the start of the nineties, watching the tortuous progress of regulation and the complex tangle of private litigation, a few state attorneys general began filing their own cases against the tobacco industry seeking tort damages for their states based on Medicaid-funded health care related to tobacco use (Daynard 1997). Progress in these cases began to gain momentum, including four cases (in Mississippi, Texas, Florida, and Minnesota) in which the tobacco industry settled out of court rather than go to trial. Thus, the idea spread among attorneys general that the states together could create a coordinated settlement of claims and behavioral restrictions on the tobacco industry to help reduce the cost of treating tobacco-induced illness and to reduce the prevalence of smoking by minors.

STATES' REGULATORY CONTROL OF TOBACCO

As already noted, tobacco control as a state health policy issue differs from much of the activity discussed in other chapters of this book due to reasons that are both structural and political. These factors range from the typically limited character of public health programs in our society (see Chapter 10), the division of legislative and executive regulatory power within each state and between states and their own municipalities, and legislative preemption of particular tobacco control measures by the federal and state legislatures. The first two of these factors are structural and so are immune from short-run strategic consideration because they are broader in scope than tobacco control policy and more deeply rooted in American governmental practices. Legislation, as we shall discuss further here, is very much a political decision and as such is subject to contention by interests affected by state and local regulatory provisions that are addressed to tobacco sale and use.

Because tobacco control rests on the notion that tobacco use is a threat to the public health, most state-level activity in this area grows out of the police power of the state. This exercise of the police power is most often delegated to municipalities as creatures and agents of the state at the local level, where the hazard to health is discovered and can be managed. Within the power to restrict behavior hazardous to the public health, the most profound factor determining how a particular state will approach tobacco is the state constitutional provision for home rule. States vary widely in their provisions for local home rule by cities, counties, and other local governments. Practices range from Hawaii, which has effectively no local government, to North Dakota, which has a state legislature meeting only for 60 days every other year and constitutional provisions that allow chartered cities and counties to override state law without state consent.

In general, there are three types of home rule charter: first, many states explicitly articulate areas of law in which control is uniformly passed to municipal authority; second, some states grant home rule to individual municipalities (cities, towns, villages, special purpose districts, and counties) that meet specified prerequisites; and, last, there are states in which municipalities are required to file home rule petitions regarding most matters, thus granting or withholding local autonomy on a case-by-case basis. While it would be tempting to suggest that a ranking exists among the three approaches of the degree to which localities are free to manage their own affairs, there is probably more variation in local autonomy within each group than across the three groups. Still, this aspect of state-local relations affects how tobacco use is controlled in any state.

This variety of provisions shapes the locus of power to control health-related activity and thus the envelope around state and local initiative. This framing of the power to regulate tobacco use is critical to the strength of restrictions over particular activities because tobacco does indeed fit one characteristic of health hazards in general: the hazardous behavior occurs within a close distance of the harm that follows. For example, the environmental tobacco smoke caused by a person smoking in an enclosed place causes harm only to those also present in the same place. As a result, all effective regulation of tobacco for the benefit of public health must occur at the local level, whether legislated by a state or mandated by a local legislature or board of health. This feature, combined with a highly variable public opinion about tobacco use, tends to make states with liberal home rule provisions more likely to have effective tobacco control that is responsible to local values and interests.

Again, however, states operate within a range of choices circumscribed by federal preemption of tobacco control. Most significantly, the Cigarette Labeling and Advertising Act (1965) and the Synar Amendment (1994) combine to limit severely the ability of the states to control the marketing, sale, and distribution of tobacco products and to require proactive restrictions of the sale of tobacco to minors. In particular, while it may be well known that tobacco used according to the manufacturer's directions can cause illness and death to the consumer, states are prohibited from passing laws that interfere with the advertising and sale of tobacco except to the extent that state legislatures may carve out a specifically public health restriction, usually by proscribing advertisements within certain distances of schools.

As a result of these limits, much of the tobacco control activities of states and localities focuses on restrictions of the use of tobacco, particularly in public places. These regulations vary widely in scope and rationale. The earliest and most widespread tobacco use restrictions are based on the concern that smoking in crowded areas is a fire hazard; hence, smoking in theaters, department stores, and some workplaces was an early target of regulation based on public health concerns. As evidence grew about the harm to nonsmokers by environmental tobacco smoke (secondhand or sidestream smoke) caused by people smoking in public places, state restrictions, whether by state legislative or executive action or ballot intiative or local regulation, began to include other indoor spaces. Not all of these prohibitions, however, have been based on a pure public health protection theory. Some such smoking has been restricted by states invoking OSHA requirements for workplace safety, provisions of the Americans with Disabilities Act (Tobacco Control Resource Center 2000), extension of the prohibition of tobacco use by minors to restrict smoking where minors are employed or expected to be otherwise congregated, or simple concern for tort liability potentially faced by states as employers and providers of public accommodations.

These regulatory efforts, of course, vary widely by state. Not surprisingly, for example, states with significant tobacco industrial or agricultural activity tend to have weak or nonexistent tobacco controls. In North Carolina, for example, restaurants are required to assure a minimum portion of seating for smoking customers if they choose also to have nonsmoking sections. On the other hand, states without major economic interests in tobacco but with strong public health traditions—particularly California and Massachusetts—have generally strong state and local tobacco use restrictions. Still, using economic or political characteristics to predict tobacco control patterns among the states can only explain so much. For example, 11 states prohibit smoking in state government work sites, but only 2 of them are among the 21 states that regulate smoking in private workplaces. Only 2 states prohibit smoking in restaurants, and neither of them is among the states restricting workplace smoking (CDC 1999b).

Nor is the level of tobacco control *by* states a clear indicator of the condition of tobacco control *in* states, since the amount of local tobacco control may vary widely among states with similar stances toward smoking in particular settings. As noted earlier, 16 states have enacted preemption laws that prohibit localities from enacting stronger provisions than the state as a whole, while the other states either have chosen to leave tobacco control to their municipalities or have enacted laws that explicitly or implicitly invite local regulations supplementing state provisions.

The net result of this situation is that there are thousands of state and local tobacco control provisions—exactly how many the CDC and Association of State and Territorial Health Officers (ASTHO) have declined to estimate because of the complexity of defining "one" regulation unambiguously—as well as a wide variety of state laws. Enforcement being necessarily a local effort (Enrich and Davidson 1998, 108), the number of laws may well be moot, since many may be honored mostly in the breach as a result of lack of political will or resources for local enforcement. Realistically, state regulation is not about to bring anything resembling an end to uses of tobacco that are hazardous to bystanders, to say nothing about uses deadly to the users. Just as the power of the tobacco lobby has shelved national tobacco control except in very restricted settings and under conditions favorable to the continued strength of the industry, the combination of a weaker but still evident industry lobby in state legislatures, and the ultimate necessity for local enforcement at local expense, has rendered state tobacco control effective only in specific places and under limited circumstances.

CIVIL TRIALS IN STATE COURTS

For most aspects of public health policy, the role of government is to seek balance among groups contending for their respective best interests in the allocation of resources while protecting the health of the citizenry and well-being of the state's finances. Albeit instances exist in which parties do conflict to the extent of civil litigation, for the most part civil litigation is not a significant aspect of the standard setting of state health policy. The control of tobacco, however, is not a matter of adjusting differences among parties who are largely united in the effort to improve health, but rather a conflict between a large cartel whose profit motive is directly antithetical to public health, on the one hand, and public health advocates and individuals with impaired or endangered health, on the other. Parties to tobacco control activities consider civil litigation not only as a way of resolving individual grievances against the tobacco industry but also as an extension of public health politics by other means.

When the political process fails to protect a large segment of the citizenry from harm to their health, such as those people experiencing health damages caused by tobacco, the aggrieved may come to frame their problems no longer as mere political claims but as rights that have been abridged. Such people tend to be individuals interested first and foremost in their own individual grievance and only secondarily in a political cause. They are driven by the desire to have their personal harm redressed rather than to make social change. For this purpose, they must turn to the courts, in most instances state courts, and try to persuade the court that their problems arise out of the misbehavior of others, that, in the language of the law, a tort has been committed against them by the defendants. In the case of health damages caused by tobacco use, the torts would have been committed by the tobacco companies that manufactured and sold the cigarettes smoked by the plaintiffs.

Typically, this legal process pits relatively poor individual plaintiffs against wealthy corporations. Invariably, the powerful corporate defendant, which has a long-range interest in how the legal process handles such cases, is motivated to invest more in any one case than the case itself would justify. As a rule, its teams of attorneys have the material resources, professional skills, and experience, as well as the personal and professional ties to members of the court community, sufficient to defeat any individual who comes to the court for the consideration of one single case (Galanter 1974).

Nonetheless, when political activity fails and when public opinion is sufficiently alienated from the defendants in such trials, attorneys committed to social change (cause-oriented lawyers) (Galanter 1974, 1975; see also Sarat 1998) will attempt to select cases with particularly compelling stories for trial in the hope that the resulting decision will not only redress the harm suffered by the individual plaintiff but will also set precedents restraining the defendants in the future (Mather 1998). The civil rights movement is rife with cases of this kind, *Brown v. Board of Education* being the most famous. The tobacco wars are similar, and beginning in the 1950s and 1960s, the use of litigation joined the use of legislative and executive action as a vehicle for efforts to control the health-related hazards created by the tobacco industry (Rabin 1992).

It is important to consider the history of antitobacco litigation, which arguably came in three waves (Cupp 1998), in order to properly understand developments in the state health-related tobacco control strategies. The first antitobacco trial *(Cooper v. R. J. Reynolds)* was filed in 1954 (Schwartz 1992, 135). In the five decades since, none of the plaintiffs in succeeding trials has ever collected any monetary award from the tobacco industry. Thus, from a cause-oriented litigator's perspective, all of these cases on the surface appear to be failures at attaining social change (Galanter 1974). However, seen in the broader historical context of state health-related tobacco control activities, this litigation has had distinct impact, albeit slowly and indirectly, by changing the public view of smoking as well as restructuring and reconstituting the culture of courts toward tort litigation (Cupp 1998; Mather 1998).

To appreciate the political quality of antitobacco litigation, it is important to know, as we do now only because of the lawsuits themselves, that the tobacco industry understood as early as 1953 that its product was addictive and dangerous

(Glantz et al. 1996, 31). What is worse, the industry decided to manipulate the conduct and reporting of its scientific research into the dangerous and addictive aspects of tobacco and agreed to a joint strategy of legal stonewalling clearly described in early industry documents (Daynard 1997). Tacitly, this strategy included an invariable rule against settling out of court as well as employing every delaying tactic available. When one recalls that the plaintiffs in the first wave of lawsuits were individuals or their survivors, that their attorneys were mostly small law firms working for a contingency fee, i.e., payment of a percentage (usually 33%) of a potential plaintiff's award, and that the defendants were among the richest corporations in the world, it is hardly surprising that things worked out as they did on a case-by-case basis (Givelber 1998).

This first wave of tobacco litigation also marked a defeat for the tobacco control effort writ large. In the process of siding with the tobacco lawyers, judges in the cases of this first wave raised the bar for cases to clear in several areas, most importantly in determining just what kind of product could be regarded as sufficiently dangerous to warrant a tort claim. The standard, eventually worked into the American Law Institute's *Restatement (Second) of Torts* (1979), was framed in the form of a determination that liability could attach to a product that is in a "defective condition unreasonably dangerous" to the user. In a related comment, the American Law Institute noted that the term "defective" had been inserted because, according to them, good tobacco was not excessively dangerous simply because smoking had harmful effects. While this round of tort suits had raised some awareness of the health hazards of tobacco in the population at large, the state courts rendered decisions with an altogether chilling effect on efforts to obtain from the judiciary that which was not forthcoming from the legislative and executive branches. The ensuing 20 years were notable for the absence of litigation against tobacco.

By 1983, however, the three major obstacles to tort litigation against the tobacco industry had developed certain weaknesses. First, the tobacco companies' insistence that each plaintiff go to trial isolated from all other plaintiffs was much more difficult to enforce because of changes in some state civil trial procedures over the previous 20 years. Also, plaintiffs' attorneys, having learned a great deal from similar cases fought over asbestos in which they brought class action suits, decided in *Cipollone v. Liggett Group, Inc.,* to work jointly in responding to the blizzard of procedural demands routinely issued by the tobacco attorneys.

Second, the course of substantive state product liability laws had drifted in ways highly favorable to plaintiffs complaining of dangerous products. In particular, many states, including New Jersey, where the *Cipollone* case was brought, now held to the notion that a manufacturer of a product could be held liable for its damages even if its dangerousness was integral to its function, provided that the maker had been reckless or negligent in its means of marketing the product (Mather 1998). In the case of tobacco, then, the law had moved to the point where the industry could be sued for producing a product that, even if not defective in design or manufacture, was in fact inherently dangerous to use. State courts also grew more critical of the tobacco industry's defense that it had done everything required of it in the way of protecting consumers simply by complying with the 1965 Labeling Act designed by the U. S. Congress (Kluger 1997, 650ff).

Still, in this landmark *Cipollone* case, federal law preempted state law, and the Third Circuit Court of Appeals reversed the state court's finding in favor of the plaintiff (Kluger 1997, 674). Further, efforts to sue the tobacco industry into submission failed on the remaining limitation that juries simply did not believe that smokers, however addicted, were unable to make a rational decision to quit. The more time that passed following the effective date of the Labeling Act, the harder it became to make the case that the user, however much deceived and harmed by the tobacco industry, was not also sufficiently negligent to bear a substantial burden of responsibility for the health consequences of smoking.

Strategically, the second round of tort trials may have done little except raise the awareness of the public to the health dangers of tobacco. To a large extent, it may be the case that these disappointing results could not have been prevented by a more coordinated and carefully selected set of cases. Development of grand strategy by a group of attorneys for individuals may be too much to ask. It may be, indeed, that it is in the nature of tort litigation that the defendant reaps the benefit of being a large organized interest, which, in the case of the tobacco industry, is capable of using its status as wealthy repeat litigants to the fullest effect (Galanter 1974). In any event, the second round of tobacco litigation yielded little direct effect on the tobacco industry and at best inadvertently developed a solid cadre of well-trained cause-oriented lawyers. Meanwhile, juries in these cases established a solid impression that the American public had little willingness to assign liability to the manufacturers of tobacco on behalf of the individual smoker (Kluger 1997, 678ff).

One should not conclude from this history that the second wave of litigation is over. At this writing, numerous cases are still at trial, and others continue to be filed. This issue of how and in what courts to handle class actions is being addressed along with the basic issues of liability (Givelber 1998). While the message is muted, the effort continues unabated, and the positive aspect of litigation as a social change strategy is that each trial is considered individually. However much law may congeal around doctrines and findings, each case is potentially a landmark that could change the topography of the landscape on which trials are staged.

Historically, however, there is an alternative reading of the first two waves of tobacco litigation. No money may have passed hands and no resounding change in legal attitudes toward the producers of a noxious product has occurred. Still, these cases may combine in significant ways with ongoing legislative and executive efforts to control tobacco as a health hazard. This line of reasoning follows from the role of the state courts as a forum for bringing to trial the facts germane to the object of litigation, and those facts in the health-related tobacco litigation include the behavior of the tobacco industry itself. Cases beginning with *Cipollone* and following through the nineties produced documents that successively revealed to the public and, most important, to tobacco control advocates at all levels the full extent to which the tobacco industry was engaged in a concerted effort to manipulate what the public knew, believed, and felt about tobacco products (Glantz et al. 1996).

Thus, this second wave of tobacco litigation yielded a set of documents that went a long way to reframe public consciousness of the nature of tobacco and the role that the tobacco industry played at large. Much publicity was created around these documents with the help of Surgeon General C. Everett Koop and Dr. Lawrence Kessler, the director of the Food and Drug Administration in 1994 (Daynard 1997). A well-publicized congressional hearing resulted in which the CEOs of the tobacco companies all swore that they did not believe nicotine is addictive. Yet the documents disclosed in tobacco tort trials stated, in the industry's own words, that the CEOs not only knew nicotine was addictive but also regarded its dosage as an important marketing strategy. This revelation promoted public consciousness of the notion that the continuing antitobacco litigation was not about negligent smokers who were blameworthy for their indulgence in smoking but rather about the well-organized tobacco industry selling a product it knew full well for over a half century was addictive and deadly (Hilts 1996). It is exactly this shifting public perception that currently appears to be the most salient accomplishment of the decades of lost tort cases and that set the stage for the next phase of health-related tobacco control.

SUITS AND SETTLEMENTS BY ATTORNEYS GENERAL OF THE STATES

Discovery of the State-Initiated Suit

In the mid-nineties, the evolution of law and public opinion outlined earlier led several tobacco control advocates to consider ways that the states might become parties to lawsuits against the tobacco industry. The record of private suits, combined with the discovery from those suits and congressional action prompted by documents filed in the private suits, provided attorneys general with a tantalizing opportunity. They would develop a novel theory capitalizing on the advantage the states had in not having chosen themselves (as fictive persons) to smoke or not to smoke. Thus, they could pursue the emerging pattern of deceit by the industry without having to engage the issue of a smoker's own responsibility. A lever was needed with which to make the health-related harms of smoking an issue to the state, and the fact that the states pay a major portion of the costs for health care delivered to their poorest citizens gave them that lever.

According to this perspective, the tobacco industry was being unjustly enriched because it was not compensating the state for the cost of delivering health care to poor smokers, amounts that came to roughly $100 million a year for the average state. Under this theory, the tobacco industry should have known that its reckless behavior—demonstrated by its own documents showing awareness and manipulation of the dangerous contents of cigarettes—would harm not only the smokers, whose own habits may have contributed to their illness, but also the states, which had taken no part in the decision of smokers to smoke. Further, the tobacco industry was also on the wrong side of laws designed to regulate commerce, including antitrust laws against unfair or deceptive commercial practices (Mather 1998).

This mix of circumstances opened the door to a flood of state suits against the tobacco industry. Starting on May 23, 1994, with *Moore v. American Tobacco,* filed in Jackson County, Mississippi, Chancery Court, state attorneys general began to file a host of similar suits against the industry. Three states had filed by the end of 1994, 5 by 1995, 17 by 1996, and 39 in 1997 (Kelder 1999). As new states joined the movement, attorneys general became more creative in discovering theories of law under which to sue the industry. For example, suits based on antitrust or deceptive commercial practices carried with them the power of the state to sue not only for its own losses but also as *parens patriae* for losses suffered by all its citizens. Given the degree of conspiratorial behavior involved, states also invoked racketeer-influenced corrupt organization (RICO) statutes (Mather 1998).

Finally, the states were in a position to seek "equitable relief" as well as monetary damages because, unlike the individual smoker with tobacco-related illness, the state was in the position to demand future restrictions on the behavior of the industry. In short, through the courts, the states had an unprecedented opportunity to do what they had not done by legislation or executive decision, i.e., impose by court order or consent decree restrictions that lay beyond the reach of the legislature and executive either because of federal preemption or lack of political will.

The Rise of the Global Settlement

At first, the tobacco industry took on the states in the same mode they had employed for decades in dealing with individual plaintiffs. But a combination of factors—the astronomical awards faced by the industry upon a loss at trial, the relatively large scale of resources a state can mount in comparison to an individual, several unfavorable procedural decisions, a spate of class action lawsuits paralleling the state suits, and rising public distaste for the industry's connivances—brought the industry to the unprecedented decision to negotiate a settlement, signed on June 20, 1997. This first settlement, made between industry attorneys, most of the attorneys general who had filed suit, and private attorneys representing classes of plaintiffs, is commonly referred to as the "Global Settlement." However, because only 44 of the 50 states and eight miscellaneous jurisdictions that would be affected were participating, and because some of the provisions involved changes in federal law, this resulting global settlement had to be ratified by Congress to ensure full state and federal cooperation with its terms. This was a condition the tobacco industry needed to protect it from continued and costly liability exposure, not only from states but also from classes of smokers.

Moreover, bringing the tobacco industry to the table, of course, also did not constitute a resolution to the many issues involved in the large number of lawsuits, which numbered upwards of 500 at the time of the signing, or the political contests that surrounded the settlement. A large number of interested parties—lawyers, the medical community, 39 states, the U.S. Department of Health and Human Services, smokers and nonsmokers, and even the unborn—plus the giant size of the monetary settlement ($368.5 billion) created tremendous pressure for settlement. Senator John McCain (R-Ariz.) and a bipartisan group of cosponsors filed a bill, one of many in Congress, that in effect would have ratified the contents of the agreement signed by the parties to various lawsuits. The McCain Bill, however, was amended extensively in congressional deliberation, including an increase in the tobacco industry's liabilities to $516 billion. Congress generated a great deal of heat in the form of hearings and press coverage but not much light in terms of actual policy decisions. The tobacco industry advertised heavily against passage of any bill, and a raft of alternative bills were filed and considered, chewing up the time from June 22, 1997, until final defeat on June 17, 1998.

Whether to Sue or Settle: States' Choice

Meanwhile, the states, although signatories to the Global Settlement, were not thereby prevented from continuing with their individual suits. While Congress and the federal executive branch were engaged in battle over who would spend how much for what and what protections the industry would reap, the state suits went forward.

The early trial dates set for several state suits, combined with the protracted and dilatory debate in Washington, resulted in strong pressure for the tobacco industry to do what it promised never to do: settle a tort liability case out of court. On the eve of the trial date and regardless of the Global Settlement, in early July 1997, the tobacco industry settled out of court with the state of Mississippi for $3.6 billion plus legal fees to attorneys for the state and other expenses. This sum of $3.6 billion represents about 10% of the bottom line for the Global Settlement and four times the state's allocation under the agreement, a heady windfall for Mississippi and a strong indication that the industry was abandoning its usual courtroom bravado. On August 28, 1997, the industry came to terms with the state of Florida for a total of $11.3 billion, conceding billboard restrictions, the release of secret industry documents, and yet more limitations on industry practices.

The Decline and Fall of the Global Settlement

It may be too cynical to say that the deal was dead on arrival, but prospects for a congressionally brokered Global Settlement were dim from the outset. Projects ranging from juvenile lockups to emphysema clinics for aged smokers emerged from the wish list of every lobbying group in the District of Columbia. Ironically, even the tobacco industry got into the act by seeking tax credits to help pay for the costs of the settlement.

While money was the undoubted "star" of the hearings on the tobacco settlement, the health-related provisions also were important and vulnerable to congressional redefinition. Basically, Congress was unwilling to offer the Food and Drug Administration the power to regulate tobacco, whether as part of a $368 billion settlement or otherwise. The tobacco lobby's influence led Congress to so vitiate the equitable—i.e., nonmonetary—provisions of the settlement that neither the executive branch nor the attorneys general who had negotiated the deal could accept the outcome. As a result, the Global Settlement dissolved with a whimper.

During and after the Fall of the Global Settlement

State tobacco control advocates had few options left to them by 1998. Aside from ballot initiatives in Massachusetts and California (the two most active states in the antitobacco movement), state-based efforts at controlling tobacco had continued to produce public health laws filled with exceptions and loopholes or worded in ways that made them easy targets for tobacco industry lawsuits to invalidate them. Under a Republican Congress, appropriations for federal support for state tobacco control had little prospect of exceeding their already nominal amounts. Incremental local tobacco restrictions encouraged by state agencies were partly successful, and research into those processes was beginning to provide a sense of what strategies work and in what context. Nevertheless, federal support for local tobacco control was also wanting.

All that remained were the individual state suits against the tobacco industry, and for those more than 40 states with cases pending, the focus shifted back to the state of affairs antecedent to the Global Settlement. For Texas and Minnesota, their trials each ground away until the industry agreed to settle. On January 16, 1998, Texas received $15.3 billion, and on May 8, 1998, Minnesota received $6.5 billion. Both settlements occurred figuratively on the courthouse steps on the way to trial. Other states continued to prepare for trial, but the tobacco industry was secretly negotiating with nine of the state attorneys general to develop a patterned settlement bringing a comprehensive end to continuing state and personal litigation, which was expanding to include labor unions, corporations, and other entities speaking for whole classes of individuals as well as for themselves. The tobacco industry was being charged for damages not only for smokers but also for others necessarily exposed to environmental tobacco smoke, which has become recognized as carcinogenic in itself (Kluger 1997, 748ff.)

If money were the only objective sought or gained by the two states, the tobacco industry might have come to a low-profile settlement. However, the Minnesota case, in particular, was as much about industry practices as monetary damages. Most crucially, the attorney general of Minnesota sought access to 30 million documents generated by the tobacco industry in its 50-year campaign of concerted deception, organized, ironically, around the abuse of its privilege of communication with the attorneys (Hilts 1996). As a rule, such communication is not subject to subpoena because the attorney and the client need to communicate freely in order to prepare an adequate defense. One exception to this protection is the so-called crime fraud rule. In effect, if an attorney is in communication with a client for the purpose of planning or committing a fraud or a crime, the secrecy between the two can be broken. Courts have been chary of applying this rule, and several judges had already rejected other states' pleas for discovery, a pretrial process of entering as much ancillary documentation and testimony as possible. In the discovery process in Minnesota, however, the judge agreed to review specific documents to determine if they were subject to the crime fraud exception, ruling that over 3 million pages of documents were indeed evidence of conspiracy between the tobacco companies and their lawyers and so were available to public scrutiny. The states that were continuing their contests with the tobacco industry, meanwhile, were developing a growing pile of documents secured through discovery that would make the industry increasingly likely to lose any lawsuit that might come to trial.

Adding to this pressure on the industry was the settlement reached independently by the Liggett Group, one of the smaller tobacco producers, in which it disclosed to a Florida judge extensive evidence not only of its misbehavior, but much of the structure of the industrywide conspiracy as well.

The Rise of the Master Settlement Agreement

Beginning in June 1998, with the fall of the Global Settlement, initiative in the matter of the remaining lawsuits between states and various combinations of tobacco companies returned to the states' attorneys general. Each case was an entity in itself, with its own complex maneuverings about discovery, pretrial motions, and, inexorably, setting a trial date and, if needed, a trial. Various states took different courses of action that brought the tobacco issue back from Congress to the states, and more specifically to their attorneys general. Significantly, many of the attorneys general were engaged in some way in a partisan election coming up in November 1998. Indeed, four of them were active candidates for governor of their states and may have been motivated to use the rhetoric of their antitobacco achievements in their campaigns.

States with the strongest legal cases pressed forward, including Minnesota in particular. Simultaneously—and evidently seamlessly with the failed Global Settlement negotiations—eight state attorneys general, more or less speaking for all the remaining states, undertook to redefine the nature of the "Settlement." Whereas the word had become, whether intentionally or through serendipity, an icon connoting a "final resolution of the tobacco liability issue," the attorneys general sought to restrict it to the narrower notion of a settlement of the litigation. They also promoted the idea that the settlement this time would be the beginning of tobacco reform, not its end (National Association of Attorneys General 1999).

At this point, the politics of tobacco control had effectively passed from the hands of the legislatures, executives, and people of the states to their attorneys general and the state courts, which were to execute the terms of the Master Settlement Agreement (MSA). As with any other agreement, each party gained some benefits at the expense of losing others. In the MSA, the settling states sought to receive a total of $206 billion and limited restrictions on tobacco industry behavior in exchange for substantial industry immunity from prosecution for prior misconduct and many categories of future misconduct. In fact, it contained $130 billion less in settlement payments and dropped most of the effective provisions of the Global Settlement including, but not limited to, FDA regulation, many provisions regarding advertising, and the "look back" provision increasing tobacco company payments if youth smoking is not reduced in future years. Last, but by no means least, the MSA was left to the state courts to interpret and enforce.

Since the document is extensive and is carving new legal territory, the likelihood of conflicting interpretation and contradictory court orders is extremely high. Still, by February 1, 1999, 50 states, 6 territories, and the District of Columbia had received trial court approval of the Cigarette Master Settlement Agreement and the Enforcing Consent Decree (National Association of Attorneys General 1999). Meanwhile, the advocates of the Master Settlement Agreement are seeking to meet its remaining endorsement requirements in order to start the flow of money to the states and to end certain industry advertising strategies aimed at the youth market (however defined). At the same time, state legislators, the National Association of Attorneys General, and the Council of Governors are struggling with each other to establish who will control the windfall $206 billion and to what ends. Meanwhile, state courts continue to hear increasing numbers of cases from organizations such as Blue Cross and Blue Shield, HMOs, labor unions, and assorted classes of plaintiffs who are not hampered by the MSA.

WHERE HEALTH POLITICS ABOUT TOBACCO IS NOW

Settlements apparently are being reached, though in tobacco politics, little is as it seems. The landscape of health politics about tobacco is littered with ongoing contests. The U.S. Department of Justice is presently seeking to sue the tobacco companies following the lead of the states on the theory that they are innocent bystanders injured because tobacco companies and individual smokers both acted recklessly. Fifty states, with funding from the Department of Health and Human Services, the Robert Wood Johnson Foundation, other external sources, and, in some instances, money from tobacco taxes, are engaged in a range of legislative activities to restrict the sale and use of tobacco. Finally, some, but by no means most, states are proposing to use portions of their revenues from the MSA for education and cessation efforts addressed to smokers and people anticipating taking up tobacco use.

The Master Settlement Agreement has preoccupied most tobacco control activists during the period from November 1998 to the time of this writing in June 2000. According to the logic of this agreement, an important justification of the settlement was that it would compensate states for the Medicaid expenses they suffered because of smoking while distributing resources to reduce smoking by, for example, discouraging teens from taking up the habit in the first place. A great deal of oratory has been devoted to this latter line of reasoning, but, while data are difficult to obtain and interpret, the states do not seem to be responding to this original intent of the MSA. Indeed, states are using their new funds for widely varied uses, from a dike surrounding Great Forks, North Dakota, to juvenile prisons in several places.

Among the health-related uses to which settlement money has been put, the most common are funding for prescription insurance for the elderly and universal health insurance for children. Predictably, the states using the largest proportion of their funds for smoking-related purposes are precisely those that were already actively engaged in tobacco control. In this way politics and policymaking for tobacco control have come full circle, returning the issue to the distinctive legislative arenas of 50 states, where inconsistency and inattention have been more the rule than the exception.

REFERENCES

American Law Institute. 1979. *Restatement (Second) of Torts.* Philadelphia, PA.
———. 1995. *Restatement (Third) of Torts: Product Liability 2 cmt c,* at 21 (tentative draft no. 2). Philadelphia, PA.
Borio, G. 1995. "Economic Aspects of Tobacco During the Colonial Period 1612–1776." *http://www.tobacco.org/History/colonialtobacco.html.*
———. 1999. "Tobacco Timeline." *http://www.tobacco.org/History/Tobacco_History.html.*
Centers for Disease Control and Prevention. 1990. "State Tobacco-Use Prevention and Control Plans." *Morbidity and Mortality Weekly Report* 39 (8): 133–136.
———. 1999a. *http://www.cdc.gov/nccdphp/osh/initfact.htm.*
———. 1999b. *http://www2.cdc.gov/nccdphp/osh/state.*
———. 1999c. *http://www.cdc.gov/tobacco/data.htm.*
———. 1999d. "Cigarette Smoking Among High School Students—11 States, 1991–1997." *Morbidity and Mortality Weekly Report* 48 (31): 686–692.
Cupp, R. L., Jr. 1998. "A Morality Play's Third Act: Revisiting Addiction, Fraud, and Consumer Choice in 'Third Wave' Tobacco Litigation." *Kansas Law Review* 46 (April): 465–506.
Daynard, R. A. 1988. "Commentary: Tobacco Liability Litigation as a Cancer Control Strategy." *Journal of the National Cancer Institute* 80 (1): 9–13.

————. 1994. "The Third Wave of Tobacco Products Liability Cases." *Trial* (November): 34–40.

————. 1997. "Litigation by States against the Tobacco Industry," a presentation to the 10th World Conference on Tobacco or Health, Beijing, P.R.C., August 26.

DiFranza, J. R., T. H. Winters, R. J. Goldberg, P. M. Paulman, N. Wolf-Gilespie, C. Fletcher, R. D. Jaffee, and D. Murray. 1991. "R. J. Reynolds–Nabisco's Cartoon Promotes Camel Cigarettes to Children." *Journal of the American Medical Association* 266 (22): 3149–3153.

Dillow, G. L. 1981. "The Hundred-Year War against the Cigarette." *American Heritage* 32 (3): 1–11.

Ellison Qualitative Research, Inc., for R. J. Reynolds Company. 1991. "A Qualitative Assessment of Camel Advertising Equity." *www.library.ucsf.edu/tobacco/mangini.html/k/053.*

Enrich, P. D., and P. A. Davidson. 1998. "Local and State Control of Tobacco: The Effects of the Proposed National Settlement." *Harvard Journal on Legislation* 35:87–121.

Fishman, J., et al. 1999. "State Laws on Tobacco Control—United States, 1998." *Morbidity and Mortality Weekly Report* 48 (SS-3): 21–62.

Galanter, M. 1974. "Why the 'Haves' Come Out Ahead: Speculations on the Limits of Legal Change." *Law and Society Review* 9 (1): 95–160.

————. 1975. "Afterword: Explaining Litigation." *Law and Society Review* 9 (2): 347–368.

Givelber, D. 1998. "Cigarette Law." *Indiana Law Journal* 73 (Summer): 867–901.

Glantz, S. A., J. Slade, L. A. Bero, P. Hanauer, and D. E. Barnes. 1996. *The Cigarette Papers.* Berkeley: University of California Press.

Hilts, P. J. 1996. *Smokescreen: The Truth Behind the Tobacco Industry Cover-Up.* Reading, MA: Addison-Wesley.

Johnson, L. D., P. M. O'Malley, and J. G. Bachman. 1987. *National Trends in Drug Use and Related Factors Among American High School Students and Young Adults, 1975–1986.* Pub. No. ADM 87-1535, pp. 248–255. Washington, DC: National Institute on Drug Abuse, U.S. Dept. of Health and Human Services.

Johnson, L. D. 1986. "Prepared Testimony Regarding Cigarette Advertising and Its Likely Impact on Youth," Subcommittee on Health and the Environment, House Committee on Energy and Commerce, report of the hearing of July 18 and August 1.

Kagan, R. A., and D. Vogel. 1992. "The Politics of Smoking Regulation: Canada, France, the United States." In *Smoking Policy: Law, Politics, and Culture,* ed. R. L. Rabin and S. D. Sugarman, pp. 22–48. New York: Oxford University Press.

Kelder, G. 1999. "The Logic of Local Action and Enforcement." *Tobacco Control Update* 3 (2 and 3): *http://www.tobacco.hev.edg/tcu/3-2/oveviews__msa/htm.*

Kluger, R. 1997. *Ashes to Ashes: America's Hundred-Year Cigarette War, the Public Health, and the Unabashed Triumph of Philip Morris.* New York: Vintage.

Mather, L. 1998. "Theorizing about Trial Courts: Lawyers, Policymaking, and Tobacco Litigation." *Law and Social Inquiry* 23 (4): 897–940.

Middleton, A. P. 1953. *Tobacco Coast.* Newport News, VA: Mariners' Museum.

National Association of Attorneys General. 1999. *http://www.naag.org/consent.html.*

National Institute for Occupational Safety and Health (NIOSH), Centers for Disease Control and Prevention (CDC). 1991. *Current Intelligence Bulletin 54: Environmental Tobacco Smoke in the Workplace—Lung Cancer and Other Health Effects.* Publication no. 91-108, June.

Ndubisi. B. U. 1999. "Tobacco Smoking and Health Consequences." *http://www.jaxmed.com/dcms/jax-medicine/jax-mag-header.htm.*

Philip Morris Companies. 1999. "Quarterly Balance Sheet and Income Statement for Quarter Ending 9.30.99." Philadelphia, PA.

Public Citizen. 1998. "Blowing Smoke: Big Tobacco's 1998 Congressional Lobbying Expenses Skyrocket." *http://www.citizen.org/tobacco/oct98lobby.htm.*

Rabin, R. L. 1992. "Institutional and Historical Perspectives on Tobacco Tort Liability." In *Smoking Policy: Law, Politics, and Culture,* ed. R. L. Rabin and S. D. Sugarman, pp.110–130. New York: Oxford University Press.

Rabin, R. L., and S. D. Sugarman. 1992. *Smoking Policy: Law, Politics, and Culture.* New York: Oxford University Press.

R. J. Reynolds Companies. 1999. *Annual Report.* Winston-Salem, NC.

Rochefort, D. A., and R. W. Cobb, eds. 1994. *The Politics of Problem Definition: Shaping the Policy Agenda.* Lawrence: University Press of Kansas.

Sarat, A., ed. 1998. *Cause Lawyering: Political Commitment and Professional Responsibilities.* Oxford: Oxford University Press.

Scharf, T. J. 1967. *History of Maryland: From the Earliest Periods to the Present Day.* Hatboro, PA: Tradition Press.

Schwartz, G. T. 1992. "Tobacco Liability in the Courts." In *Smoking Policy: Law, Politics, and Culture,* ed. R. L. Rabin and S. D. Sugarman, pp. 131–160. New York: Oxford University Press.

Stauber, J., and S. Rampton. 1996. "Why Philip Morris Hates Trial Lawyers." *PR Watch* 3 (3): *htttp://www.prwatch.org/prw_issues/1996.93/philip.html.*

Substance Abuse and Mental Health Services Administration. (SAMHSA). 1998. *Synar Regulation Implementation: Report to Congress on FFY 1997 State Compliance.* DHHS pub. no. SMA 97-3143. Rockville, MD: U.S. DHHS, SAMHSA Center for Substance Abuse Prevention.

———. 1999. National Clearinghouse for Alcohol and Drug Information. *http://www.health.org/res-brf/index.htm.*

Tobacco Control Resource Center. 1964. *Reports on Policy Aspects of the Smoking and Health Situations in U.S.A.* October. *http://www.tobacco.neu.edu/Extra/1964memo.htm#VI,1999.*

———.1999. *http://www.tobacco.neu.edu/msa/TCRC-ACS%%20Analysis-Version%20Twenty.htm.*

———. 2000. *http://www.tobacco.neu.edu/ETS/adainfo1.htm.*

Torabi, R., W. J. Bailey, and M. Majd-Jabbari. 1993. "Cigarette Smoking as a Predictor of Alcohol and Other Drug Use by Children and Adolescents: Evidence of the 'Gateway Drug Effect.'" *Journal of School Health* 63 (September): 302–306.

U.S. Department of Health, Education, and Welfare (U.S. DHEW). 1964. *Smoking and Health: Report of the Advisory Committee to the Surgeon General of the Public Health Service.* Washington, DC: Government Printing Office.

U.S. Department of Health and Human Services (U.S. DHHS), Food and Drug Administration. 1996. "Regulations Restricting the Sale and Distribution of Cigarettes and

Smokeless Tobacco to Protect Children and Adolescents; Final Rule." 21 CFR, pt. 801. *Federal Register* 61: 44396–45318.

U.S. House of Representatives. 1986. *Advertising of Tobacco Products.* (Serial no. 99-167), pp. 860–886. Washington, DC: Government Printing Office.

———. 1997. Committee on Government Reform and Oversight, *Minority Staff Report,* June 12.

University of California at San Francisco. 1999. Tobacco Control Archives, Mangini Collection.

10

Promoting Public Health: Challenges for the States

William J. Waters Jr.

In the past, public health has been far too insular, well known by its practitioners but little understood by everyone else. In this chapter, I attempt to outline what public health is and what its major policy and infrastructure challenges are as we enter the twenty-first century. Essentially, the potential of public health to improve the health of the public is not matched with a commensurate level of public commitment and resource investment. In the twenty-first century, public health practitioners will have to do a better job of communicating the strengths and opportunities inherent in public health. Throughout my presentation of these issues, I weave vignettes from the state of Rhode Island to provide concrete examples of the practice of public health at the state level. Rhode Island is a somewhat unique public health jurisdiction because it has no county or city health departments. Nevertheless, Rhode Island's experience is reflective of the central public health issues of our day. Hopefully, the articulated policy and infrastructure challenges and the Rhode Island vignettes taken together will provide the reader with a window into the world of public health practice at the state level today.

CONCEPTUAL AND POLICY ISSUES

Public Health

Public health is an extremely vital but little understood area of human endeavor. And yet—the history of public health goes back some 4,000 years to the ancient Indian cities of Mohenjo-Daro and Harappa, which were consciously planned with bathrooms, drainpipes, and sewers (Rosen 1958, 25). Rosen, one of the key public health historians, states that "throughout history, the major problems of health that men have faced have been concerned with community life, for instance, the control of transmissible disease, the control and improvement of the physical environment (sanitation), the provision of medical care, and the relief of disability and destitution. The relative emphasis placed on each of these problems has varied from time to time, but they are all closely related, and from them has come public health as we know it today" (1958, 25). The *American Journal of Public Health* and the *Annual Review of Public Health* have highlighted the key issues facing public health in the United States for over the past 88 and 19 years respectively. For the serious student of public health, there is an enormous professional literature to consult covering an amazing array of public health topics from laboratory science to social marketing.

In its 1988 landmark report entitled *The Future of Public Health,* the Institute of Medicine (IOM) defined the mission of public health as "fulfilling society's interest in assuring conditions in which people can be healthy" (1988, 7). In 1994, the U.S. Department of Health and Human Services' Public Health Functions Steering Committee further elaborated on the mission of public health as follows: prevents epidemics and the spread of disease, protects against environmental hazards, prevents injuries, promotes and encourages healthy behaviors, responds to disasters and assists communities in recovery, and assures the quality and accessibility of health services. In addition, the steering committee defined essential public health services: monitor health status to identify community health problems; diagnose and investigate health problems and health hazards in the community; inform, educate, and empower people about health issues; mobilize community partnerships to identify and solve health problems; develop policies and plans that support individual and community health efforts; enforce laws and regulations that protect health and ensure safety; link people to needed personal health services and assure the provision of health care when otherwise unavailable; assure a competent public health and personal health care workforce; evaluate the effectiveness, accessibility, and quality of personal and population-based health services; and conduct research for new insights and innovative solutions to health problems.

"Thus, public health is not so much defined by any given set of institutions or services as it is defined by the prevailing disease patterns in the population and the pragmatic opportunities for prevention that exist at any given point in time" (Rhode Island Department of Health 1999, 2). Public health is built on the scientific foundation of epidemiology, which is "the study of the distribution of determinants and antecedents of health and disease in human populations; the ultimate goal is to identify the underlying causes of a disease and then apply findings to disease prevention and health promotion" (Turnock 1997, 365).

Public health focuses on the population rather than on the individual. It emphasizes prevention rather than treatment. Its targets shift with changing demographics and disease patterns. Its interventions change with new research findings. Public health's constituencies are disproportionately members of poor and minority communities, the highest risk populations. Its successes are frequently nonevents; for example, proper immunization results in a reduction in the incidence of infectious and communicable diseases such as polio and measles. All of these characteristics tend to make public health somewhat distant or invisible to the general public. As a result, the public recognition of and support for public health are not commensurate with its importance to the quality of our collective lives. The health of the population is largely dependent on the success of public health efforts, but people today associate health progress with high-tech medical services. Yet, the health gains of Americans over the last 100 years have been largely due to public health measures such as systems for clean drinking water distribution, human sewage disposal, and sanitary food production.

A strong and vibrant public health system must have complementary components at the federal, state, and local levels. The state level public health component has its unique characteristics and challenges, serving as a bridge between national and local public health practice. It is less distant than the federal component, but it has more perspective than the local components (i.e., county and city public health departments). Moreover, the state level has much of the machinery needed for public health practice: statistics, expertise, legislative and regulatory authority, human resources, and fiscal resources. However, as we cross over from the twentieth century into the twenty-first century, the practice of public health faces many significant challenges at the state level and at all the other levels as well.

Populations

Public health starts with populations, the denominator of public health rates. To a great extent, changing demographics will drive the public health agenda in the future. First, the so-called minorities are the fastest growing segment of the population (for example, see Figure 10.1). The federal definition of minorities includes Native Americans, African Americans, Hispanic Americans, and Asian Americans. These groups taken together will constitute 40% of the population by the year 2030. They already represent the majority of schoolchildren in many urban communities. These rapidly growing minority populations represent a couple of very significant challenges to public health. Most of these minorities experience a disproportionate amount of poverty and disease. Unless significant progress is made in minority health, public health will be faced with a growing burden of disease, much of it concentrated in the inner cities.

In 1998, the Clinton administration announced the President's Initiative on Race to eliminate health status disparities in the minority populations by the year 2010. This is an extremely ambitious target, given the huge gaps in health status that currently exist. Minority groups experience significantly greater rates of infant mortality, heart disease, cancer, diabetes, HIV/AIDS, and many other disease (for example, see Figure 10.2). In addition, there is the critical issue of cultural competence. If public health is to be successful in preventing disease and promoting health in the minority populations, it must understand the minorities' cultures

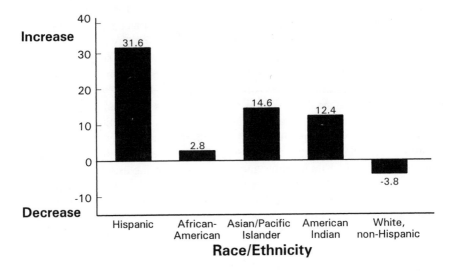

Figure 10.1 Rhode Island's Population: Percent Change, 1990–1997
Source: Rhode Island Department of Health

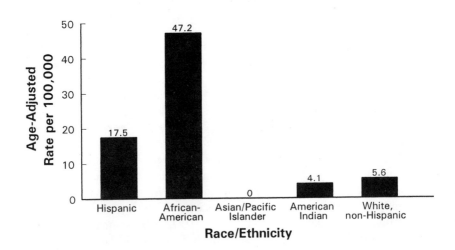

Figure 10.2 Rhode Island HIV/AIDS Mortality, 1993–1997 Average
Source: Rhode Island Department of Health

and be able to communicate effectively with minorities using their languages and concepts. In the final analysis, progress in minority health will necessitate an increase in the number and percentage of minorities participating in the public health workforce and serving on public health advisory groups.

In 1992, the Rhode Island General Assembly created the Minority Health Program in the Department of Health, including a minority health coordinator and a Minority Health Advisory Committee. The Minority Health Program has funded community-based minority health promotion/disease prevention programs through a Request for Proposals (RFP) process; it has conducted an internal assessment of minority health policies and practices in the Department of Health; and it has launched a departmentwide cultural competence training program. The Department of Health is making measurable progress in terms of minority representation on its associated boards and commissions and among its own staff members. However, the department recognizes that it has a long way to go to redress disparities in minority employment, representation, and health status.

Second, the aging baby boomers represent a human tidal wave that is coming at us. Will we be prepared? Today the 65 and older population constitutes about 13% of the total; by the year 2030, that population could be as much as 22% of the population (Robert Wood Johnson Foundation 1998, 1) (see Figure 10.3). Because the elderly also experience a disproportionate amount of disease, they will contribute to a growing burden of population illness. The rates of mortality and morbidity for almost all diseases increase with age. The service demands of aging baby boomers (those born between 1946 and 1964) will severely strain our health service systems and require an unprecedented level of cohesion in our health policies. Substantial shifts in the composition of the population cannot be accommodated by individual actions; they require collective response at the system level.

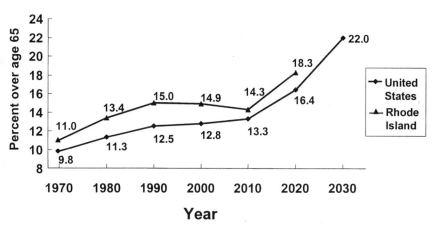

Figure 10.3 Population Projections, Age 65 and Older, Rhode Island and United States

Primary Prevention

The main mission of public health is primary prevention, preventing the inception of disease in the first place. In order to practice primary prevention, public health must follow shifting disease patterns. At the last turn of the century, the leading killers in the population were infectious diseases, such as pneumonia and influenza, tuberculosis, and acute intestinal infections and diarrhea. The burden of disease in the United States today is quite different. The leading causes of death are chronic diseases (heart disease, cancer, and stroke) and injuries, including both unintentional injuries (highway and falls) and intentional injuries (homicide and suicide).

While environmental sanitation was the most appropriate public health strategy 100 years ago, the main concern today is lifestyle change (McGinnis and Foege 1993) (see Figure 10.4). Our contemporary leading causes of death are rooted in certain societal conditions and personal habits: cigarette smoking, fatty, low-fiber diets, lack of physical activity, alcohol and drug abuse, lack of safety precautions (e.g., seat belts, bicycle and motorcycle helmets), and unhealthy sexual behavior. Although engineering was and is the key to environmental sanitation, behavior change is the key to healthy lifestyles.

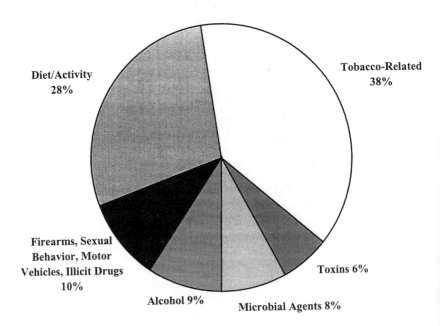

Figure 10.4 Major Causes of Death Among U.S. Residents
Sources: J. M. McGinnis and W. H. Foege, "Actual Causes of Death in the United States," *JAMA* 270 (1993): 2207–2212; J. A. Meyer and M. Regenstein, *How to Fund Public Health Activities*, Partnership for Prevention, Washington, DC, 1994.

In order to bring about lifestyle change, we need to reach people where they spend most of their time, which means that public health must reorient its priorities. In a Centers for Disease Control and Prevention (CDC) report, it was determined that only 3% of state health department expenditures were devoted to chronic disease control (1997, 287). Lifestyle change will require public health agencies to reach out and work closely with schools, work sites, the mass media, and other social and religious organizations. The dramatic reduction (50%) in tobacco use and the widespread adoption of automobile seat belt use (70%) in the United States over a period of about 30 years demonstrate that lifestyle change is certainly possible. The main challenge is to give it a high priority in policymaking and resource allocation.

In 1995, the Rhode Island Department of Health initiated the formation of the Worksite Wellness Council of Rhode Island (WWCRI), which is the first such council in New England. WWCRI includes representatives from business, health plans, insurers, labor, and the Department of Health. The council is working with the Wellness Councils of America (WELCOA) to make Rhode Island the first "Well State" in the United States. In order to accomplish this goal, 20% of Rhode Island's workforce must be employed by companies that are certified by WELCOA as well workplaces. WWCRI will be informing and training Rhode Island employers to make this happen.

Quality Assurance

Just as we have experienced an epidemiologic revolution, we are also experiencing a health care system revolution. From 1950 to 1980, retrospective cost-based reimbursement was the dominant approach to financing of personal health care services; since 1980, prospective payment (e.g., diagnostically-related groups and capitation) and managed care (e.g., health maintenance organizations and preferred provider organizations) have redefined how providers are reimbursed. With reimbursement based on diagnostically-related groups (DRGs), hospitals receive a fixed amount of payment per admission regardless of their costs. Under capitation reimbursement, managed care plans and various health care providers receive a fixed amount of payment per member per year regardless of their costs. As a result, cost containment has become less of an issue and quality assurance has become more of an issue. Fee for service is inherently cost-generating since the financial incentive is to do more, while capitation is inherently cost-constraining since the financial incentive is to do less.

In the era of fee for service, state health departments were drawn into the cost-containment movement through certificate of need programs for hospital and other health care facility capital expenditure review and through rate-setting programs to control hospital charges and costs. Now, with all the downward pressure on costs and expenditures associated with managed care, capitation payment, and for-profit medicine, state health departments are increasingly being called upon by the political process to measure and protect the quality of health care services. The political process is attempting to put checks and balances into place to counter the prevailing cost-containment incentives in the health care industry today. This new challenge will require state health departments to come up to speed on the theory and practice of clinical quality and patient satisfaction measurement and improvement.

In 1996, the Rhode Island General Assembly passed the Health Care Accessibility and Quality Assurance Act, or Zainyeh law, named after its prime sponsor, Representative George Zainyeh. This comprehensive law (Chapter 23-17.13) requires the Department of Health to regulate all managed care plans operating in the state but also to provide the public with information about their respective organizations, benefits, and operations. To date, the Department of Health has certified all managed care plans operating in the state, published a generic "Consumers' Guide" to managed care, and required a specific "Consumer Disclosure" for each health plan. In addition, comparative statistical performance indicators have been collected from each health plan and have been made available to the public. All of this information is now available on the department's web site, *www.healthri.org.*

In 1998, the Rhode Island General Assembly passed the Health Quality Performance Measurement and Reporting Program, or Fogarty law, named after its prime sponsor, Senator Charles Fogarty. This law (Chapter 23-17.17) requires the Department of Health, in conjunction with a new Health Care Quality Steering Committee, to develop standardized measures of clinical quality and patient satisfaction for licensed health care facilities, starting with hospitals. The Department of Health is working with the regional professional review organization Qualidigm, the Hospital Association of Rhode Island, the Joint Commission on the Accreditation of Healthcare Organizations, and the Health Care Financing Administration to standardize health care facility performance measures in Rhode Island. This is a pivotal opportunity for the department that could enhance its public profile if the department is perceived as doing a credible job, or it could result in serious conflict with the affected parties if its performance is seen as shoddy or biased. The department has consciously chosen to pursue this new legislative challenge in a collaborative rather than a regulatory manner. This collaborative approach is in recognition of the fact that the department does not have the expertise, the resources, or the political support to do this important job in a unilateral fashion.

System Development

State health departments have played important roles in health care system development for over 50 years. These roles have included planning, resource development, and regulation. Beginning in 1946 and extending into the 1960s, state health departments were very instrumental in the planning and funding of hospital facilities under the federal Hill-Burton Act (P.L. 79-725). In the 1960s and 1970s, state health departments played key roles in health system planning and review under the federal Partnership for Health Act (P.L. 89-749) and the federal Health Planning and Resources Development Act (P.L. 93-641). In the 1980s, the federal government eliminated its 40 years of financial support for health planning at the state level, which represented a significant change in U.S. health system development strategy.

The states began to pass certificate of need (CON) legislation in 1967 to regulate hospital capital expenditures. New York State was the first. About 20 years ago, almost all of the states had CON legislation. Today, 13 states have no CON legislation, and another 16 have very weak CON programs reflecting a shift in the U.S. health policy paradigm from regulation to competition (American Health Planning Association 1998, 3). Currently, health care system development at the state level is very problematic because there is no unifying macro strategy. Are we attempting to build a Canadian-style health care system based on external government regulation, or are we attempting to build a health care system based on "managed competition" with incentives for internal discipline (Enthoven 1993)? The reality is that we are pursuing both of these health policy objectives simultaneously, creating a great deal of confusion and conflict in our health care system.

The biggest problem in health care policy today is the lack of consensus on what type of system we want. We lack a shared vision of the future. As a result, we are implementing legislative, regulatory, and administrative policies that are contradictory. For example, CON review does not fit very well with HMO competition. Should health care facility expansion decisions be made in a command-and-control fashion through the CON program, or should the laws of supply and demand in the health plan marketplace make them? There is no right answer to this question; each approach has predictable and documented advantages and disadvantages. A national health strategy is needed to guide these and many health policy decisions.

In 1968, Rhode Island was the second state to pass certificate of need legislation for hospital construction review. By 1980, Rhode Island had one of the most comprehensive CON laws in the nation covering virtually all licensed health care facilities. Moving in the opposite direction, in 1996 the Rhode Island General Assembly passed the so-called Hanaway law, named after its prime sponsor, Senator Sandra Hanaway. This legislation (Chapter 23-15.2, 4, 6) eliminated certificate of need for all health care facilities except hospitals and ambulatory surgery facilities and placed a legislative moratorium on the construction of new nursing homes. The downsizing of CON again represented a bow to the prevailing paradigm of health care competition and opened up a flood of new, for-profit home health agencies in the state.

However, the commitment on the part of the state to market competition was obviously less than a full embrace, because the Hanaway legislation also incorporated a provision that a licensure review would be required for tertiary services where there was a documented nexus between utilization volume and quality. In addition, the General Assembly, fearing the perceived negative consequences of the potential emergence of for-profit hospitals in Rhode Island, passed legislation in 1997 that required review by the attorney general and the Department of Health of all hospital conversions (Chapter 23-17.14). So far, three proposed hospital conversions have been reviewed under this new law, but none has been successfully completed as yet. To this day, Rhode Island has no acute-care general hospitals run by for-profit companies.

INFRASTRUCTURE ISSUES

The 1988 Institute of Medicine report entitled *The Future of Public Health* stated that public health was in "disarray" and that the disarray constituted a "threat to the health of the public" (1988, 19). The huge promise and potential of public health are not being realized at the state level, not because of a lack of rational concepts, knowledge, or information but in part because of a weak infrastructure. There are very serious deficiencies in the financial and human resources committed to public health at the state and other levels.

Intergovernmental Relations

The public health system in the United States has three distinct levels: federal, state, and local. Local includes both county and city health departments. The federal level of public health is focused on program design, funding, and technical assistance. The public health community depends primarily on two federal agencies: the Centers for Disease Control and Prevention (CDC) and the Health Resources and Services Administration (HRSA). CDC funds are used at the state and local levels for the prevention and control of communicable disease, chronic disease, and injuries. HRSA funds are used at the state and local levels for maternal and child health, human resource development, and primary care access.

The state level is geared to program development, monitoring, regulation, and program funding as well. The states have always had a high profile in the licensing and regulation of health care facilities and professionals. Managed care has now been added to the sphere of state regulation. The local level is involved for the most part in service delivery and community development. The local level (i.e., county and city) has been noted in the past for the delivery of personal health care services to the indigent. However, with the ongoing movement of state Medicaid programs to the use of private managed care companies, local public health agencies are being challenged to refocus their missions more on population-based primary prevention activities.

In any event, there is no clear-cut, agreed upon division of responsibilities between the three levels. It is more like a marble cake. For example, in some cases the federal level provides program funding directly to the local levels without state involvement, such as federal funding for community health centers that goes around the state level. Higher levels in this tripartite system tend to treat the next level down as subcontractors rather than equal partners. Historically, there has been a fair amount of distrust between the three levels. Each of the three levels seems to feel a need to protect itself from the perceived incompetence and/or abuses of the other two. Thus, the public health system as a whole would benefit from a more formal agreement between the three levels as to the respective roles and responsibilities of each level in the public health enterprise.

Rhode Island has no county or city health departments. (This is also true in a few other states.) In Rhode Island, all local public health functions were consolidated into one statewide Department of Health in 1966. In addition, the leadership of this newly consolidated Department of Health made a conscious decision to contract for services in the private sector rather than build a separate system of public health services that would have required the public health system to hire a large cadre of physicians, nurses, social workers, and other health professionals. As a result, 40% of the Rhode Island Department of Health's budget is distributed to private, community-based agencies in the form of program grants and contracts. This system, consisting of one statewide Department of Health contracting on a large scale with the private sector, has certain advantages and disadvantages. On the positive side, there are many opportunities for economies of scale, such as in the recruitment of a comprehensive and expert team of public health specialists. On the negative side, the lack of official local public health structures and the extensive use of contracting makes public health that much more invisible to the public and their elected representatives, which in turn exacerbates a meager funding situation.

Planning

As noted previously, the federal government provided financial support for health planning at the state and regional levels beginning in 1946 and ending in 1986. During those 40 years, the states and regions put a great deal of effort into the identification of health status and health service problems, the adoption of health objectives, and the recommendation of health system interventions. The states and the regions had a systematic way of taking stock of the health system and charting a direction for the future in a participatory way. In addition, the federal government has created health objectives for the nation three times over the past 20 years for the decades ending in the years 1990, 2000, and 2010 (U.S. Department of Health, Education, and Welfare 1979; U.S. Department of Health and Human Services 1990, 2000).

This federal leadership in health planning has stimulated the states to create health objectives at the state level that emulate the national objectives (Rhode Island Department of Health 1993). The problem with the health objectives process is that there has been no federal financial support for the creation or implementation of these objectives at the state level. Consequently, the follow-through has been anemic. The confusion that exists in health policy today cannot be addressed without a strong, interconnected commitment at the federal and state levels to on-going, systematic health planning that identifies problems, establishes objectives, and implements strategies for positive change. While market forces do hold significant potential for shaping of the health care system, the nature of health economics is such (e.g., widespread health insurance protection) that health planning will be a critical part of any future national/state health policy.

The "Reagan Revolution" in the 1980s led to the collapse of health planning in Rhode Island. Prior to that era, Rhode Island had been receiving $1 million per year from the National Health Planning and Resources Development Act to conduct health planning for both health status improvement and to address access, cost, and quality issues of the personal health care delivery system. These efforts led to the creation of three state health plans in 1980, 1983, and 1986. In addition, Rhode Island had been receiving $1 million per year from the National Center for Health Services Research and the National Center for Health Statistics for the operations of a health data consortium, SEARCH. This statewide health data consortium produced a wide range of health statistics, which were utilized in the health planning processes. When these federal programs were dismantled, the health statistics and health planning programs in Rhode Island were all but wiped out and have never been restored to anything like their former strength. This represents a gaping hole in the public health system in the state. While the states do vary in their commitment to health planning, Rhode Island's experience is not unique but illustrative of the fact that the health planning infrastructure in the states is weak at best.

Financial Resources

There is a huge gap between the epidemiology of public health and the financing of public health. Epidemiological studies demonstrate to us that the health of the U.S. population is primarily related to lifestyle (i.e., individual and societal smoking, eating, drinking, exercise, and transportation behavior patterns) and that healthy lifestyles can be promoted through population-based approaches such as school health, work site wellness, mass media health education, and health-promoting legislation (e.g., cigarette taxes) (Rhode Island Department of Health 1997; Chapman 1999). It has been estimated that 70% of premature deaths could be prevented by population-based public health approaches. And yet, in the states, we allocate roughly 1% of our health care expenditures to population-based public health activities (see Figure 10.5).

Our national and state health objectives for 1990, 2000, and 2010 have placed special emphasis on promoting health, preventing disease and premature death, and fostering healthy lifestyles. Yet the nation continues to pour its resources into acute care services while neglecting population-based public health programs. We have not put our money where our rhetoric is. Why not? Is it because the successes

Proportion of health expenditures going to the population-wide core functions of public health v. medical treatment.

Proportion of early deaths that could be prevented by population-wide public health approaches v. medical treatment

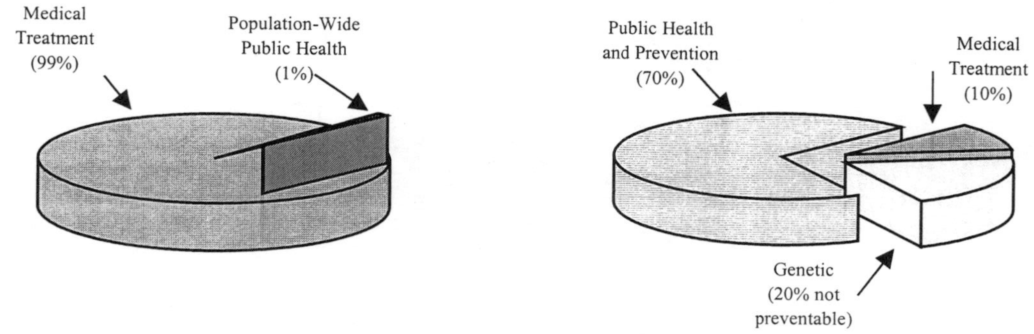

Medical
Treatment
(99%)

Population-Wide
Public Health
(1%)

Public Health
and Prevention
(70%)

Medical
Treatment
(10%)

Genetic
(20% not
preventable)

Figure 10.5 Is This a Rational Investment Strategy?
Source: Prevention Report, "A Time for Partnership: Report of State Consultations on the Role of Public Health,"
U.S. Public Health Service, December 1994/January 1995.

of public health are largely invisible events that do not happen? Is it because we are mesmerized by the glamour of high-tech medical care? Is it because we are lazy and would rather not bother ourselves until there is a crisis? (It is striking to see the number of men who take up walking *after* their first heart attack!) Are there systemic things that we could do to overcome this inertia?

Public health is funded on a so-called "discretionary" basis, which means that public health lives and dies by the annual appropriation process at both the federal and state levels. On the other hand, the two largest U.S. medical service funding programs, Medicare and Medicaid, are funded on an "entitlement" basis, meaning that individuals have a legal right to services and financial coverage. Medicare and Medicaid are the fastest growing parts of public budgets at both the federal and state levels, while public health funding has had to struggle just to hold its own. One way out of this dilemma would be to fund public health as a fixed percentage of the entitlement programs. It would not take a huge percentage to do a good job. The U.S. Public Health Service (1993) estimated that the United States would need to triple current expenditures on public health—to around 3% of total health expenditures—in order to achieve a "fully effective" public health system. It will take political wisdom and leadership to close this gap.

From 1990 to 1998 in Rhode Island, the state's total budget increased by only 28%, while the Department of Health's budget increased by a meager 8%, obviously losing ground to inflation. During that same period, the budget of the Department of Human Services, the Medicaid agency, has increased by 52% (Rhode Island Department of Health 1999). At the same time, the Department of Health faced a tight personnel cap on hiring full-time employees, making it very difficult to staff programs even when federal dollars are available. As a result, the public health infrastructure in Rhode Island is now perilously thin.

In 1994, the Department of Health determined that only 63% of its "optimal" program requirements were being met (Waters 1995, 110). To this day, health care facility inspections, environmental inspections such as food inspections, and many other areas are seriously compromised. The 1999 tobacco settlement of the states' attorneys general presented Rhode Island with a golden opportunity to rebuild and enhance its public health infrastructure. However, the state budget for fiscal year 2000 allocated only $1 million for tobacco control, which represents only 2% of the $56 million in annual revenue that Rhode Island will receive as a result of the tobacco settlement. The historic underfunding of public health is repeating itself even in the face of the largest public health bonanza in the history of this country.

Human Resources

One of the hallmarks of public health is the turnover at the top. The Association of State and Territorial Health Officials has reported that the average tenure of state health officers is only three years. This appears to be a higher turnover rate than all state department directors taken together, which is reported as five years

(Bowling and Wright 1998, 433–434). Serving as a state health officer is a complex undertaking (Mullan 2000; Novick, Woltring, and Fox 1997). The increasingly controversial nature of public health work, the relatively low pay, and the political nature of the role all contribute to constant loss of leadership at the top of state public health organizations. Many former state health officers go into the private sector or into academia. No industry or sector of the economy could achieve lasting success with the ongoing brain and leadership drain experienced by public health. Continuity in leadership is needed for institutional learning, memory, experience, and commitment. If the leadership is constantly trying to master the basics, then it is not possible to move on to more sophisticated strategies.

Steps need to be taken to prevent turnover from equating to outright loss to the public health field as a whole. Portable pension systems and interlocking public health personnel systems at the federal, state, and local levels would help to alleviate this problem by making it much easier for top public health officials to migrate from one part of the public sector to another instead of leaving the field altogether. As previously stated, state public health agencies are also plagued by full-time equivalent personnel caps, which have become common in this era of government downsizing and shrinking budgets. These personnel ceilings are forcing state public health agencies to do more subcontracting and outsourcing in order to get the work done. In addition, the combination and interaction of civil service requirements, union rules, and political interests make the recruitment and hiring of state public health workers very difficult. Public sector personnel systems need a fresh look in order to promote more flexibility and professionalism.

Rhode Island has enjoyed relatively good stability in the leadership of public health due in part to the fact that the director of health is appointed for a five-year term of office. However, the last two directors served for fewer years than their predecessors (i.e., tenures of seven and four years, respectively). The previous director of health left office with the election of a new governor in 1994. That same governor is the first elected for a four-year term (previously, Rhode Island governors were elected for two-year terms), and he was reelected for a second four-year term in 1998. The current director of health was reappointed for a second term of office in 2000. Looking ahead, the tenure of directors of health in Rhode Island may track with the political fortunes of their appointing governors (which appears to be one national pattern).

On another front, in 1992, the Rhode Island General Assembly passed legislation authorizing the Department of Health to create the Rhode Island Public Health Foundation (RIPHF) in order to increase federal and private foundation investments in state public health initiatives. This type of mechanism has also sprung up in about a dozen other states. As a private, nonprofit organization, the Rhode Island Public Health Foundation has a greater degree of flexibility in hiring and purchasing professional services than state government and as a result can be more responsive to external demands. Over the last five years, the RIPHF has increased its annual budget from $5,000 to $950,000 and has undertaken public health programs in all of the following areas: health care for foster children, lead poisoning prevention, school-based health centers, substance abuse services, youth development services, and physical activity promotion. The RIPHF does research, development, evaluation, and service delivery through subcontractors.

Collaboration

There is increasing recognition in the field that public health cannot achieve its objectives in a unilateral fashion. First, the resources are not there at the present time; and second, it is impossible to achieve health promotion and disease prevention without strong cooperation from all facets of the community. In order for public health to succeed, official agencies must give public health away. As the landmark 1966 report of the same name stated, "Health Is a Community Affair" (National Commission on Community Health Services 1966). Actually, there is a substantial reservoir of interest and goodwill toward public health and prevention in the community. It just needs to be tapped in an effective way. Schools, work sites, police departments, minority institutions, voluntary agencies, churches, and many more organizations have exhibited a willingness and a desire to contribute to public health. After everything is said and done, this reservoir of public health potential is probably public health's most underutilized resource. However, it should be noted that the health care regulatory activities of state health departments, which are adversarial by nature (vis-à-vis private sector providers), complicate their health promotion and disease prevention activities. Health promotion and disease prevention must be based on collaboration between the public and private sectors. Balancing these two functions is an ongoing struggle for state health departments.

In 1995, the Department of Health initiated the development of the Rhode Island Prevention Coalition to give more emphasis in the state to population-based primary prevention. The Prevention Coalition is made up of the state's leading health plans, hospital systems, and voluntary health agencies as well as the Department of Health. These agencies selected physical activity as their first priority and pooled their resources to fund community-based and environmental physical activity promotion programs. In addition to the general population, minority, elderly, and physically challenged population groups in the state have benefited from this highly collaborative program, which is administered by the Rhode Island Public Health Foundation.

Performance Standards

In the 1940s, the functions of public health were defined by Emerson's conceptualization of six essential public health services that included vital statistics, communicable disease control, environmental health, laboratory services, maternal and child health, and health information (1949, 473). However, in the decades following World War II, public health drifted farther and farther away from a common sense of mission, with the states organizing and conducting public health in a wide variety of organizational structures. This development, as previously noted, led the Institute of Medicine in 1988 to say that public health was in "disarray." Now, there is a movement back to the concept of common expectations for public health practice at the state and local levels. The Centers for Disease Control and Prevention is working with the National Association of County and City Health Officials, the Association of State and Territorial Health Officials, and other national partners to create performance standards for public health (American Public Health Association 1999, 3; Centers for Disease Control and Prevention 2000). While the initial thrust of this effort is for quality improvement purposes, the adoption of performance standards will probably lead to an accreditation process for state and local public health agencies.

Throughout the history of the Rhode Island Department of Health, which was founded in 1878, the department has been judging the performance of other agencies and individuals through the licensure and/or certification of health facilities (such as hospitals and nursing homes), health professionals (such as physicians and nurses), and businesses (such as restaurants and food markets). And yet, the department itself has been relatively free from any type of overall accountability standards. In 1997, the Rhode Island General Assembly created a special legislative commission "to study all aspects of the Department of Health." This commission included members from both the Senate and House and held meetings over the span of three legislative sessions. It investigated various aspects of the health department's programs including school health, environmental health, and the public health laboratory. However, in the absence of agreed upon performance standards for public health, the commission had a hard time determining what to focus on and deciding on what basis to judge the department's performance. The adoption of national performance standards for public health would assist legislative bodies and the public at large in sizing up the performance of public health departments.

CONCLUSION

At the end of the twentieth century, two things are very clear about public health at the state level. First, public health has tremendous potential to improve the health of the public. By taking into account demographic trends and epidemiological realities, public health can fashion population-based interventions that address disease prevention, risk factor reduction, and health promotion in a systematic fashion. Our best chances for protecting and improving the health of the population exist in our collective actions, not in isolated individual efforts. Second, it is also clear that public health is very far from reaching its potential contributions to the public good. Public health is lacking public and political support, resources, and organizational cohesion, which represents a failure on the part of the public health community to communicate what it is all about and what it has to contribute. However, it also reflects a public and political value system that is overly focused on the short-term fix rather than on long-term gains.

In the twenty-first century, public health professionals, the public, and the political system will have to work together much more effectively if we are to address the many challenges that we face: a more diverse population, an aging population, growing numbers of people without health insurance coverage, severe budgetary and cost constraints, confusion in health policy, and the unnecessary human and economic burdens of preventable diseases. Historically, policymakers have faced many challenges in protecting and promoting the health of the public. Hopefully, present and future generations will be able to improve upon the performance of the past. No less than the health of the people is at stake.

REFERENCES

American Health Planning Association. 1998. "1998 Relative Scope and Reviewability Thresholds of CON Regulated Service." April 27. Falls Church, VA.
American Public Health Association. 1999. "APHA Innovations Project Eyes Performance Standards." *Nation's Health* 29 (February): 3.
Bowling, C. J., and D. S. Wright. 1998. "Change and Continuity in State Administration: Administrative Leadership Across Four Decades." *Public Administration Review* 58: 429–444.
Centers for Disease Control and Prevention. 1997. "Resources and Priorities for Chronic Disease Prevention and Control, 1994." *Morbidity and Mortality Weekly Report* (April): 286–287.
———. 2000. "Draft State Public Health System Performance Instrument, Version STATE 8.0." Atlanta: Public Health Practice Program.
Chapman, L. S. 1999. *Proof Positive Analysis of the Cost-Effectiveness of Worksite Wellness.* Seattle: Summex Corporation.
Emerson, H. 1949. *Selected Papers.* Battle Creek, MI: W. K. Kellogg Foundation.
Enthoven, A. C. 1993. "The History and Principles of Managed Competition." *Health Affairs* 12 (Supplement): 24–48.
Institute of Medicine. 1998. *The Future of Public Health.* Washington, DC: National Academy Press.
McGinnis, J. M., and W. H. Foege. 1993. "Actual Causes of Death in the United States." *Journal of the American Medical Association* 270:2207–2212.
Mullan, F. 2000. "Don Quixote, Machiavelli, and Robin Hood: Public Health Practice, Past and Present." *American Journal of Public Health* 90:702–706.
National Commission on Community Health Services. 1966. *Health Is A Community Affair.* Cambridge, MA: Harvard University Press.
Novick, L. F., C. S. Woltring, and D. M. Fox. 1997. *Public Health Leaders Tell Their Stories.* Gaithersburg, MD: Aspen Publishers.
Rhode Island Department of Health. 1993. *Healthy People 2000 Rhode Island.* Providence, RI.

————. 1997. *Health Promotion/Disease Prevention: Venues for Making It Happen.* Providence, RI.

————. 1999. *Public Health in Rhode Island.* Providence, RI.

Robert Wood Johnson Foundation. 1998. "Eldercare: Where Medicine, Economics, and Demographics Collide." *Advances* No. 3:1.

Rosen, G. 1958. *A History of Public Health.* New York: MD Publications.

Turnock, B. J. 1997. *Public Health: What It Is and How It Works.* Gaithersburg, MD: Aspen Publishers.

U.S. Department of Health and Human Services, Public Health Service. 1990. *Healthy People 2000 National Health Promotion and Disease Prevention Objectives.* DHHS (PHS) pub. no. 91-50212. Washington, DC: Government Printing Office.

U.S. Department of Health and Human Services, Office of Public Health and Science. 2000. *Healthy People 2010: Conference Edition, Vol. I/II.* Washington, DC: Government Printing Office.

U.S. Department of Health, Education, and Welfare, Public Health Service, Office of the Assistant Secretary for Health and Surgeon General. 1979. *Healthy People: The Surgeon General's Report on Health Promotion and Disease Prevention.* DHEW (PHS) pub. no. 79-55071. Washington, DC: Government Printing Office.

U.S. Public Health Service, Office of Disease Prevention and Health Promotion. 1993. *Health Care Reform and Public Health: Population-Based Core Functions.* Washington, DC: The Core Functions Project.

Waters, W. J. 1995. "Public Health in Rhode Island: A Strategic Allocation Perspective." *Medicine and Health Rhode Island* 78:109–112.

PART III
Conclusion

11

State Health Politics and Policy: Rhetoric, Reality, and the Challenges Ahead

Thomas R. Oliver

In the American system of government, state policies are the foundation that lowers or elevates national intentions and actions. What states do to promote and regulate systems such as health care, education, and environmental protection is a critical determinant of the effectiveness, efficiency, and equity of those systems. The choices of state policymakers often set the tone for what policies other levels of government and the private sector pursue as well. This chapter begins by reviewing these and other reasons why health politics and policy in the states command our attention today. Ideology, institutional capacity, and federal gridlock on key issues all increase the activity and importance of states in health policy.

The discussion then focuses on several patterns in state health politics and policy, based on the earlier chapters in this book and other research, in an attempt to understand what factors shape state agendas and policy approaches. States and the federal government share a fairly common agenda, influenced heavily by market dynamics in the health care system and by changing perceptions of social problems, population groups, and industries. Even though the health policy agenda is essentially national, the strategies for policy change do vary considerably from issue to issue. In addition, different patterns in federal-state relations influence where problems will be addressed first and the degree to which action in one jurisdiction is likely to trigger action elsewhere. The patterns of federal and state action suggest that the concept of states as laboratories for policy innovation must be substantially modified. On most issues, there is a great deal of interaction across levels of government as well as between public and private sectors, and a combination of substantive and situational learning produces policies that resemble one another in purpose but seldom in exact design.

The chapter concludes with an analysis of the challenges for state health policy at the turn of a new century. In order to overcome the limits and dysfunctions of incrementalism, state officials must adopt new policy tools that focus on incentives for healthy behavior, provide more reliable data on the outputs as well as inputs to governmental programs, and facilitate the exchange of information and lessons across jurisdictions. States must more readily establish partnerships with the federal government, and more important,with private organizations and citizens at the community level to increase the net benefits from public health resources and regulations. Finally, states must consider whether it is necessary to consider broader, more radical interventions to achieve health gains by reducing social inequalities, providing universal health insurance, and giving priority to primary prevention over amelioration of health problems.

THE RATIONALE FOR FOCUSING ON STATE HEALTH POLICY

A great deal of research in the field of health policy takes the central role of states as a given, without considering either the normative or empirical justifications for this role. While Howard Leichter (1996) addresses many of the underlying issues in depth, the following section attempts only to highlight a number of reasons why scholars and practitioners alike are focused on state health policy.

First and perhaps foremost, the ideology and politics of this era continue to support decentralization of power and autonomy for states vis-à-vis the federal government. Certainly, the historical trend has been away from "dual federalism"—where federal and state responsibilities remain distinct and uncoordinated— toward "cooperative federalism" with shared responsibilities and a strong federal role (Rich and White 1996). Yet, Richard Nathan (1989) points out that there are cycles within this longer trend. Indeed, for three decades, U.S. politicians, with considerable backing from the courts, have promoted different versions of a New Federalism aimed at preserving or restoring state autonomy, even when equity is severely compromised.

Second, there is simply more policy activity in the states than ever before. The agenda of issues under consideration is broader and the level of state expertise and administrative capacity is greater. Legislatures are more professional, with a variety of formal and informal sessions throughout the year and more staff with policy expertise. There are also more and better trained staff in administrative agencies and standing commissions in the health arena. The growth of state government personnel has greatly exceeded growth in the federal government workforce in the last quarter century (Weissert and Weissert 1996). The number of interest groups and the scope of their activity in states has dramatically expanded, paralleling similar developments at the national level (Petracca 1992). As the chapters by Michael Dukakis and John McDonough and Robert McGrath note, more policy ideas are developed and disseminated among state organizations like the National Governors' Association, the National Conference of State Legislatures, the Association of State and Territorial Health Officers, and less mature organizations like the Reforming States Group and the National Academy of State Health Policy. William Brandon,

Rosemary Chaudry, and Alice Sardell argue that the National Governors' Association has been a particularly active and influential participant in policy development for Medicaid and children's health insurance.

These institutional changes are important, obviously, for increasing the scope and sophistication of state policy. They are equally important, however, for state health politics. Two decades ago, Arnold Relman (1981) warned of a new "medical-industrial complex" emerging where market forces, especially for-profit ownership, would undermine professional ethics and compromise patient well-being. In a similar vein, Paul Starr (1982) observed the "coming of the corporation" and the shift of power that accompanies the concentration of money and information. What was not predicted was that the same forces that empowered medical care organizations would also empower governments, which over time would increase their monitoring and regulatory capabilities. Ironically, the growth of the health care system, the source of what Frank Thompson calls the "Medicaid colossus," has also spawned a colossus of state officials, advisers, consultants, and managers who exercise countervailing power as regulators of the private sector. Although it may appear that the proregulatory forces are Lilliputians to industry's Gulliver, there is more micromanagement than ever before, not only in health care but also in the manufacture, distribution, and use of automobiles, tobacco, guns, pesticides, and other threats to public health. McDonough and McGrath acknowledge the dominance of health care provider interests but also point out many factors that limit interest group influence in the legislative process.

The long-term capacity of states for policymaking and administration is not assured, however. Robert Hackey argues that only a few states have "imposed regimes" that wield real power vis-à-vis private interests. Even in states with considerable commitment and capacity for problem intervention, Thompson warns of a "hollowing out" of state government, due to the increasing number of responsibilities assigned to a relatively stable number of administrative personnel. The threat may be even more acute on the legislative side, as nearly half the states have adopted term limits that force the most seasoned lawmakers to seek other elected office or leave government altogether. Although Thomas Oliver and Pamela Paul-Shaheen (1997, 740) argue that continuity in leadership priorities, personal trust, institutional memory, and other forms of "connective tissue" in state health policy communities are inevitably lost by the onset of term limits, their impact on the quality and effectiveness of policymaking is not yet clear.

A third reason for focusing on states is that their increasing policy activity is in part the result of some specific policies of the federal government. As the chapters by Thompson and by Jonathan Oberlander, Lawrence Jacobs, and Theodore Marmor highlight, state-designed changes in Medicaid were one of the hallmarks of health policy over the past decade. The Clinton administration and, later, a Republican-controlled Congress have supported state Medicaid reforms under the guise of "research and demonstration" authority in the Social Security Act. The Balanced Budget Act of 1997 did away with much of that fiction, as it eliminated the requirement for many program waiver applications. It also established the State Children's Health Insurance Program (SCHIP), which offered generous federal matching funds even as it allowed states great flexibility in program design. Brandon and his colleagues illustrate how such policies have produced substantial variation in different state settings.

The federal welfare reforms of 1996, following on expansions of Medicaid eligibility in the 1980s and early 1990s, delinked cash assistance programs from benefits such as health insurance and food stamps and endorsed a variety of state approaches to reduce welfare rolls. Some aspects of state program design and administration have been problematic, as intended drops in welfare enrollment have been accompanied by unintended drops in Medicaid enrollment; millions of families have not retained health benefits they are still entitled to, even after leaving welfare and finding employment (Ellwood and Ku 1998; Ku and Bruen 1999; Hudman 2000). Thompson argues that nearly all states must improve their commitment and capacity to increase the "take-up rate" of individuals eligible for Medicaid and SCHIP.

As both Thompson and McDonough and McGrath note, one area in which the federal government has been reluctant to intervene on behalf of states is the insulation, provided by court interpretations of the Employee Retirement Income Security Act of 1974 (ERISA), of self-insured health plans from state mandates. Under intense pressure from business interests, devolution in this area of policy has been to the private sector, not states. But the Health Insurance Portability and Accountability Act of 1996 served as a minor breakthrough, and the continuing federal debate over patient rights under managed care may further roll back the protective cover of ERISA.

Fourth, states become important when there is gridlock on key issues at the federal level. Oliver (1991, 160) observed: "In the natural order of our political system, inaction at the top begets action below. The burden of problem solving and fiscal responsibility falls on states and communities, which have no choice but to deal with the disarray on their doorsteps and are bound by their constitutions to balance budgets." During the early and mid-1990s, states pushed ahead with Medicaid reforms in response to their own budget crises. Even in a strong economy, the problem-solving role for states remains. David Rochefort's analysis of the managed care "backlash" is a perfect illustration of the phenomenon, as is Suzann Thomas-Buckle's and Leonard Buckle's survey of tobacco control efforts. On both issues, activists gained critical momentum at the federal level but thus far have failed to secure decisive action in a bitterly divided Congress.

While it is an overstatement to say that states and communities are responding to a "vacuum" in federal policymaking, Hackey correctly highlights the importance of state and local responsiveness when federal policymaking breaks down. Perhaps the most tragic example of the downward shift in responsibility is how, by default, California and New York as well as hard-hit communities were left to devise responses to the AIDS epidemic when the Reagan administration failed to recognize the urgency of the problem or give it priority (Benjamin and Lee 1989). Currently, state and local officials convinced of the effectiveness of needle exchange programs in preventing HIV and hepatitis cannot call upon federal authority or resources to assist in program development.

Finally, failure to achieve agreement in Washington leaves problems to be addressed not only by state and local government but also by the private sector, which further turns our attention to state and local services and delivery systems. As Hackey notes, in a "market era" state policies are often a response to developments in the private sector. Some of the most important private-sector developments, such as the conversion of hospitals and health insurance plans to for-profit status and the emergence of voluntary multiemployer insurance purchasing programs, have considerable impact and are a central part of state health policy even as federal policy remains silent in these areas. Thus, regardless of where policies emerge, states and communities almost always strongly influence how they are implemented and perform.

PATTERNS IN STATE HEALTH POLITICS AND POLICY

The individual contributions to this book make clear the importance of states in developing and implementing specific health policies. Across this diverse set of policies, what patterns can be observed in the issues that states are addressing and how they are addressing them? What is creating the policy agenda for states? What, if any, issues are new, and what, if any, issues are exclusively or predominantly state and local concerns? The following sections attempt to address those questions. The patterns of state action suggest that while health policies are increasingly narrow and technical, the processes that lead to the formation of policies remain highly amorphous, complex, and difficult to base predictions on.

Issues and Interventions

Thomas Anton (1997) argues that one of the most widely held myths about American government is that there is considerable separation between the responsibilities and actions of states and the federal government. In fact, most of the issues raised in this book are essentially national in scope—for example, maintaining or expanding health insurance coverage, adjusting the practices of managed care plans, reducing tobacco use and its many costs, and strengthening the capacity of public health agencies—but are engaging policymakers in virtually every state. Even where governmental responses vary considerably, a set of central issues commands the attention of public officials and other participants in the health policy community at both the state and federal levels and across nearly all jurisdictions. The following discussion examines how this common agenda is the product of market dynamics, social construction, and policy learning, and other factors.

Market dynamics. As the American health care system entered an era of rapid change in the late 1970s, close observers noted the disharmony between its scientific progress and its simultaneous excesses and inequities. Studies by the Graduate Medical Education National Advisory Committee indicated that an oversupply of physicians, accompanied by specialty maldistribution, was in the offing (U.S. DHHS 1980). There was much doubt that the solutions of the 1960s and 1970s— comprehensive planning in regions and states—would suffice to control costs, direct resources to the areas in greatest need, and improve the quality of health care systems (Brown 1983).* A paradigm shift in academic, professional, and policy circles was under way from centralized planning to "consumer choice competition," with a less overt role for government and a stronger role for large-scale private corporations offering their services to individual consumers (Ellwood 1971; Enthoven 1980; Fox 1986).

What we are witnessing today is the consummation of a generation of policy and programming based on the new paradigm. The "creeping revolution" foreseen by Paul Ellwood two decades ago has taken a good while to gain a foothold and establish itself across public and private institutions. It is still not clear whether Medicare will fall to the insurrection, but the war is now settled across most states and communities outside of rural America. Managed care in one form or another dominates employer-sponsored insurance and Medicaid, and as Chris Koyanagi and Joseph Bevilacqua describe, it now dominates the field of mental health as well as somatic health services.

As one surveys the health policy landscape at the opening of a new century, there is a striking familiarity in the general picture. Like an earlier generation, in many areas we are "doing better and feeling worse" (Wildavsky 1977). Despite steady progress in health care, improving both longevity and quality of life, there is considerable unrest among health professionals, policymakers, and the general public. The accomplishments of technological progress do not quite meet all of our expectations.

In the market era, consumers are supposedly empowered with information and choice, but instead they act beleaguered. For decades, health care organization and financing remained invisible or opaque to the vast majority of Americans. Now it is all too visible, as the market paradoxically generates many new rules of behavior for all parties. Tens of millions of people remain uninsured, and even those with insurance coverage are not assured that the for-profit mentality and methods of the modern health care system will provide them with needed care

---

*It might be argued that comprehensive health planning never was fully established in most jurisdictions, and that planning relied on universal health insurance as a source of authority and financial resources, which never materialized.

and that their caregivers are trustworthy. Rochefort notes the irony that as managed care becomes the norm, evidence of this discontent metastasizes throughout popular culture.

Social construction of problems and target populations. Along with market dynamics, the state health policy agenda is shaped in many ways by the social construction of problems and targets of governmental intervention. Rochefort captures the shifting image of health insurers and links the managed care backlash directly to the rise of for-profit institutions in the health care system, understanding how seeds of distrust can easily take root in an individualistic, antiauthoritarian culture that resists private regulators every bit as much as government regulators.

The story of the Oregon Health Plan has many unexpected twists and turns, as Oberlander, Jacobs, and Marmor report. Oliver and Paul-Shaheen (1997, 749) describe how John Kitzhaber, the president of the state Senate and an emergency room physician (who later was elected governor), recognized the futility of basing health policy on the "rescue principle." When a seven-year-old boy died from leukemia after the state Medicaid program ended its organ transplant program, the easy solution would have been to restore the transplant funding. But Kitzhaber demonstrated the inherent ambiguity of a situation that seemed quite clear to most of his fellow Oregonians. He redefined the issue from uncaring government—which would require policymakers to come up with money to pay for identifiable "needed services" without respect to other unmet needs—to an issue of fair allocation of scarce resources and how to establish an ethically defensible process for determining what medical needs were most deserving of governmental assistance. From there, Kitzhaber set up a process to determine priorities for explicit rationing of services that, according to Oberlander, Jacobs, and Marmor, has distracted attention from the real innovation of the Oregon Health Plan: a major expansion of enrollment in the state's Medicaid program (Kitzhaber and Gibson 1991; Fox and Leichter 1991).

Brandon, Chaudry, and Sardell observe that recent expansions of children's health insurance are also the products of social construction. It is indeed surprising to find a new social program, however small, within the framework of fiscal retrenchment in the Balanced Budget Act. In Washington, D.C., and in the states they examined—New York, Ohio, and North Carolina—the image of children's health insurance was converted from one of economic redistribution and activist government to one of earned benefits and individual responsibility. Even though the initiative came from liberals, ultimately SCHIP became a bipartisan trophy. Partisan conflict was muted except in the unique case of North Carolina, where Republicans had captured a majority in one of the houses of the legislature for the first time since the Civil War. The key was framing the program as a benefit for working families, distinguishing it from welfare. The description by Nancy Johnson, a Republican congresswoman from Connecticut, could easily have come from the Clinton White House: SCHIP was for "families with uninsured children who are working hard, paying taxes and playing by the rules. They need and deserve our help."* Another policy image helped SCHIP along, as it was supposed to be funded by an increase in the federal excise tax on cigarettes. The cause of so much harm, in other words, was to be tapped to create some good for an innocent, deserving population.

William Waters argues that although the public health field is built on a core foundation of science, political perceptions and support are the key to the future of public health agencies in this country. This is because most public health problems are no longer a matter of engineering; rather, they require behavioral change that can only be achieved through education. Healthy lifestyles, as well as long-term understanding of the contributions of public health, can only come from engaging people in schools, work sites, mass media, and social and religious organizations. The weak presentation of the public's interest in prevention is illustrated by the use of state tobacco settlement funds for general health care or even nonhealth purposes. As Waters puts it, "The historic underfunding of public health is repeating itself even in the face of the largest public health bonanza in the history of this country."

No issue has seen the course of public policy affected more by shifts in social construction than tobacco control. Thomas-Buckle and Buckle chronicle how the images of tobacco, the tobacco industry, and tobacco users have been framed over the past century by morality, by politics, and by health concerns. Their analysis is consistent with the work of Frank Baumgartner and Bryan Jones (1993), who show how the shifts in policy image often correspond with shifts in the arenas of decision-making and opportunities for policy change. The full impact of litigation by individuals, class action groups, and state and federal officials is yet to be felt, as is the unsuccessful effort of the FDA to claim regulatory jurisdiction over tobacco products. The social construction of tobacco has been shaped in large part by a long-term research effort, which has clarified the multiple risks, direct and indirect, that individuals face from smoking. The causal connection between industry behavior and public health has been strengthened as legal discovery and whistleblowers revealed a variety of unsavory practices related to addiction and to tobacco use by minors. This new information established an even stronger threat of the kind that Constance Nathanson (1999) argues is integral to the success of public health initiatives in tobacco and gun control—and created much more doubt about individual responsibility for the damages of tobacco use.

Strategies for Policy Change

Reforms in a given area of health policy may commence in a distinctive pattern. Programs that involve a significant amount of funding and redistribution, for example, virtually require a top-down, inside-out strategy built on the investment

---

*Given these considerations, it is ironic that a program supported precisely because it was not Medicaid should be so closely integrated with Medicaid in most states purely for pragmatic reasons.

of high-level officials. Dukakis points out that in the few states that undertook comprehensive health care reforms a decade ago, the commitment of governors and their extraordinary array of political resources was a necessary ingredient. In contrast, Thomas-Buckle and Buckle argue that the most successful examples of tobacco control have relied on spontaneous, community-based leadership, which might or might not be centered in government positions.

Once there is momentum across states and a national debate is under way, however, a combination of strategies is usually employed. In the areas of managed care, mental health, and tobacco control, reformers now have a remarkably diverse strategy, focused on all levels of government, the courts as well as legislative bodies, and the private sector.

McDonough and McGrath describe how national interest groups help inform and mobilize state-based chapters and grassroots participation of individuals. The National Alliance for the Mentally Ill, for example, developed "report cards" on behavioral health care companies that state advocates and policymakers could use in selecting contractors and developing contract provisions. The tobacco industry has sought state preemption of local regulations to avoid the relatively effective bottom-up strategies of its opponents, and its funding of local groups is often considered to be the type of "astro-turf" lobbying that holds little sway with legislators and local officials. The Robert Wood Johnson Foundation's Campaign for Tobacco-Free Kids was heavily involved in state litigation, the national settlement, and a variety of public information campaigns.

It is more common today to see governmental agencies themselves encourage and help mobilize certain constituencies. State mental health administrators have found it useful to include consumer advocates in the design of managed care reforms, according to Koyanagi and Bevilacqua. In Maryland, the health department consciously solicited the views of Medicaid beneficiaries, and it established a broadly representative task force that helped ensure that managed care organizations would be forced to include historic providers of the Medicaid population and make additional provisions to assure the quality of treatment for special needs populations (Oliver 1998).

While these patterns of state politics highlight different strategies for policy change, they do not offer clear evidence about which strategies are more effective than others. Certainly, a combination of strategies is appealing, but an issue must be of sufficient visibility and importance that a diverse, durable coalition can be organized to pursue new policies across all social institutions. Waters's analysis, for example, casts doubt on the proposition that improvements in the public health infrastructure will ever gain the attention and support of the general public. Leadership strategies are also affected by the perceived distribution of costs and benefits associated with proposals for reform (Wilson 1973, 1980; Arnold 1990), which can change dramatically over time due to new information (e.g., the risks of secondhand smoke), long-term shifts in political ideology and public opinion (e.g., attitudes toward the poor), or the achievements of leaders in other jurisdictions who demonstrate that at times an attack on a concentrated interest can be a political advantage, not a cost.

Also, the most effective strategy for policy adoption may not be an effective strategy for implementation and ongoing operations. For example, the support and resources of high-level officials are often crucial to policy change, as noted above, but implementation "fixers" who are focused on local operations dictate the performance of even the most far-reaching policy innovations (Bardach 1977; Sabatier and Mazmanian 1981). The many contributions in this volume confirm, along with Peter Jacobson and Jeffrey Wasserman (1999) and many other observers, that some of the greatest opportunities to improve health lie not in new initiatives but in more effective implementation of existing policies. In virtually every area of state health policy, the successes to date are only relative, and even fairly innovative programs are still yielding incremental improvements in public health.

Federal-State Relations in Health Policy

One of the most important questions about state and local health initiatives is how they interact with national health policies and programs. Robert Rich and William White (1996) point out that there is no single pattern of federal-state relations across all policy areas or even issues within a given policy area. The following section examines different patterns in the relationship between state and federal policy, considering whether states prompt federal action, make federal action more or less necessary, or create unwarranted variations as they adapt federal policy to their local conditions.

Sources of innovation. In addition to the propriety of state and local autonomy, a supposed virtue of decentralization is that it stimulates innovation. In the gospel of American federalism, states serve as "laboratories" for testing new policies. The most effective policies, in this view, will be emulated by other states or adopted for the nation as a whole.

There are examples that support this view. In 1960, Marion Folsom, the long-time treasurer of Kodak who had served as secretary of health, education, and welfare under President Eisenhower, forced hospitals in the area around Rochester, New York, to submit to a review process if they wanted community funds for new construction or modernization of their facilities. Folsom's influence on Governor Nelson Rockefeller helped establish the first statewide certificate of need program in New York in 1964, and the basic approach was incorporated into national health planning legislation in 1966 and 1974 (Oliver 1991). The approval of the Medicare Prospective Payment System in the Social Security Amendments of 1983 was based on the perception of federal officials that the hospital rate-setting program in New Jersey, which was initially implemented in 1980, was a successful test of the technical feasibility of DRG-based payments and their potential for cost containment (Morone and Dunham 1984). According to Brandon, Chaudry, and Sardell and McDonough and McGrath, initiatives in New York and Massachusetts to expand children's health insurance beyond the federal guidelines for Medicaid served as "models" for SCHIP, which was approved in the Balanced Budget Act of 1997.

In most situations, however, the metaphor of states as "laboratories" is misleading (Oliver and Paul-Shaheen 1997; Leichter 1997). Most state innovations are not thoroughly tested before similar policies are adopted in other jurisdictions, or even before they are modified in the state of origin. Koyanagi and Bevilacqua describe how cost pressures have led many states to adopt managed care "carve-outs" for mental health, well before their impact on the quality of care or outcomes for this extremely vulnerable population is understood. Eugene DeClerq and Diana Simmes (1997) documented the rapid spread of state bans on "drive-through deliveries," which required insurers to allow mothers and newborns to remain in the hospital for a minimum number of days, despite the lack of information about the quality and cost implications of this change. Insurance companies' criticism of this policy could be interpreted as merely self-interested rhetoric—although premiums might increase, not all subscribers will be affected (some will choose early discharge), and the overall cost impact appears to be minimal.

While relatively simple policies such as insurance mandates or indoor smoking bans may spread quite easily across states and communities, the wide variation in more complex reforms does not support the notion of states developing innovations that can readily diffuse to other jurisdictions. Oberlander, Jacobs, and Marmor note that despite its political and policy success, nothing resembling the Oregon Health Plan has been debated, let alone adopted, in another state.

What can readily diffuse are individual components, not entire packages of reforms. Thus, Massachusetts, Oregon, and Washington all followed the example of Hawaii by enacting a mandate for employers to offer health insurance to their workers, even though they employed dramatically different approaches in other areas of reform.* Koyanagi and Bevilacqua point out that about 20 states have "carve-outs" for people with severe mental illness, but there are significant restrictions by geography or groups in the population; overall, an idiosyncratic pattern of state mental health programs reflects prior public programs, internal state politics, and uncertainties surrounding private contracting. Almost every state has emphasized outreach and simplification of enrollment in SCHIP, even while there is great variation in the basic organization and financing of individual programs (Shi, Oliver, and Huang 2000). Alan Weil (1997, 1) argues: "We find that variety is, was, and will continue to be a dominant feature of children's health insurance programs. . . . Ultimately, each state will determine which method of expansion is most appropriate for that state—a Medicaid expansion, a new state program, or

*In California, both legislation and a ballot initiative proposing an employer mandate received strong consideration but ultimately failed, despite support from the state medical association (Oliver and Dowell 1994).

both—based on its unique variety of programmatic and political considerations." Thus, it is more appropriate to think of states as specialized political markets, each with its own determinants of product success or failure, than as "laboratories" with scientifically tested and generalizable results for all consumers.

In contrast to policy design, what can readily diffuse across jurisdictions is political momentum. Nearly all state health insurance reforms occurred between 1988 and 1994, during the buildup to the Clinton health plan and its collapse. Actions to regulate teen access to tobacco spread rapidly in 1996–1997, after the initial wave of state litigation to recover Medicaid costs revealed the deceptive and illegal practices of the industry toward minors (Chriqui 2000).

The rhetoric of states as laboratories assumes that innovations spread from state to state or from states to the federal government, whereas the empirical record demonstrates that there is considerable interaction between state and federal debates and policies, and some innovations diffuse from the federal level downward. In fact, states are often dependent on the federal government for research and development projects, which produce the technical instruments such as DRGs and risk adjusters for HMO capitation. Sparer and Brown (1996) suggest that state innovations are frequently the joint product of federally funded scientists and state laboratories. States also commonly depend on federal funding to support "innovations"; the Oregon Health Plan, TennCare, and the vast majority of children's health insurance expansions would not have gone forward without federal endorsement and funding.

Finally, state actions are often facilitated by federal political pressure, even when federal policymakers ultimately cannot reach agreement on reforms of their own. The president's Commission on Health Care Quality spawned a number of bills of rights for patients at the state level, for example. The 1992 Synar amendment to prohibit sales of tobacco products to minors as well as the ultimately unsuccessful attempt of the Food and Drug Administration to regulate nicotine as an addictive substance both greatly accelerated state policies to restrict teen smoking (Chriqui 2000). Thompson notes how the Health Care Financing Administration sent four separate letters between 1998 and 2000 to state officials, warning them to increase their efforts to boost enrollment in Medicaid and SCHIP*

Ultimately, it is inaccurate and simplistic to regard states as the primary engines of policy innovation. Instead, state health policy reflects a combination of three models of innovation and diffusion. The first model is based on *self-learning,* with considerable independence across levels of government and sectors. In this model, programs undergo natural, organic development, and change is based on

---

*Some philanthropic organizations also have provided inducements for states or state-based coalitions to develop new policies and programs. Hackey suggests that an important line of future research is to understand the variation in whether and how states respond to inducements (or sanctions) offered for policy innovation by the federal government and private foundations (personal communication May 23, 2000).

experience, data, and other elements of administrative capacity. Many of the reforms in state public mental health systems described by Koyanagi and Bevilacqua fit within this model; often they were supported even by consumer advocates, who saw managed care as a potential improvement over government-run mental health programs. Another example of this model is the high-cost user initiative in the Maryland Medicaid program, which attempted to move patients whose conditions might generate very high costs in the existing primary care case management system (fee-for-service) into diagnosis-specific systems of care built around case management and capitation. This reform initiative came from within the state health department and was proposed as a logical extension and addition to the existing Medicaid program, not a replacement for it (Oliver 1998).

The second model is based on *interaction*. As suggested earlier, this is a modified version of the "laboratories of democracy" model. Learning occurs across levels of government and between the public and private sectors. The scope of activity may involve federal agencies and national interest groups as well as community leaders. The John Locke Society, for example, exerted considerable influence on the peculiar design of the North Carolina version of SCHIP. In the area of managed mental health care reforms, the Bazelon Center and the grassroots National Alliance for the Mentally Ill have attempted to shape policies across the states, and the American College of Mental Health Administrators has developed performance measures for mental health and substance abuse services. Many of the early tobacco control initiatives were strictly local efforts, but in recent years federal agencies such as the National Institutes of Health and the CDC have attempted to stimulate new local programs.

In the interaction model, innovation diffuses by means of both substantive learning and situational learning (Peterson 1997). States have emulated the quality-based purchasing of managed care by entities such as CalPERS, the Pacific Business Group on Health, and the Minnesota Buyers Action Group on Health. They have simplified enrollment forms and procedures and established public-private partnerships for outreach to families eligible for Medicaid and SCHIP; to date, 41 states have dropped the asset test for children, and 39 states have dropped face-to-face interviews for either Medicaid or SCHIP. Some states have adopted limits on handgun purchases, as data on the origin of criminal weapons demonstrate an impact of those policies. Lessons can also be negative: serious problems in mental health care reforms in Tennessee, Arizona, and Montana convey important lessons about the level of provider payments, delayed access to services, restrictions on prescription drugs and inpatient care, and financial mismanagement of private contractors.

In addition, there is situational learning across sectors and jurisdictions. Besides the substantive lessons mentioned above, some of the state mental health reforms became disaster stories that increased the overall vigilance of both state policymakers and consumer advocates. Adele Kirk (2000) relates how the exit of insurers and consumers from the individual insurance markets in Kentucky and

Washington became horror stories that supposedly ridiculed standard benefit plans and community rating of insurance premiums, though the causes of each state's problems were far more complex. The Oregon rationing plan became untouchable for other states, and Kitzhaber was labeled "Dr. Death" on the cover of a national news magazine. TennCare illustrated not only the problems associated with rapidly accelerating managed care in a system with little experience in that area; it became a lightning rod for HCFA to insist on a far more open, participatory process of decision-making in states planning Medicaid section 1115 waiver reforms. Dukakis points out that Governor McWherter had very little time to move reform ahead at the end of his term, but those contingencies in Tennessee were not understood or accepted in public hearings on Maryland Medicaid reform (Oliver 1998).

A third model of innovation is based on *entrepreneurship*. In this model, innovations reflect key opportunities for market restructuring or a change in priorities. They include the creation of a new program—for example, children's health insurance or an employer purchasing coalition—or major reforms of an existing program such as the section 1115 waiver to restructure Medicaid. Unlike the self-learning model, the specific impetus for change often comes from external factors that are quite independent of conditions in the existing program or policy area. Thus, an innovation may not be left in place long enough to accurately judge the range of intended and unintended consequences. This model, recognizing tremendous variation across states and sectors, presumes that states are not commonly "laboratories" but rather specialized political markets in which individuals and groups must develop and promote customized policies and practices (Oliver and Paul-Shaheen 1997; Sparer and Brown 1996). Innovation depends on a combination of ideas, leadership, and power and is capable of producing nonincremental changes in the system (Walker 1981; Polsby 1984; Kingdon 1984; Oliver 1991; Baumgartner and Jones 1993; Oliver and Paul-Shaheen 1997). The model predicts relative independence across sectors and states, but external conditions such as an economic crisis or a media-fed "backlash" against managed care may facilitate simultaneous opportunities for innovation. The adoption of selective contracting in the MediCal program in 1982 fits this model, as do the comprehensive efforts at state health care reform in the late 1980s and early 1990s. The initial adoption and subsequent development of a children's health insurance program in New York exemplifies the idiosyncratic nature of most innovations in the entrepreneurial model.

State "preemption" of federal policy. Another pattern that can be observed is that, on certain issues, widespread state actions make federal action only marginally important or serve to raise the bar for stronger federal action on those issues. Large numbers of states have adopted basic standards for maternity stays in the hospital, access to mammography and other services, coverage for the prudent use of emergency services, and the right to see certain specialists without a referral. While President Clinton has used executive orders to introduce some reforms on behalf of federal employees, disputes between the political parties and between members of Congress and party leaders have stalled more comprehensive action in Washington, including most importantly the right of beneficiaries to settle grievances through lawsuits. An earlier example of the same phenomenon was that, prior to the passage of the federal Health Insurance Portability and Accountability Act (HIPAA) of 1996, almost every state enacted reforms to improve the accessibility and affordability of health insurance for small groups (and in a few cases, individuals). As a result, the chief accomplishment of HIPAA is that it extends similar protections to individuals and employers with self-insured health benefits. It does less than most state reforms, however, to ensure that high-risk individuals will actually be able to afford insurance even if it is nominally available (Oliver 1999).

State preemption can work in the opposite direction when states challenge or seek to undermine federal policies. In recent years, many states have attacked new rules proposed by the U.S. Department of Health and Human Services (DHHS) to reform the nation's organ procurement and transplantation network. In order to reduce waiting times for the sickest patients and to reduce enormous disparities in access to transplants across states and regions of the country, DHHS proposed new criteria for the allocation of organs. The new system spurred opposition from states with smaller transplant centers, which would see more organs go to larger centers that typically treat sicker patients. For example, a 1997 Louisiana law allows transfers of organs out of state only if a suitable in-state recipient cannot be found and if the Louisiana organ procurement organization (OPO) has a reciprocal agreement with the out-of-state OPO. In 1998, the Louisiana Senate adopted Resolution 21, directing the state attorney general to challenge the legality and constitutionality of the DHHS Final Rule (Brelvi et al. 2000).

Interaction of federal policies with state and local systems. In addition to the patterns already described, there is subtler, long-term, and often more profound interaction in how state and local policies and systems modify the operation and impact of federal policies. This interaction is perhaps most noticeable in the enforcement of occupational health and safety regulations, environmental protection, and other areas where local values and interests clash with federal priorities. In the area of health insurance, Julie Hudman (2000) shows how across states and communities, political rhetoric stressing work and public attitudes toward welfare affect whether families who leave cash assistance maintain Medicaid benefits for which they are still eligible. Thomas-Buckle and Buckle argue that the outcomes of tobacco control initiatives of the National Institutes of Health (ASSIST) and the Centers for Disease Control (IMPACT) are determined not by the initial design of national policymakers but by the skill and persistence of local leaders and coalitions.

While it is not surprising that the local impact of federal policies is subject to political culture and regulatory capture by interest groups, there are other ways in which nominally uniform federal policies have dramatically different impacts across state and local jurisdictions. These are evident in Medicare payments for graduate medical education (GME), where due to a number of factors states like New York, Pennsylvania, and Michigan get three or four times the Medicare GME payment per resident or hospital discharge that states like California, Texas, and Florida receive (Lee and Oliver 2000). These variations are often magnified by state policies, such as in New York, that dedicate further funds to major teaching hospitals.

The above examples illustrate how interstate variations in federal programs arise from local conditions, but some disparities cannot be easily explained by local conditions. For example, western states with the highest managed care penetration in the commercial insurance market and Medicaid generally have higher Medicare HMO enrollment as well (34% or higher in 1996). But states like Massachusetts and New York, which have heavy commercial and Medicaid enrollment in managed care (75% and 60% respectively in 1996), had very low enrollment (16% and 13% respectively) in Medicare managed care plans (House Committee on Ways and Means 1999, Fig. 4.25; Lee and Oliver 2000, 58–59).

Challenges for the States and Nation

There are many challenges ahead for state policymakers. In virtually every area of policy, there is greater breadth of action than depth of action. There have been significant achievements in managed care regulation, tobacco control, and insurance coverage, to highlight some of the most pressing issues. Yet, those achievements fall far short of even fairly modest expectations. In the past few years, there has been a lot of policy development and political capital expended for very little system improvement. Without further action, state policies amount to a combination of (1) symbolic action with no intent for real change; (2) real policy change but no real system reform, because of a lack of resources or unintended consequences; and (3) new layers of complexity in an unmanageable, dysfunctional system.

The contributions in this book strongly suggest that, to make further progress, state officials need to develop broader and stronger partnerships with federal agencies and particularly with private sector organizations and leaders. This is true for SCHIP enrollment, for preventing and stopping teen smoking, for improving the quality of health services and preventing medical errors, and for promoting a cleaner and safer environment.

To improve on current policies and programs, state officials also need new policy tools built around information and investment. Thompson argues that improving programs in health insurance and other areas will require substantially better data that measure program outputs as well as inputs and allow for comparison across states. The current data systems available to state officials and to federal officials who oversee shared programs such as Medicaid and SCHIP are so poor or complicated that they prevent a great deal of learning from program experience.

Finally, state and federal officials will eventually need to engage in broader, outside-the-box thinking. Even in the strongest economy in decades, there is little apparent appetite for primary prevention or economic redistribution. There is a dearth of debate about the socioeconomic determinants of health, the justice of a wealthy country without universal health insurance coverage, and the long-run health of the environment and human populations. As Waters notes, the national tobacco settlement with the states is a sobering example of how a major financial windfall, coming at a moment when most states are already flush with cash, can be frittered away in many locations. In this episode, devolution of authority is failing the public's health. Across the states, the decisions of officials resulted in the dissolution of a major public health initiative into pork barrel politics that rewards traditional clients such as hospitals and schools. The chance to dramatically affect the course of tobacco use and its related health and economic damages was squandered. Until states and other partners in the health policy community commit themselves to primary prevention in this and other areas, and until there is improved access to care for all social groups, the potential health gains from policy will greatly exceed the progress actually achieved.

REFERENCES

Anton, T. J. 1997. "New Federalism and Intergovernmental Fiscal Relationships: The Implications for Health Policy." *Journal of Health Politics, Policy and Law* 22 (June): 691–720.

Arnold, R. D. 1990. *The Logic of Congressional Action.* New Haven, CT: Yale University Press.

Bardach, E. 1977. *The Implementation Game.* Cambridge, MA: MIT Press.

Baumgartner, F., and B. Jones. 1993. *Agendas and Instability in American Politics.* Chicago: University of Chicago Press.

Benjamin, A. E., and P. Lee. 1989. "Public Policy, Federalism, and AIDS." In *AIDS: Principles, Practices, and Politics,* ed. I. Corless and M. Pittman-Lindeman, pp. 489–503. New York: Hemisphere Publishing.

Brelvi, S., N. Egbuniwe, B. Sakagawa, and T. Oliver. 2000. "The Ethics and Politics of Organ Transplant Policy." Paper prepared for the annual meeting of the American Political Science Association, Washington, DC, September 2000.

Brown, L. D. 1983. "Common Sense Meets Implementation: Certificate of Need Regulation in the States." *Journal of Health Politics, Policy and Law* 8 (Fall): 480–494.

Chriqui, J. F. 2000. "Restricting Minors' Access to Tobacco Products: An Examination of State Legislation and Policy Innovation." Ph.D. diss. University of Maryland, Baltimore County.

Declercq, E., and D. Simmes. 1997. "The Politics of 'Drive-Through Deliveries': Putting Early Postpartum Discharge on the Legislative Agenda." *Milbank Quarterly* 75 (2): 175–202.

Ellwood, M. R., and L. Ku. 1998. "Welfare and Immigration Reforms: Unintended Side Effects for Medicaid." *Health Affairs* 17 (May–June): 137–151.

Ellwood, P. M., Jr., N. Anderson, J. Billings, R. Carlson, G. Hoagberg, and W. McClure. 1971. "The Health Maintenance Strategy." *Medical Care* 9: 291–298.

Enthoven, A. C. 1980. *Health Plan.* Reading, MA: Addison-Wesley.

Fox, D. M. 1986. "The Consequences of Consensus: American Health Policy in the Twentieth Century." *Milbank Quarterly* 64 (1): 76–99.

Fox, D. M., and H. M. Leichter. 1991. "The Ups and Downs of Oregon's Rationing Plan." *Health Affairs* 12 (Summer): 66–70.

Hudman, J. A. 2000. "Predictors of Health Insurance Coverage After a Welfare Exit." Ph.D. diss., Johns Hopkins University.

Jacobson, P. D., and J. Wasserman. 1999. "The Implementation and Enforcement of Tobacco Control Laws: Policy Implications for Activists and the Industry." *Journal of Health Politics, Policy and Law* 24 (June): 567–598.

Kingdon, J. W. 1984. *Agendas, Alternatives, and Public Policies.* Boston: Little, Brown.

Kirk, A. M. 2000. "Riding the Bull: Reform in Washington, Kentucky, and Massachusetts." *Journal of Health Politics, Policy and Law* 25 (February): 133–173.

Kitzhaber, J., and M. Gibson. 1991. "The Crisis in Health Care—The Oregon Health Plan as a Strategy for Change." *Stanford Law and Policy Review* 3 (Fall): 64–72.

Ku, L., and B. Bruen. 1999. *The Continuing Decline in Medicaid Coverage.* No. A-37 in the series on "New Federalism: Issues and Options for States." *http://newfederalism.urban.org* (December). Washington, DC: Urban Institute.

Lee, P. R., and T. R. Oliver. 2000. *Understanding the Evolution of Medicare: Patterns of Policy Making and Their Consequences.* Report to the Commonwealth Fund and the California HealthCare Foundation, University of California–San Francisco and Johns Hopkins University, January 2000.

Leichter, H. M. 1996. "State Governments and Their Capacity for Health Care Reform." In *Health Policy, Federalism, and the American States,* ed. R. F. Rich and W. D. White, pp. 151–179. Washington, DC: Urban Institute Press.

———. 1997. "State Health Policy Analysis: On the Abuse of Metaphor and the Pathology of Variation." *Journal of Health Politics, Policy and Law* 22 (June): 897–906.

Morone, J. A., and A. Dunham. 1984. "The Waning of Professional Dominance: DRGs and the Hospitals." *Health Affairs* 3 (Spring): 73–87.

Nathan, R. P. 1989. "The Role of the States in American Federalism." In *The State of the States,* ed. C. E. Van Horn, pp. 15–32. Washington, D.C.: Congressional Quarterly.

Nathanson, C. A. 1999. "Social Movements as Catalysts for Policy Change: The Case of Smoking and Guns." *Journal of Health Politics, Policy and Law* 24 (June): 421–488.

Oliver, T. R. 1991. "Ideas, Entrepreneurship, and the Politics of Health Care Reform." *Stanford Law and Policy Review* 3 (Fall): 160–180.

———. 1998. "The Collision of Economics and Politics in Medicaid Managed Care: Reflections on the Course of Reform in Maryland." *Milbank Quarterly* 76 (1): 59–101.

———. 1999. "The Dilemmas of Incrementalism: Logical and Political Constraints in the Design of Health Insurance Reforms." *Journal of Policy Analysis and Management* 18 (Fall): 652–683.

Oliver, T. R., and E. B. Dowell. 1994. "Interest Groups and Health Reform: Lessons from California." *Health Affairs* 13 (2): 123–141.

Oliver, T. R., and P. Paul-Shaheen. 1997. "Translating Ideas into Actions: Entrepreneurial Leadership in State Health Care Reforms." *Journal of Health Politics, Policy and Law* 22 (June): 721–783.

Peterson, M. A. 1997. "The Limits of Social Learning: Translating Analysis into Action." *Journal of Health Politics, Policy and Law* 22 (August): 1077–1114.

Petracca, M. P. 1992. "The Rediscovery of Interest Group Politics." In *The Politics of Interests,* ed. M. P. Petracca, pp. 3–31. Boulder, CO: Westview Press.

Polsby, N. W. 1984. *Political Innovation in America.* New Haven, CT: Yale University Press.

Relman, A. S. 1981. "The New Medical-Industrial Complex." *New England Journal of Medicine* 303:963–970.

Rich, R. F., and W. D. White. 1996. "Health Care Policy and the American States: Issues of Federalism." In *Health Policy, Federalism, and the American States,* ed. R. F. Rich and W. D. White, pp. 3–35. Washington, DC: Urban Institute Press.

Sabatier, P. A., and D. A. Mazmanian. 1981. "The Implementation of Public Policy: A Framework of Analysis." In *Effective Policy Implementation,* ed. D. A. Mazmanian and P. A. Sabatier, pp. 3–35. Lexington, MA: Lexington Books.

Shi, L., T. R. Oliver, and V. Huang. 2000. "The State Children's Health Insurance Program: Expanding the Framework for Evaluating State Goals and Performance." *Milbank Quarterly* 78 (September): 403–446.

Sparer, M. S., and L. D. Brown. 1996. "States and the Health Care Crisis: Limits and Lessons of Laboratory Federalism." In *Health Policy, Federalism, and the American States,* ed. R. F. Rich and W. D. White, pp. 181–202. Washington, DC: Urban Institute Press.

Starr, P. 1982. *The Social Transformation of American Medicine.* New York: Basic Books.

U.S. Congress, House of Representatives, Committee on Ways and Means. 1999. *Medicare and Health Care Chartbook.* Washington, DC: Government Printing Office.

U.S. Department of Health and Human Services. 1980. *Summary Report of the Graduate Medical Education National Advisory Committee.* Washington, DC: Government Printing Office.

Walker, J. L. 1981. "The Diffusion of Knowledge, Policy Communities, and Agenda Setting: The Relationship of Knowledge and Power." In *New Strategic Perspectives on Social Policy,* ed. J. E. Tropman, M. J. Dluhy, and R. M. Lind, pp. 75–96. New York: Pergamon Press.

Weil, A. 1997. *The New Children's Health Insurance Program: Should States Expand Medicaid?* Washington, DC: Urban Institute.

Weissert, C. S., and W. G. Weissert. 1996. *Governing Health: The Politics of Health Policy.* Baltimore: Johns Hopkins University Press.

Wildavsky, A. 1977. "Doing Better and Feeling Worse: The Political Pathology of Health Policy." In *Doing Better and Feeling Worse,* ed. J. H. Knowles, pp. 105–123. New York: W.W. Norton.

Wilson, J. Q. 1973. *Political Organizations.* New York: Basic Books.

———. 1980. "The Politics of Regulation." In *The Politics of Regulation,* ed. J. Q. Wilson, pp. 357–394. New York: Basic Books.

Contributors

JOSEPH J. BEVILACQUA, state initiatives director at the Bazelon Center for Mental Health Law. He has 21 years of experience as state commissioner of mental health services in Rhode Island, Virginia, and South Carolina. He served as president of the National Association of State Mental Health Program Directors for two terms and currently serves on the board of directors of the Human Services Research Institute located in Boston, Massachusetts. He is chairman of the board, Fellowship Health Resources, Inc. (a private, nonprofit community service agency), a board member of the Rhode Island chapter of the National Alliance for the Mentally Ill, and a consultant to the Erna Yaffe Foundation.

WILLIAM P. BRANDON, the Metrolina Medical Foundation Distinguished Professor of Public Policy on Health at the University of North Carolina at Charlotte. He has been a Robert Wood Johnson Faculty Fellow in health care finance at the Johns Hopkins Medical Institutions and the Office of the Assistant Secretary of Health and Human Services for Planning and Evaluation. He was also a National Endowment for the Humanities Fellow for a year at the Hastings Center, a bioethics research institute.

SUZANN R. THOMAS-BUCKLE, associate professor and codirector of the law, policy, and society program at Northeastern University and coprincipal investigator for the Effective Responses to Challenges to Local Tobacco Control Efforts project funded through the Tobacco Control Resource Center by the Robert Wood Johnson Foundation. She has written two books, *Bargaining for Justice* and *Standards Relating to Planning for the Juvenile Justice System,* and several articles. Her current research project provides an opportunity to study the social construction of law at the local level in the context of the tobacco control movement and to investigate the links between local conflicts and events in the global arena.

293

LEONARD G. BUCKLE, coprincipal investigator of the Tobacco Control Resource Center's study of effective responses to the tobacco industry's legal challenges to local tobacco control efforts, which is sponsored by the Robert Wood Johnson Foundation. His research interests have included strategic decision-making by participants in professional fields, interorganizational settings, and other social realms with loosely designed normative systems. With Suzann Thomas-Buckle, he has written about negotiated order in trial courts, community organizations, and juvenile justice agencies. Since 1985, he has served as associate professor and codirector of the law, policy, and society program, an intercollegiate Ph.D. program at Northeastern University.

ROSEMARY V. CHAUDRY, health services policy supervisor in the Bureau of Health Plan Policy, Office of Ohio Health Plans, Ohio Department of Job and Family Services. Her research interest is the provision of community-based health services to disadvantaged populations. She has been involved in previous research projects focusing on community-based services for adults and children with severe mental disabilities, collaboration between public health and community mental health agencies, and health care for Medicaid recipients in Ohio. She was a member of interdisciplinary teams investigating patient and system outcomes in a mandatory managed care program for Medicaid recipients in North Carolina and the impact of organizational structure on role identity and job satisfaction of public health nurses.

MICHAEL S. DUKAKIS, distinguished professor of political science at Northeastern University. Dukakis won his party's nomination for governor of Massachusetts in 1974 and beat Frank Sargent decisively in November of that year. In 1986, his colleagues in the National Governors' Association voted him the most effective governor in the nation. Dukakis won the Democratic nomination for president of the United States in 1988 but was defeated by George Bush. Dukakis joined the Northeastern faculty in the spring of 1991, where he teaches courses on health policy and politics, public policy analysis, and public management.

ROBERT B. HACKEY, associate professor of health policy and management at Providence College, where he has taught since 1999. Prior to joining the faculty at Providence College, he taught political science at the University of Massachusetts–Dartmouth from 1993 to 1999 and at St. Anselm College from 1991 to 1992. In 1993, he served as the program manager for trauma systems development at the Rhode Island Department of Health. He is a member of the board of the American Health Planning Association and is the author of *Rethinking Health Care Policy: The New Politics of State Regulation.* His work on national health care reform, state hospital rate-setting, health planning, and state regulation has appeared in *Critical Sociology; New England Journal of Public Policy; Polity; Journal of Health Politics, Policy and Law; Spectrum: The Journal of State Government;* and *Journal of Trauma.*

LAWRENCE R. JACOBS, associate professor of political science at the University of Minnesota, where he has taught since 1988. He is the author of *The Health of Nations: Public Opinion and the Making of Health Policy in the U.S. and Britain* and has published more than 30 articles on the presidency, public opinion, and health policy. His work has appeared in *Domestic Affairs; PS; American Political Science Review; Journal of Health Politics, Policy and Law; Public Opinion Quarterly; Comparative Politics;* and *Health Affairs.* He serves on the editorial board of the *Journal of Health Politics, Policy and Law* and on the national advisory committee for the Robert Wood Johnson Foundation's Investigator Awards in Health Policy Research program.

CHRIS KOYANAGI, director of legislative policy for the Judge David L. Bazelon Center for Mental Health Law in Washington, D.C., a legal advocacy organization concerned with the rights of persons with mental impairments. She is responsible for the legislative advocacy agenda of the Bazelon Center, which since 1996 has prioritized nondiscrimination in mental health benefits and under health insurance policies, financing of mental health services (Medicaid and state actions on managed care), and rights of children with mental and emotional disorders to income support benefits and children's mental health issues. She has 27 years of policy advocacy experience in Washington on behalf of human services initiatives, and in addition to her legislative policy work at the Bazelon Center, she serves on several mental health policy advisory committees and has authored numerous articles and other publications regarding mental health policy.

JOHN E. MCDONOUGH, associate professor at the Heller School, Brandeis University, and a senior associate at its Schneider Institute for Health Policy. From 1985 to 1997, he served as a member of the Massachusetts House of Representatives, where he chaired the Joint Committee on Health Care. In 1996, he led the campaign for passage of landmark health access legislation to cover uninsured children, funded by new tabacco taxes, legislation which served as a model for the federal Children's Health Insurance Program. He holds teaching appointments at the Harvard School of Public Health and the Boston University School of Medicine. His articles have appeared in *The New England Journal of Medicine* and *Health Affairs.* He has published two books, *Experiencing Politics: A Legislator's Stories of Government and Health Care* and *Interests, Ideas, and Deregulation: The Fate of Hospital Rate Setting.* He serves as a board member of Harvard Pilgrim Health Care.

ROBERT MCGRATH, AHRQ fellow and doctoral post resident at the Heller School at Brandeis University. His dissertation explores state-level implementation of the SCHIP program. He is an adjunct professor at the University of New Hampshire in the department of health management and policy. He worked as a health policy advisor to New Hampshire governor Jeanne Shaheen and as a research assistant at Harvard University and the University of New Hampshire. He also worked as a health planning analyst for Healthsource, a managed care insurer now part of the Cigna Corporation.

THEODORE R. MARMOR, former editor of the *Journal of Health Politics, Policy and Law* and currently professor of politics and public policy at the Yale University School of Organization and Management. He was an adviser to the health policy transition team for the Clinton administration in 1993 and was a senior policy adviser for the presidential campaigns of Walter Mondale, Bill Clinton, and Michael Dukakis. He has published extensively in the area of health care reform with a particular emphasis on single-payer health insurance reform and Medicare policy. His books include *Understanding Health Care Reform* and *The Politics of Medicare.*

JAMES A. MORONE, professor of political science at Brown University, where he has taught since 1982. He is the former editor of the *Journal of Health Politics, Policy and Law* and the author of numerous monographs and scholarly articles on state health policy. His book *The Democratic Wish* won the Gladys Kammerer Award for the best book in domestic politics and policy in 1990 and has recently been reissued in an updated edition by Yale University Press. He received an Investigator Award from the Robert Wood Johnson Foundation for his current research on the politics of sin. He is also completing a study of school-based health care delivery systems in the United States.

JONATHAN OBERLANDER, assistant professor in the Department of Social Medicine, University of North Carolina at Chapel Hill. He received his Ph.D. with a specialization in health policy from Yale University and is a former Robert Wood Johnson Postdoctoral Fellow in Health Policy. His articles have appeared in the *Journal of Health Politics, Policy and Law; Health Affairs; International Journal of Health Services;* and other journals.

THOMAS R. OLIVER, associate professor of health policy and management at the Johns Hopkins University School of Public Health. He has published widely in the area of state health policy, and his work has appeared in the *Journal of Health Politics, Policy and Law* and other prominent journals in the field. He received an Investigator Award from the Robert Wood Johnson Foundation for his research on the politics of health policy innovation in the states.

DAVID A. ROCHEFORT, professor of political science and public administration at Northeastern University. His books include *The Politics of Problem Definition, From Poorhouses to Homelessness: Policy Analysis and Mental Health Care, Handbook on Mental Health Policy in the United States,* and *American Social Welfare Policy.* In addition, he has authored or coauthored numerous articles on health and mental health care issues that have appeared in *Health Affairs; Journal of Health Politics, Policy and Law; Public Administration Review; Policy Studies Journal; Journal of Public Health Policy; Hospital and Community Psychiatry; International Journal of Law and Psychiatry;* and other journals. Honors received for his work have included the Theodore Lowi Award for Outstanding Policy Studies Article of 1994, winner of the Pioneer Institute's Better Government Research Competition, and a Fulbright Scholar Award to Canada.

ALICE SARDELL, associate professor in the Department of Urban Studies at Queens College of the City University of New York. She received a Ph.D. in politics from New York University, where she was a DHEW fellow in political science and health policy. Her broad research interests are in the politics of social policy. She has published articles on the welfare rights movement, the politics of primary health care, physicians' networks, federal child health policy, and health policy in New York State. Her book, *The U.S. Experiment in Social Medicine,* analyzes the policy history of the community health center program from 1965 to 1986. She is currently working on a study of U.S. children's health policy during the last two decades.

FRANK J. THOMPSON, interim provost of Rockefeller College at the State University of New York at Albany. He has published extensively on issues of health policy, policy implementation, public personnel policy, and administrative politics. His books include *Personnel Policy in the City; Health Policy and the Bureaucracy; Public Administration: Challenges, Choices and Consequences; Revitalizing State and Local Public Service;* and most recently, *Medicaid and Devolution: A View from the States.* He has also served as consultant to various government agencies and as executive director of the National Commission on the State and Local Public Service, and is a fellow of the National Academy of Public Administration.

WILLIAM J. WATERS JR., deputy director of the Rhode Island Department of Health, where he has worked since 1974. He has more than 25 years of experience as a health planner and policymaker and served as president of the American Health Planning Association from 1989 to 1990. He is the author or coauthor of more than 60 articles on public health and state health policy that have appeared in such journals as *American Journal of Law and Medicine, Journal of Public Health Policy, New England Journal of Public Policy,* and *Rhode Island Medical Journal.*

Index

Aaron, Henry, 211
Access to care, 10–12, 71, 106, 126, 171, 196,
  219
  barriers to, 105, 144, 158
  community involvement in expanding, 289
  expansion of, 12, 84, 85, 125, 207, 214
  free care pools, 82
  gatekeepers and direct access laws, 24
  through health insurance coverage, 217
  initiatives of states for, 102
  limitations on, 22
  managed care barriers to, 118
  to Medicaid, 209
  to mental health services, 191, 193, 197–
    200, 203
  and the mentally ill, 187
  OB/GYN providers, 18
  Oregon Health Plan expansion of, 221
  private health insurance, 11
  Reforming States Group role in, 101
  state economic health considerations, 84
Accountability, 20, 30, 90, 171, 219
  of contractors, 196
  federal initiatives for, 201
  in the health care industry, 17
  of health insurers, 25, 29
  legislative elections for, 91
  for mental health care, 186
  through North Carolina's administrative
    hierarchy, 171
  of Oregon health reform politics, 221
  performance based, 42, 60, 65, 67
  state assessment and enhancement of, 89
Activists, 276
  consumers, 133
  religious conservatives, 4

ADA (Americans with Disabilities Act), 211,
  236
Administration for Children and Families, 55
Advertisement, 228, 236
  of anti-smoking and child health care, 147
  of Children's Health Insurance Program,
    55
  for tobacco industry, 229, 233
Advocacy groups, 151–153, 155–159, 192–
    195, 216, 244
  anti-tobacco, 147, 241
  Citizen Action, 153, 157
  for children, 151, 155, 156, 159, 161, 170,
    179
  for consumers, 128, 285
  for the elderly, 27
  grassroots organization of, 193
  for the mentally ill, 192, 193
  national level, 194
  for the Oregon Health Plan, 210, 214
  Statewide Youth Advocacy, 152
Agenda setting, 88
  influence of social construction on,
    279
Aid to Families with Dependent Children
    (AFDC), 52. See also Temporary
    Assistance to Needy Families
Alliances, 133
All-payer regulatory systems, 14, 152
AMA. See American Medical Association
American Academy of Pediatrics, New York
  chapter of, 152
American Board of Medical Specialties,
  public access to board certification
  records, 18
American Cancer Society, 147

299